THE REPUBLIC OF MEN

GEOFF READ

THE REPUBLIC OF MEN

GENDER AND THE POLITICAL PARTIES IN INTERWAR FRANCE

LOUISIANA STATE UNIVERSITY PRESS
BATON ROUGE

Published by Louisiana State University Press

Manufactured in the United States of America
FIRST PRINTING

Designer: Michelle A. Neustrom
Typeface: Chaparral Pro
Printer and binder: Maple Press

Library of Congress Cataloging-in-Publication Data
Read, Geoff, 1975–
The republic of men : gender and the political parties in interwar France / Geoff Read.
pages cm
Includes bibliographical references and index.
ISBN 978-0-8071-5521-9 (cloth : alk. paper) — ISBN 978-0-8071-5522-6 (pdf) — ISBN 978-0-8071-5523-3 (epub) — ISBN 978-0-8071-5524-0 (mobi) 1. Political parties—France—History—20th century. 2. Masculinity—Political aspects—France—History—20th century. 3. Sex role—Political aspects—France—History—20th century. 4. Women—Political activity—France—History—20th century. 5. Citizenship—France—History—20th century. 6. France—Politics and government—1914–1940. I. Title.
JN2997.R43 2014
324.24409'041—dc23

2013039054

The paper in this book meets the guidelines for permanence and durability of the Committee on Production Guidelines for Book Longevity of the Council on Library Resources. ♾

For Sarah

CONTENTS

ACKNOWLEDGMENTS

As is always the case with such a project many people and institutions contributed to the completion of this manuscript.

The following institutions or funding agencies helped support this research financially: York University (Canada), Lakehead University, Huron University College at Western University, the Ontario government, and the Social Sciences Research Council of Canada.

The author gratefully acknowledges the *Journal of the Canadian Historical Association,* the *Canadian Bulletin of Medical History,* and *Historical Reflections/ Réflexions Historiques* for granting permission to publish material previously published with them.

The following librarians and archivists helped me in diverse ways: Dominique Parcollet, Audrey Meheut, the staff at the interlibrary loan department of York University's Scott Library, the staff of the Media Commons at Robarts Library at the University of Toronto, the interlibrary loan departments at the Lakehead University Library and Western University's Weldon Library, and the staff at the Huron University College library.

These administrative assistants at York, Lakehead, and Huron were universally helpful: Julie Bennett, Gail Fikis, Lisa Hoffman, Lauren Hogg, Rebecca Mudge, and Brenda Sefeldas.

The following friends and/or colleagues contributed in ways big and small to the writing and conceptualizing of this project: Anna Agathangelou, Jack S. Blocker Jr., Chris Blow, Bettina Bradbury, Caroline Campbell, Kristen Stromberg Childers, Michel Dobry, Chris Dooley, Jason Ellis, Christopher E. Forth, Steve Gamester, Samuel Houston Goodfellow, Christine Grandy, Nathaniel Greene, Craig Heron, Ian Hesketh, Dan Horner, Geoff Hudson, Eric Jennings, Julie Johnson, Michael Kater, Laurent Kestel, Marilyn Kidd, Robert Kreiser, Rob Kristofferson, Ben Lander, Cindy Loch-Drake, Pascal Maeder, Steve Macleod, Dave Mizener, Deborah Neill, Karen Offen, Jason Reid, Yann Rigolet, Clifford Rosenberg, Mark Rosenfeld, Daniella Sarnoff, Marlene Shore, Michael Sibalis, Pierre Simoni, David Slavin, Charles Smith, Stéphane Spoiden, Marc Stein, Shannon Stettner, Bruce Strang, Eric Strikwerda, David Watson, Todd Webb, Sandra Whitworth, Terry Wilde, and Donald G. Wileman.

A group of friends and colleagues I affectionately think of as "The Kanadiens" have been especially supportive of my work: Samuel Kalman, Sean Kennedy, and Cheryl Koos. Cheryl is not actually Canadian but we are working on it.

Stephen J. Brooke and Suzanne Langlois were especially helpful with this project in its formative stages.

William D. Irvine's influence on this project has been foundational. He is a great mentor, colleague, and friend whose knowledge of interwar French politics is second to no one's.

Mary Lynn Stewart gave me excellent advice about preparing this manuscript for publication. She also suggested I submit it to Louisiana State University Press.

Alisa Plant, the acquisitions editor at Louisiana State University Press, was supportive of the manuscript from the get-go and unbelievably patient as I revised it. The press's copy editor, Jo Ann Kiser, was very thorough, efficient, and easy to work with.

Rachel G. Fuchs was the reader for the press. As a peer reviewer, she offers a model for others to follow. Her commentary was detailed, constructive, and fair: it strengthened the book immeasurably. Following the review process she has been, moreover, very encouraging and supportive.

Kristin Burnett, my friend and former colleague at Lakehead, read and commented diligently on every chapter of the book as I revised to answer Rachel Fuchs's critique. Her help is deeply appreciated.

My extended family has been a bedrock of support. This includes my mothers- and fathers-in-law Kathy and Mike Arnold and Terry and Sandra Tombs; my brothers and sisters-in-law (especially Hillary Tombs); my supportive mother and frequent babysitter, Jackie Read; my father, fellow historian, and dog sitter, Colin Read, and his partner Sydney Reid; my children, Zachary, Zoe, and Parker Read; and above all, my wife, Sarah Read, who has supported this project financially and emotionally from its inception. Her strength is an inspiration.

It is customary to end the acknowledgments by accepting responsibility for any errors that appear within the manuscript. I happily do so: any mistakes that appear herein—including "egregious factual errors"—are mine.

THE REPUBLIC OF MEN

Prominent French Political Parties/Movements, 1919–1940

NAME OF POLITICAL MOVEMENT*	POLITICAL ORIENTATION	AFFILIATED NEWSPAPERS	PROMINENT LEADERS
Communist Party	Communist	*Humanité, Ouvrière*	Marcel Cachin, Maurice Thorez
Socialist Party	Socialist/social democratic	*Populaire, Femme Socialiste*	Léon Blum, Paul Faure
Radical and Racial-Socialist Party	Center	*Ère nouvelle, Lumière*	Édouard Herriot, Édouard Daladier
Alliance démocratique	Republican center-right	*Alliance démocratique*	Pierre-Étienne Flandin, Paul Reynaud
Parti démocrate populaire	Catholic republican center-right	*Petit Démocrate*	Georges Thibout, Jean Raymond-Laurent
Fédération républicaine	Republican and nationalist right	*Nation, Devoir des femmes*	Auguste Isaac, Louis Marin
Action française	Monarchist right	*Action française*	Georges Maurras, Léon Daudet
Jeunesses patriotes	Fascistic right	*National*	Pierre Taittinger
Croix de feu/Parti social français	Fascistic right	*Flambeau, Petit Journal*	François de La Rocque
Faisceau	Fascist	*Nouveau siècle*	Georges Valois
Solidarité française	Fascist	*Solidarité française*	François Coty, Jean Renaud
Parti populaire français	Fascist	*Émancipation nationale*	Jacques Doriot

*Movements are listed from the political left to the right, in descending order.

Introduction

GENDER AND RACE IN THE INTERWAR REPUBLIC

On November 11, 1918, the *président du conseil,*[1] Georges Clemenceau, stood up first in the Chamber of Deputies and later in the Senate to announce the armistice with Germany, signaling the end of a conflict that had caused the deaths of 1,310,000 young French soldiers and an additional two hundred thousand civilians.[2] Moreover, as observers would repeatedly remark in the years ahead, roughly 1.4 million births that normally would have occurred from 1914 to 1918 had not. The war, in short, in addition to all the financial, human, and physical destruction it had wrought, had caused a massive demographic disruption, the implications of which would be felt for decades.

Despite this, Clemenceau and his fellow parliamentarians struck a triumphant tone. The mood in the Chamber was euphoric. This was so for many reasons. The politicians rejoiced because the war was over and France victorious; many were elated at the prospect of the return of the "lost provinces" of Alsace and Lorraine—ceded to Germany at the end of the Franco-Prussian War—a cherished goal since 1870;[3] and many shared an optimism that the end of the war heralded the dawn of a new and brighter era. In fact, Clemenceau, the *président de la chambre*[4] (Paul Deschanel), and others portrayed the armistice as the inauguration of a new utopia made possible by the courage, fortitude, and manliness of France's soldiers. In Clemenceau's words,

> For me, with the conventions of the armistice read, it seems that at this hour, at this terrible, great and magnificent hour, my duty is accomplished. . . .
>
> And then, we must honor our great dead, who gave us this victory. (*New unanimous acclamations—All the deputies stand.*) Because of them, we can say that before any armistice, France was liberated by the strength of arms. (*Unanimous and prolonged applause.*) . . .
>
> With regard to the living, to whom, from this day forward, we extend our hand and whom we will welcome when they pass on our boulevards en route to the Arc de Triomphe, they must be saluted in advance! . . . Thanks

> to them, France, yesterday the soldier of God, today the soldier of humanity, will always be the soldier of ideals! (*Enthusiastic applause. The deputies stand and acclaim the président du conseil at length.*)

Deschanel seconded Clemenceau's sentiments, focusing on the long-awaited return of the lost provinces:

> Here it is finally, the sacred hour for which we have been living for forty-seven years!—forty-seven years during which our souls have not ceased to retain the cry of pain and revolt of Gambetta, of Jules Grosjean and of the deputies of Alsace-Lorraine, that of Victor Hugo, of Edgar Quinet and of Georges Clemenceau. (*Lively applause.*) Forty-seven years during which bayoneted Alsace-Lorraine never stopped crying out to France. Half a century! And tomorrow we will be in Strasbourg and in Metz! . . .
>
> And you, sublime combatants of the Great War, your superhuman courage has made of Alsace-Lorraine, in the eyes of the universe, the very personification of right (*Prolonged applause.—The deputies stand*); the return of our exiled brothers is not only a national revenge, it is the appeasement of humanity's conscience (*Lively acclamations*) and the preview of a higher order. (*Unanimous acclamations.—All the deputies rise and applaud at length.*)[5]

At the heart of these exultant declarations were conceptions of nation, race, and gender. Deschanel, for example, invoked a line of masculine forebears, an ancestry of great men,[6] and deliberately (and somewhat disingenuously given his personal dislike of Clemenceau)[7] included Clemenceau on that list, in order to incorporate France's soldiers within the national and republican narrative and tradition. These men, like Léon Gambetta, Victor Hugo, and others before them, had shown their manly fortitude and thus ensured victory and the return of Alsace and Lorraine to the fatherland. Clemenceau, meanwhile, insisted on the need to honor the dead for their sacrifice, and he summoned the imperial image of the Arc de Triomphe to remind his listeners of the glory of France and the seemingly immemorial tradition of victory parades down the Champs Élysées. He thereby neatly elided the differences between France's republican, Bonapartist, and royalist traditions and erased the memory of the defeat to Prussia in 1870; Clemenceau also disregarded France's considerable class conflict, portraying the nation as a united organic whole.

Thus began the interwar period.

★ ★ ★

Clemenceau and Deschanel's November 11, 1918, speeches provide a good introduction to many of the themes of this book. Most obviously, the masculinist construction of republican citizenship that characterized their words typified interwar French politics, particularly in republican circles of the left and right. By studying the gender discourses of interwar France's most important political formations—the Communist Party, the Socialist Party, the Radical and Radical-Socialist Party, the Alliance démocratique, the Parti démocrate populaire, the Fédération républicaine, the Croix de feu/Parti social français, and the Parti populaire français—it becomes apparent that the republican parties, defined as extending from elements of the Socialist Party on the left to the Fédération républicaine on the right, shared a masculinist vision of citizenship. This tradition, as Joan Landes and others have shown, began with the French Revolution itself. In Landes's argument, with the collapse of the old patriarchy of the *ancien régime,* republicans constructed more inflexibly gendered private and public spheres: the public was masculine, the private feminine. Symptomatic of this, a public man was an individual of civic virtue who dedicated himself to the common good, while a public woman became synonymous with a sex worker or a woman lacking in virtue. This discursive shift had a profound impact on the lives of women, who were denied access to the city, held to be intellectually inferior, and given, in lieu of citizenship, the role of "republican motherhood."[8] Propagators of the republican ideal enjoined women to impart virtue to future male citizens as mothers but excluded them from full citizenship.[9] Judith Stone, Judith Surkis, and Patricia Tilburg have demonstrated that this separation Landes documents persisted and, in some ways, rigidified during the prewar Third Republic (1870–1914). Surkis, in fact, argues that women's subordination was necessary to control men's heterosexual desires. Mothers had to pass on a sense of civic responsibility to their sons to counteract the potentially dangerous individualism inherent to republicanism. Women, in short, had to remind their sons that a measure of selflessness (and self-control) was necessary in order for a society of free individuals to function. Tilburg, on the other hand, asserts that while the Third Republic's school curricula consigned women to the private sphere, they also held some emancipatory potential, thanks to the contradictions inherent in teaching girls the ethos of republican citizenship while effectively excluding them from it.[10] Other historians have also emphasized themes similar to Landes's. For example, Karen Offen's extensive work on French feminism demonstrates that its champions nearly universally subscribed to what she dubs "relational feminism," which emphasized, like republicans, the essential biological differences between the sexes: instead of arguing that women were absolutely equal to men and basing their claims on notions of individual rights, French feminists largely chose to insist they were "different" but equal.[11] Joan Scott similarly demonstrates that French feminists accepted the masculine definition of the citizen and the biological difference of the sexes while, unlike Offen, emphasizing the limitations of this approach.[12] Francine Muël-Dreyfus, addressing different questions, has likewise shown that Vichyites believed that their counter-revolution hinged on a return to an "eternal feminine."[13] The concept of separate spheres and socially constructed notions of biological difference is central to these works, and, intriguingly, both Offen and Scott's feminists and Muël-Dreyfus's collaborators embraced biological essentialism. In the same vein Laura Frader finds in her study of the construction of the French welfare state in the interwar years that a desire to reinforce the position of male breadwinners was a primary goal of French policy makers, whether in government or organized labor, and Kristen Stromberg Childers maintains that idealized notions of fatherhood underlay policies in a diverse range of fields in the Third Republic.[14] In combination with Rachel Fuchs's work on paternity cases in the nineteenth and twentieth centuries,[15] Frader's and Childers's studies suggest the centrality of fatherhood, and therefore of gender, to France and the French welfare state.

The insights of these historians and others raise fascinating questions about gender and citizenship as well as gender and politics in the years between 1918 and 1940 (and beyond)—what exactly were the virtues that male citizens were meant to possess? What were those destined for female subjects? How did this vary across the political spectrum? This study addresses these questions, outlining exactly what sort of man a republican citizen was supposed to be, showing how this message was conveyed in language as in ritual, and demonstrating how masculine republicanism functioned in the interwar years, including, significantly, how it affected important policy decisions.

Recent contributions to the historiography have also emphasized that in addition to particular constructions of gender, French republicanism rested on conceptions of race. Elisa Camiscioli, for example, posits that in the late nineteenth and early twentieth centuries, notions of racial hierarchy shaped a plethora of policies and popular attitudes in fields ranging from immigration to the economy to marriage. She suggests that a consensus had emerged among governing elites that to "reproduce" the French race only certain kinds of immigrants—white Europeans—should be admitted into France and only these racially desirable individuals should be encouraged to intermarry with French women and integrate fully into society and the economy.[16] Camiscioli's findings cohere with Frader's, which emphasize that the breadwinner model excluded not just women from well-paying professions but nonwhite men as well.[17]

Both Camiscioli's and Frader's scholarship on race builds, in part, on the work of historians of immigration, eugenics and racial theory, pronatalism, and neo-Malthusianism which has increasingly illustrated the importance of the idea of the French or white European race in all four fields. On immigration, for example, Vicki Caron's research on the Jewish refugee crisis of the 1930s demonstrates the widespread influence of distinctions between racially "desirable" immigrants and those—particularly eastern European Jews in her study—thought to be racially "undesirable."[18] While Caron emphasizes that there were principled opponents of such views,[19] other historians have shown the deep penetration of racial prejudices into centrist and left-wing circles as well as the corridors of power. Clifford Rosenberg's examination of Albert Sarraut, for instance, shows that the centrist and Radical,[20] who served variously and frequently during the interwar years as the minister of colonies, minister of the interior, and even twice interim *président du conseil,* was deeply influenced by race science and sought to limit the influx of racially undesirable North Africans into France as a result.[21] Mary Dewhurst Lewis's study of the policing of immigrants in interwar Marseille, meanwhile, shows how such prejudices could play out at the local level. While she stresses that officially the Republic's policies were not racist, there was considerable overlap between those targeted as "strange" and the categorization of racial undesirables—an overlap that increased over time as local authorities followed the dictates of the central government and cracked down on unwanted immigrants in the late 1930s.[22]

The findings of these and other historians of immigration mirror those of historians of eugenics and racial theory. One of the unsettling findings of analyses of the French eugenics movement by Anne Carol, William Schneider, and others, for example, is surely that the French Eugenics Society attracted many of the leading lights of the Republic upon its founding in late 1912. The Radical and former *président du conseil* Léon Bourgeois, for example, served as the society's first honorary president, and Paul Doumer, a Radical deputy, the past governor of Indochina, and a future president of the Republic, addressed the society's inaugural meeting; there were also many Socialists among the society's early adherents.[23] Members of the society, moreover, would continue to be influential in the interwar period.[24] Similarly, while Andrès Horacio Reggiani's work on the famed but flawed Nobel Prize-winning scientist Alexis Carrel indicates that his influence on French policies and government reached its apogee under the Vichy regime, it also makes clear that his eugenicist book, *Man, the Unknown,* was a highly influential best-seller in the interwar years.[25] The influence of the eugenics movement on interwar French politics and policy was great indeed.[26]

Carole Reynaud Paligot's work also buttresses the impression that social Darwinist conceptions of race increasingly structured French politics and culture. Her 2006 book, *La république raciale,* shows that polygenists who saw human races as fundamentally different from each other populated the French social sciences and anthropology in particular. These scholars constructed elaborate racial hierarchies and typographies accordingly. Paligot, moreover, demonstrates the impact such thinking had on colonial policy.[27] Her follow-up to *La république raciale,* 2007's *Races, racisme et antiracisme dans les années 1930,* pursues the argument further and demonstrates that in the 1930s despite the mounting evidence of its fallaciousness racial theory increasingly dominated French anthropology and psychology as well as colonial and immigration policies.[28]

Similarly, the mountain of scholarship on the pronatalist movement in France—referring to those who sought to increase the population by promoting the birthrate—has unearthed evidence that many pronatalists were concerned not just for the well-being of the nation or national economy, but also for the health of the French race. Camiscioli's first chapter outlines the connection between conceptions of race and French pronatalism, and many others, including Cheryl Koos and Miranda Pollard, have offered similar observations.[29] Thus, many influential pronatalists, such as Fernand Boverat of the powerful lobby group the Alliance nationale pour l'accroissement de la population française, stressed that they wished to raise the "French" birthrate and increase the "French" population: theirs was not an indiscriminate pronatalism.[30]

Demonstrating the pervasiveness of the racial paradigm, historians have discovered that notions of race influenced even pronatalists' most strident opponents. The neo-Malthusians were sexual radicals who believed that to avoid a Malthusian crisis, working-class men and women should be educated about methods of contraception. Foremost among them was the schoolteacher Paul Robin, a member of the first socialist international and a one-time associate of Karl Marx and Mikhail Bakunin. As Elinor Accampo shows, Robin, active at the turn of the century, was concerned about the health of the race as well as the well-being of the working class. This anxiety, moreover, was shared by many of his followers, including the feminist Nelly Roussel, who invoked horticultural imagery to argue that faulty human seeds should not be allowed to grow.[31]

This historiographical trend toward emphasizing the importance of race alongside gender, then, informs another goal of this study: to bring together the insights of historians of race and of gender in France, as Frader and Camiscioli, among others, have begun to do. Race and gender intersected in the discourses of the political parties in France, producing a myriad of policies and arguments not properly understood without studying both the racial and gender ideologies that lay behind them. Class too, while it is not a central focus of this study, remains important to understanding the material. Class identities informed the gender and racial discourses of the parties, and many of those discourses aimed to elide class differences and incorporate workers, in particular, into political movements, parties, the nation, and the Republic.

Another ambition of this book is to address the historical interpretation of gender and fascism—another topic where conceptions of race are highly relevant. A great deal of work has been done in this area, and its authors have typically explored a number of themes, including the essentially masculine character of fascist movements.[32] In so doing, they have argued persuasively that fascism advocated the advent of a "new man" who would possess a series of apparently distinctive traits. There was an emphasis placed on the physicality of this fascist man—he was to be youthful, vigorous, virile, aggressive, warlike, a man of action, homosocial, and generally hypermasculine.[33] In keeping with this, some, such as Klaus Theweleit, have portrayed fascists as misogynists run amok, and they have therefore suggested that hypermisogyny was both a particular characteristic of fascism and one possible path to it.[34] In contrast, others, while not denying the misogynist elements of fascism, have instead emphasized the role that women could and did play in fascist movements, forging, in Julie Gottlieb's words, a "feminine fascism."[35] Caroline Campbell's recent contributions to historians' knowledge of women in the Croix de feu adopt this perspective, as is especially clear in the introduction to her dissertation.[36]

While this literature has contributed substantially to our understanding, significant gaps remain in our knowledge. Most importantly, this vast scholarship on gender and fascism broadly and in the French case specifically rarely compares fascism to other political traditions. Relatively little attention, for example, has been paid by gender historians to the mainstream French political parties, which received more popular support than did the fascist leagues throughout the interwar period,[37] which dominated France's political institutions and governments, and which, by implication, exercised more direct influence on policy than did the extreme right. Historians can both improve their understanding of the nature of fascism by examining how its gender discourse did and did not differ from other political organizations and learn more about the impact of gender on politics by studying parties outside the fascist fold. Further, while there is an emerging literature on masculinity in France—stimulated, in part, by Robert Nye's pioneering work[38]—few have looked at the interwar period in depth.[39] As Christopher Forth's book on the Dreyfus Affair has illustrated, the politics of masculinity in that instance were equally crucial to all elements of the political spectrum,[40] suggesting by extension that more attention needs to be given to nonfascist parties and organizations in the 1920s and 1930s. Yet, no study to date offers an examination of the political parties' gender discourses, how they changed across the spectrum, how they transformed over time, and what impact they had on policy formation. Therefore, this book sheds new light on gender in interwar French culture broadly speaking, on how gender interacted with and shaped politics, the utility of gender for delineating different political traditions, how gender helped to form debates on a wide range of issues, how gender intersected with concerns and discourses of race and nation with respect to those issues, and, perhaps most interestingly, how French politicians' ideologies of gender affected the lives of ordinary French men and women.

Perhaps the most obvious implication of this analysis is that gender matters as Scott first argued in the 1980s.[41] Gender did have a profound impact on the way parties conducted business, on how they reached out to voters, on what policies they advocated, and on their members' and leaders' senses of identity and group cohesion. Hence, *The Republic of Men,* as a political history itself, strengthens the work of more traditional political histories by augmenting historians' understanding of the formative influence of gender on France's political formations.[42] It is to be hoped that this study makes it clear that it would be a mistake for political historians to overlook gender in the future.[43]

In order to make this point and others the evidentiary base must be broad. Some gender histories, while provocative, are based on relatively few sources. Lucia Re, for example, offers a theory of gender and fascism based on five Italian texts, while David Carroll advances his own based on a survey of the secondary literature and Pierre Drieu La Rochelle's *Gilles* and *Notes pour comprendre le siècle.*[44] These sources can be informative to be sure, but they lack the breadth to draw definitive conclusions about the broader phenomenon of fascism. *The Republic of Men,* therefore, does not concentrate on intellectuals alone, as their impact can be difficult to measure, but focuses instead on the utterances of politicians at rallies, at funerals, in letters, and in parliament, and the wider party presses, which featured diverse commentary from militants and leaders, including from hundreds if not thousands of women. The political parties and their politicians were the leaders of French society who, cumulatively, had literally millions of followers: their influence was profound. The newspaper research, moreover, was not restricted to particular sections of the parties' publications as gender scholarship sometimes is:[45] material has been drawn from editorials, sports sections, women's pages, youths' pages, essays, news stories, and obituaries over a twenty-one-year period.[46]

Chapter 1, "'The Eminent Virtues of the Citizen': Gender and Virtue," examines the gendering of virtue across the political spectrum in interwar France. In France, or "The Republic of Virtue,"[47] certain qualities were widely prized. These virtues were highly gendered. Commentators thought some to be specifically male characteristics, others to be specifically female in nature, and still others to be virtuous in both men and women but with different implications for the two sexes. There was, as well, considerable continuity across the political spectrum in the definition and evaluation of virtues, particularly with regard to those pertaining to women, while there were also important and revealing divergences along political and class cleavages. One item common to all the parties was that they appealed to men as breadwinners, a phenomenon that grew with time and reached its apex during the Great Depression and the Popular Front.[48]

Among the divergences, on the other hand, was that the political formations of the right held a profoundly paternalist view of French society, while those on the left, including the centrist Radical and Radical-Socialist Party, embraced a rhetoric of brotherhood or "fraternalism."[49] Notably, both envisioned male domination of the political world in one form or another. Fascism's contribution was its attempt to marry these two traditions. Fascists tried to maintain the paternalist authority of the leader characteristic of the right while invigorating their movements with the sense of fraternity found on the left. This marriage was contradictory and in many respects irreconcilable; it was nonetheless, at least for the Croix de feu, quite successful.

Chapter 2, "New Men, New Women: Gender and the Totalitarian Drift," explores this as well as fascism's other related innovation, "the new man." The construction of a novel masculinity by the Parti populaire français and Croix de feu clearly set them apart from the republican right. This man was, as George Mosse and others have illustrated, to be virile, militaristic, obedient, physically fit, anti-intellectual, and potentially violent.[50] However, as Mosse himself intimated but never fully explored, the fascist new man was in many respects anticipated by the Communists.[51] The Communists too needed such a man in order to be able to carry out a successful revolution. Particularly with the Bolshevization of the French Communist Party in the mid-1920s, Communist masculinity acquired a militaristic, unquestioning, violent, and anti-intellectual form. This is not to say that the communist and fascist "new men" were one and the same, but that the fascist version does appear as an adaptation of its communist predecessor. Moreover, with the increasing popularity of the totalitarian alternatives in the mid-to-late 1930s, ever-greater numbers of French men were being exposed to and presumably partly indoctrinated by masculinities at odds with republicanism and democracy. Their very identities were assuming authoritarian characters. This cannot have been healthy for the Third Republic.

Furthermore, chapter 2 queries whether alongside the new men of the extremes "new women" also appeared. In the Communist Party, a truly unconventional and militant femininity did arise for a time. While it never became the norm in the party the articulation of this vision of communist womanhood did open an exciting and liberating space for some women; however, with the onset of the Great Depression even the communists distanced themselves from the new woman and adopted a more conservative gender ideology. As for the fascists, while they too opened important spaces for women within their ranks, their articulation of ideal femininity remained staunchly traditional.

Studying the new men also provides some insight into the impact of World War I on French culture. While the war's impact on French masculinities cannot be measured definitively without a study that looks both at the pre- and postwar years, it seems obvious that the new men of the fascist and communist traditions were at least partly products of the Great War. For one, without the war the Russian Revolution might not have taken place; by extension, the French Socialist Party might not have split, and the Communist Party might not have come into existence; without the communist threat, French fascism would have been without its raison d'être. In a more abstract sense, both the far right and left's new men were militarized, disciplined, and aggressive—characteristics whose connection to the war seems obvious. Surely it is no coincidence that the Croix de feu began life as a veterans' organization. Thus, provocatively it would appear that just as World War I "disarmed" France, in the words of Mona Siegel, by spurring integral pacifism,[52] so too it engendered an opposite reaction: the communist and fascist new men.

Chapter 3, "'The Savagery of the Barbarians': The Politics of Race," begins to explore how the gender ideologies outlined in chapters 1 and 2 intersected with prevailing thoughts about race. Building on the work of Camiscioli and others, this chapter reveals how this intersection affected the political parties and leagues' positions on a host of issues, including immigration, colonialism, and sports and physical fitness. By consequence, moreover, ideologies of gender and race also shaped government policy. In addition to exploring the practical impact of these attitudes, the chapter remains attentive to variations across the spectrum and time, and discovers that there was a widely-shared acceptance of the idea of race, that this bipartisan understanding of race increased with time and especially with the onset of the Depression and the formation of the Popular Front, and that this convergence begat a France that was much more hostile to racial and gender difference by the late 1930s.

This phenomenon inevitably influenced the politics of pronatalism. Chapter 4, "'Warning! The Cradles Are Empty!': Gender and the Politics of Population," explores the practical implications of the prevalence of racial thinking further, including on the parties and leagues' support for and government policy on pronatalist measures. In the 1920s, the political right was the champion of raising the birthrate while the socialist left—the Socialist and Communist parties—rejected such measures. By the mid-1930s, however, that partisan split began to break down. Historians, especially those with progressive sympathies, have heretofore emphasized that while the Popular Front ultimately disappointed its supporters, it nonetheless spurred considerable social progress during its brief time in power.[53] Yet, contrary to some who view Léon Blum's government as the "least pro-natalist of the interwar era,"[54] evidence suggests the Popular Front represented the triumph of pronatalism and adopted a pronatalist course. In this light, the Popular Front appears less as a moment of progressive ascendancy and more as a turning point in French politics toward a path of racial regeneration and its attendant politics of exclusion.

The final two chapters of the book explore these racial and gendered discourses' impact on French women. The study reveals both that women could and did successfully resist the powerful discourses that worked against their emancipation and that sometimes those discourses proved too powerful to overcome. Chapter 5, "Women in Public Space: Women's Work and Women in Politics," presents just such a mixed bag. On the one hand, the breadwinner ideal, which suggested that women did not need to work, dominated the parties and leagues' rhetoric on women in the public sphere. On the other hand, women continued to work in large numbers in interwar France and women within the political parties and leagues successfully convinced almost all of their organizations to embrace the principle of equal pay for equal work. This success enjoyed by women within the political parties and leagues in influencing policy suggests another finding of this chapter: that women were visible and, to varying degrees, influential in every major political organization in interwar France. Thus, Sîan Reynolds's call for the inclusion of women in the political narrative is answered here.[55] As numerous studies have illustrated, women were making inroads during this period into the professions, education, and other previously male domains.[56] In line with other recent contributions,[57] *The Republic of Men* shows that the political parties were no different in this regard. Women held leadership positions in parties and leagues, founded and ran their own organizations and journals, appeared regularly in all the parties' publications, and lobbied party leaders behind the scenes to promote "feminist" policies such as the reform of the civil code or the enactment of women's suffrage. Thus, histories that have either ignored the role of women in the parties altogether,[58] or those that have nearly done so,[59] are seriously flawed and deny the presence and agency of these politicized women. Women made significant contributions to their parties and their activities should be recorded for posterity.

Despite women's activism, however, women's suffrage remained unattained by the outbreak of World War II. Women's suffrage was, quite simply, a casualty of the increasingly prevailing racial and gender conservatism of the interwar years. As chapter 6, "'Veritable Prisoners of Their Sex': Gender and

Race in the Debates over Women's Suffrage," suggests, female suffrage was opposed on a plethora of grounds, but underlying these concerns was a suspicion that women's voting was both unnatural and detrimental to national and/or racial hygiene. The campaign for the family vote—wherein male heads of households would receive one vote per member of their families—was but one indication of how the breadwinner ideal sabotaged suffragists. Daniella Sarnoff explores the fascist leagues' stances on women's suffrage and examines the gendered aspects of the interwar debates on the issue. This chapter goes beyond Sarnoff's work in its political scope and by demonstrating how racial concerns shaped those discussions alongside gender.[60]

THEORY AND DEFINITIONS

In addition to supporting this study's arguments, one of its aspirations is to remain as accessible as possible without sacrificing complexity or sophistication. That said, some terminology appears herein that begs unpacking.

First, gender is understood as the social construction of sexual difference. As Joan Scott famously puts it, "Gender is a constitutive element of social relationships based on perceived differences between the sexes, and gender is a primary way of signifying relationships of power."[61] In her analysis, moreover, Scott makes clear that both men and women have gendered identities, which scholars have subsequently dubbed "masculinity" and "femininity." R. W. Connell's explanation of masculinity is informative: "Rather than attempting to define masculinity as an object (a natural character type, a behavioural average, a norm), we need to focus on the processes and relationships through which men and women conduct gendered lives."[62] Masculinity and femininity, then, are inherently unstable understandings of maleness and femaleness. They are socially constructed and mutable.

Scott maintains that there has been, historically, a gender binary between masculinity and femininity.[63] She emphasizes that one was constructed in opposition to and in conjunction with the other. Yet, many gender historians have tended to focus on femininity.[64] Conversely, studies of masculinity have likewise demonstrated a propensity to examine only half the equation.[65] This tendency has provoked some to discuss masculinity studies as the reemergence of phallocentric history, with its exclusion of women from the narrative.[66] This project accordingly seeks to integrate these two scholarly traditions by covering both masculinity and femininity, asserting that a proper understanding of one can be achieved only alongside the other.

In addition, while Scott's binary is accepted here as the basic though socially constructed and variable framework, attention has been paid to Connell and to Judith Butler's teachings about the multiplicity of genders that can exist in competition with one another.[67] As Scott explains, "'man' and 'woman' are at once empty and overflowing categories. Empty because they have no ultimate, transcendent meaning. Overflowing because even when they appear to be fixed, they still contain within them alternative, denied or suppressed definitions."[68] Thus, while much of *The Republic of Men* focuses on the dominant or "hegemonic" varieties of femininity and masculinity within the parties, the advent and progress of competing "femininities" and "masculinities" has also been charted when applicable.

The language of race is similarly complex and, if anything, more loaded. While most scholars today rightly reject race as a biological category the concept had its origins in the early modern period and enjoyed near-universal purchase in late nineteenth- and early twentieth-century Europe.[69] Certainly, in interwar France most commentators reified race, believing the existence of biologically different races to be a scientific fact. Such people are defined in this book as "racialists"—meaning people who thought in terms of essentialized racial categories. Likewise "racialism" denotes the ideology of race—the racial paradigm nearly all accepted. In fact, however, like gender race is a socially constructed category based on perceived rather than real biological differences between groups of people. As Paligot emphasizes in her work on anthropologists, the first clue that races are pure abstractions should have been the impossibility of defining their boundaries.[70]

Racialism was often the gateway to racism, unsurprisingly. Pierre-André Taguieff defines racism as "the absolutizing of difference, the naturalizing or the essentializing of differences, whether perceptible or imagined."[71] He elaborates by explaining that racism is defined by five features:

> (1) the rejection of the universal [the idea of a universal humanity];
> (2) the fixed categorizing of individuals;
> (3) the absolutizing of collective differences;
> (4) the naturalizing of differences, whether by scientific biologization, ethnicization, or "culturalist" rigidification;
> (5) the inequitable interpretation of differences, measured on a universal scale of worth.[72]

Racists, in short, were those who discriminated or were prejudiced against those they perceived to be racially different (and usually racially inferior). By this definition there were certainly many racists in interwar France.

Finally, the term "fascism"'s utility and meaning have been debated endlessly by specialists.[73] Robert Paxton provides a useful definition:

> Fascism may be defined as a form of political behavior marked by obsessive preoccupation with community decline, humiliation, or victimhood and by compensatory cults of unity, energy, and purity, in which a mass-based party of committed nationalist militants, working in uneasy but effective collaboration with traditional elites, abandons democratic liberties and pursues with redemptive violence and without ethical or legal restraints goals of internal cleansing and external expansion.[74]

With regard to the task of deciding which parties or leagues were "fascist" this definition is helpful, but not definitive. The two fascistic—meaning "fascist-like"—parties or movements examined in detail in this book are the Parti populaire français and the Croix de feu/Parti social français. The latter is by far the most controversial case, as historians have long argued over how to characterize it.[75] Using Paxton's definition, the organization would appear to qualify as fascist except that it did not espouse external expansion; it might also be argued that it pursued its goals with some restraints, although these were notably imposed on it by the state. Paxton, for his part, describes the Croix de feu as belonging to the "fascist right" but also casts doubt on the movement's fascist bonafides.[76] Following his lead, however, the present study treats fascism as a creature of the interwar period (although it has since persisted), wherein political movements loosely fitting the above definition proliferated.[77] Certainly, both the Parti populaire français and the Croix de feu/Parti social français were part of this phenomenon.

THE POLITICAL PARTIES AND LEAGUES

In order to understand the ground this book covers, readers should have a clear picture of interwar France's political parties and leagues. First off, the Third Republic had a two-ballot electoral system (as does the Fifth Republic). In this system, any number of parties could run candidates for single member constituencies on the first ballot, but on the second, only the candidates who received the most and the second-most votes on the first ballot were eligible. Usually, this meant that between the first and second ballots alliances of relatively like-minded parties kicked in and mobilized their supporters behind their preferred candidate.[78] This system encouraged a proliferation of political parties and ensured that no one party could form a government on its own. Further, beyond the parties there were also extraparliamentary leagues, usually on the extremes, which did not run candidates in elections but sought to influence politics nonetheless.

The Communist Party was founded in December 1920, following the split in the old Socialist Party between the majority of the delegates at the Congress of Tours, who wanted to adhere to the Third International and thus follow Moscow and the Bolsheviks' lead, and the minority who did not. The Communist Party became the party of the majority. At the time of the "schism" as it is widely known, the Socialist Party had 180,000 members.[79] Initially, the fledgling Communist Party appeared to be in good shape. It had successfully attracted the more youthful members of the old Socialist Party, and by October 1921 it could boast roughly 110,000 members. This figure, however, had shrunk to eighty thousand by the spring of 1922, as the Comintern[80] exerted its influence to push out those it felt to be too socially democratic.[81] The party then entered a long period of steady decline, particularly as it was Bolshevized in the mid-1920s, and by the early 1930s it was a marginal force, with only twenty-five thousand members in 1932.[82] With the birth of the Popular Front, however, the Communists enjoyed a resurgence, jumping from eleven to seventy-two seats in the Chamber of Deputies, as their votes increased from 795,000 to 1,487,000, and their membership expanded to 328,457 in 1937. Thereafter, the figures are uncertain, but it is clear that the party was losing members from 1938 onward, and doing so precipitously following the signing of the Molotov-Ribbentrop Pact in August 1939.[83] The Communist Party had a steady succession of leaders who fell in and out of favor with Moscow, but in the 1930s Maurice Thorez emerged as the party's secretary-general and acknowledged leader, while the party's most constant figure throughout the period was Marcel Cachin, the editor of the Communists' tribune, *L'Humanité*. This study accordingly uses Marcel Cachin's personal papers, Thorez's autobiography, twenty-one years of *L'Humanité* (including the 1918–20 period prior to the schism), which had a circulation much wider than the party membership, and *L'Ouvrière,* the on-again, off-again women's journal that reportedly never had more than 800 readers.[84]

The Socialist Party left the schism at Tours seemingly enfeebled. It exited the congress with only fifty thousand devotees in tow[85] and minus *L'Humanité,* the paper of founder Jean Jaurès; yet, as early as the 1924 elections it trounced the Communist Party and returned as the party of choice for the majority of France's socialistic voters. By 1931, party membership had climbed to 135,000,[86] and in 1936 the Socialists emerged as France's foremost party, with 2,200,000 votes and 147 deputies, although they did possess a slightly lower membership than the Communists with around 285,461 militants at their 1937 peak.[87] The party's masthead with the loss of *L'Humanité* was *Le Populaire,* which was edited by the Socialist parliamentary leader and the party's dominant interwar personality, Léon Blum. Its circulation was a paltry twenty thousand in 1922,[88] but it increased steadily to forty thousand in 1932[89] and enjoyed a rapid expansion during the Popular Front. This study surveys this newspaper along with Léon Blum's personal papers, as well as those of Blum's friend and the party's financial expert, Vincent Auriol, as well as the pages of *La Femme Socialiste,* which, though not an official party publication, was the organ of Socialist-feminist Louise Saumoneau and an important center of exchange and debate for Socialist women and their male allies.

The Radical and Radical-Socialist Party was interwar France's party of power. No one could form a government without the cooperation of at least some of its members. Unlike the Socialist and Communist parties, the Radicals only partly resembled a modern political party, as they lacked a mass-mobilizing organization and showed a distinct lack of party discipline. Their membership during the 1930s fluctuated between seventy thousand and 120,000,[90] but the Radical Party's electoral strength was impressive. Even after the loss of some four hundred thousand votes and fifty seats in the 1936 elections,[91] it remained the second largest bloc in the Chamber of Deputies with 116 representatives.[92] The Radicals had no official press, but *L'Ère nouvelle,* surveyed here, began life in the early 1920s exemplifying the opinions of the party's left and ended in 1940 as the voice of its right, while *La Lumière,* also examined herein, assumed the mantle abandoned by *L'Ère nouvelle* on the left in 1927 and also published prominent Socialists.[93] The party's two dominant interwar personalities were Édouard Herriot and Édouard Daladier: accordingly, this study considers Daladier's personal papers as well as Herriot's influential *Pourquoi je suis radical-socialiste.* In addition, the archives of the Ligue des droits de l'homme, France's highly influential civil liberties union, also provide good insight into the thinking of the prominent Radicals and Socialists who dominated it.

On the right, the picture was more confused. There was the Alliance démocratique, reborn as a proper political party in 1933. Its previous incarnation was the Alliance républicaine et démocratique, which had been a loose coalition of parliamentarians. It represented the interests of the haute bourgeoisie and recognized that the Republic was the best guarantee of that class's privilege.[94] Led by Charles Jonnart until 1923, and Antony Ratier from 1923 to 1933, the Alliance made no attempt to mobilize the masses, either as members or for elections, and its parliamentarians were free to belong to other political parties.[95] But when the relatively young and charismatic Pierre-Étienne Flandin was installed as leader in 1933, the Alliance reinvented itself as a modern political party, taking the name of the Alliance démocratique.[96] Of the parties on the right, the Alliance was the most moderate, the most committed to the Third Republic, and the party most often participating in government. Its membership was negligible, but it alone among the parties of the right gained electorally in the pivotal 1936 elections, and its roster of parliamentarians produced no fewer than three *présidents du conseil* in the 1930s: Flandin, André Tardieu, and Paul Reynaud. The party's weekly, *L'Alliance démocratique*, provides a good sampling of the party's discourse, as do its archives and Flandin and Tardieu's papers.

The Fédération républicaine, standing to the right of the Alliance démocratique, was a coherent political party throughout the interwar years, although party discipline was limited and its boundaries were fluid as its members often belonged to multiple political organizations.[97] Still, the Fédération was, as William Irvine's study makes clear, consistently the largest political party on the French republican right. In the heyday of the nationalistic Bloc national following World War I,[98] the Fédération was a regular partner in government; yet following the elections of 1924 and the definitive shift to the left in French politics, it was often excluded from power. The party was very Catholic and intensely nationalistic. Its leader after 1924 was the anthropologist Louis Marin, whose papers, along with the party's weekly, *La Nation*, and its post-1935 women's monthly, *Le Devoir des femmes*, have been taken as indicative of the party's discourse.

In terms of membership and representation in the Senate and Chamber, the Parti démocrate populaire was much less significant than either the Alliance démocratique or the Fédération républicaine. Never boasting more than a handful of parliamentarians,[99] the party's roots can be traced back, arguably, as far as the Second Empire, when socially conservative but politically democratic Catholics rallied to the republican cause.[100] Formed in response to the triumph of the Cartel des gauches in the 1924 general elections by a group of Catholic politicians and intellectuals, including Robert Cornilleau, Jean Raymond-Laurent, and Georges Thibout, who served as the party's first president, the party remained relatively small but disproportionately influential.[101] Contemporaries recognized *Le Petit Démocrate,* the Parti démocrate populaire's newspaper, as a site where key debates took place on a number of issues, including women's suffrage; the party was at the forefront of all post-1924 discussions about the family. What makes the Parti démocrate populaire of even greater interest is that it was the forerunner of the post–World War II Mouvement républicaine populaire and therefore the "grandfather" of Christian democracy in France.[102] *Le Petit Démocrate,* a weekly, as well as some party pamphlets and programs serve as emblematic of the Parti démocrate populaire's discourse. Additionally, Catholic feminist Marie Maugeret's monthly newspaper, *Questions féminines et questions féministes,* while not officially affiliated with the party, can be read as indicative of the same conservative Christian democratic milieu.

The Croix de feu/Parti social français is something of a special case. First, it did not become a political party as the Parti social français until 1936, and then only under duress (it, along with the other fascistic leagues, was outlawed by the Popular Front and thus had to reinvent itself). That said, while it may not have stood for election prior to 1936, the Croix de feu was undeniably political in nature and provided important support to candidates of the right and their agendas. The Croix de feu was originally a veterans' organization, founded in 1927 by Maurice d'Hartoy, but it was when Colonel François de La Rocque became the group's president in 1931 that it began to expand rapidly and, arguably, take on a fascist tone.[103] The Croix de feu attracts a great deal of scholarly attention in French historiography because, alone among the fascist or quasi-fascist formations of France's interwar right, it enjoyed undeniable mass support, boasting a membership of, according to Robert Soucy, roughly five hundred thousand by the end of 1935 and nearly 1 million by 1937. By French standards of the time, this was enormous and made the Croix de feu/Parti social français the country's most populous political party.[104] Thus, historians who argue that homegrown French fascism was a significant phenomenon begin with the Croix de feu, while those seeking to classify domestic fascism as of marginal importance attempt to demonstrate the movement's republican credentials.[105] For the Croix de feu, its monthly and then weekly newspaper, *Le Flambeau,* has been consulted, as have the personal papers of François de La Rocque; these include, in essence, the organization's archives.

Finally, there remains the Parti populaire français, the one political formation of note that all observers agree was fascist. It appeared in 1936, under Jacques Doriot's leadership, and briefly attracted a good deal of support. Jean-Paul Brunet hypothesizes that it enjoyed a membership of roughly a hundred thousand by early 1938.[106] Thereafter, as the threat to private property of the Popular Front receded, and as Doriot entered a spiral of alcoholism and dissolution, the party's support melted away rather markedly. The organ of the Parti populaire français, *L'Émancipation nationale,* as well as the writings of party intellectual Drieu La Rochelle function well to exemplify party ideology and gender construction.

These were the parties and organizations that shaped politics in interwar France. Their conceptions of gender and race accordingly affected the lives of French citizens and subjects, just as, to some degree, they reflected the wider mentality of French society.

I
GENDER

1

"THE EMINENT VIRTUES OF THE CITIZEN"

GENDER AND VIRTUE

Gender historians agree that popular conceptions of gender "matter." Prevailing gender norms, scholars argue, have a profound influence on men and women's identity formation, on their upbringing, on their educations, on their career paths, in short, on their lives in the broadest possible terms. An obvious way in which gender can shape people's lives is through public policy. Politicians adopt gender ideals, allowing of course for variation depending on their ideologies, sexual and ethnic identities, and class backgrounds, and the laws they enact reflect their conceptions of gender. These laws then replicate and reinforce gender norms, or, in some cases, help to reshape them in important ways. It seems crucial then, to understand how gender informs policy formation if you want, as Karen Offen once put it, to "understand what was really going on."[1]

In order to understand "what was really going on" in interwar French politics, it seems essential first to explore what the gender ideals of France's politicians were. What did French political opinion makers think of as the ideal man and the ideal woman? Did this vary across the political spectrum? Did it change over time?

This chapter explores these questions through the prism of virtue. Paul Jankowski has deemed the Third Republic the "Republic of Virtue,"[2] and indeed the political parties' commentators and leaders spent a great deal of time praising and defining virtuousness. President of the Republic Albert Lebrun, for example, celebrated "the eminent virtues of the citizen" in dedicating a monument to former president Émile Loubet.[3] Needless to say, Lebrun and others' articulations were highly gendered, although there were virtues defined as common to and desirable in both sexes. Equally predictably, there were virtues, whether coded as masculine or feminine, that commentators agreed upon irrespective of party affiliation, while others were particular to given sections of the political spectrum. "Masculine" virtues were profoundly shaped by widespread understandings of fatherhood, brotherhood, and the breadwinner ideal; conversely, "feminine" virtues were frequently defined by conceptions of motherhood. By outlining the political contours of the gendering of virtue in interwar France this chapter lays the foundation for a better understanding of the policies pursued and in some cases enacted in the period.

COMMON VIRTUE: THE CULT OF SELFLESSNESS

Some virtues were universally prized and considered suitable for both men and women. Perhaps the most interesting of these was "selflessness," most often expressed as "self-abnegation" or "disinterestedness." Whether praising friends, colleagues, party militants, family members or historical figures, male and female, left- and right-wing political commentators invariably touched on their selflessness as proof of an individual's worth. This particular virtue also evinced little change over time—it was as celebrated in 1940 as in 1919. Further, invocations of selflessness frequently evoked the memory of World War I when French soldiers had—so the logic went—saved the nation through their spirit of self-sacrifice. This tendency to reference the Great War was more pronounced on the right than on the left but could be found across the political spectrum. It also reveals the degree to which the legacy of the war loomed large in the 1920s and 1930s.

As a leader of a movement that began as a veterans' organization, and which constructed a powerful cult of heroism around veterans of World War I, Colonel François de La Rocque, leader of the Croix de feu and Parti social français, often expressed this theme of selflessness in his correspondence. On October 13, 1936, for example, he wrote Raymond Guenard, a party member from the Marne who was reportedly shot by a Communist Party agitator: "I don't doubt for a second, my dear friend, that you remain devoted to our cause. But, after the sacrifice that you have already made in so generously spilling your blood for our Country, I hesitate to again abuse your self-abnegation."[4] La Rocque thus focused on Guenard's virtuous spirit of self-sacrifice and suggested that service to the Croix de feu was akin to service to the "country."

Figures from the conservative right likewise extolled selflessness as a virtue verging on the sublime. Speaking in the Chamber of Deputies after becoming *président du conseil,* conservative Alexandre Millerand declared that "in order to derive from the victory [over Germany in World War I] our due and legitimate benefit, we will have to expend no less effort, and evince no less selflessness than was needed to win it." He continued, "To save the fatherland, his children, in an admirable spirit of faith and self-abnegation, offered him everything, including their lives."[5]

A sense of duty was inextricably tied to this self-effacement. It was a virtue that could be invoked in almost every circumstance, providing individuals with a moral compass to guide them in their lives. In the traditional right's paternalist worldview men had duties to fulfill to their country, to their party, and to their wives and families. Louis Marin's eulogy for prominent Fédération républicaine parliamentarian and former minister of finance Charles de Lasteyrie, for instance, stressed his faithful work for the nation and his "sense of duty."[6] Renowned philosopher Henri Bergson, whose theories, though he was a republican, approached proto-fascism, similarly applauded his friend André Tardieu for his having "patriotically undertaken his duty."[7] Duty was the companion to the power vested in men in the patriarchal order espoused by conservatives. If men, in this view, enjoyed certain privileges, they also had well-defined responsibilities.

Leftist men too enjoyed advantages in exchange for obligations. That said, speaking generally, leftists exhorted men to be selfless not in the service of an organic hierarchical social order, embodied in the nation or "fatherland," but in the interests of the Republic, their social class, or "the revolution." As always, the line between left and right blurred somewhere in the center, in the space occupied by the Radical Party, wherein unregenerate conservatives coexisted with progressive liberals. The right's vision of a conservative selflessness buttressing the social order was, after all, not altogether different from the solidarism that had become the Radicals' primary sociopolitical philosophy in the 1890s. Léon Bourgeois and other solidarists, as Judith Stone explains, posited fatherland and family as the pillars of interclass solidarity.[8] Few rightists would have disagreed.

Yet, while a definitive left/right divide can be difficult to delineate, there were subtle but important differences. Certainly, "disinterestedness" and "self-abnegation" were considered virtuous on the left. A true man of the left, for example, was self-denying, self-abnegating, and generally selfless just as on the right. As a small sample demonstrates, the terminology was near ubiquitous: Boris Souvarine, later expelled from the Communist Party for his defense of Léon Trotsky,[9] extolled Lenin in a memorial as "the most disinterested man one could ever imagine";[10] supporters praised Radical *pré-*

sident du conseil Édouard Daladier for his selflessness in stepping down in the wake of the February 6, 1934, riots;[11] Communist Marcel Cachin, in a speech delivered on the anniversary of his friend Paul Vaillant-Couturier's death, declared his fellow Communist a "disinterested soldier, who stood for the defense of all human causes."[12] The valorization of selflessness in men was, suffice it to say, universal in French politics.

The chief difference on the right and left in this regard thus lay not in the language of selflessness per se but in the substance of the duties that this selflessness entailed. On the socialist left, for instance, there was much less focus on paternalist duties than on the right, as befitted the left's fraternalist rhetoric versus the right's paternalism. Cachin, for example, frequently reminded his male readers and listeners of their duties in a manner that might seem identical to right-wing commentators. Yet Cachin referred not to men's duties to their families or nation, but to, for instance, "the working class."[13] Similarly, in a 1932 poster thanking those who had voted for him in the recent election, Socialist Party grandee Vincent Auriol used language that superficially echoed the militarized evocations of World War I on the right: "The battle is over. Duty begins." However, Auriol referred not to a duty to defend the fatherland or the French family but to pursue the "social renovation" desired by his party.[14] Therefore, while both the French right and left praised selfless men, they saw that selflessness as leading to different ends.

Nor was selflessness a desirable characteristic in men only. Both men and women were expected to be self-effacing; however, what this meant for each gender could be radically different: there were separate spheres of self-effacement. In the right's ideal, for example, a man showed his self-abnegation by acting as a responsible *père de famille,* taking the decisions necessary for his family's welfare and ruling over his wife and children benevolently. Thus, while his self-effacement meant a communitarian and familial outlook, privileging the needs of his dependents over his own, he retained a degree of power and freedom of action. A woman, on the other hand, showed her spirit of self-sacrifice by embracing her "natural" role, following her husband's lead and generally letting her individual identity be erased. This was symbolized by the way women's names were publicly recorded. Even when ostensibly the focus of praise women usually found their identities subordinated to men's. The Parti démocrate populaire's masthead, for example, *Le Petit Démocrate,* printed a telling obituary. In this piece, the deceased was identified as "Madame Paul Duguet" and her given name was never noted.

Her husband's full name appeared, as it would have in his own obituary, but hers did not.[15] Of course, at least Madame Duguet was visible to the degree that her obituary was featured in the paper: for the most part, women passed on without comment—the vast majority of obituaries in the political press were for male politicians, militants, and public figures. Even when profiling important women within their respective parties, newspapers like *L'Alliance démocratique* usually did not give their first names, instead identifying them with either Madame or Mademoiselle, thus defining them in terms of their relationships to men.[16] This effacement was predictable. The Fédération républicaine's Fernande Hartmann made it abundantly clear in her treatise on the education of young girls that a spirit of "obedience" and "discretion" was absolutely essential in a woman's life, as was "thoughtfulness, right up to the forgetting of oneself." Hartmann continued that women experienced the most "heroic hour" of their lives when, after having "lived for others," they gave up their children to adulthood and let go of their maternal role. As she proclaimed, "A woman must know how to be dead to herself."[17] A woman must, in other words, allow her own identity, her own aspirations, and her own dreams to be entirely submerged within the family.

As with men, "duty" was a component of this selflessness. Again, however, women's "duty" was quite different from men's. "*Le devoir des femmes*" (women's duty) was a favored catchphrase on the right and was unique to it. In fact, *Le Devoir des femmes* was the name of the Fédération républicaine's women's journal, which took its title from an earlier publication of the Catholic feminist right, founded in 1901.[18] The name was likely a response to *Le Droit des femmes* (women's right), the feminist and suffragist paper of the Ligue française pour le droit des femmes, most famously edited by noted feminist (and Radical) Maria Vérone.[19] The title also reflected the right's typical juxtaposition of citizens' "duties" and "rights." Thinkers tended to view the latter as individualistic and divisive; Senator A. Lefas of the Fédération raised this theme in his article "Duties Trump Rights: Duty First!" in which he congratulated the Fédération's women for performing their duties selflessly without selfishly pursuing their rights.[20] Likewise, speaking to a meeting of the Croix de feu's feminine section in Bordeaux in 1934, National Volunteer G. Feraud went on at great length and to acclaim about "the duty of women" toward the nation and their families.[21]

As on the right, self-abnegation meant something quite different for leftist women than it did for men. *La Femme Socialiste,* for example, fêted the

Hungarian socialist couple Koloman and Paula Wallisch and stressed that both "devoted themselves selflessly to propaganda and educational work."[22] Koloman, however, had become a leader of Styrian socialism, while Paula had gravitated into party social work, organizing a society that took orphans off the street and relocated them in good socialist homes. Paula, like her husband, had sacrificed for the cause but had done so in what was seen as an appropriately feminine manner, helping children as befitted her maternal femininity (this was underlined by the fact that she apparently liked to "play with the children and dance around with them"). These divergent masculine and feminine paths, both selfless, led Koloman to be executed by the Miklos Horthy dictatorship while Paula escaped with incarceration. Dying for one's cause was a masculine prerogative.

A narrative of female subordination to leftist male domination was oft-repeated (and praised) under the guise of selflessness. Socialist Georges Boris, for instance, remembered Thérèse Blum, Léon Blum's much-beloved wife, as someone with "ardent convictions" and with a strong sense of "what is just and good," which explained her "attachment to a cause and her devotion to her man."[23] Thérèse's femininity, like Paula Wallisch's, dictated that, properly selfless, she evinced her commitment to socialism by supporting her husband. Her selflessness was passive: Léon's was active.

Thus, selflessness, though it was a universally prized virtue, was far from gender neutral. A close reading reveals that just as its meaning varied for men and women, so too it changed somewhat from right to left.

MASCULINE VIRTUES

In addition to selflessness, of course, there were other virtues celebrated within interwar French politics. Many of these were gender specific. The case of expressly masculine virtues is especially complex, as some virtues were applauded as manly across the political spectrum with subtle changes in nuance and context, while others might be celebrated, for example, on the left but not on the right. The key to understanding the way these virtues fractured politically lies in the distinction between the traditional right's paternalist discourse as opposed to the left's fraternalist one. The traditional right's hierarchical familial vision of society led it to espouse different virtues than the left with its view of a brotherhood of men, or in some cases, to interpret the same virtues in differing ways.

Perhaps the most universally applauded virtue that was specific to men in the discourse was a strong work ethic. French politicians and political commentators—from communists to fascists—celebrated hardworking men and enjoined their male followers to work hard for their causes. This, of course, does not mean that women could not be hardworking or that, on occasion, commentators did not extol a given woman's hardworking nature; but "hardworking" was not a stock descriptive for praiseworthy women the way it was for men.

On the right, Catholic syndicalists had long promoted the value of hard work to working-class identity (as had, indeed, other unionists), stressing that it provided labor with a dignity lacking in the confrontational militancy promoted by leftists.[24] In keeping with this tradition, the right-wing parties all promoted a strong work ethic as a key masculine virtue. Such was the case in the first-ever issue of *Le Devoir des femmes*. Outlining the lessons that Marcus Aurelius had supposedly learned from the parental figures in his life, an anonymous author listed "to love work and to do it assiduously."[25] Similarly, then President of the Republic and Alliance républicaine et démocratique member Paul Doumer wrote to the minister of agriculture, André Tardieu, to recommend one Gustave Hannoun for employment and declared, "Mr. Hannoun is very serious, hardworking, and intelligent."[26]

On the fascistic right, hard work was more overtly politicized. The Croix de feu, in particular, stressed that devotion to the cause and tireless effort would ensure the movement's triumph and thus the rejuvenation of France. This was particularly evident in calls on men to labor unfailingly for the movement. The Croix de feu, adherents were consistently told, would return France to glory through the common enterprise of its cadres. Jean Ybarnégaray, for example, the leader of the then nascent Parti social français's parliamentary group, called on the party's men, in October 1936 to "work intensely for our goals in the ranks of the PARTI SOCIAL FRANÇAIS . . . follow LA ROCQUE, and lead France behind him."[27]

The Parti populaire français echoed this theme. And like the Croix de feu's writers and leaders, the Parti populaire français saw work as both delivering France from republican-inspired decadence and as forging the unity necessary for the party's victory. Jacques Doriot, for example, drummed up enthusiasm for the party's 1938 congress by touching on both work and unity:

> After eighteen months of common effort, the men who have had the mission of welding the party together present themselves in front of it in total unity of thought, doctrine and action.
>
> This intimate union of men from all points on the political horizon is a major asset for our party and unique in the political annals of our country.[28]

On the left, the picture was both similar and distinctive. Certainly, commentators saw an ability to work hard as a masculine virtue. Obituaries, for example, typically celebrated the hard labor performed by their subjects in support of various causes. *La Lumière* cofounder Émile Glay's, for example, written by his good friend and collaborator Alfred Bayet, revealed that "death had surprised him still hard at work" and that he had given "himself completely to the study of the great problem of education."[29] Likewise, *La Femme Socialiste* remembered its departed contributor Charles Vérècque, the husband of noted Socialist-feminist Marguerite Dupuis-Vérècque, as a man "issued from the world of work, who remained faithful to that world all his life" and whose life's "work was great."[30] Although he was not yet dead, the Communists portrayed Stalin in a similar light. Tragicomically, *L'Ouvrière* carried an interview with his mother, translated from its *Pravda* original, wherein Mrs. Stalin lovingly recalled her son's taking time out from his intense working schedule to pay her an unsolicited visit. Apparently, "our comrade Stalin" was not only a very hard worker, but a loving son to boot.[31]

Men on the left could also draw attention to their merit by highlighting their many years of work. Radical supporter A. Bernard, for example, began his letter to Édouard Daladier by saying "I am 69 years old and have worked for 53 years."[32] Bernard hoped to establish his worthiness to Daladier and thus have him take his words seriously. This was a letter to a high official, but more private correspondence also often revealed this tendency to emphasize one's industriousness. In a letter to his daughter written from La Santé, where political prisoners were held, for example, Communist Marcel Cachin painted himself and his fellow internees as working hardily in the service of the revolution: "I am surrounded by ten good comrades in the struggle with whom I get along perfectly: we work, and we hold discussions."[33]

Cachin's comments hint at a similarity between the Marxist left and the fascistic right. While being hardworking was admired across the political spectrum the purpose of men's labor was more openly politicized on the margins. Socialist Party secretary Paul Faure's memorial for Jules Guesde, a founder of France's first Marxist party, the Workers' Party in 1880 and therefore a grandfather of both the Socialist and Communist parties, was instructive. As he wrote, Guesde "was still reading everything, he knew the smallest details of the life of the party and the international situation. He truly died while still fighting, certain of the final victory of the proletariat, providing his brothers in arms with a magnificent example of a life entirely devoted . . . to the socialist ideal. . . ."[34] Faure thereby constructed Guesde as the ideal socialist man—working hard for the revolution until the bitter end. Thus, while the Croix de Feu and Parti populaire français pushed their men to work hard for their movements in order to help rejuvenate an ailing France, the Socialists and Communists did likewise to facilitate the advent of social revolution.

Laboring faithfully for the revolution frequently meant demonstrating "sangfroid," which emerged as a vital masculine characteristic on the left and the right. *L'Humanité* editor Cachin was especially given to invoking this masculine virtue. In 1920 alone he authored three editorials entitled "Sangfroid," calling on his readers to display this manly quality in a variety of circumstances but especially in considering the ongoing debates about whether or not the Socialist Party should adhere to the Third International.[35] Cachin's heavy reliance on this term betrayed his view of the importance of keeping cool under pressure to a Socialist (and later a Communist) man's masculinity.

Leftists, like rightists, most frequently invoked the need for sangfroid in moments of crisis. For instance, in the wake of the March 1937 clash between Communist and Croix de feu militants at the Place de Clichy in Paris, Socialist André Février, desperately hoping to keep the Radicals from abandoning the Popular Front over Communist violence, called on his readers to, "give proof of their sangfroid and their discipline" by waiting for the authorities to complete their investigation of the incident before drawing hasty conclusions.[36] Similarly, Vincent Auriol entreated his detractors in the Chamber of Deputies to show a little "sangfroid" and to stop interrupting his speech on the need to reverse his deflationary policies in 1936,[37] and the editorialist at *L'Ère nouvelle,* who, admittedly, had drifted noticeably to the right by this time, called for "courage and sangfroid" as the Battle for France reached its pivotal stage in mid-May 1940.[38] Leftists saw sangfroid as crucial to the masculine qualities of perseverance, courage, and clear thinking in times of crisis.

Right-wing commentators similarly exhorted men of the right to keep a cool head in the face of challenges. As the Parti démocrate populaire senator Armand Champetier de Ribes declared in 1936: "In the disarray of men and things, we are proud to conserve our sangfroid, to preserve our confidence, and to remain faithful to our program."[39] Not only did the senator stress the party's masculine sangfroid in the face of the challenges of 1936; he implicitly attacked the masculinity of other parties in deploring the "disarray of men and things."

The Croix de feu and Parti populaire français shared Champetier de Ribes's admiration of this trait. Colonel de La Rocque, for example, wrote an essay lamenting its disappearance among the general population and asserted that only his movement retained it as a dominant characteristic. He was sure that this would attract people to the Croix de feu banner.[40] The Parti populaire français's Maurice Lebrun meanwhile, specifically lauded the sangfroid of the "*gardes mobiles*" in holding them up as an example for party faithful to follow in the fight against Communist disorder.[41]

What made a capacity for hard work and an aptitude for sangfroid discursively masculine attributes, likely, were two social phenomena, both related to the so-called "doctrine of separate spheres." From the French Revolution forward, as Joan Landes and others have shown, politics was gendered as within men's sphere, while women's sphere was thought to be "in the home."[42] Accordingly, when envisaging political militants who would work hard and show sangfroid for their cause, interwar French politicians and pundits thought of men, not women. Similarly, the gendering of work more broadly, in which policy makers and others viewed earning income for the family as a male responsibility—as the role of a male breadwinner—no doubt had an impact on the discourse as well.[43] Thus, the public, political, and breadwinning sphere was gendered as masculine and thought to be a male domain. As this tendency only grew more pronounced following the onset of the Depression, it is unsurprising to find that interwar figures continued to perceive being hardworking as a highly desirable and specifically masculine trait.

As the breadwinner ideal suggests, fatherhood represented another point of convergence on the right and the left. Being a father brought men praise in both camps, and exhibiting properly fatherly attributes did likewise. Again, however, there were variations on the theme that corresponded to political affiliation; moreover, more notably than with a capacity for hard work, the perception of fatherhood, especially on the left, evolved over the period.

Within its paternalist framework, the traditional right emphasized the many responsibilities and duties of husbands as heads of their families. As Kristen Stromberg Childers has observed, "Linguistically, fathers in France were accorded a special status as *pères de famille,* or 'fathers of a family,' an expression that symbolized the father's unique collective and relational identity and finds no direct translation in the English language."[44] This discursive distinction signified the centrality of fatherhood to a French man's masculinity at this time. As a Parti démocrate populaire writer offered, fatherhood and fatherly love were the pinnacle of a man's life: "Only the love of a father for his children is a perfect love: it is disinterested and pure. Fathers do things for their sons they would do for no other. A son is a father's oeuvre . . . and before this new being, . . . he feels creative, benevolent, powerful, and happy."[45]

The right assumed that all men were, or would be, fathers. Fatherhood was so prized, in fact, that letter writers and others used it to signify their worthiness much as they did when they highlighted their hardworking nature. Louis Marin, for example, in his letter pleading for clemency for a Mr. de Wasels stressed repeatedly that de Wasels was the head of a large family, implying thereby both that he must be a good patriot and that his case deserved mercy for the sake of his charges.[46] Likewise, a supporter of right-wing President Alexandre Millerand began his letter by identifying himself as the father of nine children.[47]

Fatherhood as a mark of suitable masculinity was also evident in interwar obituaries. The death of a son in the Great War was frequently offered as proof of the father's patriotism and once again demonstrates the impact of the war on French society and culture. The eulogy in the Senate for the conservative Senator Lesgranges from the Saône-et-Loire, for example, highlighted the loss in the war of the senator's "tenderly loved" son,[48] while that for Deputy Henri Roquette declared that he "paid a very heavy tribute to the war. Father of a family of 12, he saw two of his sons fall for France."[49]

The right's affinity for fatherhood coalesced with its paternalism. Even the former Communist and increasingly dissolute Jacques Doriot liked to posture as the "father" of the Parti populaire français "family."[50] The Croix de feu's Colonel de La Rocque was especially given to these fatherly fantasies. In one instance, for example, he inaugurated a new page of *Le Flambeau* dedicated to the "Sons and Daughters of Croix de feu," the party's youth group, in the following manner: "My children, my friends, I give you *your* journal," and he signed the message "Your old President-General who loves you so much."[51] Indeed, evidence suggests that La Rocque took an active interest in the welfare of his Croix de feu children.[52] La Rocque's right-hand woman, Antoinette de Préval, for instance, explained that "the Colonel desired" that she and Madame de Gérus, the leader of the feminine section, become the godmothers of a young boy whose *Croix de feu* father had recently died.[53] As *Le Flambeau*'s I. Montaudoin proudly reported on the occasion of the opening of a Croix de feu children's center in 1935, this paternalist attention paid dividends: "The children give all their affection to the colonel. One of them even told me, 'I love him like a second father.'"[54]

As on the right, meanwhile, leftist commentators assumed men to be fathers. War brought out this tendency most poignantly. Radical *président du conseil* Édouard Daladier, for instance, in one of his radio broadcasts meant to maintain public morale in World War II's early days, referred to soldiers at the front who had gone to defend "their households," thereby evoking the image of the father fighting to protect his wife and children.[55] Similarly, Socialist Vincent Auriol evinced his concern for fathers by intervening personally with Daladier in 1939 to point out the incongruity that among the *gardes mobiles, pères de famille* had been sent to serve on the frontlines while *célibataires* (single men) remained stationed in the interior.[56] Clearly, fatherhood carried increased responsibilities and therefore increased privileges in Auriol's mind. Even the Communists, supposedly the enemies of the traditional family, insisted that the joys of fatherhood were enhanced in the Soviet Union.[57]

The most crucial difference between the right and the left regarding fatherhood lay in the right's exaltation of large families. On the right, men were not just expected to be fathers and heads of families but to be fathers of four, five, or more children. On the left, this was not the case before the mid-1930s. This divergence was largely due to the fact that the politics of pronatalism dominated the right while achieving limited penetration on the left until the Popular Front. Generally speaking, prior to the mid-1930s, the further left one was on the political spectrum, the more hostile one was likely to be to the promotion of large families. In the 1920s, for example, the Communist Party's view was essentially that France's low birthrate reflected the misery of the working class—life was so hard that workers could neither afford more mouths to feed nor justify introducing children to lives of deprivation.[58]

What is certainly true is that there was no cult of the *père de famille nombreuse* (father of the large family) on the left as there was on the right. Obituaries on the left, for instance, did not mention the size of a man's family as a signifier of his masculinity, unlike those on the right.

While the left only belatedly embraced some pronatalist measures such as family allocations, the Radicals, Socialists, and Communists did explicitly appeal to fathers as breadwinners in a number of ways. The Communist and Socialist parties, for instance, both capitalized on the Great Depression by lambasting the "bourgeois parties" for failing to look out for the interests of working people and workingmen in particular. In turn, of course, the parties presented themselves as able to defend the workingman's interests. In the images that appeared in the parties' press, for instance, the party was invariably personified as masculine and as standing up, aggressively, to the forces of rapacious capital. Figure 1.1, for example, appeared in *L'Humanité* in July 1935 and featured right-wing Pierre Laval, *président du conseil* at the time, divvying up the ill-gotten gains from his much-maligned "decree-laws" (he had received emergency powers to deal with the economic crisis in the face of leftist opposition) with an overweight capitalist complete with tuxedo, top hat, and cigar. Unbeknownst to Laval and his portly companion, however, a large muscular-looking worker was standing behind their screen,

Fig. 1.1. *L'Humanité*, July 23, 1935, 1.

Fig. 1.2. *L'Ouvrière,* March 4, 1926, 1.

inscribed with the words "Equal Sacrifice for All," and rolling up his sleeves, getting ready, one presumes, to force the miscreants to live up to their false egalitarian rhetoric. Such appeals specifically targeted male workers with families. The party, its militants, and workers were all personified as male. Figure 1.2 made this appeal to breadwinners explicit. Showing a bare-chested man holding a sledgehammer, flanked by a widow holding a dead soldier, a female worker, and a mother with two children, the artist appealed to the reader to join the party in order to fight taxes, the high cost of living, fascism, and colonial wars and to attain the protection of mothers and children and his or her full political rights. Again, despite the fact that this image appeared in the Communist Party's women's journal, the central Communist in the picture is the man, and one of the primary appeals to that man was as breadwinner. Through communism, the picture implies, he would be able to protect and provide for his wife and family.

FEMININE VIRTUES

If interwar French politicos saw working hard, having sangfroid, being a father, and behaving in a fatherly fashion as specifically masculine virtues, then these qualities certainly had feminine corollaries. There were any number of virtues that commentators perceived to be inherently feminine in nature and which came up continuously in discussions of worthy women, women's social roles, and related subjects.

It is interesting to note that even in the early 1920s, when the socialist left maintained untraditional positions with regard to a number of "women's issues"—including the issues of women working and women's suffrage, for example—the virtues that left-wingers regarded as feminine rarely differed much from those admired on the right. Thus, the road was paved, so to speak, for the Socialists and Communists to shift, as they did in the early to mid-1930s as part of the Popular Front strategy, to a more conservative gender politics by their strikingly conventional view of femininity. For most commentators, it would seem, the apparent radicalism of some of the positions of the immediate postwar period went only skin deep.

For the centrist Radicals, meanwhile, no such shift proved necessary. The party was always, during the interwar years at least, France's most retrograde political formation of significance when it came to "women's issues," particularly women's suffrage. The Popular Front, therefore, while it pushed the Socialists and Communists to retreat to convention simply brought others into conformity with views long held by the Radicals. Profoundly conventional, the embrace of a conservative vision of gender sat very comfortably with the Radical Party.

Accordingly, men and women of both the left and the right believed a litany of virtues, which they associated with motherhood in particular, to be innately feminine. The most prominent of these included purity—meaning both chastity and a purity of spirit—a capacity for caregiving, and a pacifistic nature. These were the virtues, combined with the selflessness described above, that defined the interwar period's ideal woman.

On the right, unsurprisingly, conventional views of women and feminine virtues predominated. In keeping with Catholic traditions in particular, women were expected to be pure, faithful within and chaste outside of marriage. Fédération républicaine leader Louis Marin, for instance, pointedly titled an essay he penned on Saint Margaret, "Saint Margaret, Virgin and

Martyr."[59] For Marin, Margaret's dying unspoiled rendered her a worthier example of ideal womanhood. Purity also extended beyond the sexual: women were supposed to be pure of sentiment as well. "Annie," a regular contributor to *Le Petit Démocrate,* advised prospective brides to be practical about their men's inquiring after their dowries and to be equally pragmatic about having their fathers check out their beaus' financial situations. She assured her readers that such realism "does not detract at all from the purity of your sentiments."[60] The Croix de feu's La Rocque also often invoked the language of feminine purity, such as in an article addressing, "My girl students," about the "home" that they had established (a sort of sorority house for the movement's women students), when he remarked that it was "welcoming, pure, [and] joyous."[61]

The left also focused on female purity. Accordingly, female columnist Fanny Clar's call for the end to the exaltation of feminine purity was a voice in the left-wing wilderness.[62] Indeed, the language of purity was as frequently invoked in acclamations of leftist women as of their right-wing counterparts. Socialist Alice Jouenne claimed (dubiously given that the majority of Socialists rallied to the war effort) that Socialist women had "piously consecrated" international women's day during the war to building international solidarity.[63] Marcel Cachin raved about Karl Liebknecht's "courageous struggle" against World War I, while emphasizing, in counterpoint, Rosa Luxemburg's "noble and pure soul."[64] Cachin's (then) fellow Communist Paul Guitard likewise praised Josephine Baker as representing "pure dance"[65]—a classification that reflected both Guitard's conception of femininity and his racialization of the African American Baker as a "noble savage," a stereotype that Baker, of course, played to with her "*danse sauvage.*"[66] Even the fiery Socialist feminist Louise Saumoneau referred to Charlotte Osmin as a "model wife and mother" and as "one of the purest women of our Party."[67]

This exaltation of women's purity on the left also meant chastity outside of reproductive marriage as it did on the right. There was, however, a considerable nonconformist tradition in this regard on the political left. Léon Blum, for example, advocated in his 1908 treatise *Of Marriage* that young women experiment in their youth so as to find sexual fulfillment.[68] Nor was Blum entirely exceptional, as there were a number of commentators on the left, including Socialist then Communist Louise Bodin, who argued for a more open sexual education for women.[69] The most celebrated case of nonconformism regarding sexual politics was Madeleine Pelletier, onetime member of both the Socialist and Communist parties, a medical doctor, and a committed neo-Malthusian, who has been much discussed in the historiography.[70] Pelletier, who had been sexually abused by her father, argued contrary to Blum that women could be emancipated only if they suppressed their sexual appetites and thereby became totally independent from men. She, in fact, made this argument in *L'Ouvrière* in 1924.[71] Opinions such as Pelletier's and Blum's could be advanced only on the left—the right was more bound by a conservative sexual politics. This relative openness was certainly significant and did allow for some debate in a society that was extremely censorious of discussions of sexuality (especially female sexuality). Birth control literature, for example, was outlawed in 1920.[72]

But this progressiveness was limited, as one might expect from Angus McLaren's study of the increasing hegemony of conservative French attitudes to birth control.[73] Much more typical, especially after the early 1920s, were opinions such as leftist and medical doctor Jenny Héricourt's, that sexual education sounded great in theory but led to increased promiscuity in practice. Héricourt stated that women were not ready for sexual egalitarianism.[74] In a similarly conventional fashion, Socialist Danièle Vindor advised mothers to police their daughters' sexual activity rigorously so as to guard their virginities and avoid them falling into "an abyss."[75] Moreover, the golden era of frank discussion of sexuality, if there was one in the interwar years, was clearly in the early 1920s; thereafter, sexual radicals like Pelletier found their views decisively marginalized even in the Communist Party. Pelletier for example left the party in 1925, and radical perspectives like hers disappeared from the party press. Such ideas could now be expressed only within the increasingly marginal anarchist movement.[76]

Indeed, this is one instance where the evidence shows a clear change over time. As the space disappeared on the far left for radical discussions of sexual freedom for women, so too the left increasingly came to adopt a rhetoric of feminine selflessness indistinct from the right's. Thus, on the left commentators came to extol sexual purity and a spirit of self-abnegation within motherhood. Their logic was fairly straightforward. As Socialist Alice Jouenne explained to her readers, the Socialist woman "has many duties to her child because the child of today will be the man of tomorrow and will continue the task that we have begun."[77] Sacrificing her needs, including her sexual needs, for her child, therefore, was how a good Socialist woman evinced the necessary self-sacrifice for the cause.

Indeed, if purity defined feminine virtue, there was no clearer expression of the purity of a woman's soul than motherhood. If men on both the left and right were to strive for fatherhood then a woman's mission in life, in most reckonings, was to be a mother. Accordingly, a host of virtues associated with motherhood were coded as feminine, including a boundless capacity for caregiving and an innate pacifism.

There were some partisan differences in this discourse. For one, the change over time evident above in discussions of sexuality was apparent here too. On the right, motherhood, always prominent in portrayals of feminine virtue, became ever more so from the early to mid-1930s onward; the language around motherhood on the left likewise evolved. Gone, for the most part, were the suggestions, found in *L'Ouvrière* in the early 1920s about a new Communist motherhood, which would see fathers and the community assume many of the traditional housewife's burdens. Instead, readers of leftist papers by the mid-1930s found, much more typically, homages to angelic mothers, devoting their lives to their children and families. These portrayals differed not a whit from their right-wing counterparts.

Second, while both sides of the political spectrum perceived one of mothers' most crucial duties as educating their children, again, as with selflessness, what this meant differed from right to left. This was particularly obvious around the question of religion.

The value that the right placed on motherhood was highlighted when commentators praised women for abandoning other pursuits in order to raise families. For example, Louis-Alfred Pagès's mother's *Le Petit Démocrate* obituary emphasized that while she had attended university in the early 1880s and was a woman of considerable ability, she had left school in order to start a family.[78] Another telling illustration came when Yves Dautun of the fascist *L'Émancipation nationale* interviewed "Claudine," a peasant girl whom he held up as an example for others to follow. Dautun asked how French girls could best serve their country. Claudine replied, "In learning, as seriously as possible, an intellectual or manual trade, but with the fierce will to do everything in our power in order to never have to use our diplomas and certificates."[79] In other words, Claudine believed, and Dautun agreed, that women should set aside their careers and their work outside the home in order to pursue their true "trade": motherhood. As a young *Alliance démocratique* woman proclaimed, in lamenting the dearth of husbands available for young women wishing to found families thanks to the war, husbandless young women had no choice but to "persevere in our thankless task, while waiting for marriage that will make us true Frenchwomen in permitting us to give sons to the Fatherland."[80]

Daniella Sarnoff argues that "woman as mother" was a central component of the fascist project, as women embodied the fascist spirit and were crucial to the desired regeneration of the French family and race.[81] Certainly, the Croix de feu fit this mold convincingly. *Le Flambeau*'s appeals to women were dominated by images of motherhood, such as the one in figure 1.3. This image typified the movement's aesthetic and supports Sarnoff's contentions in that it was titled "The Work of the Croix de Feu," implying, thereby, that the movement's objectives were captured by the image of a youthful mother. A happy mother with a healthy baby was the end goal of the Croix de feu's activities.

Fig. 1.3. *Le Flambeau,* May 23, 1936, 1.

In truth, though, members of the conservative Alliance démocratique, Fédération républicaine, and Parti démocrate populaire were also susceptible to such appeals and would have shared this apparently fascist objective. Madame Pagès's obituary, cited above, was typical, for example, of another indicator of the importance of motherhood to a woman's identity across the interwar right: in such memorials a woman's children were invariably mentioned, when possible, as proof of her worthiness, and, naturally, the more she had had the better. Such was the case with the Parti démocrate populaire's tribute to Madame Paul Duguet, for instance, who not only bore several children, apparently, but tirelessly inculcated them with the proper spirit of self-abnegation.[82]

Perhaps more surprising is the degree to which the virtues of motherhood defined the left's image of women. Just as on the right, motherhood dominated women's identity in Radical, Socialist, and Communist discourses. While it is true that there was a group of Communist women who advanced a vision of a new Communist woman, as discussed in chapter 2, who eschewed traditional femininity, this was a vision shared by only a minority of Communists. Moreover, the Communist Party silenced this minority by the 1930s. For the vast majority in the political parties of the left, including the Communist Party, motherhood was inseparable from femininity: to be a woman was to be a mother. The Socialist Party, for example, wholly embraced the trope of woman-as-mother. In 1919, *Le Populaire* reprinted an eight-piece essay by the German Henri Schulz entitled, "Advice to a Socialist Mother," originally published in Stuttgart in 1913, which the newspaper introduced with the words, "All our readers, and especially our female readers, will appreciate, we are certain, these admirable pages, . . . from which all proletarian women who desire to turn their sons and daughters into noble and good combatants for our great cause, can learn."[83] All women were or would be mothers and thus all would appreciate Schulz's counsel. Notably too, the goal of these mothers was not just to produce good sons and daughters, but to produce good Socialists.

That Socialists regarded women primarily as mothers in the home was most obvious in the women's section of *Le Populaire,*[84] which was variously called, "The Life of the Home," "The Interior of the Home," "The Homemaker's Life," "The Woman's Page," "Woman and the Home," "Woman, Militant," and simply "Woman." With the exception of the last two titles, featured in the mid- to late 1930s, these headers appealed to women as homemakers, and throughout the interwar period (including the mid- to late 1930s) columns providing recipes, sewing tips, fashion advice, and childcare information dominated the section. The page was, in other words, decidedly aimed more at "woman" than at "militant." A persistent feature was medical advice from those such as Dr. Emmeline Weill-Raynal about protecting and maintaining children's health, once again indicating the conflation between women and mothers in the Socialist mind.[85] This is not to suggest that talented feminists did not contribute to these pages or that significant political issues were not raised or debated there. In fact, party women and men made important contributions on a variety of "women's issues" in this section. But these instances did not negate the consistent identification of women with mothers, nor were they intended to.

The Communists shared this Socialist predilection. The striking resemblance between *L'Humanité*'s and *Le Populaire*'s women's pages captured this fact. *L'Humanité* introduced its women's page in 1925. Like its Socialist counterpart, the Communist journal published its women's section weekly, and it too sported many different names over the years: "The Women's Tribune," "Woman," "For the Woman Worker," "Our Home," and finally, "Woman and Child." While the first three titles might seem relatively gender-neutral, and the third might even imply a degree of militancy, the substance of these sections was nearly indistinguishable from those of *Le Populaire*. The exception to this rule was, following the wider pattern within the party, that the women's page struck a more militant tone in its early days. By the mid-thirties, however, the adoption of "Our Home" and "Woman and Child" signaled, in tandem with the Popular Front strategy, a decided *embourgeoisement* of the section as the Communist Party sought, in competition with the Radicals and the Socialists, to attract middle-class women to its ranks. It represented the triumph of the more traditional conception of Communist femininity and the suppression of a potentially revolutionary gender politics in the Communist Party.

L'Ouvrière reprinted a Guy de Maupassant tale that demonstrated the inseparability of the categories mother and woman in Communist parlance.[86] Written in the style of a popular crime novel, the article, "A Parricide," chronicled the story of an illegitimate son abandoned by his upper-class mother and raised by a good-hearted working-class woman. As an adult, he killed his real parents upon discovering their "bourgeois hypocrisy." That the roots of this tragedy lay in the inadequate femininity of his biological mother was clear from his testimony: "The woman who breastfed me was honest, more a woman, nobler, more a mother than my mother. She raised me." His adoptive mother was properly feminine and therefore a good mother; his biological mother was selfish, lacking in maternal instinct, and sowed the seeds of her own murder. As her son explained about killing her, "It was my legitimate right."[87]

Most examples of the Communist veneration for motherhood were less grim. In his private correspondence, for example, Marcel Cachin praised his mother-in-law thusly: "Your mother is doing very well: she is caring for me like a child."[88] Her continued capacity for caregiving was evidence, in Cachin's mind, of his mother-in-law's well-being: as a good woman, so long as she breathed, she would mother. Likewise, Maurice Thorez's autobiographical *Son of the People* virtually ignores women but when they do appear in the narrative it is as mothers fighting for their children's welfare.[89]

Motherhood was no less central to the Radical conception of the ideal woman. Radical senator Louis Martin stressed in his plea for Senate approval of women's suffrage, that, far from fearing that voting would pull women from their homes and children, senators should recognize that women would vote as mothers and thereby make the wisest choices possible for the future of their offspring.[90] On the other hand, Janine Louis-Merlet used very similar logic to argue that women did not want or need the vote: "Nature, stronger than free will, performs the miracle, and after the arrival of the child we see a new being appear, . . . who is physically and morally 'a mother.'" This new being's world was necessarily and rightly confined within the walls of her home, where all her energies needed to be concentrated in raising her children; it was better that women allow their husbands to speak for them. As Louis-Merlet advised her women readers: "Remain, in the home, the mother and wife, . . . Be the soul of the house, tender and wise. If politics interest you, discuss them in your home."[91]

The Radical rank and file shared the identification of women with motherhood. Sibille Brésart certainly understood the importance of maternity to her standing. She began her letter to Édouard Daladier by establishing her credentials, describing herself as a "mother of two sons." She then proceeded to commend Daladier for his selfless decision to step down as *président du conseil* in the wake of February 6, 1934, and added, "I dare hope that many French mothers would add their voices to mine to thank you."[92] Motherhood was Brésart's function and the signifier of her worth: no woman began a similar letter by declaring herself a career woman with no children.

Thus, with rare exceptions, the perception of women as mothers was truly hegemonic in interwar France. The duties associated with motherhood were many; that said, the one on which commentators focused most relentlessly was a mother's responsibility to educate her children, to inculcate in them, in other words, desirable values. These values of course, differed greatly depending on the commentator's political affiliation.

The right-wing parties and leagues placed a great deal of value on religiosity, particularly those most openly Catholic in orientation—the Croix de feu, Parti démocrate populaire, and Fédération républicaine. As the primary caregivers within the family, women thus had to be suitably religious themselves and to tend diligently to their children's religious educations. Monsignor Julien of the Parti démocrate populaire made this abundantly clear, writing that educating her children was a mother's primary responsibility and that, for girls, "in education, the most educational principle is religion."[93] Fédération républicaine enthusiast the Princesse de Robech echoed the monsignor's sentiments in applauding the efforts of Quebecoises in civilizing the new world. In particular, claimed the princess approvingly, French-Canadian women had ensured the continuing dominance of the Catholic Church in Quebec society by raising their children in piety.[94]

On the left, in contrast, mothers were in charge of the equally crucial task of protecting the secular Republic by keeping the nefarious influence of the Church at bay in their children's schooling. Communists, Socialists, and Radicals were all overanxious in this regard. Communist Marie Rabaté, for instance, addressed "mothers or future mothers of families" about her concern over the Boy Scouts, an institution that she felt was dominated by "*cléricaux*," the leftist term denoting the actual Catholic Church and its conservative supporters. She urged mothers to keep their sons out of this "pre-fascist" organization, which she maintained was preparing young boys to be strike breakers and fascist thugs.[95] A female comrade of Rabaté's likewise directed Communist women to militate against the Church's influence in their children's formation.[96] The Socialists' Berthe Fouchère, meanwhile, remembered Austrian socialist Adelheid Popp's lifetime of battling the pernicious power of the Catholic Church in her homeland, holding her up as an example for Socialist French women to follow.[97] In short, opposition to the Church, especially in educating children, was fundamental to left-wing femininity. As one Radical called to her fellow women, "To work for the Republic!"[98]

Mothers, then, were to ensure that their children's development was ideologically suitable. Commentators also believed that women as mothers embodied many virtues. Two virtues, in particular, surfaced persistently within political circles in discussions of women generally and motherhood in particular. Commentators consistently lauded women and mothers' loving and caregiving natures as well as their presumed pacifism. Authors, politicians, and others, moreover, assumed and asserted that these characteristics defined all women, or at least all proper women, even though they clearly associated them with motherhood; they thereby revealed their belief that all women were or would be mothers.

Women's natural proclivity for maternal love, according to the predominant logic, gave them a nearly inexhaustible capacity for caregiving. A 1918 obituary written for the aunt of conservative politician Alexandre Millerand, journalist Valerie Boyer, by her collaborator and husband portrayed her as the ideal woman and evoked her boundless ability to care for others, especially children: "for children, her arms were always open, ready to embrace all those who were brought to her. Her maternity was without limits."[99]

One trope of this celebration of women's natural nurturing was the representation of the nurse as the feminine ideal. Nursing was one of the few professions that politicians of all political stripes could agree was suitable for women, as it seemingly agreed with women's natural inclinations. Moreover, the memory of World War I, in which tender and devoted nurses were front and center, also colored the overwhelmingly positive view of nurses. Conservative and later Alliance démocratique supporter Edmond Lefebvre du Prey, for example, speaking in the Chamber of Deputies in 1919, perversely held up nurses as embodying the feminine ideal in order to argue against women's suffrage:

> It is impossible to find more delicate beings. No one knows better than they the secret to consoling a patient, to applying with gentleness a bandage that brings relief, to finding the right words to convince the patient to bear the treatment that is inflicted upon him in order to improve his health, and to rekindling hope when the bell tolls signaling the departure from this world.
>
> Only a woman could accomplish this mission.[100]

Somehow, so went Du Prey's logic, if women could vote nurses' patients would suffer from their inattention. That Du Prey highlighted nurses as well as the statement that "only a woman could accomplish this mission" revealed his belief that nurses' caregiving was a uniquely feminine virtue. The fact that he received applause following that statement suggests his view was widely shared by his fellow deputies.

The crucible of war brought women's "natural" caregiving to the fore in other ways too. In particular, it was common practice for the political parties to organize women to send aid to either soldiers at the front or civilian victims of war. For example, during the Spanish Civil War the Communist youth organization for girls and young women was very active in sending condensed milk to Spain for malnourished republican babies.[101] This Communist campaign was, in turn, a mirror reflection of the later Croix de feu, Parti populaire français, Fédération républicaine, and Parti démocrate populaire women's campaigns to send care packages to France's men at the front during World War II.[102]

Indeed, war was thought to bring out the best of the feminine virtues. Just as motherhood, so contemporaries reasoned, prepared women for caregiving in other capacities such as nursing or charitable pursuits, so too it made them instinctive pacifists. The entire political spectrum, from fascists to communists, held that an ideal woman was a pacifist. Quite simply, commentators of all political affiliations and both sexes believed that women as mothers "naturally" opposed war, as any good mother would not freely send her sons to their possible deaths. On the conservative right Alliance démocratique writer Maurice Vincent's lament in September 1939 was typical: "How French mothers were right to fear the worst from the Germans."[103] Likewise, in 1929 the Fédération républicaine's *La Nation* inveighed against Aristide Briand's policies of disarmament and rapprochement with Germany, in a column addressed, "To a French Mother." Reminding women of all those husbands, brothers, and sons who did not return home in the Great War the author claimed that Briand's recklessness made another war more likely and thus had to be opposed by French mothers.[104] The Parti démocrate populaire's Marie-Thérèse Archambault explained the logic succinctly: "Women, whose physiological function is to create life slowly and painfully, . . . consequently have a penchant for instinctively hating all that threatens to destroy it."[105]

This reasoning was, for the most part, no different in the fascistic Croix de feu or Parti populaire français. A Croix de feu pamphlet in 1934, for instance, addressed to "French Women," urged them to join the party, "so that your sons—workers, peasants, or students—have a guaranteed future, with their work finally encouraged, and peace finally consolidated."[106] The movement appealed to women as mothers and to their corresponding (it was thought) pacifism. This was also true of a flysheet the feminine section employed, which called on women to join the movement in order to fight "for your children" against the coming of war, and "disorder."[107]

The Spanish Civil War provided the opportunity for the Parti populaire français to pursue a particularly gendered strategy against the left. In a campaign previously commented upon by Paul Schue,[108] the party undertook to prevent what it claimed was the forcible recruitment of young French boys to fight for the Spanish Republic. For this, *L'Émancipation nationale* published a series of impassioned pleas such as one from "J.R.": "'Thorez, Return my Child to Me!' Says a Mother of a Boy of 18, off to Fight in Spain."[109] When this effort reportedly bore fruit, one grateful *père de famille* apparently declared upon his son's return, "I have just offered my life to Doriot, for his having returned the little one to his *maman*."[110] The image of women/mothers as pacifists was so pervasive in the party that even the misogynist Pierre Drieu La Rochelle felt compelled to respond to a letter he received from a mother in Normandy accusing the party of warmongering: "I am like all the men of the PPF and like their chief: none of us likes war."[111] Drieu discreetly omitted that the glorification of war was the primary theme of his novels.[112]

The left shared the belief that women as present or future mothers were naturally opposed to war. The protective maternal instinct dictated against women's remaining passive in the defense of peace. This device was universal: no commentator deviated from it; no one claimed women were naturally warlike. Radicals like Louis Martin and feminist Cécile Brunschvicg, for example, hoped that granting women's suffrage would see the abolition of war.[113] As feminist-Radical lawyer Germaine Malaterre-Sellier proclaimed at a disarmament demonstration in Trocadéro Palace, "There isn't a single woman in France who doesn't hate war or wish ardently for peace."[114] Thus, all women, regardless of political affiliation, could stand united in their antagonism to war.

Nor was it just with the printed word that left-wing journalists and politicians portrayed women/mothers as naturally inclined to pacifism. Figure 1.4 from *L'Humanité* showed a group of desperate mothers pleading with a general and a capitalist to "Return our children." Figure 1.5, also from the Communist daily, portrayed a skeletal mother in the foreground with her hands raised in grief-stricken agony over the body of her murdered child. In the background a battle raged, complete with aerial bombardment (which

Fig. 1.4. *L'Humanité,* May 29, 1925, 1.

Fig. 1.5. *L'Humanité,* August 8, 1923, 1.

the left consistently decried as brutal to civilians), and featured the caption, "Dedicated to the Mothers of France," in reference to the French military communiqué, "Our planes dropped 10 tons of ordnance on enemy positions." This cartoon addressed the ongoing suppression of rebels in Morocco, and the artist intended to pull on the heartstrings of French women by showing them a mother grieving for her dead child.

The Socialists' cartoonists employed similar devices. One image, for instance, entitled "Mothers' voting ballot," featured a protective mother, her arm around her son, angrily waving a ballot at a menacing man in military uniform and exclaiming, "We will no doubt make ourselves better understood with this than with our tears." Figure 1.6 was even more arresting. It appeared with a Socialist call for youthful militants to attend a rally for "peace and disarmament." The drawing featured a crowd, including Marianne, the female embodiment of the Republic, demonstrating peacefully. Such de-

Fig. 1.6. *Le Populaire,* October 16, 1930, 6.

pictions of leftist crowds by Socialists and Communists were typically masculinist, showing highly male crowds and displaying physically strong men in the foreground. On this occasion however, a peace rally, the crowd was envisioned as composed entirely of women, suggesting the degree to which pacifism was seen as a feminine domain and as a virtue to which women, as mothers, were presumed to be naturally inclined.

CONCLUSION

In the Republic of Virtue a swathe of qualities could show an individual's caliber. From selflessness to a hatred of war, there were many virtues that commentators regularly celebrated. The silhouette of these virtues, however, changed depending on the light in which it was seen. The observer's political ideology and the sex of the subject could both have a profound impact on what was seen as virtuous and on how virtues were understood. The "eminent virtues of the citizen," in other words, were variable and in the eye of the beholder.

The virtuous citizen was above all to live in a spirit of selflessness. French men and women of all political persuasions prized a willingness to sacrifice self-interest for the greater good. This commonality, however, should not elide variations on the theme. There were, for example, separate spheres of selflessness. Women's selflessness was passive and involved submission to male domination, especially within the family and especially on the right. Women were expected, quite simply, to live for their families and to devote themselves wholeheartedly to them. Men's selflessness, on the other hand, required, on the right, male citizens to act responsibly on behalf of their families as well as to provide and care for them. It also necessitated a willingness to sacrifice for the nation, which sometimes meant for the political party or movement by extension. In the center of French politics, the Radicals interpreted this virtue differently. They too believed men should act as responsible household heads, but they tended to emphasize the need to sacrifice not for the nation but rather for the Republic, which they conceived of, generally speaking, as a band of brothers rather than a paternalist hierarchy. The Socialists and Communists, meanwhile, sometimes stressed the demands of fatherhood and the corresponding need for self-abnegation, but they more frequently called on their men to be selfless in the pursuit of social and political revolution. They, as did the right with service to the nation, frequently conflated service in the cause of revolution with devotion to their parties.

Selflessly devoting oneself to the national or a political cause required hard work and sangfroid as well as devotion. Given that paid labor and politics took place in the public sphere and were both male-dominated, commentators gendered both a capacity for hard work and the ability to remain calm under pressure as masculine. Politicians and party militants perceived industriousness and sangfroid as highly desirable masculine virtues, praised them in the men of their parties, and exhorted fellow-travelers to follow the examples of their hardworking and determined peers. As with selflessness, the key difference between the left and the right in this regard lay in the objects to be pursued with hard work and sangfroid—national regeneration, for example, on the right and social revolution on the left—rather than in the value placed on the virtues themselves.

Similarly, both the left and right praised the virtues of fatherhood; both assumed men were or would be fathers; and both urged their male followers to embrace the responsibilities of paternity and a breadwinner identity: good fathers made good citizens. This discourse, however, while it was present across the spectrum, was undoubtedly more pronounced on the right, with its profoundly paternalistic outlook, than on the left. In this case as in others, however, the left came to more closely resemble the right in the mid-1930s with its embrace of the Popular Front strategy to fight fascism.

Specifically feminine virtues were even clearer than their masculine equivalents. If fatherhood was largely assumed for men, motherhood defined women. Divergences from the hegemon of woman as mother were few and far between with the most notable departure appearing within the Communist Party in the early to mid-1920s. That deviation aside, for the great majority a host of attributes associated with mothering were accordingly synonymous with feminine virtue. Thus, just as motherly love was pure, so were women expected to be sexually chaste outside of marriage and to evince a purity of spirit in other matters. Similarly, as mothers cared for their children so should women apply their (believed to be) inherent capacity for nurturance to select professions—such as nursing—and in their daily lives. Finally, all mothers' greatest fear, commentators assumed, was the death of a child; accordingly, observers uniformly believed that women were inherently pacifistic. No mother could desire war because no mother would want to see her children perish in warfare. In a society deeply traumatized by World War I this discourse of motherly pacifism had a potent appeal.

These were the eminent virtues of the citizen in interwar France. They would play a defining role in shaping attitudes and the parties' policies and public policy by extension. Thus, it is clear that the gendering of virtue helps historians to understand "what was really going on" in interwar France.

2

NEW MEN, NEW WOMEN

GENDER AND THE TOTALITARIAN DRIFT

One of the seminal political developments in the western world at the end of World War I was the advent of international communism. The birth of communism destabilized Europe by introducing a genuinely revolutionary element to mass democratic politics and sowing fear among the middle and upper classes, thereby opening the door to right-wing authoritarianisms. The presence of the Soviet Union, which refused to participate in multilateral institutions such as the League of Nations, also undermined the international order. Many of the defining features of interwar Europe, including the rise of fascism and Nazism and the breakdown of the international security system established by the Treaty of Versailles, can accordingly trace their origins at least in part to international communism and, by extension, the Russian Revolution.

During the second meeting in 1920 of the communist or Third International in Moscow, Lenin outlined the twenty-one conditions that socialist parties would have to meet in order to join the Comintern, as the organization came to be known. These conditions amounted to agreeing to follow Moscow's lead and embracing the strategy of violent revolution rather than the gradualist reformism espoused by more moderate voices.

In France, the result of the twenty-one conditions was the "schism at Tours" in December 1920, which saw the Socialist Party split in two. Led by Marcel Cachin and Ludovic-Oskar Frossard, those willing to submit to Lenin's conditions formed the nascent Communist Party; while those who wished to maintain their independence from Moscow, led by Léon Blum and Marcel Sembat, stuck with the Socialist Party and the Second International.[1] Thus, French politics underwent a profound shift whose effects would be felt throughout the interwar period and beyond.

Perhaps in no area was this impact more obvious than in the politics of gender. The Communist Party introduced new visions, at least at times, of both masculinity and femininity, which historians have sometimes referred to as the Communist "new man" and, less frequently, the Communist "new woman."[2] These deviations from mainstream gender ideals threatened to destabilize cherished institutions such as the French family just as communism itself threatened the social order. Contemporary critics worried most about the at-times unconventional view of femininity that was articulated in the Communist Party, which cast aside biological essentialism and envisioned a society where women would be men's intellectual, social, cultural, and physical equals. In these ways, the Communist woman was indeed a radical departure. This perceived threat proved fleeting, however, as the party silenced its advocates by the 1930s; it was in fact the new man who made the more long-lasting and indeed subversive impact.

Thus, this chapter primarily focuses on the phenomenon of the new men. The Communist new man helped inspire a fascist equivalent and together the fascist and Communist new men aroused a creeping totalitarian drift within French politics. In an attempt to staunch the bleeding of popular support from the center to the margins centrist parties began to flirt with the new men, as their own youths, in particular, adopted political masculinities more typically found on the extremes.

The substance of these new men was problematic for French democracy. The Communist new man embodied the fraternalist rhetoric of the left, while giving that fraternalism a more militant, youthful, revolutionary, and violent gloss. The fascist new man borrowed heavily from the Communists' rhetoric of brotherhood but abandoned their underlying egalitarianism, preferring instead to fuse the left's fraternalism with the traditional right's paternalism via the militarized language of discipline and order. So while the Communist new man was meant to be disciplined in aiding the overthrow of the political and social order so as to establish an egalitarian utopia, the fascist new man was instead directed to follow orders unquestioningly within the social and political hierarchy. He, however, retained the violent predispositions of the Communists' new man without directing those energies toward social revolution; rather, his violence targeted the nation's enemies, as defined by fascist leaders.

The timing as well as the substance of the emergence of these new gender identities in French politics, moreover, suggests strongly that both the fascist and Communist new men were products of World War I. Their emphases on physicality, youthfulness, manly camaraderie, and discipline appear to reflect millions of men's wartime experiences in the military and the militarization of politics more generally. Given that the Russian Revolution itself emerged in part from the Great War, in fact, World War I's influence on interwar politics, including on gender politics, was acute indeed.

NEW WOMEN

On the two extremes of the political spectrum, there were attempts to construct new men; these endeavors led or at least contributed to a totalitarian drift within interwar French politics. One might expect, accordingly, to find a similar phenomenon with regard to femininity, to discover, in other words, that the Communists and fascists also tried to construct "new women" and that these deviations from the norm of woman-as-mother made a significant impact in mainstream circles.

For a time in the Communist Party, this was indeed the case. In the early to mid-1920s, some Communists, particularly the women involved with the newspaper *L'Ouvrière,* attempted to create a new woman akin to the Communist new man. This Communist new woman both built upon and was a departure from the new women of the fin-de-siècle like Marguerite Durand.[3] On the one hand, like Durand the Communist new woman transgressed traditional gender boundaries and asserted her independence. On the other, the Communist new woman was far more radical both because she eschewed norms of feminine beauty, which Durand for example had embraced, and because she was a revolutionary activist: the women at *L'Ouvrière* sought to refashion femininity to enable women to engage in revolutionary struggle as men's equals. They did not adopt the more conventional "different but equal" strategy of relational feminists who argued for an equality of difference. Rather, these Communists, perhaps following the lead of unorthodox feminist pioneers such as Nelly Roussel, set out to construct a femininity that included characteristics normally coded as masculine, including strength of character and body, aggressiveness (with its corresponding thirst for action), and leadership.[4] Given these emphases, these commentators did not place motherhood at the center of the new feminine identity they sought to craft, which represented a major departure from predominant notions of femininity.

In its inaugural year, 1922, *L'Ouvrière* carried several articles by Russian Katia Palianoff that signaled the journal's promotion of a new femininity. In particular, Palianoff profiled Russian women workers and emphasized the degree to which these figures were indistinguishable from their male counterparts. They cut their hair short, were "robust," and had "strong and assured" voices.[5] They wore men's clothes and "developed the habit of referring to [themselves] in the masculine."[6] They were abandoning prostitution, getting educations hitherto reserved for men, and advancing rapidly in the workplace.[7] Russian women were, in short, shedding the constraints of traditional femininity and asserting themselves as men's equals. Palianoff, notably, never mentioned motherhood. The Revolution would bring a similar liberation to French women, so she implied.

Nor was it just Russian imports who advocated such gender radicalism on *L'Ouvrière*'s pages. Germaine Sillon, for instance, argued that women should not enter into marriages as men's subordinates. She then stressed that the Communist Revolution would provide women with the necessary economic independence to allow them to wait to marry at a later age and to choose partners who would respect their individuality and opinions.[8] Working-class women should, as she outlined, learn a trade and thereby avoid "prostitution" of both the streets and traditional marriage.[9]

The paper also celebrated women doing more conventionally masculine things, such as the commune of Roubaix's Marie Buisine, who died saving twelve children "with ferocious energy" from a fire. Buisine's actions were "heroic."[10] Similarly, Augustine Ben of Calonne-Ricouart in the Pas-de-Calais apparently gave blood eight times to her husband who was dying of anemia while continuing to support their family as a glass blower in a local factory. She did this "in spite of the diminution of her strength."[11] She persevered and assumed the breadwinner role.

L'Ouvrière also called consistently for women to be more like men in terms of their workplace activism. Women had to, authors repeatedly insisted, join their union, fight for their rights, and become members of the Communist Party. As Jeanne Vendras put it, women needed to abandon their "apathy" and perform their "duty" like men to fight their "exploitation."[12] In this vein, contributor and party notable Suzanne Girault was held up as an example to follow in 1930 when she was imprisoned and confined to solitary confinement for singing the International after lights out.[13]

Within this new militant femininity, motherhood was significantly diminished as a virtue in a clear departure from the hegemonic trope of women as mothers outlined in chapter 1. Some pointed out, truthfully enough, for example, that while wealthy conservatives glorified motherhood actual working-class women tended to find it a less than glorious condition, as did one mother of five whose husband had abandoned her and taken the family's meager savings with him.[14] In a similar attempt to explode the fantastical vision of motherhood that dominated most interwar discourse, another reporter asserted that many single mothers contemplated suicide when refused welfare by the state.[15] Yet another lambasted the insensitivity of midwives who criticized working mothers for not breastfeeding given that breastfeeding while holding down full-time employment was nigh impossible.[16] Through such commentaries, the women authors at *L'Ouvrière* articulated a novel vision of femininity and offered a cogent critique of the indignities and hardships women, especially working-class women, had to endure in French society as then constituted.

As commentators promoting the new woman downplayed the otherwise overweening emphasis on motherhood in representations of ideal femininity, so too they, like those who embraced the new man, sometimes cast the new woman as youthful. Thus a Jeunesses Communistes' call to arms urged young female workers to engage in an "energetic struggle against [their] exploitation" and suggested they follow the example of Russian women who had taken up arms against their oppressors.[17]

As with young men, the Communists created auxiliary organizations for young women. In particular, in 1935 the party founded the *Jeunes filles de France* in an attempt to attract young women to communism. By 1938, the *Jeunes filles* claimed 16,500 members, 5,000 of whom were clustered in Paris and its environs, and were capably led by such figures as Danielle Casanova, Claudine Michaut, Jeanne Vermesch, and Paul Vaillant-Couturier's daughter Marie-Claude.[18]

Historians should not, however, see this organization's relative success as proof of the perseverance of the new woman. The photographs of young women that appeared in the party press offer a hint that new womanhood was not triumphant. While such photographs did show young women and girls engaged in physical activity such as playing basketball or performing calisthenics, they were often slightly sexualized and portrayed their subjects in tight-fitting tops and shorts, for example; certainly, the photographers represented young women in a manner consistent with traditional notions of feminine beauty.[19] This objectification of young women ran counter to the egalitarianism of the new woman ideal; it also coheres with Susan Whitney's finding that the Communists did precious little to recruit young women to the party prior to the Popular Front and "embraced" the "status quo" in reaching out to them thereafter.[20] Accordingly, while the Jeunesses Communistes would be a bastion of support for the Communist new man, the Jeunes filles de France did not play a similar role for the new woman.

Indeed, even at *L'Ouvrière* this new woman was never unabashedly ascendant, representing, at its height only a competing femininity to the traditional hegemon. Even on the newspaper's own pages, and even in its most radical period in the early to mid-1920s, a much more traditional view of femininity with motherhood at its heart continued to be expressed.

One way in which this manifested itself, for instance, could be found in the Communist Party's attempts to reach out to women workers. To the party, motherhood remained a potentially powerful propaganda tool. Thus, for instance, Communist calls to action targeting women on *L'Ouvrière*'s pages (and elsewhere) usually included a cry "for the protection of mothers and children."[21] Equating mothers with children and portraying them as passive actors in need of protection rested uneasily with calls for female militants to take their place as new women at the barricades alongside their male comrades. Similarly, one persistent recruiting technique the Communists pursued was to emphasize the social services made available to mothers in municipalities with Communist administrations. A 1922 piece, for example, stressed that women in the Communist-led municipality of St. Ouen got free midwifery services when pregnant, large families there received stipends from the municipal government, and St. Ouen's mothers had access to public health nurses who dispensed childcare advice without charge.[22]

With time the view of maternity as women's most "natural function," in the words of Communist journalist and politician Jean-Marie Clamamus, began to take precedence.[23] This was especially evident from 1934 onward, with the Popular Front strategy and the Communists' adoption of pronatalism. As part of the shift in tactics, for example, page 4 of *L'Ouvrière* began to feature a fashion section, most of which was aimed at advising mothers how to dress themselves, their children, and their husbands fashionably but economically.[24] This page was virtually indistinguishable from its equivalents in the mainstream press, and if anything, was less overtly political in orientation and certainly less feminist than its Socialist counterparts in *Le Populaire* and *La Femme Socialiste*. The paper's authors, meanwhile, such as regular contributor A. Gilles, continued to employ the pathetic figure of the impoverished mother unable to care properly for her children to engender disgust with government policies and sympathy for the Communist Party.[25] In the same vein, Marguerite Michard lambasted the fascist regimes of Germany and Italy for the "dupery" of their rhetoric of returning women to the home; as she pointed out, in the fascist states mothers continued to toil in misery while in the Soviet Union the state, by providing daycare and other social services, had allowed women to enjoy "all the joys" of motherhood without any of the "worries."[26] This was a far cry from the heady days of the early 1920s when *L'Ouvrière* urged French women to emulate their Soviet counterparts and refer to themselves with masculine pronouns.

If this shift was discernible in the Communist Party's women's newspaper, it was even more so in its main organ, *L'Humanité*. While odes to motherhood had always been featured in the paper, as in a 1921 homage to the temporarily Communist Séverine,[27] there can be no doubt that woman as mother became the dominant image of womanhood by the mid-1930s if not before. This was perhaps clearest when the women's page was renamed "Woman and Child" in November 1935.[28]

Why did this transition to a more conservative view of femininity occur? The answer is multifarious. For one, many historians have noted a creeping conservatism in interwar French society, particularly with regard to women's roles in the family and workforce.[29] This became especially pronounced following the onset of the Great Depression, which led many to theorize that if women would just return to the home and stop taking men's jobs, so to speak, the high rate of unemployment for men would return to normal levels.[30] To some extent then, the convergence of the feminine ideal on the left with the right can be seen as a reflection of wider social attitudes and trends.

Other factors also played a role, however. Given that the Communist Party had, in the early 1920s, been the primary political haven for free thinkers like Pelletier, Louise Bodin, and others, the conversion of the party to a rigid Stalinism in the mid-1920s had a necessarily dampening effect.[31] Toeing the party line and stressing class conflict above all else became de rigueur; it was no coincidence that this period witnessed the exit of Pelletier from the party. The 1934 adoption of the Popular Front strategy to combat fascism, moreover, mandated by Moscow, necessitated the Communist Party reaching out to middle-class and republican voters for the first time. Accordingly, the party's vision of femininity became decidedly conformist, symbolized succinctly by *L'Ouvrière*'s evolution.[32] The party used such devices as the paper's women's page to signal its unthreatening normality to potential supporters.

Communist women were now to be equal but different and therefore, properly feminine in the traditional sense. The project of the new woman was thus abandoned by the Communist Party leadership.

Among the women of the Parti populaire français and Croix de feu, meanwhile, while there is some evidence of a yearning among women for a fascist new woman, there is none of it gaining either widespread traction or the official sanction of the two movements' leaders. Both movements placed clear limitations on the roles that women could perform. As Croix de feu commentator "Nenassou" put it, "What a woman must know" consisted of cooking, cleaning, managing the household, and raising her children.[33] Donning a uniform and becoming a defeminized new woman was not considered.

Mary Jean Green's study of the writings of Thérèse Delhaye de Marynhac provides a hint that at least some far-right women desired a revolutionary fascist new woman. The main character of de Marynhac's novels, "Bouboule," was a Croix de feu adherent and expressed a thirst for action. Initially in the series, for example, Bouboule engaged in seemingly masculine street activism but was later relegated to the margins and expressed resultant dissatisfaction. As Green concludes, through Bouboule de Marynhac conveyed her frustration at the limitations of fascist gender discourse for women such as her. Confined by the Croix de feu's overwhelmingly traditionalist articulation of femininity, the best Bouboule could hope for was to take on a supporting role to the movement's men.[34]

It is true that both the Croix de feu and the Parti populaire français had organizations for young women. The Parti populaire français founded the "Jeunes filles françaises," one of whose leaders was Dora Sabiani, the daughter of Marseilles party boss Simon Sabiani.[35] The Jeunes filles françaises appears to have been organized in early 1939. The young women's group outlined its goals as fourfold: to counteract the Jeunes filles de France, the Communist group; to defend the rights of young French girls; to win back the standing of same within their families; and to apply the social action program of the party.[36] What this translated into was a highly gender-specific set of activities for the group's members: while the Parti populaire français held cycling rallies, soccer, basketball, and water-polo games for its young men, the Jeunes filles françaises undertook such tasks as assembling care packages for men in the army. Further, tellingly, the supervisor of the Jeunes filles françaises' athletic activities, such as they were, was a man. A young party woman, Jacqueline Girard, was the president of the St. Denis section of the Jeunes filles françaises; given St. Denis was Doriot's home base she was likely, therefore, a key figure in the national organization.[37] Certainly, however, there is no evidence that the Jeunes filles françaises sought to craft a new fascist woman.

The Croix de feu was very energetic in its efforts to recruit young women. In June 1930, the movement set up its youth group, "The Sons of Croix de feu,"[38] and, by 1932 the organization had morphed into "The Sons and Daughters of Croix de feu," reflecting the inclusion of girls.[39] Although both boys and girls fell under the aegis of this organization, they were, for the most part, rigidly segregated within it. The boys flew planes, did athletic activities, and generally fashioned their manhood in suitably manly ways. That the girls were subjected to a different regime is clear in an outline of the Croix de feu's "Home for Young Girls," which offered courses for girls ages 14–25, in three categories. The first covered "homemaking" and included cooking, home economics, hygiene, and sewing. The second category, "intellectual courses," encompassed classes in history, literature, typing, stenography, foreign languages, physical education, rhythmic dance, and swimming. This did include some physical activity but absent from the girls' regimen were all the militaristic and intensely competitive pursuits of the boys. Classes on typing and stenography, meanwhile, while they did offer girls practical skills that undoubtedly helped them in the workforce, prepared them less for careers and more for the sort of low-paid work that leaders likely saw as a transitional phase in young women's lives before they married and raised families. Admittedly, professional careers were still largely closed, in practice, to women, but the Croix de feu did not appear to be intent on changing that situation. The third category covered cultural activities and included visiting museums and taking voice lessons.[40] All indications are that, despite this fairly traditional approach to forming femininity, the Croix de feu was successful in recruiting young women. The party ran summer camps for young girls (and boys, although, again, the sexes were rigidly separated),[41] and in 1937 it set up a monthly newspaper for Parti social français women students.[42] Yet, successful though the recruitment of young women may have been, the Croix de feu, like the Parti populaire français, was clearly not engaged in constructing a new fascist woman.

Daniella Sarnoff's research, on the other hand, illustrates that in some of the fascist leagues such as the Solidarité Française, women did sometimes wear uniforms like the men, and, by extension, it would appear that the possibility existed for them to take on militant functions such as physical combat with Communist foes.[43] However, the marginality of the aforementioned fascist leagues as well as the absence of such fascist new women in the much more significant Croix de feu or Parti populaire français suggests the overwhelming hegemony of the traditional image of femininity on the far right. There was a fascist new woman but she was a rare sight in interwar France.

Needless to say, given that attempts to construct new women were abortive on the far right and smothered on the far left by the early to mid-1930s, they achieved limited penetration in mainstream French politics. Accordingly, while observers fretted over the Communists' promotion of an unconventional womanhood,[44] the Communist new woman made little impact on the broader discourse, at least in the short term. In interwar France, political femininity continued to be overwhelmingly defined by motherhood and housewifery. The ideal French woman was, like Jacques Doriot's wife Madeleine, "in her kitchen."[45]

THE COMMUNIST NEW MAN

The Communist new man's impact, however, was more considerable than the new woman's. Prior to the advent of the Communist Party, the masculine ideal in French politics was embodied in the exemplar of the virtuous male citizen. This citizen personified the masculine virtues of selflessness, a fatherly outlook, and a capacity for hard work. These were, generally speaking and with allowances for differences of nuance, virtues admired across the political spectrum. Thus, in keeping with the studies of Judith Stone, Judith Surkis, and others, there was, in interwar France, a vision of the respectable male republican citizen.[46]

Thus, mainstream politicians displayed a measure of interparty solidarity around their vision of a respectable, patriotic, democratic, and male republican citizen. While there were those at the margins who did not conform to this ideal, such as Senator Dominique Delahaye or Deputy Henri Ferrette,[47] they did not represent a genuine threat to the political order and therefore did not pose a significant challenge to the hegemonic ideal.

The emergence of the Communists in late 1920, however, did both these things. The party, enjoying a significant measure of mass support, represented a genuine threat to the Republic. The new, militant brand of masculinity of the new man that it often espoused diverged significantly from the vision of the respectable masculine citizen.

Perhaps the most obvious way in which the Communist new man differed from the virtuous masculine republican citizen was his youth. While the Communists certainly celebrated fathers and generally embraced the breadwinner ideal, the new man represented a departure in this regard. He was too young to have a family and was therefore unattached and more willing to engage in violent revolution. The new man was a competing ideal to the breadwinner, one that was free of familial ties and subversive to fatherhood. He was, moreover, proudly proletarian, while the breadwinner aspired to bourgeois respectability.

The Communist Party anticipated the fascists in its unreserved recruitment of young men and its adoption of a youthful guise. Party commentators liked to contrast Communist youthfulness and virility with the supposed ancient and decrepit Socialist Party in particular. Albert Treint, for example, invited readers to ponder the "agedness of the 'newborn of socialism,'"[48] while a *L'Humanité* cartoonist contrasted the "chatterboxes" of the Socialist Party with the "men of action" of the Communist Party, displaying an anemic and hunched-over Léon Blum across from an upright and vigorous male figure at the Communist tribune.[49] The Communists were masculine and youthful; the Socialists were feminine and geriatric.

In keeping with this youthful image, the Communist Party was quick off the mark in the race to enlist young men. Susan Whitney documents the considerable energy the Communists expended mobilizing and organizing youth.[50] In fact, from its very inception in late 1920, the party inherited a youth organization from the formerly unified Socialist Party, and its militants were hyperactive from the outset, getting arrested by the dozens for seditious activities.[51] These young men advanced a less respectable, more violent, and more confrontational masculinity than the breadwinner ideal often promoted by the party leadership. A willingness to face imprisonment or worse in the party's service became an important hallmark of the Jeunesses Communistes' masculinity. As famed feminist and journalist Séverine, who adhered to the Communist Party until 1923,[52] enthused about some youths incarcerated for their activities: "Having behaved like men, they would not accept being treated like kids."[53] Thus, an unhesitating willingness to sacrifice oneself for the Communist cause became paramount to Communist youths' identity. As Maurice Lebrun explained of Lucien Carré, then just recently transferred to solitary confinement for smuggling party literature into prison, he had first been arrested at age eighteen and had taken part in illegal actions and strikes ever since. Lebrun enthused, "The life of this young comrade provides a complete education for the working class."[54]

Party literature excitedly followed the exploits, trials, and tribulations of Jeunesses Communistes leaders like Jacques Doriot and Gabriel Péri, always underlining both their manliness and self-abnegation.[55] This spirit led Péri to die in the service of communism and the Resistance in World War II, declaring "my comrades know that I have remained faithful to my ideals all my life" in a letter before his execution by the Nazis in 1941.[56] Conversely, the same militant masculinity spurred the by then fascist Doriot to join the Wehrmacht in fighting the Bolsheviks on the eastern front before dying when an allied fighter pilot strafed his car.[57]

This hypermasculine discourse apparently held some appeal. It is difficult to test the veracity of such claims, but Doriot maintained in September 1923 that the Jeunesses Communistes had had 4,500 members in early 1922 and could boast 10,000 odd at the time of his article.[58] Edward Mortimer states that the Jeunesses' greatest period of growth came in the summer of 1936, as membership exploded from 38,000 in May to 100,000 in October.[59]

This apparent success was facilitated by the comprehensive nature of the Communist Party's youth organizations. The party started young. One program for Communist members' children saw them sent on exchange to provincial towns to live for a few weeks in the summer with other Communist families.[60] Likewise, from as early as 1925, the party set up a boys' and girls' summer camp accommodating roughly 560 kids.[61] The Jeunesses Communistes also participated in the Third International's yearly "International Youth Week," staging rallies and protests,[62] had their own newspaper—*L'Avant-garde*,[63]—and founded, in 1933, the Pioneers, a group explicitly meant to counteract the influence of the "pre-fascist" boy scouts.[64]

The Pioneers sought to promote brotherly solidarity among Communist boys. The Communist emphasis on fraternity, therefore, was both a key element of the Communist new man and an inheritance from left-of-center political traditions. The Radicals, for example, used fraternalist rhetoric with some frequency. Radicals often invoked the third component of the republican trifecta—liberty, equality, fraternity—to arouse their men to defend the Republic and defined themselves as the inheritors of the revolutionary legacy. As the Radical (and moderate Socialist) founders of *La Lumière* decreed, they desired "a better city where the exploitation of man by man would give way to brotherly work."[65] Likewise, Premier Édouard Daladier called on "that noble sentiment of French fraternity that has always ensured the salvation of the fatherland" when announcing the formation of his government of national defense in 1938;[66] he reiterated that it was this same "fraternity" that led French men to leave aside all that divided them in standing ready to fight Germany in September 1939;[67] he claimed in October of the same year that "French fraternity will permit us to overcome all obstacles and vanquish all perils once more."[68]

The Socialists shared the Radicals' notion of a republican fraternity responsible for the defense of the Republic. But they also spoke the language of the international brotherhood of socialism and the working class. This was particularly acute in their discussions of international pacifism, as they stressed that through building feelings of international fraternity Socialists could avoid a repetition of the carnage of World War I. Socialists therefore saw it as their duty to promote, as Suzanne Lacore, later one of Léon Blum's three female deputy ministers, explained, "the virile and fraternal feelings that foster pacific desires."[69] Socialists believed that "fraternal education" would keep war at bay.[70] Accordingly, the "tasks of the [party] militant" included "to contribute to proletarian cohesion and fraternity."[71]

The Communist Party made this fraternal pacifist rhetoric its own, going to the extent of encouraging French soldiers to disobey their orders and lay down their arms rather than abuse their German, Soviet, or colonial brothers. This sort of Communist activity was especially prominent during the French occupation of the Ruhr in 1923 and 1924. The party's youth—exemplifying the spirit of the Communist new man—dominated the campaign to encourage disobedience in the French army. The Communist Youth's 1923 manifesto encouraged youthful militants: "Join the army to be the soldier of communism. You are the brother of those who, under the red banner, defend Soviet Russia, the only workers' fatherland."[72] In other words, the party pushed its young men to enlist in the French army in order to spread sedition in the service of the fraternity of the international working class. Ironically, given his later fascism, Doriot, as the secretary of the Communist Youth, led this fight and endured incarceration as a result.[73]

In the Communist Party, in keeping with the aggression of the new man, a properly fraternal spirit could lead to the espousal of violence despite this pacifist campaign. In 1927, for example, Communist leader and militant André Marty went to trial for inciting his readers to kill Ferdinand Foch, the former generalissimo of France's armies in World War I. Marty had targeted Foch to silence his view that France should prepare for war with the Soviet Union. *L'Humanité* celebrated Marty as the personification of the new man and outlined the "exasperation" of the judges faced with the "male attitude of our comrade Marty."[74] Exasperated or not, the judges sentenced him to four years in prison.

The threat that new men like Doriot or Marty posed to the established order was heightened by their physicality. Forth indicates that the new men of the turn of the century were physical fitness enthusiasts.[75] Similarly, Joan Tumblety locates a concerted effort to "remake" the "male body" on both the left and right in the interwar period.[76] The Communists certainly fit this mold, placing great emphasis on robust, physically fit, male bodies and encouraging young Communist men to be athletic. Paul Vaillant-Couturier, for example, the prominent Communist author, leader, and war veteran, declared, "Sport is an essential manifestation of the life of the masses. . . . [It promotes] endurance, and heroism."[77] The Communists were concerned, however, that the proper values be imparted in sporting associations and were especially uneasy in later years about fascist penetration into sporting circles. L. Robert, for example, warned against the tendency for unsavory "bourgeois" sporting organizations to disseminate hierarchical and authoritarian values.[78] Such teaching did not construct the proper Communist masculinity. As Doriot explained, "Contrary to the opinion of some scholars, the young Communist is not an ascetic. He loves sports, because they are a manifestation of strength and life. But he must do everything in his power to destroy bourgeois sporting organizations, which are manifestations of the capitalist exploitation of muscle, athletes and spectators. He works for the dissolution of the 'neutral' sporting societies for military preparation, because they are active agents of fascism and reaction."[79]

To avoid the threat of exposure to fascist or "bourgeois" values, the Communists provided multiple outlets for athletic interests and energies. *L'Humanité* consistently dedicated a weekly and then a daily page to sports throughout this period, covering both party-sponsored activities and commercial ones. In this, they outmaneuvered *Le Populaire,* which always hesitated to give too much attention to professional sports.[80] In its use of sports to attract converts, the Communist Party benefited greatly from the fact that the Fédération sportive du *travail* (FST), founded in 1908, adhered to the

Communist rather than the Socialist Party upon the schism at Tours.[81] The FST regularly hosted sporting events at locations such as the Bois de Vincennes or the Vélodrome d'hiver, featuring a mixture of "popular" activities in which all members could participate and spectacles involving high-profile athletes from France itself or from the U.S.S.R.[82] The Communist Party and FST organized leagues and competitions in a variety of sports, which received ample coverage on *L'Humanité*'s pages.[83] That the images of sports and youth commingled in the Communist consciousness was evident at the funeral of Maurice Thorez's ten-year-old nephew Lucien, where the "good little comrade['s]" colleagues from the FST (renamed, by this time, the Fédération sportive et gymnique du travail) sent an official delegation.[84]

Not only did the Communists exalt the revolutionary (and often violent) activities and physicality of Doriot and others, but they also created a cult of the Red Army soldier. One image of a Soviet infantryman standing on guard with his rifle featured the following quotation from Stalin, "No fortress exists that the Bolsheviks cannot breech," indicating the conviction that if the revolution could not be spread throughout Europe by uprisings, the U.S.S.R. would deliver it through military conquest.[85] After all, the army had proven its mettle in the past. As Marcel Cachin wrote from La Santé prison, it was "thanks to the courage of the Red Army . . . that the revolution was saved in 1918 and 1919," in the Russian Civil War.[86] This was a courage that Communist leaders intended the new man to emulate, and one that even Madame Cachin admired in a letter written during one of her trips with her husband to the Soviet Union.[87] Indeed, *L'Humanité* proudly predicted that the Red Army would smash fascism in the spring of 1939.[88] This was just prior to the signing of the Molotov-Ribbentrop Pact that August, which saw Stalin and Hitler agree to a pact of nonaggression while divvying up Poland between the two totalitarian powers.

The celebration of a youthful, physically robust, and courageous masculinity—such as that supposedly evinced by Red Army soldiers—was meant to prepare young French Communists to be the shock troops of the coming Revolution. This was perhaps most apparent in some of the images of men the party produced, particularly in calling on its members to join street demonstrations, marches and the like.

A key day on the Marxist left's annual calendar was May Day. On that day, Communist militants took to the streets to demonstrate Communist strength. The numbers could be impressive as workers were urged to take the

Fig. 2.1. *Le Premier Mai,* May 1, 1927, 1.

day off work in order to claim the boulevards of Paris under the red banner. These images in figures 2.1, 2.2, and 2.3 all picture the party militant as a defiant male worker. This male character epitomized the Communist new man with his threatening posture and physically fit body, and he was frequently portrayed bare-chested as in figure 2.1. Thus, the new man's masculinity was equated with rebellion and physical strength. Figure 2.3 is also revealing, as, on the eve of the Popular Front it portrays the unity of the Communists, Socialists, and presumably the Radicals through men's arms emblazoned with the parties' logos (with the exception of the Radicals' as they had no such insignia), holding aloft a flag announcing the first of May. Again, the parties'

Fig. 2.2. *Le Premier Mai,* May 1, 1929, 1.

strength is represented in physically imposing male form, and notably, the Communist arm is given priority of place.

In short, there was a radical masculinity with violent overtones within the Communist Party, a masculinity that was especially prevalent in the party's youth cadres. This image of a youthful proletarian street fighter therefore existed alongside that of the breadwinner—almost by definition a member of the so-called labor aristocracy[89]—in the party, although the breadwinner remained predominant. Perhaps it was less than totally surprising that Doriot, as well as onetime Secretary-General of the Jeunesses Communistes Henri Barbé,[90] founded the Parti populaire français, bringing with them such *L'Humanité* contributors as Paul Guitard[91] and Maurice Lebrun.[92] That these

Fig. 2.3. *L'Humanité,* May 1, 1935, 1.

men could abandon communism for an ethos as opposed to its tenets as fascism suggests that ideological explanations of their left-to-right trajectories are insufficient.[93] Rather, one important factor was arguably that these men were political creatures driven by a lust for power who embraced the action-based and combative virility of the Communist Party, particularly its youth groups, and saw in fascism an ethos entirely similar to communism in its masculine (and youthful) orientation. As Guitard wrote, "The style is the man."[94] Fascist masculinity fit these former Communists very comfortably.

THE FASCIST NEW MAN

The fascistic parties studied here—the Croix de feu and Parti populaire français—like the Communist Party desired the creation of a new man. Given that one of fascism's raisons d'être, and arguably its most crucial one, was to combat communism both by literally battling Communists in the street and by, it was hoped, converting Communist militants to fascism, it was natural that the fascists would emulate some of the Communists' appeals, rhetoric, and esthetic. But the fact that the fascists borrowed from the Communists means neither that the fascist new man was identical to his Communist counterpart nor that fascists' espousal of a new man was purely cynical. Fascists, like Communists, believed they were building a new and better world, or at least a new and better France; the new man was to be the agent of the fascist revolution.

As George Mosse writes, like the Communist new man, the fascist one was young so as to contrast with, "muddleheaded, talkative, intellectualizing liberals and socialists—the exhausted, tired old men of the old order."[95] Accordingly, the Parti populaire français, for example, poured much of its organizing energy into its youth formations. The Popular Union of French Youth (UPJF), formed in October 1936, was the umbrella organization and aspired to form sections all over France. It defined its mission as doing battle with the Jeunesses Communistes and as providing "action, education, [and] amusement."[96] By December, the party had set its sights on younger children, setting up the Jacques Doriot Pioneers, a name clearly borrowed from its Communist predecessor, for kids aged 7 to 13.[97] The party went on to found a weekly journal for its youth,[98] establish a sporting association explicitly for them—divided into forty-five "phalanges" that would compete with one another,[99] thus demonstrating the links between an emphasis on physicality and a glorification of the young, and create summer camps for children and adolescents where campers engaged in a variety of robust activities.[100] To what purpose? As the members of the national bureau of the party's youth declared on the eve of World War II, "We will fight for the purity of our blood, and for the genius of our race, which for five centuries has enlightened the world." This was the primary goal of the Parti populaire français's mobilization of boys and youths: to prepare them for war and combat. Upon the German invasion of Poland it was important to reassure party members that that mission had been accomplished. As the title to one declaration to this effect stated, "The Youth of the UPJF will die, if necessary, for France."[101]

Of course, another possible purpose of the fascist new man was to prepare men for a coup d'état. As Kevin Passmore's research makes clear, the Croix de feu staged military maneuvers where volunteers would storm into city centers in motorized columns and seize temporary control of town squares, often in front of the town hall.[102] These certainly appeared to detractors as dress rehearsals for a violent seizure of power.[103]

Croix de feu members were likewise involved in the riots of February 6. 1934, when a demonstration involving far-right groups protesting the infamous Stavisky corruption scandal got out of hand, whether by design or accident, and moved on the Palais Bourbon, housing the Chamber of Deputies.[104] True, Colonel de La Rocque himself opposed this violence, but not from a principled objection to such tactics; rather, the Colonel felt that public opinion was insufficiently prepared for a coup d'état.[105] Moreover, in the period prior to February 6, La Rocque continuously suggested to his underlings that "the hour will sound, for the Croix de feu and Briscards, to save the country a second time."[106]

La Rocque's movement, like the Parti populaire français, especially post-1934, went to great lengths to mobilize and organize youthful adherents in order to prepare them for some future conflagration, whether domestic or international. As Forth's research suggests, at the turn of the century, the French right began to show interest in a "new man" who would embody a "culture of force."[107] Accordingly, fascistic movements focused on cultivating physical fitness and military discipline among their youthful followers. The Croix de feu set up summer camps, established clubhouses in urban areas, ran activities, organized picnics, and created student groups, complete with their own press.[108] As a document outlining the goals of the group for children under thirteen specified, "The purpose is to introduce the youth to the Croix de Feu movement and to develop in them the national spirit."[109]

As with the Parti populaire français or the Communist Party, within the Croix de feu the glorification of youthful masculinity intersected with an emphasis on physically fit male bodies. This tendency has long been noted by observers as central to fascist gender discourse,[110] and some, such as Theodor Adorno and Jean-Paul Sartre, have even used it to denigrate fascists as effeminate homosexuals.[111] More recently, thankfully, scholars have distanced themselves from such unfounded and value-laden classifications,[112] but the consensus remains that fascism involved a celebration of the male body. The Croix de feu certainly made sports and physical activities the focus of its cultivation of young boys and men. The constitutive meeting of the "Sons of Croix de feu" decreed that the following activities would instill the proper sense of "honour" and "duty" in participants: "Hiking, camping, swimming, running obstacle courses, high, long and lateral jumping, pole-vaulting, Greek and Roman wrestling, ball games, packing lunches, flying, and swimming in teams, fencing, discus, javelin, and spear throwing, archery and target shooting, cycling, and military preparation at summer camps."[113] The documentation suggests that the Sons of Croix de feu's subsequent activities followed this intensely physical regimen quite faithfully.[114] As Gäetan Maire, the president of the Society for Preparation and Sporting Education, a Parti social français organization, explained, "The physical perfecting of a race is indispensable in order to maintain it among the first rank of great modern nations."[115] The movement organized its manhood accordingly. Indeed, as seen in figure 2.4, even *Le Flambeau*'s masthead conveyed a sense of youthful and manly vigor.

The Parti populaire français and the Croix de feu also glorified "action," which they associated with youth, versus oratory and debate, which were classified as the purview of "mediocrities and incompetents."[116] Dynamism and energy, coded as youthful qualities, were highly valued within both organizations. As the Croix de feu's R. Fallay commented approvingly in a report on the Federation of the Somme, its leader, "comrade Bouchet," was "full of good will, [and] very dynamic."[117]

La Rocque, in fact, made a point of privileging youth in his movement. This led him, for example, to withdraw the Croix de feu's support from the campaign of respected deputy and ardent champion of pronatalism Louis Duval-Arnould in the 1936 elections, with the result that the septuagenarian Duval-Arnould lost his seat to a much younger man who enjoyed La Rocque's patronage.[118]

Such a betrayal would have been unimaginable in any of the conservative right-wing parties, where age and experience were not just respected but venerated. This was clear in the *Le Petit Démocrate* series "Our Militants."

Fig. 2.4. *Le Flambeau,* June 1, 1931, 1.

On October 30, 1927, for example, the six men profiled were all in their forties, fifties, or sixties, and "his experience" was oft-listed among each man's virtues.[119] In fact, respect for one's elders was institutionalized in the republican system: at the opening session of both the Chamber of Deputies and the Senate, the eldest among the members of the House presided as speaker and gave a speech to his colleagues, imparting the wisdom of his years.[120] It is difficult to imagine that this tradition would have persisted in a future Croix de feu or Parti populaire français state.

Thus, while fascist movements retained the hierarchical structure typical of the French right's paternalism, and while leaders endeavored both to evince a fatherly care for their followers and to guide them with an unyielding paternal hand, the fascists also embraced the fraternalist rhetoric of the left. *Le Flambeau,* for instance, the Croix de feu's mouthpiece, urged the movement's militants to work towards national reconciliation with the following passage: "Remain calm. Remain firm. Guard each house, each home with our vigilant, fraternal, and protective presence."[121]

Colonel de La Rocque, in fact, argued that it was the Croix de feu that embodied fraternity—a concept that had been corrupted by deceitful centrists and leftists. He, moreover, linked the movement's sense of brotherhood to its war veterans' experiences:

> The Croix de Feu spirit has returned fraternity to us. Not the fraternity dishonestly inscribed on the faces of public buildings.[122] But that which we all discovered in the tense moments before an artillery barrage, during the headlong rush onto the "billiard table" of the field of attack. Through the storm of shells, the burst of machine guns, what did our stripes, our origins, our faiths represent if not a call to higher duties, the tenderness of a tragic cooperation, the order of the brotherhood[?][123]

The new Croix de feu man, in other words, forged in the fires of military combat, knew the true spirit and value of fraternity. Interestingly, as Chris Millington demonstrates, this was a theme that other veterans' organizations also emphasized.[124]

In a similar manner, Parti populaire français commentator J.-M. Aimot urged his readers to go camping in groups in the countryside. This, he assured them, was "the surest method" to rediscover "the ties of brotherhood." Notably, Aimot's title suggested that in the party camping excursions, the

French people would "rediscover their youth."[125] Thus, a youthful brotherhood would rejuvenate the nation.

One visible sign of this fascist attempt to graft the fraternalist spirit of the left onto the fascist project was the use of the term "comrade." This term denoted equal status and a shared camaraderie, typical of an ideal fraternity; it surfaced constantly in fascist materials, both public and private. In his letters to his underlings, for example, La Rocque used the term incessantly, as did his correspondents.[126] The Parti populaire français, meanwhile, always referred to adherents as "comrades," as in a 1939 memorial to a French soldier and Parti populaire français member killed in action. Like a good fascist new man, Albert Roux was killed, gun in hand, fighting for the nation. He was mourned by his fascist "comrades."[127]

As with Roux, the Croix de feu and Parti populaire français saw in their youthful brethren future or present soldiers of France and possibly a fascist revolution. This was particularly evident in the Croix de feu's virile cult of martyrs. Unsurprisingly perhaps, for a group that began as a veterans' organization, this cult of martyrs reflected a wider militarization of masculinity within French fascism. This militarization as well as the exaggerated reverence for the dead was a legacy of World War I. Good men conducted themselves as soldiers, showing discipline, following orders, and sacrificing for the greater good. By recreating the fraternity of the trenches within a suitably hierarchical organization, fascists hoped to attract a popular following while avoiding social change. Additionally, as seen through the figure of Jean Mermoz below, this militarized youthful masculinity—typical of the new man—could also be fused with the fascist identification with modernism and technology.

The Croix de feu constantly evoked the memory of those who had died in World War I as a reminder to its followers to honor them. The Great War tangibly set the tone for the movement, as La Rocque and his fellow travelers' compulsion to remember those who had fallen for France between 1914 and 1918 translated smoothly into doing the same for the movement's own dead. The official anthem of "The Association of Those Decorated to the Peril of Their Own Lives" revealed clearly the links between the war, masculinity, and the movement's paramilitarism.[128] As the last verse declared,

> Are we going to lose the benefit
> Of our twenty centuries of glory and honor?

> Will we have made a vain sacrifice,
> Of so much blood and so much pain.
> This insignia adorning our buttonholes[129]
> Must remind us, Friends, at all times
> That the Fatherland wants that our proud souls
> Work together for its greatness.[130]

Even Édouard Daladier—a figure generally despised on the right—was partially redeemed through his service in the war. La Rocque wrote him several times over the years and paid his respects to Daladier for his "having understood his duty during the war."[131]

While the Parti populaire français was not a veterans' movement and did not, accordingly, place quite the same emphasis on wartime service as did the Croix de feu, its writers and leaders were nonetheless given to extolling the wonders of martial masculinity. Bertrand de Jouvenel, for example, the son of noted journalist and diplomat Henri de Jouvenel and a former Radical, opined after a trip to the Francoist front lines in Spain that "men at war demonstrate virtues that one would never have seen in them during peace." In turn, Jouvenel asserted that this rediscovered virility was regenerating Spain, a hitherto decadent nation: "Suddenly, this degenerated nation is providing examples of heroism that are astounding the entire world. These men, from whom one did not dare to ask any effort, now give their lives with . . . simplicity."[132] This theme of a resurgent military masculinity redeeming the male individual and the nation was similarly central to Drieu La Rochelle's work, especially his seminal novel, *Gilles*.[133]

The Croix de feu's obsession with remembering the war dead translated very smoothly into the construction of a cult of martyrs to the movement. Such was the case with Charles Muntz, a member from Mulhouse, who was killed by a Communist bullet in 1936. The article mourning his passing was entitled "A New Martyr."[134] *Le Flambeau* followed Muntz's death with a bitter condemnation of the Popular Front government for not finding and prosecuting Muntz's killer(s).[135] The irony of a paramilitary movement posturing as uniquely able to deal with Communist aggression turning to a Popular Front government, dominated by Socialists and left-wing Radicals, for protection from the Communist Party was lost on the author.

The Parti populaire français liked to highlight its manly exploits in the face of Communist violence. In September 1936, for example, Communist agitators apparently attacked a party rally. One member was evidently gravely wounded, and *L'Émancipation nationale* emphasized the heroic bravery of the party's men in the face of superior Communist numbers. Particularly highlighted, of course, was Doriot's own courage and levelheadedness in directing his troops to protect Parti populaire français women and children.[136] With these tales of sangfroid and militaristic action against the Communists, the Croix de feu and Parti populaire français advertised their utility in the counter-revolutionary struggle to potential backers in the haute bourgeoisie and gave their men a hypermasculine mystique unique to fascism on the right.

While the Croix de feu revered a past captured by its cult of martyrdom, it also, like the National Socialist Party in Germany, sought to blend the past, the present, and the future in its innovative use of technology. Sean Kennedy has documented the affinity for aviation in the movement.[137] La Rocque, for example, like Hitler, would travel the country by plane, and, on grander occasions the Croix de feu would use airplanes in its exercises. No man more embodied this aspect of the movement's masculinity than Jean Mermoz, who became the living embodiment of the fascist new man in Croix de feu literature. Mermoz was one of France's great interwar pilots. His daring exploits, particularly in crossing the South Atlantic, were legendary. In 1935, he was recruited to the movement and placed in charge of its aviation program.[138] Mermoz quickly ascended to a place of privilege in the Croix de feu hierarchy, becoming one of four members of the executive committee of the Parti social français upon its formation.[139] On December 7, 1936, however, his plane disappeared while traversing the South Atlantic.[140] A cascade of tributes to him followed in party literature and continued intermittently long after his death. La Rocque himself signaled Mermoz's martyr status in the days following his disappearance: "Not having the honor to be a pilot, I will not describe in detail here his professional virtuosity or science. My respect for faithful heroism, for simple self-abnegation, for technical expertise, forbids me all profane incursions into his noble profession. [I recall instead] the inner flame of his ardor, of his intelligence, and of his purity."[141]

The cult constructed around Mermoz's memory was formidable. Revealingly, the Parti social français was particularly aggressive in pushing his example upon its youth. Party flying clubs, targeting youths for recruitment, were set up in February of 1937, named the "Jean Mermoz Aero-Clubs."[142] *Le Flambeau,* in part, no doubt, in tribute to Mermoz, and in part to capitalize on his popularity following his death, began to dedicate an entire page to aviation; its youth page regularly featured pieces such as, "Young Men of France: Listen to . . . Mermoz, Your Guide."[143]

Mermoz lived on in other publications. On July 14, 1937, the party assumed direction of *Le Petit Journal,* a Parisian daily with wide circulation; the date chosen for the official launch of *Le Petit Journal* under the party's auspices was timed, as Kennedy has said, for "maximum patriotic effect": July 14 is Bastille Day, France's national holiday.[144] The first issue was also full of stories and images of Mermoz. Bernard Boringe's text was typical of the paper's hyperbole in its praise of Mermoz's masculine qualities: "Mermoz had to have a legendary end worthy of a superhuman hero."[145] Similar tributes likewise appeared in the party's youth publications, indicating the omnipresence and persistence of "the cult of Mermoz."[146]

Provocatively, the Parti populaire français also appropriated Mermoz's memory. Not only did the party's paper, *L'Émancipation nationale,* eulogize him repeatedly in near-identical terms to the Croix de feu,[147] but the Parti populaire français also used him as an example to its youth, naming one of the six "phalanges" of the Sporting Union of French Youth, founded in December 1938, after the dead pilot and telling its young summer campers to emulate him.[148] This use within the two parties of Jean Mermoz as a masculine model suggests both his highly utile image for those promoting the fascist new man and the ideological proximity of the Croix de feu to the Parti populaire français.

The images of the two movements' leaders were also novel. La Rocque, for instance, cultivated an image of steely determination, discipline, and commanding presence. Accordingly, he did not present himself as a great or fiery orator, but rather as a plain-speaking military man who preferred action over words.[149] As he told an audience in Bordeaux, "If I have had citations, it's because, more lucky than others, I was not killed. . . . But apart from all that, I, quite simply, did my duty."[150]

This kind of heroic masculine stoicism, in fact, was both similar and dissimilar to the image cultivated by Doriot. He forged a decidedly hypermasculine persona, full of martial imagery, which epitomized the fascist new man in many respects. Like La Rocque, Doriot and his henchmen drew attention to his wartime heroism and his cold determination in the armed struggle.[151] Unlike La Rocque, Doriot was a charismatic speaker and was often, like Mussolini, portrayed doing physical activities.[152] This difference should not be taken to suggest that Doriot was a fascist while La Rocque was not; after all, Hitler's public image was similarly unlike the Duce's.

As in the realm of image and discourse, the Croix de feu arranged its men into militaristic formations. There was a rigid, well-defined hierarchy with La Rocque at its apex. The authoritarianism (and paternalism) of this elaborate apparatus was underlined by La Rocque's insistence that everyone in the movement was responsible to him personally.[153] In short, as Kennedy remarks, the Croix de feu set about constructing a "counter-society" in opposition to its democratic pluralistic counterpart.[154]

This was mirrored in the Parti populaire français. While the party maintained a fairly traditional structure with departmental federations, which, in turn, were broken into local sections,[155] it later created a corporatist organization with "secretariats" dedicated to propaganda, the middle classes, the liberal professions, peasants, women,[156] "documentation," and children. These were in addition to the party's sizable youth group (with many subdivisions) and its fighting phalanges.[157]

The fascist man emerges, therefore, as youthful, disciplined and unquestioning in a military fashion, physically fit, and ready for action at the beckoning of his leaders. This new man was ready to fight his Communist equivalent in the streets or to defend France against invasion. He was also meant to appeal to Communist youths seduced by the élan of the Communist new man. Given the Croix de feu's meteoric rise post-1936 to a membership of over a million, it would seem the fascist new man won some converts.

THE TOTALITARIAN DRIFT

Philippe Burrin's study of Gaston Bergery, Marcel Déat, and Doriot, *La derive fasciste* (The fascist drift) sought to explain how it could be that three erstwhile leftists—once leading lights of the Radical, Socialist, and Communist parties respectively—made their way into the fascist camp by the late-1930s, while also hinting that this "drift" was representative of a wider phenomenon in French society.[158] By concentrating on leftists cum fascists, however, Burrin missed an arguably more significant phenomenon. The drift in French politics, though by no means absolute, was not simply from left to extreme right, but from the political center to the totalitarian margins. This, moreover, did not exclusively involve people moving from the centrist parties to the fascist parties and leagues and the Communist Party—although that certainly was a noteworthy trend in itself—but also the "totalitarianization" of the centrist parties themselves. This totalitarianization was halting, partial, and sometimes in retreat, but it was real and alarmed some contemporary observers.

This development becomes especially obvious when one focuses on the politics of masculinity in interwar France, as the Communist and then fascist new men infiltrated, or at least found imitators in, the parties of the center-right, center, and center-left. Additionally, the mainstream parties mimicked the extremes in encroaching ever more comprehensively on the private lives of their followers. The totalitarianization of French politics, in other words, witnessed an increasing politicization of daily life and a growing radicalization of political masculinities.

An emphasis on youth, as seen above, was crucial to both the Communist and fascist new men. In the 1920s, there was disagreement between the democratic left-wing parties on the question of youth. Interestingly, the situation was a mirror reflection of that on the right: the farther from the center the party, the more prevalent were youthful constructions of masculinity and the more enthusiastic it accordingly was in its mobilization of youth. By the 1930s, however, centrists became much more concerned with recruiting youth in response to the threat posed by the fascists and Communists.

The Radicals, in this respect, were more similar to the formations of the center-right than to the Socialists and Communists. The Radicals' ideal man remained, largely, respectable and experienced. As Édouard Herriot claimed of the then recently deceased Deputy Paul Elbel, "In listening to him, I observed once more how experience gives a man authority."[159] Similarly, in his speech at the party congress in 1933 Édouard Daladier praised the Radicals' elder statesmen, including Herriot, Maurice Sarraut, René Renoult, and Joseph Caillaux, saying of Sarraut, for example, that "he remains for us a much-loved, respected, and clairvoyant guide."[160]

This sedate vision of masculine virtue did not lend itself easily to a wholehearted embrace of youth or youthfulness within the party. Until the mid-1930s, in fact, the Radicals did not have an official youth wing, contenting themselves instead with loose affiliations with independent youth organizations, including the Jeunesses républicaines et laïques, which had Radical Gaston Bonnaure at its head.[161] There were occasional articles in *La Lumière* or *L'Ère nouvelle* celebrating youth or groups such as the Boy Scouts, but on the whole, the Radicals remained either indifferent to or suspicious of the young.[162] No doubt, this tendency was reinforced by the behavior of the so-called "young Turks" of the party, including Bertrand de Jouvenel and Gaston Bergery,[163] who both gravitated toward fascism in the 1930s, and more sincere leftists like Pierre Cot, Jacques Kayser, and Pierre Mendès-France. What united these men, aside from their age, was a desire to modernize the party and the state—the party hierarchy generally viewed them as noisome troublemakers, successfully, it would seem, co-opting most of them and sidelining their agenda over time.[164]

This indifference changed somewhat in 1933, with the founding of the Jeunesses Radicales. The subsequent comportment of this group may very well have confirmed the prejudices of the party's elders. Peter Larmour contends it was a fascistizing influence and the National Council felt compelled in 1937 to disband it after several violent incidents, including an assault on Cot at the party congress in 1937.[165] It had, at least after the original left-of-center president Roger Huss was pushed out in 1934, two dominant figures. One was Roland Manescau, who served as the group's secretary-general, and the other was Marcel Sableau, its president after Huss's ouster. Both men opposed the Popular Front and were at the fore in moving the Radicals to the right, although Larmour identifies Manescau as the more insidious personality of the two (Sableau appears to have been, in the manner of the young Turks, successfully bought off, becoming a vice-president of the party in 1937).[166] Whatever its nature, the Jeunesses Radicales was quite successful, boasting twenty thousand members by 1935–36. Manescau and Sableau also contributed regularly to *L'Ère nouvelle,* which, in conjunction with its own shift to the right, became the unofficial mouthpiece of the Jeunesses Radicales.

There can be no doubt that the Jeunesses Radicales introduced a brand of masculinity hitherto foreign to the party. They were militant, uncompromising, and less than respectable. Manescau, for example, called for the government to imitate Cardinal Richelieu and seek out and "exterminate" France's internal enemies.[167] He described the Jeunesses in starkly masculine terms, extolling, "the combative temperament of their militants, the virile energy of their leaders, their tireless tenacity."[168] It is difficult to imagine even the somewhat authoritarian Daladier mimicking this intemperate language.

The symbolic nadir of the Radical Party, when it was most obviously affected by the totalitarian drift, came in late 1936 at its party congress in

Biarritz. There, right-wing Radicals, members of the Jeunesses Radicales no doubt prominent among them, interrupted the proceedings to protest the Radicals' adhesion to the Popular Front and sang the "Marseillaise" while making a gesture that was unsettlingly similar to a fascist salute. In response, the Radical left-wing rose, sang the "Internationale," and gave the Communist clenched-fist salute.[169] At that moment, observers could have been forgiven for believing that the totalitarian drift was pulling the Radical Party apart at the seams.

That said, the fascistic tendencies of the Jeunesses Radicales and by extension the totalitarian drift within the Radical Party, though striking, should not be overstated. Yes, the Jeunesses engaged in tactics at odds with Radical traditions, tactics reminiscent of extremist politics, but they also possessed some attributes clearly republican in nature. Most importantly, they stood in defense of the Republic and democracy. A 1937 call for readers to join the organization proclaimed, for instance, "And so, join the Jeunesses Radicales in order to give even more vigor, even more dynamism and enthusiasm to radicalism, and to help us build a France that is the most beautiful and happiest of democracies."[170] In fact, even Manescau, that would-be brownshirt in Radical clothing, saluted Louis Besse, the aged Party treasurer who died in 1937, as "a noble old man whose entire life was devoted to an ideal."[171] That ideal, of course, was the Republic. The Jeunesses Radicales did employ some of the tactics of the fascists, and they did try to emulate, to some degree, their style and their élan, but they did so in defense of the Republic in the tradition of their republican forefathers during the Dreyfus Affair. This may not have been a particularly noble development, and it may indeed have signaled, as Larmour argues, the decline of the moral and political Radical fabric, but if Sableau and others were successfully integrated into the traditional party apparatus by the late 1930s through their obtaining plum jobs and respected positions, that transition was facilitated by their perception, shared with the Radical Party mainstream, that their political identity was defined by their fealty to the Republic. Thus, while the totalitarian drift was evident within the Radical Party, it was not fully ascendant. On the other hand, in the mid- to late 1930s the Radicals hemorrhaged supporters, and historians have concluded that at least some made their way to the totalitarian Croix de feu.[172]

If the Radicals were a little slow off the mark in mobilizing youth, and if the experience of the Jeunesses Radicales was not an entirely happy one, the

Socialists' record with youth was more successful. First, the Socialist Party had the precedent of the prewar Jeunesses Socialistes, so they were involved in organizing youth from a much earlier date than the Radicals. Granted, the party's efforts had to overcome the split in the Jeunesses Socialistes with the majority of its delegates voting to join the Third International in 1920, but still, the foundations for post-1920 success were well-laid.[173] The party continued to have an annual "Week of Studies" for its youth,[174] as well as yearly national congresses.[175] By January 1931, the Jeunesses Socialistes claimed ten thousand members.[176]

But the Socialists' advantage was not just organizational; it was attitudinal. In 1927, Suzanne Caille, a member of the party's National Mixed Committee, which brought together leaders of both the young men and women's sections, requested in a personal letter to Léon Blum that he devote a weekly page of *Le Populaire* to the party's youth: the Socialist leader agreed and such a page remained a constant in the paper thereafter right up to 1940.[177] The Socialist Party, in short, embraced youth with an enthusiasm evinced only reluctantly by the Radicals. In fact, as with the Communists, there was a concerted effort to portray socialism itself as an inherently youthful ethos. In Louis Levy's words, "Socialism appears as the youth of the world."[178]

The party's relative success in mobilizing youth snowballed in the 1930s, partly fueled by enthusiasm for the Popular Front and partly out of a recognition on the part of the leadership that a key to Nazism's rise had been its ability to attract youthful adherents and thus that an effort to forestall similar fascist gains in France was required.[179] By 1940 the Jeunesses Socialistes were targeting a membership of forty-five thousand.[180] In fact, the zenith of the group's success seems to have come in the wake of the Popular Front's ascendancy, as its president, Bernard Chochoy claimed seventy thousand members in the spring of 1938.[181] The fall in membership from 1938 to 1940 was probably due to several factors, including of course the outbreak of the war and the general drift to the right of French politics

The Socialist Party's youth, much as in the Croix de feu, enjoyed an elaborate and well-organized apparatus providing them with myriad opportunities for involvement. Paul Faure, in his capacity as secretary-general of the party, called in the fall of 1931 and in early 1932 for Socialists to donate money to enable the establishment of a "home" for Socialist youth in Paris; this institution opened its doors in 1932.[182] In the summers, the party, in cooperation with the Workers' International, organized a summer camp at Draveil along the Seine, bringing together young socialists from all over Europe and fostering a spirit of international brotherhood: "The fraternity that unites these future citizens bodes well for the future." Camp attendees heard speeches by party dignitaries—Léon Blum and Jean Longuet, in 1931—organized concerts and plays, and sang songs.[183] There was also a Socialist student organization, the National Federation of Socialist Students, who saw themselves as a sort of vanguard of the proletariat and whose primary objective was to educate and mobilize the masses.[184] This group held annual congresses beginning in 1926 and maintained its own journal, *L'Étudiant Socialiste.* Consistent with the party's ethos of masculine international solidarity, the National Federation invited "fraternal delegates" from brother European socialist parties to address its congresses.[185] The party also maintained a more general youth journal as of the mid-1930s, the *Cri des jeunes.*[186]

Notably, within these institutions above, there was no hint of the militarization of masculinity characteristic of Croix de feu youth groups. However, the Socialist Party too had its militaristic wing, which evinced a vision of masculinity in competition with the dominant breadwinner ideal and seems to have resembled the Communist new man. Founded just prior to the February 6, 1934, riots, the Jeunes gardes Socialistes (JGS) were clearly intended to confront the fascists physically, and their militant masculinity reflected this. In a sign of the Jeunes gardes' uncomfortable discursive proximity to the fascists, their secretariat for the Seine region, in denouncing the fascism of the "Solidarité française, whose members [wore] blue shirts and blue scarves," felt compelled to insert a footnote that read "The JGS wear blue shirts and red scarves."[187] Readers doubtless appreciated the clarification. Indeed, Paul Faure signaled some of the party leaders' discomfiture with the Jeunes gardes' brand of militancy by stating that Socialists should learn from the example of the *milices* of the Belgian Party, who apparently ran amok and became a fascistizing influence within the larger organization. Faure thus advocated a rigid subordination of the Jeunes gardes, who should be vetted by a "severe recruitment" and harnessed by "an absolute discipline in following the Party's orders."[188] This subordination was largely achieved, and by 1937 the Jeunes gardes were neatly synchronized into the larger Jeunesses Socialistes' organization.[189] While the far right and the Communist Party engaged in street fighting and captured newspaper headlines with their violent confrontations, the Jeunes gardes Socialistes did not; they were pacified by the party leadership.

That said, although it is surely significant that the party did seek to tame its most militant factions, if historians are to level the accusation against the Croix de feu of its construction of a "counter-society," binding militants' loyalty to the movement first and foremost, the Socialists were also guilty, to some degree, of this ambition. Not only did they have the rather comprehensive apparatus for youth detailed above, but they also started at a relatively young age, like the Croix de feu and the Communists. The Socialist Party's own version of the Boy Scouts, named the Red Falcons, seems to have been an all-male organization. They took field trips to the Spanish Republic, participated in fundraising drives,[190] and went to summer camps where they forged friendships, enjoyed the outdoors, and participated in suitably boyish activities like hiking, soccer, and rugby.[191] In short, their program was not altogether different from their Croix de feu, Parti populaire français, or Communist counterparts. This physical regime was encouraged into young adulthood, when the Socialists had in place the Union des sociétés sportives et gymniques du travail, established in 1924, which organized basketball, soccer, rugby, cycling, swimming, and cross-country running leagues and competitions.[192] Moreover, just like the fascist movements and the Communist Party, the Socialists sought to politicize children at a disturbingly young age. As a *Le Populaire* author maintained, the party did not introduce Jeunesses Socialistes–run daycare centers only out of a concern for social justice, but to "make Socialist pupils—Red Falcons—out of them." The daycare centers in question welcomed children at age four.[193] Thus, while, as in the Radical Party, the totalitarian drift never swept the Socialists away, the party clearly had some totalitarian impulses and elements in its ranks.

On a superficial level, the section of the political spectrum that was most immune to totalitarianization was the conservative right, which made at best tepid attempts to incorporate youth into its parties, for example. The values espoused by the Alliance démocratique, Fédération républicaine, and Parti démocrate populaire's youth organizations seemed more designed to stifle and contain youthful exuberance than to encourage and exploit it. The Alliance's youth group's founding manifesto, for example, called on members to, "maintain liberal traditions"[194]: a worthy goal but hardly one designed to fire youthful passions. *Le Petit Démocrate* ceased carrying a youth page altogether in 1935, deeming the announcement of the page's demise so unimportant that it buried it on page three.[195] And while the Parti démocrate populaire did go on to establish a youth paper, *La Route des jeunes*, which enjoyed moderate success,[196] Jean-Claude Delbreil's conclusion that the party's deterioration in the late 1930s was in part due to a failure to renew itself seems more than warranted.[197] Likewise, William Irvine is clear that the Fédération républicaine, though it too founded a youth group in 1935, grew uncomfortable with some of the activist (and extremist) rhetoric within it and so shortened its leash, ensuring that it did not deviate substantially from the tempered line of the party and, consequently, that it was at best a modest success.[198] The experience of this organization then appears to have been analogous to that of the Jeunesses Radicales or Jeunes gardes Socialistes, albeit on a smaller scale.

In this instance, however, focusing exclusively on the gender discourse of the conservative parties would be misleading. Facts on the ground suggest strongly that there were strong totalitarian impulses within even these organizations. Irvine provides evidence that the Fédération républicaine turned to the fascist leagues and to the Croix de feu in particular as its potential shock troops in the event of a need to resist a Communist or Socialist coup d'état, especially during the period of the Popular Front.[199] The role filled on the center left by the Jeunesses Radicales, the Jeunes gardes Socialistes, or the Jeunesses Communistes was thus effectively farmed out to external organizations. Moreover, as Irvine, Kennedy, and others have noted, membership in the conservative or center-right parties did not preclude simultaneous adherence to one of the fascist leagues. A seemingly respectable Fédération deputy like Pierre Taittinger could accordingly, for example, also be the leader of the fascistic Jeunesses patriotes; Fédération deputy Xavier Vallat could belong to the Croix de feu; conservative scion Alexandre Millerand could found his own fascistic league, the Ligue républicaine nationale; and Alliance démocratique grandee André Tardieu could build bridges to the fascist leagues and flirt with decidedly fascistic ideas of his own.[200] Regional studies, moreover, confirm that local relationships between the traditional right-wing parties and their fascist cousins could be incestuous indeed.[201] In short, to borrow Carmen Callil's description of Taittinger, many of the men of the center-right were in fact "antiparliamentarian parliamentarian[s]."[202]

Still, it must be acknowledged that there is plenty of countervailing evidence that like the Radicals on the center-left, while some on the center-right strayed from the republican camp most preferred to achieve their goals through parliamentary and democratic means and that, perhaps, alliances with the leagues were simply desperate measures meant to preserve rather than destroy the Republic as they understood it. In 1926, for instance, the

Fédération républicaine called on veterans to remember their manly and patriotic "duty" to the nation, which consisted, not of taking up arms against the left, but of defeating them at the ballot box.[203] Likewise, Louis Marin wrote party dissident Louis Adt in 1935 to remind him of his patriotic "duty" to remain politically engaged for "the interests of the country."[204] In fact, the Fédération républicaine, like the other parties of the republican right, believed itself to represent France's liberal and democratic tradition and the left, especially the extreme left, to be the real threat to the Republic. As the party's statement of domestic policy in 1935 put it: "For a third of a century, two political tendencies have divided France. On the one hand, the demagogic, étatist, internationalist, materialist, and revolutionary tendency. On the other, the traditionalist, democratic, liberal, national, and spiritual one. The Republican Federation advocates this second tendency. It sees in the Republic . . . the best possible regime."[205]

It is noteworthy that Marin, along with Millerand and Henri de Kérillis, two other right-wing notables (de Kérillis was a former member of the Fédération républicaine) oft-fingered as having fascist leanings, abstained from voting Marshall Philippe Pétain the power to abrogate the Third Republic's constitution in 1940, while many others supposedly more committed to democracy, such as the Radical Fernand Bouisson, showed little compunction in doing so.[206] Thus, there seems little reason to cast particular doubt on the center-right's fidelity to the republican order, at least as they envisioned it. There was a totalitarian drift within the republican right as there was within the left, but it was no more pronounced than elsewhere on the political spectrum.

It might be tempting to conclude that the politicization of private life and the totalitarianization of masculinity was equivalent among the parliamentary parties and the fascists and Communists, but it was not. While the Socialist Party, for example, did emphasize youthfulness as a positive masculine characteristic, and while it did, in quasi-totalitarian fashion, extend its reach into children's lives, it did not for the most part seek to militarize its young boys or men in the same manner as the fascists or encourage them to take up violent revolution as did the Communists (at least at times). Also, while the style might have been somewhat similar, the substance was different: the Socialists, Radicals, and others were not preparing their boys for a violent seizure of power: a rather significant distinction. That said, the totalitarian drift in interwar France was a sizable, noteworthy, and troubling phenomenon, both from the center to the margins and within the center itself.

CONCLUSION

World War I's impact on interwar France was profound in many respects. These included that in helping to beget the Russian Revolution, the war contributed to yielding the Communist new man and woman. The Communist new woman was a fascinating experiment in gender roles and represented a major departure from traditional notions of femininity. She was militant, physically strong, and independent, and she agitated for political and social equality. She was also, however, always on the margins of not just French political culture, but the Communist Party itself. Moreover, in its moves first toward stifling Stalinism in the mid-1920s and then the Popular Front strategy in the mid-1930s, the Communist Party sidelined and then silenced the advocates of the Communist new woman, suggesting that traditional conceptions of femininity were both strikingly resilient and pervasive.

The Communist new man, in contrast, had a more pronounced destabilizing effect on interwar French politics. First, he was youthful, physically fit, revolutionary, and either potentially or actually violent and was, therefore, a dramatic departure from the much older, more experienced, and respectable man idealized in the political mainstream. Second, there were many proponents of the Communist new man within the party—signaled by the number of party notables who fashioned themselves as new men, including Jacques Doriot and André Marty—and this newly militant masculinity bred more non-Communist imitators than did the new woman.

This was most evident in the rise of fascism—another critical interwar development greatly influenced by World War I. As many historians have noted, veterans of the war were conspicuously prominent in fascist ranks.[207] It seems likely, therefore, that the militarization of masculinity within these movements resulted in part from the wartime experiences of French men, who sought in their civilian lives the discipline and camaraderie they had experienced in the trenches. Moreover, fascism was a mimetic phenomenon, and the fascist new man resembled his Communist counterpart in many respects. The fascist new man too was youthful, physically imposing, and prone to violence, for example. Given that the Communist new man was in part a product of the Great War, therefore, the fascist new man was doubly so, via the experiences of fascist war veterans and the imitation of his Communist opposite number.

The Communist and fascist new men thus challenged and destabilized accepted norms as some young men were drawn to the political extremes by their dynamism; in response, many in the centrist parties began to imitate them. The respectable republican masculine citizen gave up some ground to the new man. This process was never completed, but it is fair to say that the totalitarian new men destabilized the hegemonic breadwinner ideal. Gender discourse accordingly emerges as one cause of the totalitarian drift evident in 1930s French politics. Not only did many voters and party members flee to the margins but also some others who did not emulated the new men in order to capitalize on the enthusiasm they engendered. This signified a radicalization of political masculinity in interwar France and was accompanied in some cases by a concomitant politicization of party members' daily lives. In a liberal democracy such as Third Republic France, premised as it was upon the free-thinking male citizen and breadwinner, the increasing effort by the political parties to shape adherents' thoughts from an early age was unhealthy.

None of which is to say that France was "decadent" or that the catastrophe of Vichy France was inevitable or organic. France was not, to quote one proponent of a variant of the decadence thesis, mired in "stagnation and sclerosis."[208] France lost in 1940 because of a military blunder, and while Vichy certainly had many indigenous origins, it seems doubtful that a similar regime would have come to power without foreign intervention. Yet, a rejection of this line of thinking should not blind observers to the very real problems confronting republican France in the interwar period. The totalitarian drift, signaled and in part inspired by the Communist and fascist new men, was one of them.

II

RACE

3

"THE SAVAGERY OF THE BARBARIANS"

THE POLITICS OF RACE

Historians of interwar France have tended to locate the home of racists and xenophobes firmly on the right. Studies of despicable figures such as Louis Darquier de Pellepoix or Robert Brasillach, for example, reinforce for many the popular and comforting assumption that the virulent racism they espoused was the purview of the far right generally and the fascist right in particular.[1] This supposition allows French citizens to view racism as a marginal phenomenon in the period.

Aside from the fact that it provides French citizens with a reassuring alibi, this identification of the far right with racism is understandable. The racially motivated crimes of the Nazi regime during World War II and the willing and at-times eager collaboration in those crimes on the part of the right-wing Vichy government of Marshal Philippe Pétain in France have left an indelible mark on the popular and historical consciousness.[2] Moreover, the number of violent racists, and especially violent anti-Semites, on the far right was undeniably striking and included such influential figures as Louis-Ferdinand Céline, Léon Daudet, Pierre Drieu La Rochelle, and Georges Maurras.[3]

Yet, focusing too intently on the most spectacular racists of the era can serve, inadvertently, to obfuscate the more subtle but also dangerous ways in which racism permeated the mainstream. Recent studies of attitudes toward immigration in interwar France have, for example, illustrated that xenophobia with racist overtones could be found at the center of the French political spectrum as well as at the extreme right.[4] Indeed, even on the Marxist left where rhetoric about the solidarity of the international working class was axiomatic, one could find the vilest racism. Speaking of the "Chinese legions enlisted in the Bolshevik army," for instance, Socialist Pierre Lainé decried "the savagery of the barbarians employed as soldiers by the Reds."[5] Lainé's language evoked the same fear of the "brutal Asiatic" found in Drieu La Rochelle's musings; that it was shared too by the conservative Robert Cornilleau, who described Soviet aggression as part of "the eternal struggle of

Asiatic barbarism against European civilization" and the typical Asiatic as "a human beast without culture or discipline, motivated by the strength of his impulsive instincts," underscores the need for a comparative analysis of the discourse of race across the political spectrum.[6]

Such an analysis allows several observations. First, the language and politics of "race" were nearly omnipresent in interwar French politics. Almost everyone assumed the legitimacy of race as a category and adopted that assumption as part of their worldview. This led to a widespread "racialism," wherein nearly everyone treated the existence of definable human races as a fact. That said, the concept of race remained unstable, with considerable confusion in evidence around what constituted the French or white race, for example, and with many commentators perhaps deliberately eliding distinctions between the two. Second, the combination of the ubiquity of racialism with the social Darwinism of the age and the unprecedented influx of visibly different immigrants into France in the interwar years produced a flourishing of overt racism,[7] which, though not so universal as simple racialism, could be found across the political spectrum nonetheless. Third, while both racialism and racism were prominent on the left and in the center as on the right, it remains true that the far right attracted the most pronounced racists. Drieu La Rochelle found his political home in the Parti populaire français for a reason. Finally, the Communist Party, to its credit, was the political formation most impervious to both racialist and racist appeals. Where Socialists might waver in their commitment to an egalitarian fraternity of peoples, the Communists were generally steadfast. Moreover, as racism was more prominent on the right so antiracism was more common on the left; that said, the left harbored many racists and the right produced some antiracists.

RACIALISM

Nearly everyone in interwar France thought in terms of race. Race, for most, was as accepted as a category as sex or nationality. Most assumed that races existed, that those races had definable characteristics, and that there was such a thing as the "French race," which had to pursue its own interests actively in order to thrive. Racialism, in short, was a defining feature of the interwar mentality. Accordingly, considerations of race permeated discussions of almost all issues.

In Radical circles, for example, discussions of physical fitness often drew upon racialized language. This tendency may have represented the outcome of medical professionals' concern, as Christopher Forth discusses, that "civilized manhood" had been defined too exclusively as an intellectual state of being in the Republic.[8] Certainly, Radicals evinced a marked interest in bodily fitness inflected with concern for the race. Proponents of physical fitness invariably talked about the health of the race when they advocated measures such as mandatory physical education in schools or heightened public participation in physical exercise. R. Le Bon's article "For the Future of the Race: Modern Industry Must Favor Sports" was emblematic of this tendency. Le Bon maintained that in promoting sports as leisure activities for the working class, industrialists would help workers sustain their "vigor and conserve their health." As a leftist, Le Bon added that reducing working hours and thereby increasing workers' leisure time would be a step in the right direction.[9] This regenerative concern was explicitly racialist—it was also widespread. Édouard Herriot, at the time the undisputed kingpin of the party, asserted that "healthy lodgings are indispensable for the formation of a healthy race," that physical education was similarly vital, and that "the French bourgeoisie is the class that conserves the virtues of the race."[10] In the 1920s Radical Deputy Dr. Georges Faugère, who was the head of the Chamber's "Hygiene Commission," was a relentless advocate for the popularization of physical education, and he linked its proliferation to a return to the virtues of "sobriety, chastity, and moderation," which he felt had fallen into disfavor with the postwar generation.[11] It was hardly out of character, therefore, when longtime *L'Ère nouvelle* contributor J. Ernest-Charles welcomed the implementation of mandatory physical education in the public school system in 1937 with the comment that "this will create a strong race."[12] That this concern with the health of the race intersected with a desire to see French masculinity revitalized was best captured by *La Lumière*'s André Glarner, who argued that the Popular Front should reorganize physical education in the public schools because this task was "that of the defense of the race. . . . Sports, in giving to their participants an esprit de corps, a sense of voluntary discipline, a taste for struggle and a desire to conquer naturally produce men apt for military service, but they also produce courageous and healthy men, capable of succeeding in life."[13] In this realm, some Radicals touted the benefits of physical exercise because they felt that it would inculcate men with the desired masculine characteristics and that these, in turn, would help revitalize the French race.

While such racialist language was less prevalent on the Marxist left, it could be found there as well. *Le Populaire*'s women's page contributor Danièle Vindor, for example, raged against the debilitating influence of urban environments and denounced modern child-rearing techniques as producing a generation "incapable of acts of will." The tonic, she proclaimed, was physical activity, which she predicted would "develop [and] aerate the race, tone it, and return to it that vigor, that suppleness, that active blood circulation, which abiding in the cities has compromised and caused to atrophy."[14] Pierre Marie, who was *Le Populaire*'s primary sports columnist from 1927 to 1940,[15] likewise approached the Radicals' racialism, hinting darkly in 1932 in social Darwinist fashion, for example, that Germans were getting fitter while French men continued their sedentary ways.[16] In 1938, Marie's racialism was more open, as he opined that "those who are preoccupied with promoting physical exercise, must make it a goal to reinforce the vigor of the race."[17] Even the Communist Paul Vaillant-Couturier, in expanding on the revolutionary virtues of sports, wrote that "when a civilization fails and decomposes—and that is both the tragedy of and the source of hope of our era—everything that is a manifestation of health, of the survival of an extenuated race, and within this race of the class exploited today but triumphant tomorrow, is highly revolutionary."[18]

Another subject in addition to physical education that tended to conjure the language of race was motherhood. *Le Populaire* regretted, for example, that industrialists were neglecting "the future of the race" in forcing expectant mothers to work late into their third trimesters.[19] In the same vein, Socialist general councilor for the Seine Jean Alessandri asserted in his article on protective legislation for mothers and children that "the protection of childhood poses a capital problem, that of the race itself."[20] At the Radical-sympathizing *L'Ère nouvelle,* meanwhile, "Bertine" proclaimed that "women have . . . a sublime role. Nature entrusts them with the race and charges them with assuring its continuity."[21] Radical deputy Joseph Garat likewise seemed particularly peeved that Judge Victor D'Uhalt had sent Basques to remove his own allegedly senile sixty-three-year-old mother from her home, as though it was especially unseemly for a mother of the French race to be mistreated in this manner by racial aliens.[22] Even Marcel Cachin was not immune to this identification of motherhood with the interests of the race (although in his case, Cachin meant the human rather than French race): "once she [woman] accomplishes her august role as the reproducer of the human race."[23] Any notion, therefore, that racialism did not penetrate the left is pure fancy. A concern for the welfare of the race underlay leftist discussions of motherhood as it did other issues, although this tendency was less pronounced in the Communist Party than elsewhere and whether commentators meant the white, French, or human race could sometimes be unclear.

On the right, as one might expect, racialism was even more apparent when motherhood was the subject. Mothers' duties, for example, were constantly defined as to their "race," as in *Le Devoir des femmes* in April 1937: "Among all peoples, it is in the family that the aptitudes and virtues of the race are acquired and cultivated."[24] Wealthy industrialist Raoul de Warren, a Fédération républicaine supporter, likewise touched on race in a *La Nation* piece. Declaring infant mortality and the declining birthrate to be a "vital problem," de Warren continued on to label reversing both trends "the problem of our race."[25]

XENOPHOBIA

This pervasive racialism, found on both the left and the right, helped to fuel a rising tide of xenophobia in interwar France, particularly in the 1930s. Beginning in the immediate post–World War I period, from 1919 to 1924, France witnessed a massive influx of immigrants, both from other parts of Europe and from the colonies. In those years, for instance, roughly 1 million immigrants entered the country, largely to answer France's labor shortage, made acute by the demand for workers created by France's postwar reconstruction and by the dearth of men of working age thanks to the Great War's horrific human toll: over 16 percent of enlisted men had died from 1914 to 1918. By 1931, the number of immigrant and foreign workers had increased threefold to around 3 million. The fact that, as Laura Frader has recently demonstrated, these immigrants played a crucial role in France's interwar prosperity did not prevent widespread anxiety and resentment at their presence.[26]

When the Great Depression began to affect France in the early 1930s these xenophobic sentiments began to be more fully expressed. One highly prejudicial outcome of this for immigrant workers was that employers tended to lay them off first, along with women workers, when scaling back production to account for reduced demand. Even the government pursued a policy of open discrimination. In 1932, France decreed that only 5 percent of public-sector jobs could be held by noncitizens.[27] This wave of xenophobia in the 1930s moreover began to take on a distinctly anti-Semitic tone as Sephardic Jews from Eastern Europe, visually and culturally distinct from the "true French," and indeed from France's indigenous Jewish population, arrived on French territory in large numbers seeking refuge from the fearsome wave of anti-Semitism that swept across eastern and central Europe at that time. According to the French government's figures, by 1938 there were an estimated sixty thousand central and eastern European Jewish refugees in the country, forty-two thousand of whom were in France illegally.[28]

It must be emphasized that while xenophobia gained momentum in the 1930s it was prominent in French political circles from an early point. It is also important to note, once again, that this was true of the left as it was of the right, albeit to a lesser degree. In 1920, for example, *Le Populaire* ran a number of articles warning of the "yellow peril": Chinese immigrants. In a typically Orientalist fantasy, the author of one piece on the Chinese quarter of London expressed racialist concerns about miscegenation and portrayed the Chinese as lascivious and diseased degenerates:

> Debauchery has become a normal state there. In a recent police raid, they uncovered repugnant orgies involving Chinese, Negroes, and women of color as well as young Englishwomen most of whom had their children (métis) with them.
>
> This quarter . . . is moreover curious for the 2,000 Chinese, the hundreds of Negroes and Asiatics who swarm there in a typically Asian dirtiness.
>
> 'One sees babies of all colours and of all origins there,' a functionary declared to a reporter, 'and 90% of the women who prostitute themselves in the area are afflicted with venereal diseases. It's horrible.'[29]

While this passage was particularly virulent, it was not as aberrant as it might seem. The Socialist Party continued to evince concern over immigration, perhaps in response to its working-class supporters' anxieties. The party program in 1924 even promised to pursue the "regulation of immigration" and, in particular, pledged to voters that the Socialist Party would ensure "equal pay for equal work."[30] Likely, this latter plank in the Socialist platform reflected workers' impression that immigrants were undercutting their wages by accepting lower rates of pay.[31] Forcing employers to pay immigrants the same as French workers, so the logic went, would remove the incentive to hire them and lead to their decreased participation in the workforce.

The Radical Party too harbored some xenophobes. Perhaps the most notable case was at the journal *L'Ère Nouvelle,* the newspaper that had emerged by the mid-to-late 1930s as the voice of the Jeunesses Radicales and the party's right wing. There those like contributor Pierre Mille could muse openly about the "colonization" of France by foreigners and lament that even European immigrants like Poles and Italians did not integrate into French society. Similarly, "Norpois," likely a nom de plume for editor Léo-Abel Gaboriaud, could opine, "At present there are 400,000 [unemployed]. But you will notice that we are nourishing 1,300,000 foreign workers. If they weren't here, unemployment wouldn't exist."[32]

On the center-right this sort of xenophobia was yet more common and touched on similar themes. Perhaps the most frequent xenophobic trope appeared in discussions of one of the right's pet issues—the birthrate. While fretting over France's stagnant population growth, right-wingers, both those who were directly affiliated with France's powerful pronatalist movement and those who were not, consistently rejected immigration as a solution. Pronatalist Henri Roulleaux-Dugage, for example, in his remarkable and lengthy discussion of women's suffrage and the family vote in the Chamber of Deputies in 1923, rejected Communist André Berthon's call to deal with population decline by increasing immigration: "Whatever elements you might appeal to would never replace the French of France, born on ancient French soil."[33] Roulleaux-Dugage's sentiments were oft-repeated by other conservatives in the Alliance démocratique, Fédération républicaine, and Parti démocrate populaire. Some like the Parti démocrate populaire's Etienne Martin St.-Léon, while regretting the "crimes or thefts committed by certain Arabs and Kabyles in our workers' neighborhoods in Paris,"[34] allowed that *European* immigrants like Poles and Belgians were hard workers. St. Léon's comments appear to be indicative of the phenomenon Elisa Camiscioli discusses, wherein policy makers distinguished between racially desirable and undesirable immigrants.[35] Most commentators however, such as the Fédération's Jean Bourdon called on readers "to be clairvoyant in [their] hospitality" and realize that immigration of any kind was a threat to France rather than a solution to its problems.[36] This pervasive logic is an indication of the hegemony of racialist thinking: commentators were so wedded to the notion of the French race that they could not conceive of the French nation in any but racial terms. Thus, while the Croix de feu's language around issues of immigration, as in the following extract, was generally more extreme than its republican counterparts, its sentiments were far from unique. Writing of "all the horde from ethnic areas, steppe or desert, who burden our economy, our social laws, our hospitals, our asylums and our prisons," the movement declared that "immigration and nationalization are not remedies to the continued decline of the birth rate. They are not even palliatives."[37]

As this quotation suggests, the fascist right was the ugly cousin of conservatism on this and other issues. What they said was undeniably related to and often substantially the same as conservative discourse, but the fascists phrased their views in blunter and more inflammatory terms. The Croix de feu's E. Anxionnat, for example, argued that being xenophobic was simply a matter of patriotism. It was time, in his view, to reconsider the "excessive naturalization" of 350,000 "foreigners" in recent years as these people along with the fifty-five thousand children they had produced on French soil had become a "heavy and dangerous burden."[38]

While such xenophobic invective was a notable feature of the Croix de feu's rhetoric, it was a central pillar of Parti populaire français ideology. Party intellectual Drieu La Rochelle was one champion of the party's anti-immigrant rhetoric and paranoia. On one occasion, he painted an alarming picture of what he dubbed an "atrocious reality" for his readers, pointing out that even France's already anemic birthrate and unimposing population were artificially high, as they were distorted by the presence of 3 million naturalized foreigners and their offspring; ergo, Drieu proclaimed, France's real population was only 38 million. He tied this, moreover, to the Communist threat, suggesting that Marcel Cachin and the Communist Party leadership were deliberately flooding France with "North Africans, Poles, and Negroes," in preparation for an attempted revolution.[39]

While quixotic, this connection of xenophobia to anticommunism was familiar on the right, including the center-right. The common thread tying the two together was that both were seen as internationalist rather than nationalist and foreign rather than French elements. In decrying a Communist electoral victory in 1926, for example, a *La Nation* author attacked those he saw applauding the victory thus: "The results of the election . . . were welcomed at the Variety Theater by some 'refugees.' In the orchestra seats . . . women covered in pearls and diamonds applauded to no end. Three quarters of them were foreigners. They were saluting the success of the foreigner in France."[40] Thus, fascist Jacques Doriot was expounding on a familiar theme when, in indicating the Parti populaire français's support for the Munich Accord, he declared that "WE MUST PURGE THE FOREIGN INVADERS FROM

FRANCE WHO TAKE ADVANTAGE OF HER HOSPITALITY IN ORDER TO DESTROY HER FROM WITHIN. We must suppress the odious party of Moscow, the truly destabilizing presence. WE MUST UNITE THE FRENCH IN ORDER TO REMAKE FRANCE."[41] Immigrants and Communists alike were thus to be cast out.

The outbreak of World War II provided cover for the Parti populaire français to unleash an unrestrained xenophobia. Moreover, that untrammeled chauvinism became clearly linked to another defining characteristic of the party: its anti-Semitism. The articles of party journalist Jacques St.-Germain were particularly disturbing in this regard. On January 26, 1940, for example, St.-Germain informed his readers that it was time "to regulate the serious problem of foreign merchants." He wrote that "foreigners" were "strangling" the French economy and blamed the "liberals" who had run France's interwar governments for letting them in. The term "merchants" was likely meant as code for "Jews" to fellow anti-Semites, but just in case the connection was too subtle, St.-Germain continued that foreigners were "profiting from our distress as from a good business transaction, escaping the tax of blood and sometimes even the other kind of tax,[42] to satisfy their speculative nomadism. They are here today, they will be somewhere else tomorrow just like the Rothschilds during the Napoleonic wars who made their fortune by furnishing all the belligerents with arms and credit regardless of whether or not they were friends or enemies of their momentary homeland of convenience."[43] Again, as with the spurious connection between immigration and the Communist Party, the association between the Jews and immigrants, in the fascist imagination, lay in their shared internationalism and foreignness: they were not and could never be French because they were not from genuinely French stock. As a foreign element, moreover, they had no patriotic feeling and might betray France as the Rothschilds supposedly had done.[44]

COLONIALISM AND EMPIRE

As Bertrand Taithe's recent account of the 1898–99 Voulet-Chanoine mission and the scandal it caused has reminded historians, the scramble for Africa and the new imperialism, not to mention the brutality that accompanied them, were partly produced by pseudo-scientific notions of racial superiority among the French and other European colonizers.[45] In interwar France too, attitudes toward colonialism and empire shaped commentators' thinking on race and immigration, and vice versa. Indeed, as Camiscioli and Carole Reynaud Paligot observe, one might say that attitudes toward "racial" questions at home and enthusiasm for the empire overseas were two sides of the same coin.[46]

Most studies of the French empire argue that the zenith of its popularity at home came during the interwar period. The empire had proven its worth during World War I, so the argument goes, and so ordinary French citizens embraced it with an enthusiasm that had hitherto been lacking, with this imperial zest reaching its pinnacle with the 1931 Colonial Exposition in Paris.[47] Indeed, in a December 1918 speech Paul Deschanel, the newly elected president of the Republic, singled out France's "African troops, those irresistible Moroccans," for praise and claimed that they were "proud to fight for France whose generous and humane soul sparks in all the flame of supreme sacrifice."[48] Another sign of this fresh fascination with the empire inspired by this "supreme sacrifice" was the so-called "negrophilia" that gripped Paris's cultural elites, including luminaries such as Pablo Picasso, Jean Cocteau, Jean-Paul Sartre, and Simone de Beauvoir, and helped propel Josephine Baker to stardom.[49]

Yet, despite this enthusiasm evident in other places, it must be said that the political press paid relatively scant attention to the colonies. Focused inwardly on domestic politics and, to a lesser degree, events in Europe, newspaper editors generally ignored day-to-day events in the colonies and turned their gaze on them only when some scandal or anticolonial revolt demanded notice. This inattention made a mockery of the ruling logic of French colonialism, which was that as the culmination of the "civilizing mission" the colonies would be integrated into France itself; indeed, some privileged colonies were divided into departments and sent deputies, albeit elected by a highly restricted franchise, to the national assembly.[50]

Still, when the colonies did merit attention, race definitely factored into the discussion. In 1920, an unnamed author who was likely Yvon Delbos, the editor of *L'Ère Nouvelle* and member of the Socialist Party at the time and a future justice minister and leading light of the Radical Party, provided a classic statement of the civilizing mission. Entitled "France and the Weak," the piece suggested that as a superior and stronger race, it was the French's special responsibility to protect their inferiors: "If there is a reputation that . . . France has maintained and largely deserved, it's as protector of the oppressed nationalities and races."[51] This would no doubt have been news to the subject peoples of the French empire and represented as pure a colonialist fantasy as one could hope to find, but delusional though it may have been, it was widely shared and propagated. Radical Albert Sarraut, for example, then minister of colonies in the Raymond Poincaré government, insisted that allegations of abuses in the colonies were entirely unfounded and added that the French empire was perhaps the only example in the world "of an affectionate and confident accord tying indigenous populations to the French authority that has taken them under its wing."[52] In 1939 this colonialist myth of France as benevolent educator to her colonial pupils remained powerful. Antoine Sallès, the eldest member of the Chamber of Deputies, lectured his colleagues on the beauties of the empire in the first sitting of the chamber that year. Declaring that while racism was dangerously pervasive in Germany and the United States, he continued, "we have always treated the exotic peoples that we have brought under our jurisdiction with kindness and respect." Sallès then, referring to deputies from the colonies, asserted that "we are proud to note, even here among our colleagues, sons of the black race, which has shown itself to be, contrary [to the opinions of racists] so worthy and so grateful for the didactic mission by which France introduced it to our occidental civilization."[53]

This responsibility of the French, as the superior civilization and race, to tutor and protect the colonial peoples was also celebrated on the right. Fédération républicaine leader Louis Marin, then a minister of state, delivered a eulogy for Marshal Hubert Lyautey to a crowd of Moroccan elites in Rabat in 1936 on the occasion of the inhumation of the former "pacifier" and governor of Morocco. Adopting racialized language and, typically of colonialists, cavalierly suggesting that the Moroccan race embodied certain characteristics, Marin addressed himself to the sultan, "Of old racial stock, [Lyautey] loved in Your subjects their loyalty; he declared . . . that he had never seen them fail in this virtue." He continued, "No country is more worthy of the affection of Morocco than France. For her destiny to be among one of the guides of humanity; for her more than one thousand years of glory; for her old civilization, originating in the Occident; for the benefits that she has brought to all the shores of the world."[54] Marin's usage of Lyautey's memory as a vehicle for celebrating France's colonizing mission typified the cult of celebrity around the marshal, as Edward Berenson's research on this "hero of Empire" suggests.[55]

Women, it seems, in keeping with the widespread belief in their innate aptitude as educators, could play a special role in bettering the subject peoples. Reporting on the Estates-General of feminism in 1931, for example, Parti démocrate populaire militant Cécile de Corlieu noted approvingly that under the leadership of Catholic feminist Ghénia Avril de Sainte-Croix and none other than Lyautey, the delegates had discussed the need for French women to enlighten and empower women in the colonies.[56] De Corlieu's fellow traveler and de facto leader of the party's women, Pauline Le Cormier, likewise launched an investigation into the state of women in Cameroon. She insisted that "to colonize is not to exploit the black, but to elevate him," and that thanks to some happy examples under French tutelage she could confirm that "the improvement of the black woman is not an unrealizable utopia."[57]

But, despite this civilizing mission and the apparent ideal of elevating France's imperial subjects to the lofty status of French citizens, all was not sweetness and light. That an ideology of racial superiority underlay, for most, France's colonial mission was most evident in discussions of *métissage,* which commentators generally (though not universally) abhorred. Republican Socialist deputy Victor Augagneur,[58] for example, viewed the children of "mixed-race" unions as racial degenerates who were "not even, as one might have hoped, a link between the two races." He explained, "The métis is an unfortunate accident and, as a black saying goes, 'God made coffee. God made milk, but God did not make café au lait.'" Augagneur then closed his article by calling for colonial authorities to take measures to separate the races more rigidly, and he compared French practices unfavorably with those of the British empire. In a second piece he suggested more concretely that one advantageous step would be "to expel" "black" concubines and mistresses from urban areas.[59] Augagneur's fears no doubt stemmed in part from the challenge métis peoples posed to the rigid categorization of races to which he subscribed. He notably called for a more rigorous policing of racial boundaries focusing on the need to control indigenous women's sexuality in so doing.

Others such as Pierre Mille held less negative views of the métis themselves but still viewed them as a problem and as inassimilable into the French race. Mille argued that the best that métis peoples could hope for was what had transpired in the Antilles where they had emerged as a racially distinct colonial elite acting as middle men between French masters and native subjects. He thus urged colonial authorities to establish homes reserved for métis and to encourage them to marry within their own community.[60] The Radical Mille's thinking was in keeping with that of the Fédération républicaine's Ch. Chenet, a contributor to *Le Devoir des femmes*. Taking up de Corlieu and Le Cormier's view of French women as playing imperial roles suited to their femininity, she urged the party's women to help the métis children orphaned throughout the empire by their French fathers and indigenous mothers. Particularly revealing of her racialist conception of these products of miscegenation, Chenet suggested that "just by the fact of their [half-French] origins, these métis children have a much more highly developed sense of human dignity than indigenous children." Apparently, a "sense of human dignity" was a biologically French trait. The humane thing to do was therefore to inculcate these unfortunate children with the appropriate bourgeois values and to teach them about their glorious French heritage. Left unsaid was whether or not Chenet believed these children could or should be integrated fully into French society and, by extension, the French race.[61] As Anne Carol among others discusses, French racial theorists debated whether *métissage* elevated the inferior blood of the indigenous parent or degraded that of the French one.[62]

On other issues pertaining to the colonies besides *métissage* commentators also revealed their racialist stripes. The leader of the Alliance démocratique's feminine section, Yvonne Foinant, was unambiguous, for example, in her rejection of the idea of colonial peoples voting. In 1936, she explained at the party congress that the Popular Front government was not introducing a bill for women's suffrage because leftist politicians felt that women needed further education on France's republican traditions. To illustrate the absurdity of this logic, Foinant asked, "Did you know that the Popular Front government has tabled a bill giving the vote to native Algerians?" Foinant's dismissive comment was greeted by laughter from the congress's delegates,[63] indicating their shared belief that the Algerians, as racial and cultural inferiors, could not possibly be responsible citizens.

In similar terms, Pierre Mille of *L'Ère nouvelle* revealed his doubts about the assimilability of North African women, thereby undermining the logic of the civilizing mission. In particular, Mille lamented the inability of French educators to break Muslim women's "backwards" thinking. Quoting an author who had lived in Morocco, Mille found it especially distressing that "rarely can one observe among these Muslims an 'intelligent' curiosity; rare are questions about our customs, our country, or our religion."[64] Taking Muslim women's lack of interest in French civilization as evidence of a lack of intelligence, Mille certainly viewed Islam as one impediment to their enlightenment. Yet, given Mille's many other racialist musings, it seems highly likely that he viewed these women as racially as well as culturally inferior.

In short, interwar politicos' views of the empire were strongly colored by their racialist worldviews. One can also hypothesize that the empire itself was partly responsible for the frequency of racialism across the political spectrum. Seeming to confirm the view that French civilization, populated by the racially superior French race, had a historic mission and responsibility to take lesser civilizations and beings under its wing, the empire no doubt substantiated and solidified for many their racialist outlook, which placed European races generally and the French race particularly at the apex of a supposedly natural racial hierarchy. While the empire and its attendant racialism had their critics as will be seen below, most would certainly have agreed with Radical and future president of the republic Paul Doumer that the empire was the product of "the genius of our race."[65]

RACISM

That sense of racial superiority inevitably produced a great deal of full-blown racism directed against both imperial subjects and domestic minorities seen as racially distinct, most notably the Jews. Not all racialists were necessarily overt and belligerent racists, but racism was very often a perversely logical outcome of racialist thinking. If one view was that as racially superior the French had a duty to care for and uplift their inferiors, another was that being biologically a cut above gave the French the right to dominate lesser beings. In truth, such thinking surely explained much of the brutality of French military officers and civilian officials in the colonies, for example, where slavery, mass executions, and group punishments for individual (and often specious) misdeeds remained the norm well into the twentieth century.[66]

As support for colonialism was more prominent on the right, so was racism. However, by no means did conservatives and fascists have a monopoly on racial prejudice. The licentious and sexually dangerous man of color was a specter that haunted the colonialist imagination across the imperial world, from the American south to British India to western Canada.[67] In France, the experience of World War I heightened these fears, as sexual liaisons between colonial troops stationed in France and French women had been far too commonplace for many observers during the war.[68] In 1919–20, the occupation of Germany by black African French colonial troops produced an outpouring of anxiety in the West and a great deal of sympathy for the Germans.[69] Left-wing feminist, Socialist, and later Communist Louise Bodin shared the fear that France's black troops posed a danger to German women and produced a highly charged rant in 1920 denouncing their use. Quoting her Socialist colleague L. D. Morel, Bodin wrote that in stationing black soldiers in Germany, "French militarists . . . are committing a horrible crime against white women and civilization." In her own words she continued that "it is inadmissible that women, once again, not raise protests against these assaults on their fellow women." While assailing the military for its inhumanity, Bodin gave vent to the stereotype of African men as sexually uncontrollable: "*They* [the French high command] came up with this plan to spread battalions of Negroes across Germany with their appetites and bestial natures." Worse, French generals had then forced German municipalities to organize brothels staffed by local women for the colonial troops:[70] "There must be white women for these sons of Ham."[71] Bodin then wrapped up by arguing that the French army was indifferent to the infection of German and French girls as young as fourteen with syphilis—"most of the negroes are syphilitics"—because the victims were working class. This class bias also explained the failure to prevent the black troops from raping German girls.[72] In Bodin's mind, it would seem, the civilizing mission remained incomplete.

Anti-Semitism too could be found on the left. There were celebrated instances involving high-profile personalities. André Gide, for instance, a member of the Communist Party, once used anti-Semitic language to attack his erstwhile friend Léon Blum.[73] More famously still, Socialist Party secretary Paul Faure split definitively with Blum in the late 1930s over the issue of whether to confront Nazi Germany (Faure was an integral pacifist and favored appeasement at all costs). When declaring that he would not support any government that included his former Socialist colleague, Faure reportedly said that if Blum entered the cabinet "then all Israel is with him! That would be war without end!"[74] Radical Party elder statesman Joseph Caillaux likewise proclaimed that Blum, born and raised in France, did not have "enough French soil on the soles of his shoes."[75]

As in other cases, *L'Ère nouvelle* provided a revealing glimpse at trends and attitudes in the interwar left. While prior to the late 1930s, one could not accuse the paper of advocating racist policies, anti-Semitic jokes did appear on its pages. The paper's humorist Charles Régismanset, for instance, portrayed

Jews as wealthy, duplicitous, and sexually aggressive.[76] This suggests a tolerance at the journal, which was decidedly within the mainstream of French politics, for anti-Semitic stereotypes. Moreover, as the journal drifted rightward under Léo-Abel Gaboriaud's editorship its tone become openly anti-Semitic. Gaboriaud, for example, who began to campaign for the Radicals to abandon their anticlericalism and embrace a Catholic identity, complained of "Israelites" who opposed his ideas.[77] Three years later Gaboriaud had come to endorse a xenophobic brand of anti-Semitism, proclaiming, for example, "We were shocked, at times, during the years before the previous war, to hear Israelites educated at Rabbinical schools on the shores of the Vistula, who had come here in order to be naturalized, raise their voices against our customs, our institutions, [and] the religion of our fathers, and advocate reforms and a revolution which, at the time covered them in nothing but ridicule."[78] His resentment toward naturalized Jews, moreover, paralleled columnist Pierre Mille's many columns sounding the alarm about Jewish refugees on French soil. Among his remarks, Mille most notably commented that having accepted 3 million foreigners France had "had its fill" and could not stomach the Jews.[79]

As unsettling as these musings on the left and center might have been, however, such thinking was indeed much more common on the far right. In her study of Robert Brasillach's journal, *Je Suis Partout,* Joan Tumblety, among others, has remarked on the centrality of anti-Semitism to the fascist worldview.[80] Certainly, the fascist Parti populaire français was a haven for racists and bigots of all stripes.[81] Pierre Drieu La Rochelle, as is well known,[82] was violently anti-Semitic and advocated a frankly bizarre scheme of forcing Jews either to renounce their religion in writing and commit to assimilating or to leave the country.[83] The article where Drieu outlined this plan, in the summer of 1938, was representative of a transition to a more overt racism in the party following the death of Jewish party notable Alexandre "Kiki" Abremski,[84] as Laurent Kestel has demonstrated. Yet, the potential for this turn was apparent from the party's inception in 1936 when the representative from Algeria, at the founding congress, declared that while the Parti populaire français was not anti-Semitic it would take to task all those who put their Judaism ahead of the interests of France.[85]

The party's anti-Semitism came into full bloom after the German occupation. It was, in fact, the main theme of *L'Émancipation nationale*'s first issue after the fall of France. The paper engaged immediately in the sickening practice of denouncing Jews to the authorities, for instance.[86] One might interpret this as merely a disgraceful opportunism were it not for Kestel's conclusive illustration of the deep roots of anti-Semitism in the party.

As for the Croix de feu, while it only occasionally displayed an overt anti-Semitism, following the tradition of the anti-Dreyfusards it equated "Jewishness" with effeminacy. "The Jew" for the Croix de feu represented urbanity, modernism, internationalism, finance capital, and "the intellectual": in short, all the things the radical right despised.[87] Accordingly, a "real man" could not be Jewish; or at least, if he was Jewish, he had to overcome his Semitism and abandon those very attributes that the anti-Semitic right associated with being Jewish.

This anti-Semitic element to Croix de Feu masculinity was usually covert. A favorite codeword, for example, was "parasite." An undated official propaganda pamphlet asked the question, "What Kind of Men Do We Want?" The answer was revealing:

> Let us disdain intellectuals, opportunists, combinationists, idlers, parasites, profiteers! Out with them. No more discoursing lawyers, windbag committeemen, parliamentarians!
>
> With us, men of faith and character above all. . . .
>
> Catholics, Protestants, freethinkers, good Jews![88]

The catalog—intellectuals, opportunists, and so on—contains all the typical irritants of the radical right, but the "parasites, [and] profiteers" reference, in particular, reads like an allusion to Jews and finance capital, assumed, usually, to be Jewish. The suggestion that the movement welcomed "good Jews," of course, indicates that there were "bad Jews." What made one Jew good and the other bad, presumably, was that a good Jew would not have belonged in any of the aforementioned categories, categories that mirrored the typical racist conception of "Jewishness." A good Jew, in other words, would not be a Jew.

Indeed, leaders sometimes had to define this distinction between good and bad Jews more carefully. In one such instance, for example, a member wrote the head office to inquire as to the group's position vis-à-vis the "Jewish question." The head of propaganda replied, quoting liberally from La Rocque's book *Service public*. On the one hand, La Rocque, as he did quite consistently, insisted that Jews were welcome in the movement and that French identity was not defined by religion: what mattered was "French devotion." On the other, La Rocque, and his propaganda chief by proxy, drew the classic distinction of a particular kind of French anti-Semite, between "good" French Jews, and "bad" foreign ones supposedly "invading" France: "Among the latter, numerous islets form for whom persecution is but a cover for espionage. To point this out is not to commit an anti-Semitic act. I know many Israelites for whom this latent invasion appears like a menace not only for the country, but for their coreligionists privileged with the rights of citizenship; I know many Israelites in whose eyes this rush of German Jews represents the peril of provoking an anti-Semitic reaction."[89] Thus, anti-Semitism was in fact, in this view, the fault of Jews themselves. Foreign Jews, in this case German, were flooding France causing an understandable, and in fact justified, backlash. In a speech to the Parti social français's departmental congress of the Rhône in 1937, La Rocque again blamed Jews for the spread of anti-Semitism, focusing his accusation, this time, on Blum, then the *président du conseil:* "I call on all the patriotic Israelites and Lord knows that we have many of them, very dear to us, in our ranks, and I invite them to put on trial Léon Blum, a member of their religion all of whose activity unfolds as though he wants to unleash in France an unjust and fearsome wave of anti-Semitism."[90] The colonel moreover, eventually advocated reversing a decade's worth of naturalizations of Jews.[91]

While the Croix de feu remained somewhat circumspect about its anti-Semitism in metropolitan France, Samuel Kalman has demonstrated that in Algeria its attacks on Jews were open and fierce. The movement's activities included sparking a pogrom in Constantine on August 5, 1934, that left twenty-five dead.[92] That the Parti populaire français's Algerian sections were similarly violently anti-Semitic suggests the virulence of the settler community's racism. The fact that neither La Rocque nor Doriot discouraged their Algerian followers' anti-Semitic actions and in fact encouraged them in a variety of ways stands as damning testimony to the fascist right's anti-Jewish sentiment.[93]

Sadly, anti-Semitism surfaced too, and sometimes openly, on the republican right. Parti démocrate populaire deputy Paul Archambault, for instance, penned the lead article for *Le Petit Démocrate* on June 12, 1938, "The Jewish World and Its Destiny." In this piece Archambault evinced considerable hostility to France's Jewish population, which, according to him, had "a place manifestly disproportionate to its numerical importance" in the economic life of the country.[94] Demonstrating further that anti-Semitism was considered respectable across the right, the renowned anti-Semite Xavier Vallat was variously a member of former president Alexandre Millerand's short-lived Ligue républicaine nationale,[95] a deputy for the Fédération républicaine post-1933 (and a vice-president of the party after 1936),[96] and a member of the Croix de feu.[97] Léon Blum, in particular, seemed to bring out the traditional right's worst instincts. Even the *Alliance démocratique,* whose leader, Pierre-Étienne Flandin, was at pains to distance himself from anti-Semitism, was prone to diatribes about Blum's lack of patriotism, his insidious internationalism, and his being "the High Priest" of socialism.[98] In sum, while authors like Robert Soucy are correct that anti-Semitism was present within the Croix de feu, Parti populaire français, and French fascism,[99] this fact alone hardly made the fascist right unique: French fascism's racism and anti-Semitism were very much a product of its time and right-wing milieu. What set the fascists apart was simply the frequency and virulence of their racism and anti-Semitism.

ANTIRACISM

While racialism was near-omnipresent in interwar France, and while racism could be found across the political spectrum, there were many, especially on the left, who denounced xenophobia, racism, and anti-Semitism. The leftist Ligue des droits de l'homme, for instance, championed the civil liberties of colonial peoples as it did French citizens, although less frequently or consistently.[100] Similarly, while the Radicals embraced racialism, they, like the Socialists and Communists, frequently denounced racism. In the spirit of the defense of the Rights of Man engendered by the Dreyfus Affair among other events, Yvon Delbos, at this time moving from socialism to radicalism, set the tone for *L'Ère nouvelle* in 1920 by passionately denouncing what has since come to be known as the Armenian genocide, the massacre of Jews in the Ukraine, and the international community for ignoring both catastrophes.[101] In the same spirit, *La Lumière* campaigned against both the Croix de feu and Parti populaire français's anti-Semitism, focusing particularly on their more rabid followers in Algeria.[102] Even Gaboriaud's or his collaborator Mille's diatribes against "misled Israelites,"[103] in *L'Ère nouvelle*'s last years carefully pointed out that France had given refuge to hundreds of thousands of Jews before denouncing those refugees for their ingratitude. Gaboriaud and Mille thereby tried to shield themselves from criticism from the left for their xenophobic anti-Semitism, indicating a consciousness on their part that their views were not the norm in the left-of-center camp.

There were fewer such ambiguities in the Socialist camp. As J.-B. Séverac laid out for party militants in 1939, "No doctrine more merits the hostility of socialism than racism, including its derivative anti-Semitism. None, in effect, more violently contradicts our main ideas."[104] This is not to say that there were no anti-Semites within the Socialist Party but rather that overt racism was not part of its official package. After all, despite some anti-Semitic resentment within the party at his leadership, it is surely noteworthy that Léon Blum led the party's parliamentary group and edited *Le Populaire*. It is difficult to imagine a Jewish man playing as prominent a role in one of the right-of-center parties.

The Communist Party also remained an opponent of racism. While there were certainly counterexamples, the party generally remained faithful to its doctrine of working-class fraternity regardless of race or ethnicity. *L'Ouvrière,* for example, drew readers' attention to the injustice of racial segregation in the American south, calling for the international working class to show its solidarity in some undetermined fashion with southern African Americans and help them throw off the chains of their oppression.[105] The party's leadership could be admirably unequivocal. In a statement akin to the Socialist Séverac's, Communist Party secretary Maurice Thorez told an Algerian crowd in 1939 that "we, Communists, we don't recognize races. We recognize only peoples."[106]

On the conservative or center-right, where many bigots could certainly be found, nobler sentiments sometimes also prevailed. The *Alliance démocratique,* for example, celebrated the election of Gratien Candace, a black deputy from Guadeloupe, to one of the vice presidencies of the Chamber of Deputies and did so without resorting to racist or patronizing stereotypes. Granted, the paper's chief reason for endorsing Mr. Candace appears to have been his championing of French colonialism, but given the racist sentiments of others in the party at times, one might have expected worse.[107]

Even on the fascist right, there were some who expressed antiracist sentiments. Antoinette de Préval, for instance, Colonel de La Rocque's lieutenant in the Croix de feu expressed her dismay about an employee who displayed racial "bigotry," which she described as "the worst of faults." Rather than wishing to fire this employee, who worked at the movement's rest home, de Préval hoped that careful guidance might lead her to correct her ways.[108] Likewise, the Parti populaire français, as part of its outreach to potential indigenous supporters in Algeria, printed a call for "Justice for Muslims," from an Algerian doctor and party member in *L'Émancipation nationale*.[109] Even more remarkably, the Parti populaire français's France Duspay rebuked a Parisian school principal for allowing students to taunt a black teacher from Martinique, saying instead that that teacher should be applauded and supported.[110] Such sentiments were unusual in fascist circles. Yet, their existence underlines the need to query seductive assumptions about racism as a right-wing property or as all-pervading on the right.

CONCLUSION

Racialism defined politicians' and commentators' mentalities in interwar France. With some notable exceptions—most obviously in the Communist Party—everyone accepted that races were a biological reality: race was reified. Racialism thus influenced people's thinking on a diverse array of issues, including the desirability of physical fitness, immigration, and colonialism.

Not surprisingly, one of the ways in which racialism shaped discussions of immigration was that, in combination with workers' economic insecurities and the destabilization of French identity more generally, it produced a great deal of xenophobia, particularly in the 1930s following the onset of the Great Depression. This xenophobia, moreover, while more prominent on the right, engulfed portions of the left as well, particularly within the Radical Party. Racially defined concepts of French identity, moreover, were threatened both by miscegenation and by the fallibility of racial theory. This cast doubt on the racial certainties to which many subscribed.

Equally expectedly, discussions of the empire and France's so-called civilizing mission were tainted by racial thinking. Interestingly, this racial thinking often led commentators and politicians to conclusions that directly contradicted the stated rationale for French colonialism—that it was intended to enlighten the benighted subject peoples and turn them into fully functioning French citizens within a "greater France." Many effectively concluded, although they never acknowledged the contradiction, that the civilizing mission was a doomed enterprise: those deemed biologically inferior could never hope to be the equals of their racial superiors however much civilizing education they received. Indeed, as others have observed, this contradiction lay at the heart of the education systems that the imperial powers established in the colonies.[111]

Understanding and organizing the world into fictitious races, moreover, could give way all too easily to racism. Whether it was Socialist and later Communist Louise Bodin denigrating west Africans as savage brutes unable to control their sexual appetites, Joseph Caillaux questioning the patriotic bona fides of Léon Blum, or the fascists promoting anti-Semitic violence in Algeria, racism appears to have been all too ready to bubble to the surface in interwar French politics. Certainly, the far right was the ideological and political home of France's worst racists, but racism was present elsewhere on the political spectrum as well. The discourse of the French race and French civilization standing in enlightened opposition to "the savagery of the barbarians" was one that seduced many in interwar France irrespective of party affiliation.

Still, if racialism was nearly omnipresent and racism too frequent, there were also many, especially on the left, who attacked racism both generally and in specific instances: a racialist worldview did not necessarily produce racial hatred, dangerous though it could be. Unfortunately, from 1940 to 1944 such voices were excluded from the corridors of power as the intolerance evident in interwar France took center stage. As the savagery of the actual barbarians was unleashed, the results were tragic, especially for French Jewry.

4

"WARNING! THE CRADLES ARE EMPTY!"

GENDER, RACE, AND THE POLITICS OF POPULATION

In the late summer of 1936, in the first year of its existence, the Parti populaire français sounded the alert: "Warning!" an author at *L'Émancipation nationale* declared, "The Cradles Are Empty!"[1] The two-part article bearing this alarm exemplified the widespread paranoia in interwar France about the country's stagnant population growth. The Parti populaire français, moreover, was typical of the far right in attempting to assert ownership over the politics of pronatalism; as many historians have observed, the right dominated pronatalist circles.[2]

Yet, the Parti populaire français's fears were, especially by the mid-1930s, shared by the left. This is a phenomenon that has been underestimated in the literature: the degree to which the Radicals, Socialists, and Communists came, certainly by the Popular Front era and to a considerable degree before, to share both the right's pronatalism and its broader desire to increase the population.[3] Gender historians have tended to focus on how this fixation reflected traditionalists' conceptions of femininity: conservative French men thought women's place to be in the home. This was a belief held in common with the right by most men on the left: by the 1930s even in the Communist Party "subversive" visions of femininity were silenced and marginalized. Moreover, pronatalism reflected popular conceptions not just of femininity among France's political elite but of masculinity as well. All the parties believed that good men were or would be fathers, and preferably prolific ones. In other words, the parties not only imposed a gender role upon women in pursuit of more children for the nation, they imposed one on men too. Just as women were pushed to be mothers in the home, men were pressed to be breadwinning fathers. This trend was most pronounced at the time of the Popular Front. As they tacked to the center, the Radicals, Socialists, and Communists, though they did not wholly abandon the politics of fraternalism, embraced a more paternalist outlook and adopted conservative gender ideals.

This transformation in the left's discourse also reflected something insidious: a shared belief in a French racial identity. As Elisa Camiscioli has recently demonstrated, a sense of racial hierarchy increasingly shaped French policy on a host of issues, notably immigration, in the interwar years.[4] Certainly, racialist language progressively permeated leftist anxiety about France's demographic decline; once again, the left moved in this regard considerably toward the right's position over time. Thus, a host of proposals that were introduced by the right in the 1920s as a means of ensuring population growth and increased French procreation were later adopted wholeheartedly by the left. These included more maternity benefits; protective legislation for women, especially mothers, in the workplace; and family allocations meant to augment breadwinners' wages. More negatively, racialist concerns over the nation's demographic health also slanted the views of politicians of all stripes on the availability of birth control and abortion and the treatment of hereditary diseases. As concern for the birthrate spread across the political spectrum, so too did a eugenicist mentality.

THE DEMOGRAPHIC PANIC

The pervasiveness and hysterical nature of the interwar panic over the decline in France's population growth and birthrate have been frequently remarked upon and really cannot be overstated. In Cheryl Koos's words, Fernand Boverat, the secretary-general and then president of the Alliance nationale pour l'accroissement de la population française, and other pronatalists presented the decision about whether or not to have children as "the choice between life or death" for the nation.[5] This panic was initially most in evidence in conservative circles, with the Marxist left initially rejecting populationist and pronatalist rhetoric for a variety of reasons that will be outlined below. However, over time, the left gradually dropped its objections for reasons of strategy and conviction. By the mid-1930s, the obsession with the dearth of French babies was strictly bipartisan: it could be found from the Communists to the fascists.

Concern over France's declining birthrate was long-standing. Indeed, the by-then powerful pronatalist movement had its roots deep in the nineteenth century. Anxiety over depopulation had percolated among nationalist academics before the Franco-Prussian War in 1870–71, but undoubtedly France's defeat in that conflict heightened anxiety and made the birthrate a political rather than strictly academic concern. Studies of the problem produced by a growing number of demographers fueled fears of French decline. The data seemed alarming. From 1871 to 1911, for example, the French population grew from 36.1 to 39.3 million, which represented a growth rate of just 8.6 percent over that forty-year period. Within that same time frame, by comparison, the German population expanded by 60 percent to 65 million.[6] Given the spread of social Darwinism and its ethos, coined by the Englishman Herbert Spencer as the "survival of the fittest,"[7] many took such figures as signs that France was losing ground to its fitter German neighbor and thus risked extinction. By the end of the nineteenth century, therefore, increasing the population and, in most cases, raising the birthrate were imperatives for the political elite.

Civil society began to mobilize for the pronatalist cause. The key organization, eventually titled the Alliance nationale pour l'accroissement de la population française, was founded by demographer Dr. Jacques Bertillon in 1896. The group's original membership provided a hint of the influence it would grow to exert as it included many well-known figures such as Émile Zola and the Orléanist pretender to the French throne.[8] By the end of World War I, itself a further catalyst to fear over population decline, the Alliance was positioned as the leading proponent of pronatalist policies in the country and in 1920 the energetic and well-connected thirty-four-year-old Boverat became its secretary-general.[9]

Le Petit Démocrate, which predated the Parti démocrate populaire, was a center of pronatalist advocacy. The reasons for this were clear. As a report on a festival thrown by the Maternal Mutuality Committee in Noisy-le-Sec, organized in part by the Union des femmes de France,[10] noted, "France needs children. France needs children to preserve her rightful place in the world."[11] Yet, while prominent in the crusade to repopulate France, *Le Petit Démocrate* was far from alone. Even the Radical-sympathizing *L'Ère nouvelle* joined in the sounding of the alarm over France's perilous demographic position. A favored method there and elsewhere to heighten popular fears was to publish statistics showing the number of war dead, the number of children who were not born as a consequence of the war, and, most commonly, the long-term downward trend of France's population growth compared to the upsurge in the birthrates of other European powers, especially Germany's. One such piece estimated that for every one hundred marriages France normally witnessed per year, during the war there were only thirty-seven. And, the author added, France had lost more than its share of the 20-million-odd births that did not take place across Europe because of the war.[12] That this was a military and social danger was repeated incessantly. One commentator even claimed that, if statistics followed their then current trends, by 1938 Germany would be able to field 1.2 million men in uniform to France's 120,000 and French agriculture would be all but defunct.[13] *Le Petit Démocrate* likewise reported annually on German demographics, as in 1925 when the paper noted that the German birthrate had increased in 1924 while infant mortality had declined. The French numbers, the author pointed out, were much less favorable.[14] As was common practice, Louis Andrieux, the Chamber of Deputies' *doyen d'âge* in 1924, included a reference to the problem of the birthrate in his speech opening parliament and exhorted his colleagues to take action to rectify the situation.[15]

Although the failing birthrate was also addressed in left-wing publications like *L'Ère nouvelle,* that anxiety over population decline was largely a right-wing issue in the 1920s is undeniable. Koos argues forcefully that the considerable support in the Chamber of Deputies for conservative deputy Louis Duval-Arnould's "Large Family Protection Group," 1919–24, and for his "Natality and Family Defense Group" in the legislatures of 1924–28 and 1928–32, symbolizes that right-wing domination of the issue. Groups such as Duval-Arnould's were common in French political life. They were not parties per se, but rather loose coalitions of like-minded parliamentarians who agreed to cooperate on a given issue: in this case, on efforts to protect and aid large families. Members of these two groups were deeply concerned, needless to say, with raising the birthrate. Under the Blue Horizon Chamber of 1919–24,[16] dominated by the right, Duval-Arnould attracted the support of 348 of 532 deputies. Under the second postwar legislature, on the other hand, which was further to the left under the Cartel des gauches, Duval-Arnould, much to his disgust, was able to recruit only 150 members. When the pendulum swung back to the right in 1928, he found renewed success with 359 out of 612 deputies adhering to his cause.[17]

The hysteria over population decline in right-wing newspapers was also more marked than in those of the left. "Irène," for example, who was a contributor to the fashion section of the Fédération républicaine's paper, *La Nation,* proclaimed that "the perpetuation of the French race and our prosperity depend entirely on the maintenance of the family in its traditional form."[18] Likewise, Jean Guiraud, writing in *La Croix,* a paper of Catholic nationalism, stated that his opposition to feminism was based on the fact that "feminism is the adversary of the fecundity of the home."[19] And the right also took initiatives to remedy the declining birthrate. Louis Marin's friend Lieutenant-Colonel Blaison, for example, authored a book recording the "prizes of virtue" handed out by the "Academy of Stanislas" in 1928. These included an entire category of prizes under the heading "Maternal Devotion and Large Families," wherein parents, mostly mothers, were given awards based on the number of their children.[20] These measures, like Alexandre Millerand's Mother's Day medals of the same ilk, instituted in 1920,[21] prefigured similar encouragements in Nazi Germany and Fascist Italy.[22]

In the 1920s the Marxist left was hostile to pronatalist policies. The Socialists and Communists adopted a variety of stances that can all be reduced to a common critique: pronatalism served the bourgeoisie's class interest and helped to subjugate and impoverish working families. Granted, not all sounded the same notes in this particular chorus. One refrain had it that the bourgeoisie encouraged the working class to have families in order to create a large and therefore cheap pool of unskilled labor. Marthe Bigot, for example, advanced this view in 1919.[23] A cartoon from *L'Humanité* in 1925 exemplified another critique. The drawing sported an overweight bourgeois smoking a cigar and declaring "Ah Madame, if you only knew how comforting it is for a good patriot to see a large family!" to an impoverished mother and her famished children, standing enviously in front of stores offering all the foodstuffs that they could not afford.[24] This underscored the irresponsibility of promoting childbearing without doing anything to alleviate the miserable conditions of the working class. Anatole Sixte-Quenin, for example, mocked the Bloc national's regulation of bread prices as wholly inadequate to protect workers' families in the inflationary period that followed the war with the declaration that "if after this the number of births does not go up I would despair of all remedies."[25] Elsewhere, he pointed out that in a budget in excess of five billion francs the Bloc could find only 150 million odd to help large families. He asked "whether fathers of large families . . . are beginning to realize that they've been played for fools?"[26] Similarly, a commentator at *L'Ouvrière* intoned sardonically that "the entire future of the race, they say, depends on women and mothers. In our bourgeois society, most women, before considering the race, have to work hard just to survive."[27]

Another theme of the Socialist and Communist parties was that the right wanted more children in order to pursue its criminal militarism. This was an argument aimed at the hearts and minds of parents, and its proponents frequently invoked the painful memory of losing a child during the Great War. As one cartoon in *L'Humanité* explained, "When your children grow up… the bourgeois state will make them unemployed workers . . . while waiting to send them to their deaths."[28] Jean Longuet tied the problem of depopulation in 1919 to the "frightful bloodletting that [the country] has just endured and that our exterminationist 'patriots' criminally prolonged." Longuet's message was further clarified by his title: "In Order to Save the Working-Class Children."[29] Of course, this leftist critique seems to have been at least partly justified. The right did want more children for the military, if not necessarily to send them to senseless slaughter. As Colonel de La Rocque made clear, the depopulation crisis was linked inexorably to French military vulnerability in the right-wing nationalist imagination.[30]

Something on the left changed by the mid-1930s. Gone were leftist denunciations of bourgeois hypocrisy regarding the demographic crisis; in their place appeared pronatalist articles and columns that would have seemed out of place a decade earlier. Sixte-Quenin, for example, who had so caustically lampooned the Bloc national, wrote a column in 1934 which, while it attacked then premier Gaston Doumergue for increasing breadwinners' burdens, applauded the efforts of conservative deputy Georges Pernot to increase the birthrate by helping large families.[31] The analysis of the problem was of course different among Socialists and Communists than among conservatives and fascists. Dr. Emmeline Weill-Raynal, for example, in a detailed exposé, decreed that the root of depopulation lay not in the widespread decadence supposedly endemic to the Third Republic as conservatives claimed, but in the human misery created by the Great Depression and the capitalist system. That qualification aside, like right-wing commentators, the doctor explicitly contrasted France's unimpressive demographics with Germany's healthier numbers and insisted that "Socialists must not ignore demographic problems" because they could have "profound repercussions."[32] By the time of the Popular Front, Communists also felt that they could not ignore these "problems." At the party's 1937 national congress in Montreuil, for instance, Maurice Thorez made a revealing admission:

> The Communist Party concerns itself with the problems of childhood and the family for a double reason. We want to help fathers and mothers of families who face so many challenges in raising their children decently.
>
> We also want that measures be taken in order to resolve the grave crisis of the declining birthrate that menaces the very existence of our people.[33]

Such a statement would have been unthinkable in the Communist Party of the 1920s or even the early 1930s. Not only did Thorez reveal a pronatalism that would have been anathema to the party in its earlier days, but in choosing the phrase "our people" he also displayed a nationalism that ran counter to the stated internationalism of the party. On another occasion, *L'Humanité* even announced proudly that Thorez had become the godfather to the fifteenth child of a Communist family in the Ardennes. At the child's baptism Thorez applauded the vigorous and large families of French peasants while contrasting them with bourgeois families, usually limited to one or two children.[34] Here was the leader of French communism sounding like an imitator of the Fédération républicaine's Louis Marin.

So what had changed? How did the Socialists and the Communists, hostile to pronatalism in the 1920s, become converted to the cause by the mid-1930s? In the case of the Communists, part of the explanation came from outside France. As Stalin awoke to the Nazi menace and the threat of fascism, he adopted a multi-tiered antifascist strategy. The tale that historians are most familiar with involves his attempts to form alliances against Germany with the liberal democracies. Along with this, of course, was the Comintern's "pact of struggle against fascism," which it presented to the western Communist parties in 1934, leading later, in France, to the Popular Front.[35] Less well-known is that Stalin, just like the French nationalists of the Bloc national and their successors, also decided that to prepare for war with Germany he needed as many babies as possible whom he could raise to be antifascist soldiers. He thus adopted a pronatalist course in the Soviet Union, complete with a campaign to promote the traditional family, and he simultaneously pushed the western parties to follow his lead. This the French Communist Party did.[36] This transition however, was not as radical as it might seem. The Communists had adopted a strikingly traditional discourse of femininity before embracing pronatalism. Given the party's appeals to breadwinners and its espousal of traditional motherhood, pronatalism proved to be a comfortable fit with French communism.

The same could be said of the Socialists. Like the Communists, they converted to pronatalism. They did so slightly earlier than the Communists but also less completely as befitting members of a democratic rather than democratic-centralist organization. As late as 1939, for example, Paul Faure, who was an integral pacifist,[37] and who was therefore unlikely to support sending more children to the military, suggested that far from combating fascism, a high birthrate led directly to it.[38] Nonetheless, while the Socialist Party was never as explicit publicly as its right-wing counterparts about the need for more human material for France's military defense, its conversion to pronatalism coincided very neatly with its adoption of a rigorously antifascist course. Like the Communists, moreover, the Socialists' generally traditionalist conception of gender no doubt made the passage to something resembling conservative familialism a fairly smooth one. The Socialists, as seen below, supported and indeed initiated a swath of pronatalist measures in the second half of the 1930s.

A EUGENICIST MENTALITY

The desire to fight fascism is one with which today's observers can readily identify. What should evoke less sympathy, however, is the degree to which commentators of diverse political stripes fused their pronatalism with their racialism to embrace eugenics. A good number of French politicians of all creeds conceived of the ongoing struggle between France and Germany in social Darwinist terms, in terms, in other words, similar to the Nazis' own.

The eugenics movement was broadly influential in the western world. The term "eugenics" was coined by Englishman Francis Galton in 1883,[39] but proto-eugenicism had existed in France and elsewhere since at least the early nineteenth century and theories of hereditary racial determinism had proven to have purchase amongst French anthropologists, ethnographers, pediatricians, obstetricians, puericulturalists, gynecologists, venerologists, and social hygienists.[40] Galton's definition of eugenics was "the science which deals with all influences that improve the inborn qualities of a race; also with those that develop them to the utmost advantage,"[41] while the statutes of the French Eugenics Society (founded in 1912–13) defined it more simply as "the science of the conservation and the improvement of the race."[42] What eugenicists meant by race was not always clear. Some focused on the health of the species broadly while others seemed concerned with their particular race, which in France might mean either the "French" race or commonly the white European one.[43] In sum, eugenicists were those who believed in the existence of biologically defined human races of one kind or another and held that those races could (and desired that they should) be improved through interventions ranging from selective breeding to improved social conditions to sterilization and euthanasia. Not all eugenicists, notably, embraced the entire range of measures; in particular, many shied from the "negative eugenics" of sterilization and euthanasia.[44]

Eugenics was by no means synonymous with pronatalism. Some pronatalists, for example, simply advocated raising the birthrate indiscriminately—a position eugenicists abhorred as it would encourage the reproduction of "unhealthy" racial strains. However, there was considerable crossover between the two camps. This cross-pollination was, as Andrès Reggiani has recently argued, increasingly pronounced in the 1930s and culminated in the foundation of the Fondation française pour l'étude des problèmes humaines in the Vichy years. The foundation brought together leading French thinkers from both the pronatalist and eugenicist movements.[45]

Pronatalists were racialists from the start. Radical Henry Spont, for instance, in suggesting that France should direct its efforts to lowering the infant mortality rate alongside raising the birthrate, titled his article "For the Future of the Race."[46] Spont's focus on infant mortality was typical of populationists including pronatalists, particularly of those within republican circles. Paul Strauss, for example, a turn-of-the-century physician, politician, and social reformer, dedicated many of his pronatalist and populationist energies toward reducing infant mortality rates.[47] By the 1920s, there was broad consensus—which pleased Strauss—that mothers breastfeeding as opposed to the practice of wet-nursing decreased infant mortality and so helped boost population growth. Measures to encourage breastfeeding thus enjoyed considerable bipartisan support, as they had, in fact, since the late nineteenth century.[48]

Spont was typical in his racial language as well. Duval-Arnould, for example, agreed in 1926 with *Le Populaire* administrator Adéodat Compère-Morel that measures needed to be taken to encourage the birthrate but disagreed that immigration was a solution to the problem of depopulation in the meantime: "Immigration itself cannot protect us from depopulation, it appears instead as an invasion destructive to the race and admits the most undesirable elements. We must therefore return the family to its fecundity of days past."[49] As Camiscioli observes, most French commentators, if they desired immigration at all, sought only racially suitable white Europeans.[50] Duval-Arnould's reasoning certainly carried on into the 1930s. Maurice Rondet-Saint of the *Alliance démocratique* authored an article that laid out the usual array of troubling demographic statistics from across Europe and worried about "the more prolific races," including the "semi-Asiatic" Soviet Union overwhelming

France by force of numbers;[51] the reporter on social politics for the Fédération républicaine at its 1938 congress, meanwhile, warned of a pending "national suicide," thanks to the low birthrate and foretold that "France, where three million foreigners already throng, will fall prey to its prolific neighbors";[52] Jacques Doriot insisted that a Parti populaire français state would take the necessary steps to increase French fertility and thereby "renew the race."[53]

The high incidence of racialist language around populationism and pronatalism on the interwar right is not, perhaps, particularly shocking. More remarkable was the permeation of such thinking in leftist circles. Socialist Amélie Vincent, for example, expressing concern about the conditions in which many French children were raised, asserted that it was "high time if we want to protect the race" to build sanitary urban public housing.[54]

Socialist and former public health minister Henri Sellier, like Vincent a progressive who favored a scientific approach to urban planning, took things a step further. He proclaimed that,

> in order to ensure the salvation of the everlastingness of the race, it does not suffice to promulgate seductive texts, provoking with the help of allocations the procreation of any kind of children, even defectives, but to apply to the human species the same precautions that one takes for the selection of domesticated animals and plants.
>
> We must, above all else, help healthy individuals to found homes, and give them the means to do so; assure their children, from birth, of the benefit of collective solidarity and social protection that separates them from the shame and the misery of illness; envelop them in a bundle of institutions to preserve them physically, intellectually, and morally, designed to later make of them citizens useful to their country and to humanity.[55]

Indeed, upon becoming minister of public health, Sellier penned a manifesto that made his eugenicism explicit. As he wrote,

> It is urgent that we defend the race against the certain degeneration and destruction indicated by the lamentable statistics on births, illnesses, and deaths. . . . And when I say births, I mean desirable births. France has too many hereditary syphilitics, carriers of rickets, retards, abnormals whose existence, as painful for them as it is for others, encumbers our hospitals, asylums, and prisons.
>
> We want robust children, born from healthy parents. . . .

> I am for a eugenicist politics. It is not enough to raise the birth rate, the quality of the race must also be improved.[56]

Sellier concentrated most of his efforts on measures meant to encourage racial desirables, and he devoted much of his political life, in particular, to urban planning.[57] However, there was always a sinister side to his thinking. What was to become of those whom Sellier felt to be undesirable was unsaid, but one can conjecture that he might have supported a policy of sterilization, for example. Certainly, the fact that as the minister for health he commissioned a study to discover the number of mentally and physically handicapped children in the school system provides food for thought.[58] Equally suggestive was Sellier's status as a founding member of the Association d'études sexologiques in 1931. The association's journal, *Problème sexuel,* was subtitled "morals, eugenics, hygiene, legislation" and printed several articles endorsing sterilization during its run from 1933 to 1935. Sellier was on the editorial committee of the journal as was Victor Basch, the widely respected president of the Ligue des droits de l'homme.[59]

Nor were Sellier's inclinations unprecedented in the Socialist Party. The redoubtable Louise Saumoneau, for example, declared in 1929 that "we no longer want to see alcoholics and those infected with venereal diseases perpetuate unconsciously the race of degenerates."[60] Indeed, eugenicist language advocating a process of unnatural selection penetrated the Socialist Party as early as 1922. Deputy Armand Charpentier's attack on patriotic pronatalism was informative:

> It would be truly strange if while horticulturalists are encouraged to select the most productive trees and breeders to improve the animal races, only the human race was denied the benefits of Science. Can we ask lunatics, syphilitics, alcoholics, and the tubercular to transmit their diseases? That would be nonsense, what am I saying! A crime against humanity—which no one could defend. However, our enemies don't fight us on scientific terrain. . . .
>
> —Perfect the human race, they tell us, prepare healthy and robust generations destined for life, we want it as you do; yes, but with the condition that *quality* does not trump *quantity.*[61]

Charpentier, in other words, wanted fewer children in order to ensure the healthiness of the racial strain. The idea of letting undesirables procreate was "a crime against humanity." Charpentier's fellow Socialist Alice Jouenne, writing some fourteen years later, likewise revealed herself as seduced by this sort of thinking, warning against a criminal underclass of "degenerates" who had been born malformed thanks to hereditary disease. She recommended their institutionalization.[62] Charpentier and Jouenne's thinking was, in fact, compatible with that of the father of French neo-Malthusianism, Paul Robin, who believed that smaller families would ensure the quality of French bloodlines. Robin worried that modern medicine had impeded the process of natural selection: the weak were surviving, thus human intervention had to prevent their being born.[63]

Robin's theories also informed the thinking of the Radical and medical doctor Edouard Toulouse, a friend of Sellier's. A prominent advocate of sexual education, Dr. Toulouse shared Charpentier and Robin's concerns and advocated sterilization accordingly: "If the state is going to pay the costs of births [among the working class as Toulouse was advocating to raise the birthrate] it must also control them, because it would be absurd to encourage the birth of healthy and diseased infants equally. And so, should we regulate marriage with the corollary that we forbid certain unions? How? The United States . . . does not hesitate to sterilize individuals whose products would likely be undesirable."[64] Toulouse's fellow Radical Denise Moran at *La Lumière*, meanwhile, sounded suspiciously like Sellier in her anxiety about syphilitics, alcoholics, epileptics, vagabonds, thieves, prostitutes, and other "abnormals" passing on their "mental debilitation" to their children. She claimed that children were now born (in 1926) with "abnormalities" twice as frequently as in 1914. She warned wives to watch for incontinence among their husbands: this was a sign of degeneration,[65] the fear of which, as William Schneider makes clear, had inspired the French eugenics movement in the nineteenth century.[66] Presumably, Moran hoped that a good French woman would not mate with a genetically unsuitable beau. Similarly, Radical senator Henri Michel called for women to return to the home to produce "healthy" children to "safeguard the French race!"[67]

Fear of degenerative venereal diseases among left-wing commentators like Moran most often focused on syphilis. As Daniel Pick among others has noted, syphilis exercised a particular and horrible fascination for those who feared racial degeneration.[68] Judith Surkis argues, moreover, that social and racial hygienists' fixation on venereal diseases peaked in the interwar period. She also maintains these anxieties fueled a "defense" of French masculinity by politicians and reformers.[69] The Communist "Doctoresse Nadia" explained her fears to her readers, "Syphilis is a scourge that has always devastated and decimated humanity, ravaged the population in the present, and threatened the future."[70] The fixation on syphilis had two origins: the disease came from "degenerate" promiscuity and it led to mental debilitation; syphilis was thus tailor-made for the fretful eugenicist imagination. Communist Georges Levy, for instance, labeled the disease "an important factor in our depopulation." Syphilitic parents' children were "idiots, epileptics etc." and suffered frequently from mental retardation or paralysis.[71] Late nineteenth- and early twentieth-century specialists like the German physician Iwan Bloch and his French colleague Alfred Fournier argued that syphilis was transferrable from both parents to their children through "inheritance," that the disease caused extremely high infant mortality rates, and that children who survived with syphilis carried "stigmata of degeneration," including "malformations of the nose, the ears, and the palate, dwarfism, deaf-mutism, malformations of the external and internal sexual organs, rickets, epilepsy, and mental weakness."[72] Fournier was particularly active in the crusade against syphilis, founding the influential French Society of Sanitary and Moral Prophylaxis in 1899 to campaign against the disease's spread and effect.[73] In truth, though not as common as early twentieth-century physicians and eugenicists like Fournier feared, infants can "inherit" congenital syphilis from their mothers (but not their fathers) through the transmission of the bacterium *Treponema pallidum*, fetuses with syphilis are stillborn more than 50 percent of the time, and the list of symptoms of the disease is indeed long and serious.[74] Needless to say, however, syphilis does not modify its victims' DNA and therefore does not contribute to the degeneration of the species or "race."

On the right, particularly by the 1930s, the eugenicist mentality was also evident. The Parti démocrate populaire, for instance, demanded in its founding program, "that social hygiene be ensured by a better organization of the struggles against the great social scourges: alcoholism, tuberculosis, debauchery, and gambling."[75] L. Camuzet at *La Nation* pointed out that, while encouraging births was well and good, "60 to 75" out of 100 children were born with hereditary diseases, inherited principally, he claimed, from their mothers. He suggested that preventative measures taken in advance of impregnation would do more to improve the health of the race than any monies designed to encourage procreation (which he nonetheless supported).[76] While the Croix de feu claimed that eugenicism was unthinkable in France as the French were a people too "jealous of their liberty" to pursue such methods,[77] the movement's deep concern with regenerating the race was consonant with eugenic thinking. As sports enthusiast Gäetan Maire said at the 1939 Parti social français congress, "Sports are not in opposition to a healthy PHYSICAL EDUCATION of which the only GOAL must be the REGENERATION OF THE RACE. It must fight alcoholism and tuberculosis in drawing youth away from cabarets and unhealthy pleasures."[78]

Koos comments insightfully that pronatalism provided the grounds for bipartisan alliances and cooperation.[79] Sellier and Toulouse's friendship provides a hint that eugenicism functioned in a similar fashion. In addition to Toulouse, Sellier's familiars included the onetime neo-socialist and later fascist and collaborator Marcel Déat and the Nazi mayor of Stuttgart, Karl Strölin. What bound these ideologically opposed men together was their common eugenicist mentality as well as their shared belief that the application of science to urban planning could improve the racial stock.[80] Add to these otherwise odd friendships the fact that Toulouse was friends with Alexis Carrel and a picture begins to form of a bipartisan network of eugenicist thinkers, striving towards the shared goal of perfecting the race.[81]

This is not to say that in France during the 1920s and 1930s there was a systematic campaign of sterilization of the physically or mentally unfit as there was in the United States and Germany. In the United States around sixty-four thousand people were sterilized between 1907 and 1964, and in Nazi Germany, nearly four hundred thousand suffered this fate and a further two hundred thousand were murdered outright.[82] But the evidence of widespread bipartisan sympathy for eugenic projects, combined with the near-absolute predomination of racialist thinking by the end of the 1930s, does suggest a partial explanation for the relative comfort with which French officials later participated in the Final Solution[83] and for Vichy France's ham-fisted attempt to explore the causes of the French race's supposed degeneration.[84] When everyone in France, regardless of their political sympathies, was at least somewhat concerned about racial hygiene as they defined it, and given that anti-Semitism was significant on the right and present on the left, it is not really surprising that a good number of French men's thinking evolved to embrace the notion that French blood needed to be protected not just from the hereditarily diseased but from Jews as well. This anti-Semitic trajectory was buttressed, notably, by a growing number of anthropologists who, in the 1930s, decreed Jews to be an inferior race.[85]

PRONATALISM AND POLICY

Needless to say, the widespread and, by the mid-1930s, bipartisan concern with raising the birthrate drove policy on a range of issues. One such was the campaign for the family vote, which, in turn, affected the drive for women's suffrage, as shown in chapter 6. Another, perhaps even more permanent topic of discussion in the interwar years was that of "family allocations." These consisted of a variety of schemes, some of which called for male breadwinners to have their wages indexed to the size of their families and others that instead proposed direct payments to parents every year on a per-child basis. Predictably, in the 1920s proposals of this nature came from the right. The first proposition, for example, to improve family allocations of the second variety (concerning payments to families with three or more children from municipal governments) over the levels set by 1913 legislation came from Georges Thibout, soon to become the leader of the Parti démocrate populaire. It was debated by the Chamber in March 1921. Conservative Joseph Delachenal was the chair of the commission that investigated Thibout's proposal, and his report was strongly enthusiastic. That the Blue Horizon Chamber was anxious to propagate the race was evident from the debate. As Auguste Isaac, then the president of the Fédération républicaine and later the honorary president of the Alliance national pour l'accroissement de la population française, declared in explaining why it was healthier for France to have an elevated birthrate, "The elite is a select group, and to make a selection there must be the numbers."[86] There were, however, some restrictions. Illegitimate children were not to be counted toward a family's eligibility for the payments. Traditionalism in gender relations here trumped pronatalism: as Delachenal explained, "the statistics demonstrate that rates of mortality and criminality are much higher among illegitimate than legitimate children," and Thibout added that "we estimate that only the legitimate family has the essential elements of stability, durability, dignity, and morality to form the rock upon which to base all of society."[87] While there was little objection to the exclusion of children born out of wedlock benefiting on this occasion, the proposed revision that mothers rather than fathers be paid the stipend proved more contentious. Duval-Arnould, for one, worried that this might undermine fathers' paternal authority; but in the end, this amendment passed handily as did the legislation.[88] Interestingly, although in law the allocations were to be paid to mothers, in practice it seems that among state employees, at least, in the event of divorce fathers continued to receive the benefit even when the mother had been granted custody of the children. This prompted the feminist commission of the Ligue des droits de l'homme to move for the abolition of this practice in 1928.[89] The commission, which met irregularly before fading away,[90] must have pressured league president Victor Basch to take some action because he subsequently wrote the minister of finance a note demanding the reversal of this practice.[91]

This was not the end of the discussion of family allocations in the interwar years. Fédération républicaine deputy (and independent senator as of 1936) Georges Pernot outlined the progress of allocations for his followers. Municipally administered allocations were increased in 1925, and a 1923 law gave parents with four children or more who were not eligible for the municipal payments 90–120 francs per year from the Republic. Pernot asserted that these measures, though better than nothing, were woefully inadequate.[92]

Throughout the 1920s the fledgling Parti démocrate populaire joined Pernot and other pronatalists in agitating loudly for increases to the allocations. In addition, the démocrates populaires, in particular, pushed hard for men's wages to be indexed to the size of their families. Some industrialists had voluntarily begun this practice with their employees through a complex system wherein the employers contributed to a compensation fund, usually organized by industry, which in turn paid out the allocations to eligible parents.[93] According to *Le Petit Démocrate,* the practice had been initiated in Grenoble during the war by two Catholic industrialists and was spreading rapidly across the country.[94] By campaigning in favor of these sorts of measures the right both addressed its racialist disquiet over the birthrate and appealed to the breadwinners that it coveted as voters. This sort of private initiative, moreover, suited the right as it encouraged the birthrate without invoking the visible hand of the state.

That this campaign was also linked to a conservative vision of France was apparent in the right's mounting concern to extend family allocations to agriculturalists. By the late 1920s family allocations had come to mean, principally, the indexation of wages to family size and not the direct state payments of 1913 and 1921. This extension, it was hoped, would not only encourage more babies but might furthermore stem the exodus from the French countryside that the right found so distressing.[95] Conservatives idealized rural life, believing that with *la France profonde* lay the key to preserving French traditions, including Catholicism. That rural voters were more likely to vote for the right while urbanites showed a disconcerting tendency to find their way to the Socialists and Communists was probably not lost on conservative commentators either.

This agitation was not in vain. By the early 1930s, the right, probably recognizing that private initiative was not providing a sufficient stimulus to the birthrate, decided that state intervention, in this case, might be justified. In 1931 the Parti démocrate populaire scored what it counted as a major victory when the Chamber of Deputies passed legislation that made family allocations obligatory in certain industries (although, notably, not in agriculture).[96] While the party had been crucial to the popularization of this issue, the actual bill enacted had come from a Fédération républicaine deputy, as the Fédération's Raoul de Warren took pains to point out when the Senate voiced its approval of the measure in 1932.[97]

The Socialist and Communist left's position on family allocations was predictable. While the Radicals, including Henri Michel, expressed support for family allocations from time to time,[98] and certainly most Radicals must have voted for the relevant bills in order for them to pass, the Marxist left was initially vehemently hostile to them. Louise Bodin, for instance, ridiculed Thibout's proposal for improving the 1913 legislation as absurd. In her mind, the injustice of the poor's condition was so great that nothing short of a total overthrow of the capitalist system could provide adequate redress.[99] The negative response was conditioned of course by the general hostility to the pronatalist project. As Communist Marthe Bigot put it, "Fewer children, fewer workers, fewer soldiers . . . a sad prospect for those who count on the vast human herd to cut and shoot when the need arises." Bigot also advanced the most typical leftist argument against family allocations: that they would be used as a tool to create different classes of workers and thereby harm working-class solidarity. Recipients of family allocations, Bigot implied, would make good strikebreakers as they would have increased incentives to return to work. Besides, she added truthfully, the allocations fell far short of making children a paying proposition.[100]

In accordance with this logic, the Communists and Socialists were forever warning their flocks of the insidious dangers of family allocations. As late as 1930, *Le Populaire* cautioned its readers that family allocations provided employers with "a terrible weapon" and catalogued incidents where an employer had withdrawn the allocations in order to bend a worker to his will.[101] In *L'Humanité*'s terms, family allocations remained, in reality, "loyalty bonuses."[102]

In 1933 however, somewhat in advance of the Popular Front strategy and the conversion to pronatalism, the tone began to change. *L'Humanité,* while careful to denounce employers' continued abuse of the allocations, began to advocate their extension to all sectors of the French economy.[103] Shortly thereafter, the Socialists too began to praise, rather than belittle, family allocations.[104] Indeed, though they had not advertised the fact, both parties had voted for the 1931–32 improvements, so this enthusiasm was less newfound then it might have seemed to the casual observer.[105] This was probably, as Frader has argued, due in part to the fact that, by taking the allocations out of the hands of employers and disassociating them from work attendance, the framers of the 1931–32 legislation removed trade unions' objections to family allocations as being designed to discipline the workforce.[106]

In 1935, Communist Paul Vaillant-Couturier had a well-publicized dispute with Fernand Boverat over the latter's plan to finance an increase in *pères de famille*'s pay through a tax on single men's wages. At first glance, this might have seemed like a continuation of the Communists' former opposition to family allocations but, in fact, Vaillant-Couturier proclaimed openly that he was all for augmenting fathers' incomes just not at the expense of other workers.[107] In short, Vaillant-Couturier, one of the Communists' most fiery personalities, was conceding that workers doing the same job should receive disparate compensation. The Communists had come a long way since 1930 in their support of repopulation. By the end of 1936, Jacques Duclos was hinting that the party might even reconsider its opposition to the idea of a tax on single men.[108]

In fact, one of the great ironies of the history of interwar pronatalism is that it was the Popular Front government of Léon Blum that extended family allocations to the agricultural sector. On November 14, 1936, the government decreed that compensation funds would be organized for agricultural laborers,[109] a move that even the Parti populaire français begrudgingly applauded.[110] In truth, this innovation relied on the cooperation of rural employers who had to subscribe voluntarily to the compensation funds and thus its impact was probably limited as complaints from all corners suggest,[111] but nonetheless, it is remarkable that the Socialists and Radicals, with the Communists' agreement,[112] took action that had long been sought after by right-wing pronatalists. Boverat and others had vainly hoped that the governments of Pierre-Étienne Flandin, Gaston Doumergue, Pierre Laval, and other conservatives would do this: paradoxically, it was the Popular Front that finally delivered. Defending the measure in the Chamber of Deputies, Léon Blum's close friend and minister of agriculture Georges Monnet was candid about its pronatalist rationale. As he explained, the point was to allow, "all agriculturalists, whether smallholders or farmers, to benefit . . . from an inducement to have large families."[113] This was staggering in light of the staunch opposition to pronatalist measures, including family allocations, from the Marxist left just a few years before, particularly given the identification of French rural life with conservative forces. Finally, in November 1938, the Radical-dominated government of Édouard Daladier nationalized the program and extended the benefits, in theory, to workers in all sectors.[114]

While family allocations were one of the most obvious, continuous, and at times contentious issues energized by pronatalist concerns, they constituted far from the only policy area affected by the politics of racial regeneration. The extension of maternity benefits, for example, afforded Gaston Doumergue the opportunity to posture as a pronatalist champion in 1928. Doumergue, as president of the Republic, had just signed into law a bill that extended maternity leave from eight to twelve weeks, a fact he advertised in *La Femme Socialiste* of all places.[115] The Socialists and the Communists also scored points with pronatalist voters by advocating extended maternity leaves.[116]

Daycare was another matter where there was both convergence and divergence between the left and right. Catholic aid societies, to which the right was sympathetic, had taken the lead in the nineteenth century. The first crèche in Paris was opened in 1844, for example, by the Catholic Société des crèches in 1844. By the time the Parisian municipal government joined the fray in 1874, there were twenty-three Catholic crèches operating in the city providing care to some 810 babies.[117] That 1874 state intrusion into the hitherto Catholic domain of daycare provision, however, portended the future contours of the politics of daycare as the left strongly advocated for state-controlled or subsidized and therefore secular daycare. Both the Socialists and the Communists pointed repeatedly, for example, to the need for state-run or at least state-regulated daycare. As one *L'Ouvrière* contributor phrased it, "Nurseries! Daycares! We need them everywhere!"[118] In Paris, in fact, state-run daycare was more widely available as of 1927, at least in newly constructed public housing.[119] Of course, at this stage, on the left, the push for daycare was not motivated by racialism or pronatalism, at least not openly, but rather by concern for the welfare of working families. As early as

1931, however, some Communists were beginning to link the need for daycares to the desire to repopulate the country.[120] The same year *Le Populaire* commented dryly that closing a public daycare in Paris was a funny way to encourage the proliferation of large families.[121] By 1938, with the inclusion of the establishment of daycares in the Communist list of promises to "help the family" alongside family allocations to large families and the recognition of illegitimate children, the Communist Party made it clear that it saw daycare as part and parcel of its strategy to encourage the birthrate.[122]

By the 1930s the more traditionally racialist and pronatalist right began to awaken to the need for state involvement in daycare provision. The Parti démocrate populaire was the first to seize upon the issue. In 1930 its program included a pledge to provide state subsidies for daycares. Notably, this left the door open to the state subsidizing privately run daycares, including those run by Catholic agencies.[123] In any case, in 1933 the Party's feminine section stated démocrates populaires' commitment to developing a comprehensive daycare system.[124] In 1935, the Fédération républicaine followed suit, similarly promising the promotion of daycare through unspecified means in its program. That its promise, like that of the Parti démocrate populaire, was pronatalist in origin is emphasized by its being embedded in a slew of other openly pronatalist undertakings, such as a commitment to pay baby bonuses.[125] The Croix de feu did the republican conservatives one better, using daycares as part of its strategy of establishing social outreach programs to attract the working class to the movement. The league set up two daycares: one on the boulevard du Havre in Colombes,[126] and the other on the rue Kléber in Paris. The latter is known to have serviced 350 children in 1935.[127] The Croix de feu's successor, the Parti social français, evidently maintained these institutions as several industrialists petitioned the party to accept their workers' children in 1938.[128] Similarly, *L'Émancipation nationale* boasted of the "model daycare" that Jacques Doriot had established in his fiefdom of St. Denis.[129]

The most significant piece of legislation that arose from racialist pronatalism was the "Family Code," decreed by the Daladier government on July 29, 1939. The code's scope was vast, promulgated as it was in 167 articles.[130] Among its measures was a sizable one-time payment for mothers who had their first child within the first two years of marriage, the raising of the age of children's eligibility for family allocations from thirteen to fourteen, and the alteration of a policy introduced earlier that year that paid mothers who stayed at home an allowance so that the mother, and not the husband, received the stipend.[131] Nor did the pronatalist framers of the Family Code restrict themselves to positive encouragements of the birthrate. The code also newly specified penalties for all offenses related to abortions and doubled the penalties for abortionists.[132] The bipartisan nature of the drive to sustain the race by this time was symbolized by the fact that Daladier, once ostensibly a leftist, joined hands with the conservative nationalist and Alliance démocratique member Paul Reynaud to push for the Family Code.[133] Even more tellingly, it was greeted with near universal enthusiasm—from the Parti populaire français on the far right to the Communist Party on the left. As Maurice Guérin of the Parti démocrate populaire enthused, "A large breech has been opened in the liberal individualist system."[134] Such complaints as there were, including those from the Marxist left, focused more on omissions from the code than on critiquing either its content or its pronatalist inspiration. Jean Garchery, a Socialist deputy from Paris, for example, grumbled that the code did not include strengthened rent controls and hence did not protect families adequately.[135] The Communists, meanwhile, lauded the legislation, murmuring only that family allocations should have been extended to all families with children, not just those with three or more.[136] The Communists, in other words, criticized Daladier and Reynaud for wanting in populationist vigor, not for pursuing racial regeneration.

The measures discussed so far, as incapable as they were of raising the birthrate, did no doubt provide some appreciated relief to working families. A little extra money never hurt in hard times. But there was a coercive side to these pronatalist inducements. In addition to encouraging French men and women to have children, politicians also tried to prevent them from limiting their families' size. The individual's freedom of choice and action was conspicuously proscribed in the pursuit of racial health. Politicians tried to force men and women to accept their gender roles and, particularly, to become traditional fathers and mothers.

The proscription of contraceptives, birth control literature, pornography, and abortion was nearly as severe in Republican France as in Fascist Italy.[137] When, on July 23, 1920, the Blue Horizon Chamber passed a new law meant to restrict access to such products and practices, the lines for and against were drawn clearly in partisan shades. Vincent Auriol, Léon Blum, and the other Socialist deputies (including the future Communists) voted against the legislation, with the exception of Joseph Paul-Boncour on the outermost right of the party who abstained, while the Radicals, including the Ligue des droits de l'homme's then president Ferdinand Buisson, and everyone to their right voted in favor of it.[138] This law prescribed serious punishments for those who distributed contraceptive literature: offenders faced one to six months in prison and fines of one hundred to five thousand francs. Socialist and later Communist André Berthon fired a no doubt satisfying anticlerical shot in a losing cause during the debate. He argued that "there is an entire category of citizens in full physical vigor who are dedicated to celibacy and glorify chastity," inquiring, "Will those who glorify virginity . . . fall under the hammer of this law?"[139]

The right's support for these measures was motivated principally by its desire to boost the birthrate. In a speech in Paris's Salle Wagram Georges Thibout explained the thinking clearly: "With the birthrate crisis from which we are suffering, we must use all the means that we have at hand." Accordingly, he urged, among other measures "the struggle against pornography in all its forms" by which rightists usually meant pornography as one would understand it today, plus all contraceptive literature.[140] Most right-wing commentators, in fact, remained convinced that the government was not doing enough to prevent the spread of such materials. Pernot, as he usually did over measures related to raising the birthrate, chimed in: "It is time to act. Not only do pornographic magazines, in poisoning the soul of young Frenchmen, run the risk of compromising the very future of the race, but their diffusion abroad strikes a most serious blow to France's good name and furnishes an easy argument to German propaganda."[141] How pornography poisoned young men's souls was apparently so self-evident that it did not require explanation. Historians examining European fears of degeneration emphasize how experts believed that Onanism, as they coined masturbation, caused a loss of vital energy with every nonreproductive "emission" until boys literally wasted away. Whole volumes were dedicated to identifying boys who were falling prey to the Onanist temptation.[142] One can only assume that this tradition fed Pernot's and others' racialist paranoia.

On the left the tone was much more critical and less alarmist. Louise Bodin, for one, offered some sober and thoughtful commentary that stood in contradiction to the hysteria on the right:

> It is a serious responsibility to create a life. A man should understand that his strict duty is to not create a life until he can ensure its health, with a minimum of moral and material happiness; it is not to create as many babies

> as his wife can bring into the world without losing her physical, moral, and intellectual strength.
>
> The limitation of children in the working class, far from being an immoral or illegal question, is a question of conscience and human dignity.[143]

Nor was Bodin's a solitary voice on the left. Others like *Le Populaire*'s Armand Charpentier echoed her sentiments.[144]

After the schism of December 1920, the Socialists and Communists took different approaches to these questions. The Socialists generally ignored them, offering only the occasional ironic comment,[145] despite Blum's well-publicized advocacy of birth control's usefulness.[146] A *Le Populaire* report in 1921, for instance, covered several prosecutions of abortionists and their patients in very neutral tones and no editorialist wrote on the subject.[147] The women of *L'Ouvrière,* on the other hand, spearheaded the Communists' progressive posture on reproductive issues. Most radically, and uniquely in France, members of the Communist Party openly advocated the legalization of abortion—a stance that was downright dangerous for its proponents, thanks to the often liberal interpretation of the 1920 censorship law by the authorities. The unforgiving official mood was signaled by a law passed in 1922, which gave convicted abortionists one to five years in prison and a fine of five hundred to ten thousand francs while women caught having or seeking an abortion faced six months and a penalty of one hundred to two thousand francs.[148] A 1923 bill, moreover, redirected abortion cases to be tried by magistrates and not juries in an attempt to secure more convictions.[149] Despite this, the Communists did not back down. *L'Ouvrière* adopted the now classically pro-choice argument, for instance, that the criminalization of abortion's only achievement was to contribute to the deaths of, and injuries to, women seeking the services of clandestine abortionists.[150] Similarly, coverage of a German Communist Party women's campaign argued for the legalization of abortion in strong terms: "All women must have the right to a free abortion in a hospital."[151]

The Communists also took up the cause of the victims of pronatalist repression. Trade unionist Victor Méric, for one, railed against the injustice of the persecution of those distributing birth control literature as they were only trying to help ordinary people "bring a little prudence and clairvoyance to their sexual relations."[152] More concretely, André Marty, Marcel Cachin, and others proposed in the Chamber, albeit fruitlessly, that abortionists and their clients be granted an amnesty,[153] and *L'Ouvrière* attacked Édouard Herriot for posturing as a supporter of women's emancipation in opposition but ruling as an unregenerate conservative. The unnamed author then demanded that Herriot prove him or her wrong by freeing the women incarcerated for breaking the abortion law.[154] Even in *L'Humanité,* the party's official voice, an article appeared calling for the prohibition of abortion to be replaced by its regulation for the well-being of working-class women.[155]

While there was some frustration on the part of the sexual radicals in the party that it did not adopt the legalization of abortion as part of its platform in the early 1920s,[156] it was nonetheless invaluable that the Communist Party provided a space where their voices could be heard. In a France increasingly intolerant of dissent over the politics of racial health and regeneration, only in the Communist Party could advocates of legalizing abortion carry some weight, as the Communist intervention in the Chamber suggests. Consider for a moment that even at *La Femme Socialiste* no one dared take a pro-choice stand and that the journal adopted, on occasion, a tone hostile to the legalization of abortion.[157] The Communist Party was quite literally the only refuge for proponents of freedom of choice.

Sadly, by the mid-1930s this was no longer true, for as the party embraced pronatalism, including its repressive aspects, the Communists' Stalinism precluded openness and debate. There was a relative dearth of commentary calling for abortion's legalization after 1926, but the issue resurfaced occasionally in the party's literature. In 1931, Marguerite Michard celebrated Stalin's success in raising the birthrate in the Soviet Union "in spite of" the availability of abortions,[158] as did another article in *L'Ouvrière* the following year.[159] Ironically, not long before the adoption of a pronatalist line, the Communist Party proposed a radical bill in the Chamber that included a proposal to legalize abortion.[160] Thereafter, all discussion of abortion or abrogating the laws against the dissemination of birth control literature vanished from the party's discourse. In 1939, in fact, a story appeared in *L'Humanité* that reported the case of a woman who died of a botched clandestine abortion without commenting on the larger issue. This article even used the term "maker of angels" to describe the abortionist: a term used habitually by pronatalist opponents of abortion.[161] As Stalin recriminalized abortion in the Soviet Union in 1936, the French Communists found it expedient to abandon their claim that abortion provided relief to working families.

The Communists were falling into line with the rest of France's political parties. While Radical Denise Moran did publish a couple of articles advocating the decriminalization of abortion in *La Lumière* in 1933, this was exceptional.[162] Even the Socialists' *Le Populaire,* while maintaining the Socialists' general silence on the issue, printed a salacious account of a midwife who, thanks to her clandestine abortion practice, owned an apartment in Paris's best neighborhood and maintained several domestic servants, including a chauffeur. The reporter noted her arrest with evident satisfaction.[163] The Alliance démocratique, meanwhile, endorsed the criminalization of abortion, a practice it deemed as equally threatening to the race as alcoholism and tuberculosis.[164] This was typical. The right was, unsurprisingly given the strong influence of Roman Catholicism and pronatalism in right-wing circles, resolutely hostile to abortionists and generally unsympathetic to women seeking them. A writer for the Fédération républicaine's *La Nation,* for example, called for the "pitiless" suppression of abortion and abortionists.[165] The Parti démocrate populaire's take on the matter was similar. In 1925 a party brochure referred to abortion as an "ignoble crime."[166] Nor did the 1930s fascists depart from the right-wing script on the issue. In 1939, the Parti populaire français's Gaston Guigon outlined his party's policies on depopulation and emphasized the need to throw more "makers of angels" into prison.[167] The party also cautioned young French women against joining the Communist Party with tales of Communist officials raping women recruits and forcing them to have abortions that caused sterility and death.[168] Less sensationally, the Croix de feu/Parti social français's 1939 party congress heard a lengthy discourse from executive committee member Henri Andriot in which he celebrated the movement's familial politics as in keeping with French Catholic traditions and proclaimed that the future Croix de feu–dominated state would strengthen the laws prohibiting abortion.[169]

The most celebrated victim of this pronatalist climate was Dr. Madeleine Pelletier, who had flirted with communism in the early 1920s. The prominent neo-Malthusian was charged with performing abortions in 1939. The judge ordered that she undergo a psychiatric evaluation, whereupon she was pronounced legally insane and thrown into an asylum. She died in obscurity.[170] No political journal surveyed here noted her passing and no one called for her release. The Communists, who had once enthusiastically published her work, abandoned Pelletier in their pursuit of nationalist unity and racial regeneration.

Nor was Pelletier to be the last victim of the pervasion of racialist pronatalism. The Vichy government took the Third Republic's repression of abortionists, for example, much further. In February 1942 the government made abortion a capital offense, equating it to treason. By the 1944 liberation Vichy had executed two abortionists, condemned another fourteen to life imprisonment, and sentenced a further twenty-six to terms exceeding twenty years.[171] Unfortunately too, the Parti populaire français's 1936 rhetoric portended Vichy's policies. Deploring the "immersion of foreigners in our affairs," the author of the party's founding manifesto proclaimed that "to return to the French nation its unity, its prosperity, its security and its influence in the world . . . it is necessary to purge the country of foreign influence." This purge was designed, he or she added, to "engender a stronger, healthier, race."[172] Pierre Laval and Marshal Pétain did not shrink from this undertaking; Vichy denaturalized some 150,000 "foreigners" who had obtained their citizenship post-1927. This was an important preliminary step toward the deportation to Nazi death camps, chiefly Auschwitz, of roughly seventy-six thousand French Jews; those without citizenship were the first to be so expelled.[173]

CONCLUSION

Race and gender intersected in the racialist politics of populationism and pronatalism in interwar France. There was a clear change over time in the period. In the 1920s, the Socialists and the Communists, but not so much the Radicals, were hostile to the pronatalist agenda and denounced it as a bourgeois conspiracy to keep labor costs down and cannon fodder at the ready. However, with the formation of the Popular Front against fascism, and to some degree before, the Marxist parties abandoned their objections and wholeheartedly embraced pronatalist measures that had hitherto been the exclusive purview of the right. This suggests a need to revise, at least in part, the traditional interpretation of the Popular Front, which casts it as a moment of hope and progress, however fleeting.[174] The Popular Front interlude, traditionally interpreted as engendering extreme friction between the left and the right, also saw the Radicals, Socialists, and Communists join right-wingers in their campaign for racial hygiene and repopulation; the Popular Front witnessed bipartisan conjuncture with respect to the politics of race. In uniting to fight fascism, the left eventually came to resemble the fascists with respect to pronatalism.

These pronatalist measures included innovations that no doubt benefited working families, however marginally, such as family allocations, extended maternity benefits, the provision of daycare, and the indexing of workers' wages according to family size. These were stimulated by a concern for the maintenance of the traditional family and a desire to reestablish the vitality of the French race. As the left took on the pronatalist project, it also adopted its racialism and gender traditionalism, both of which had deep roots in the parties.

The other side of the pronatalist coin was repression. Birth control literature was suppressed and its distributors arrested. Even in the 1920s, outside of the Communist Party, the left was largely acquiescent in this campaign. Abortion was also criminalized and its practitioners identified as enemies of France. For those like Pelletier the consequences of this could be serious indeed. More wide-reaching still was the imposition of traditional gender roles upon both men and women, whom the state tried to force to be fathers and mothers, without regard to their personal circumstances or preferences. As racialist thinking colored policy on an ever-widening range of issues, the right's paternalism and the left's fraternalism encompassed increasingly narrowly defined communities. Come June 1940, those defined as outside these communities proved at risk.

III
WOMEN

5

WOMEN IN PUBLIC SPACE

WOMEN'S WORK AND WOMEN IN POLITICS

France was moving toward an increasingly conservative gender politics in the 1930s. This conservative politics was, moreover, ever more shaped by racialism and a eugenicist mentality. While these discursive trends could and did have profound effects on social realities, they did not always reflect or shape them perfectly. For example, while a traditionalist gender politics would seemingly dictate that women, at least those of a childbearing age, retreat from the workforce, and while politicians did indeed take measures to encourage women's departure from paid work, women continued to labor for wages in large numbers; in fact, French women continued to be pacesetters in the western world. French women did paid work, as they had long done historically, at higher rates than other women in the West. In 1936, for example, at the height of the Depression and the racialist pronatalist consensus, women continued to comprise 37.1 percent of the workforce.[1] By comparison, just 25.4 percent of the American workforce was female in the 1930s.[2]

Similarly, one would expect that the gender conservatism that dominated French political discourse by the mid-1930s would have proven hostile to women in politics. Certainly, the climate remained chilly for proponents of women's suffrage; yet, paradoxically, the evidence is clear that just as they were denying women the vote and pushing them to stay home and raise babies, France's parties and leagues included women as members and support workers in unprecedented numbers. Moreover, these women played prominent roles in many cases and could be found, for example, featured prominently in the political press.

This chapter plays on these tensions. It explores, for example, the political parties and leagues' rhetoric about women in public space, which could at times be antifeminist and even misogynist, while at the same time emphasizing that women continued to work for wages irrespective of the opinions of male politicians and commentators and were in fact very prominent in the parties and leagues themselves. In the parties and leagues' presses, in particular, women ranging from prominent and well-known feminists to obscure political operatives to politically engaged housewives made their voices heard.

WOMEN WORKING

Historians have added nuance to the once orthodox view that World War I was a watershed moment for women and paid work in France. Jean-Louis Robert has pointed out, for example, that prior to the war women already comprised 35–40 percent of the French workforce and that "the wartime increase in female labor was not as explosive as some contemporaries believed it to be."[3] Indeed, Robert finds that women as a percentage of the workforce increased from roughly 38.2 percent in 1911 to an estimated 46 percent at war's end. Combine this fairly modest change with the facts that the increase appears to have been concentrated largely in industries already dominated by female labor and that by 1926 women once again constituted 37.2 percent of the workforce—equivalent to the prewar figure—and the narrative that the war saw a rush of women into the workforce with lasting repercussions is thrown into question.[4]

Still, although the novelty of women working might be very much in doubt, the fact remains that something like one in three women were engaged in paid employment at any given time during the interwar period.[5] It is also true, moreover, that although they were mistaken, most contemporary observers believed this to be a new or at least newly significant phenomenon. In 1926 Roger Besnard at *L'Ère nouvelle,* for instance, in musing about gendered levels of pay, repeated the trope that because of the war women had entered many professions and jobs previously unavailable to them.[6]

Thus, given the reality of women working in large numbers and given the widespread perception that this "new" phenomenon posed particular problems for policy makers, employers, and male and female workers alike, it seems imperative to ask what the political parties and leagues thought of women working and what policies they put forward relevant to women's paid labor?

In the 1920s, there was considerable divergence between the socialist left and the center and right on issues related to women's work. That said, what is interesting to note is how the contrary policies advocated by the parties and leagues rested on strikingly similar conceptions of gender and family relations. In particular, even the Communist Party, the ideological haven of unconventional thinkers in the 1920s, largely adhered to the breadwinner ideal and believed, accordingly, that preferably women should not have to work.

While there would be progress in this regard in the 1930s, in the 1920s, the right was blind to working women's situations; reflecting the class bias of their parties, conservative republicans agitated for maintenance of the traditional family without much consideration for those women who needed to work to feed themselves or their families. Commentators, their heads in the proverbial clouds, tended to assume that working outside the home was a choice women exercised free of economic constraints. A manuscript of Louis Marin's entitled "The Return of Women to the Home" certainly fit this mold. In it Marin confidently declared that women, "even the most '*garçonne*' among them" would jump at the chance to marry a good husband and raise children at home. On that day, he predicted to women, "You will abandon your balls or dances. You will banish your feminism from earlier days from your aesthetic."[7] Married women, in other words, would joyfully abandon their jobs because, once married, they would no longer need them since their husbands would provide for them and their children.

The total incomprehension of the economic situation of most working women (and men) that Marin betrayed in this essay was typical of many on the right in the 1920s. The Parti démocrate populaire, the first of the right-wing parties to consider the problem of women's work seriously, took a small step forward in the late 1920s by admitting the economic imperative behind most women's work. The party's solution however, displayed both a lack of imagination and a failure to grasp the realities of working women's lives. Louis Blain, in 1926, was among the first on the right to advocate an expansion of the practice of piece or outwork, which allowed women to remain home to tend to the children while producing (most usually) textile goods that they then sold to manufacturers for their wages.[8] Blain was confident that this would reconcile working families' need for income with the national interest involved in the return of women to the home to produce and rear children. Unfortunately, as Elinor Accampo among others has shown, such outsourcing was invariably exploitive, ensuring women sub-subsistence wages and leaving them at the mercy of oftentimes miserly employers.[9] For working-class women, Blain's idea must have seemed singularly unattractive. Still, it represented progress for a party and milieu that more typically declared that "all [women's] activity belongs to the family," when condemning mothers working outside the home.[10]

Debate continued within the party on this subject. The *Petit Démocrate*'s Annie, for one, acknowledged the need for many women to work and tried to offer some practical advice to women readers on how to choose a job or career.[11] Others, however, took the view that, were women forced to withdraw from the workplace, this would drive men's wages up, enabling them to provide for their families and obviating the need for women's labor outside *le foyer*.[12] What exactly would happen to single women in this scenario, and there were many such women thanks in part to the devastation of World War I, was unclear. That said, with the rise of the Great Depression, this began to be an ever more popular "solution" to the problem of low wages. As Louis-Alfred Pagès opined, women's return to the home would be "more humane, more in conformity with the commandments of nature and Providence."[13]

The idea of women returning to the home appeared to gain some momentum in the early 1930s as it spread to other parties. In the Fédération républicaine, Raoul de Warren, the son of influential deputy and industrialist Édouard de Warren, picked it up. In his opinion, piecework at home for women seemed "an ideal solution allowing the reconciliation of a good mother's obligations with the necessities of our modern life."[14] Warren did allow, admittedly, that often piecework created an exploitive relationship between women and their employers, and he called for the stricter regulation of these arrangements by the state. Perhaps recognizing the improbability of such action, Warren, a year later, endorsed instead part-time work for women, which he felt would allow them to earn the income needed for the family while still spending most of their time at home with the children.[15]

If the right muddled through the 1920s largely ignorant of women's need to work, the same cannot be said of the left, particularly the socialist left, which was much more attuned to the demands of working women. That said, a breadwinner ideal underlay most of the left's positions on the matter. In 1918, the Socialists modified (and thereby strengthened) a bill that guaranteed veterans the return of their prewar jobs.[16] This measure privileged the right of these men to work over that of those, including thousands of women, who had replaced them, and signaled the fidelity of the Socialist and later the Communist Party to the breadwinner ideal. In keeping with the mores of the period, there was no talk of men returning from the front to take up residence in the home while their wives and girlfriends earned their families' keep. As Mary Louise Roberts has shown, what men wanted was less a break from labor than a return to perceived normalcy, and this meant working and supporting their homemaking wives.[17] The socialist left supported these aspirations.

Yet, in 1919, it is also true that many Socialists were calling for the party to support women's right to work. Louise Saumoneau, for instance, agitated for the recruitment of women to France's powerful union movement, arguing that as women worked in ever greater numbers it was inevitable, once they experienced capitalist oppression firsthand, that they would push for revolution.[18] Teacher and later Communist Marthe Bigot asserted in the run-up to the 1919 general elections that the party had the "duty" to reaffirm its prewar support for women's right to work, an assertion that did not go unheeded.[19] Nor did this energy dissipate with the schism of 1920. Communist Party secretary-general Pierre Semard reiterated the Communists' support for women's rights, declaring that French women must "participate with the same rights as men in the economic activity and political life of the country,"[20] while in 1921, *Le Populaire* ran a series favorably profiling women's breakthroughs in a variety of professions both at home and abroad.[21] Moreover, this enthusiasm did not wane over time or with the onset of the Great Depression, at least not rhetorically. Suzanne Buisson, for example, underlined for her readers that the Socialist Party did not want to see women's gains in the workplace eroded because of the crisis,[22] and the Communist Confédération générale du travail unitaire (CGTU) continued to defend the rights of women who were laid off by their employers.[23]

Nor did the socialist parties limit themselves to general statements about the right of women to work. On the contrary, both the Socialists and the Communists were clear early on that they favored equal pay for equal work for women and men, in contrast to the parties of the right at the time. In 1924, for example, the Communists published a manifesto calling on the Confédération générale du travail (CGT), CGTU, and Socialist Party to join them in pushing for a number of measures including the legislating of equal pay for equal work.[24] The Socialists, while perhaps slightly quieter on the issue, likewise continually endorsed the principle. In 1929, for instance, *La Femme Socialiste* pointedly remarked that the right to equal pay for equal work was enshrined in article 427 of the Versailles Treaty,[25] while *Le Populaire* published a study of 1927 workplace statistics to show and decry the imbalance between men and women's pay.[26]

The Radicals were considerably more reticent. The party never adopted equal pay for equal work as part of its platform, and while occasional calls for it could be found in Radical circles,[27] the best Radical leaders could muster was an approving reference in Herriot's *Why I Am a Radical-Socialist* to Jules Guesde's support for the measure.[28] No Radical leader ever took a principled stand in favor of equal pay for equal work, and the party's record on this issue was abysmal, worse, in fact, than most of the right's.

The degree to which the breadwinner ideal also limited the Socialists and Communists' thinking is thought-provoking. Yes, they supported equal pay for equal work and women's right to work generally, but their adherence to the traditional family was near-total despite the influence of the new man among some Communists. While its very occurrence was somewhat remarkable given the mentality of the era, the discussion of women's "double shift"—working full-time for wages while still doing all the housework and childcare—was nonetheless indicative of the limitations of the socialist left's thinking. Socialist Monette Thomas, for instance, bemoaned the phenomenon of women working nine-hour days at their jobs to return to their homes where they then had to tackle the housework. This did not, however, cause her to rethink the usual division of household tasks and assert that husbands should shoulder some of the household chores. Instead, Thomas opined that women should work part-time so as to be better able to balance their responsibilities. She even suggested, in fact, that women could start their working days earlier so they could return home in time to care for the children after school and prepare dinner. This solution would have, of course, prolonged working women's hours of toil even further.[29] Party notables, such as Émile Kahn, later the secretary-general of the Ligue des droits de l'homme,[30] likewise occasionally reflected on the injustice of women's double shift, but their solutions lay in the reduction of women's work outside the home, not in men's sharing the load within it.[31] Socialist women also continued to echo this gendered reasoning. Germaine Fauchère, for instance, interviewed a nurse who complained of her double shift. Fauchère asked her if she would stay home if her husband's salary permitted it. The nurse responded, "If I could stay at home to look after my children I would. No one, you see, can replace a mother."[32] This discussion revealed the Socialist endgame: the breadwinner wage for men and the maintenance of the patriarchal family. In keeping with the logic of relational feminism, which saw the sexes as different but equal, there would be no absolute equality between the sexes in either the workplace or the home. As a 1931 article chronicling the state of women's work in *La Femme Socialiste* maintained, the steps to alleviating women's "double task" were as follows:

1. by the progressive and general diminution of the working day;
2. by improvements in home economics: the development of gas networks, the development of the electrical grid, the development of central heating, the improvement of the garbage disposal system, the increased use of washing machines;
3. by the specialization of tasks: a woman should not have to be at once a worker and, at home, a fashion expert, a dressmaker, a laundrywoman, an ironer, a cook, a mender.[33]

Evincing a naïve faith in the ability of modern technology and the rationalization of housework to lighten women's loads,[34] this piece notably did not include men's assumption of a fair portion of household tasks among its proposals.

Only the most radical group of leftist women, the Communist women behind *L'Ouvrière* in its first incarnation (1922–27), dared suggest that perhaps the sexual division of labor should be rethought. Anita Coder, for example, deplored the tensions between men and women workers and traced them at least partly to the resentment women felt at having both to work and to manage the household, suggesting that it was high time men did their fair share.[35] Still, the solution to women's double shift most often proposed at *L'Ouvrière* lay, as with point number 3 from *La Femme Socialiste*'s plan above, in the reorganization and collectivization of the household economy. Bigot, for instance, said that meals should be provided for workers' families at the workplace so that working mothers would have less to worry about,[36] while Marcelle Le Guen marveled at the labor-saving potential of new electrical devices but pointed out that only in an egalitarian society would everyone benefit from these advances.[37] These women believed that in the future Communist utopia, a collectivized egalitarian ethos would rule the domestic economy and that tasks such as meal preparation would be performed by paid employees of the factory or state.

Three things are of note here: 1) This rhetoric about women's "double shift" all but disappeared from Communist discourse by the late 1920s, indicating that just as the immediate post–World War I frank discussion of sexuality was later silenced, so too was talk of a more equal distribution of household responsibilities. 2) Even at *L'Ouvrière*, a certain whimsicality prevailed about the prewar period when supposedly women were able to remain at home due to men's earning a true breadwinner wage. As Charlotte Davy, who had stood as a Communist candidate in the 1925 municipal elections,[38] wrote, "Back then, women remained in their homes, where they occupied themselves with caring for the household, with making clothes, with washing and folding laundry, and with dedicating themselves to the care of young children. The husband provided all the resources necessary for the whole family." It was, in other words, the demands of capitalism, particularly during the war, that had, as Davy phrased it, "called women outside."[39] Presumably, in a more just society, this would not have happened and women would have remained in domestic space. 3) Even when Communists envisioned a less burdensome regime for women and mothers, they always forecast this in an imagined future Communist state. Thus, women did not need to concern themselves with their situations at present, for their deliverance was at hand. Accordingly, if anything, they were told to concentrate their energies on hastening the revolution. As Alexandra Kollontaï told French women, "In the Soviet Republic, no women workers' movement exists 'independent' from the common movement of the entire proletariat."[40] This spirit of proletarian unity, Kollontaï and others intimated, should guide Communist women's actions: for them, socialist aims must trump feminist ones. In Kollontaï's case, she learned firsthand of the dangers of pursuing feminism at what Communist leaders deemed to be the expense of socialist solidarity: she was eventually marginalized within the Bolshevik hierarchy because of her too enthusiastic promotion of the women's section as well as for her affiliation with Leon Trotsky. She was lucky to survive the purges of the 1930s.[41]

Two themes, in short, predominated in much of the Communist and Socialist parties' commentary on women's work generally: capitalism had forced women out of the home and shattered the idyll of the prewar family where breadwinning fathers worked and mothers joyously watched over the home and children; women's quest for equality in the workplace, while just, was clearly subordinated to the larger goal of revolution, whether this was to be achieved on the violent Communist or reformist Socialist model. Marcel Cachin, for example, emphasized that women were forced out of the home by the rising cost of living and that, as such, they now deserved the vote (apparently they would not have merited it had they remained homemakers), which they would attain after the inescapable Communist revolution.[42] Likewise, Socialist Marcel Bidoux told his readers, "Capitalism is perfecting its methods . . . it destroyed the family in taking mothers from their natural function in throwing them into the industrial furnace. . . . Only in socialism will the family find the conditions for development and guarantees that capitalism robs it of."[43]

Furthermore, the argument behind demands for equal pay for women was unwaveringly that the measure was necessary to prevent women's undercutting men's wages. Even noted Socialist feminist Suzanne Buisson made her case on these grounds, for example.[44] No doubt she did so to counter the widespread perception among left-wing men and, particularly among left-wing male workers, that women's work threatened their employment and drove their wages down.[45] Buisson's stance was unsurprising, really, given that she had earlier explained to Henriette Langlade that while she believed in feminist causes such as the struggle for the vote, she thought the fight for socialism must take priority, as only socialism would truly emancipate all women.[46]

Occasionally, frustration from below at the predominant breadwinner ideology in the Communist Party bubbled to the surface, as when unionist Adrienne Montegudet pointed out that the CGTU's apparent lack of enthusiasm for women in the workforce only rendered women workers the ideal strikebreakers: with the full inclusion of women and the adoption of equal pay for equal work, everyone's wages would rise and the specter of female "scabs" would disappear.[47] While Montegudet was expressing displeasure with her fellow Communists, she was nonetheless forced to make her argument for women workers' cause on the grounds that their advancement would benefit men.

Of course, these issues were largely absent in the Radical Party, given that it simply did not support the right of women to work. Suffice it to say that Radicals too, as shown above, conceived of women as mothers first and strove for the reestablishment of the one-income family. Even the redoubtable Fanny Clar rejected the campaign for the equal treatment of women in the workplace on the basis that women needed more protection and thus had to be treated differently from men.[48] Perhaps this reflected Clar and the Radicals' class position and their concordant divorce from working-class reality: Clar's solution to the problem of the double shift was for working mothers to hire maids.[49]

Clar's advice would not have seemed out of place on the right. Yet, contrary to what one might expect, while in the 1920s they were tone-deaf to working women's concerns, the right-wing parties and leagues proved surprisingly pragmatic about women's need to work in the 1930s. Undeniably, the goal, as in the socialist parties, was always a society where women would not have to work outside the home, but in the interim, right-wing politicians conceded that women must be allowed to earn wages in order to survive.

In fact, the Alliance démocratique, Parti démocrate populaire, Fédération républicaine, and Parti populaire français all came to advocate that women be paid on par with men.

Thanks, no doubt, to the advocacy of feminist Germaine Chapuis,[50] who, in the postwar cabinet of fellow former Parti démocrate populaire militant Robert Schuman became France's first female government minister (she became the minister of health—a portfolio of suitably "feminine" concern),[51] the party, somewhat unexpectedly given the avalanche of contrary opinions in the pages of *Le Petit Démocrate*, never made the forcible expulsion of women from the workforce part of its platform. On the contrary, it endorsed the principle of equal pay for equal work in 1933.[52] Likewise, the Alliance démocratique's founding manifesto that same year declared the party in support of women's right to work and of their right to equal wages.[53] The Alliance, in fact, waged a running campaign on behalf of women whose husbands owned their own businesses, agitating for them to be able to be paid employees of their spouses' companies. The main concern of the campaigners seemed to be that men could at the time employ their mistresses but not their wives: this was not a problem the average French worker confronted on a regular basis.[54] Still, while appealing to a particular class constituency and despite its traditional conception of gender, the Alliance démocratique became a champion of sorts of women workers' rights. In 1935, even the ultraconservative Fédération républicaine followed suit, coming out in support of the principle of equal pay for equal work.[55] So, while the goal of the republican right was clear—the return of women to the home—by the mid-1930s it had grappled with the realities of working women's lives sufficiently to support their demands for equal compensation, at least rhetorically. This evolution may well have been produced by the desperation of French working women during the Great Depression. Whatever the cause, the parties of the republican right chose to pursue the restoration of the traditional *foyer* through persuasive rather than coercive means.

Given the regressive records on this issue of Nazi Germany and Fascist Italy—where both regimes forcibly removed women from a variety of professions[56]—it seems reasonable to hypothesize that the Croix de feu and Parti populaire français might have been similarly authoritarian and traditional in their approach to women's work. There is, however, little evidence of this. In the case of the Croix de feu, this was simply not an issue that its journalists and politicians addressed frequently. Clearly, the movement shared the republican right's ideal of women returning to the home, but, as one piece in 1936 made clear, "women cannot stay [in the home] unless a sufficient wage is provided for homemaking," and the movement, accordingly, favored the same persuasive methods advocated by the republican right.[57] It is perhaps notable, however, that, to this author's knowledge, the Croix de feu never endorsed the principle of equal pay for equal work.

The Parti populaire français, however, was unequivocal. In 1938, the party program simultaneously declared that "the objective of the Parti populaire français is women in the home" and called for equal pay for equal work for both sexes.[58] In fact, despite its stated desire to see women homemaking, *L'Émancipation nationale* was surprisingly receptive to the image of the woman worker, running favorable stories on the work of female social workers, police officers, and secretaries, while also highlighting the special difficulties of women mobilized in heavy industries for the war effort in 1940.[59] One female author even tackled the problem of the double shift and called for husbands to be more supportive.[60] There was, in other words, no evidence that the two key French fascist formations of the 1930s would have followed the Nazis or Fascists in expelling women from the workforce. Granted, it is possible they would have done so nonetheless, for, as Robert Paxton emphasizes, fascisms tended to mutate significantly during the transition from movement to regime;[61] but there was no marked divergence between the far-right parties of the 1930s and their more moderate counterparts on the issue of women's work.

As for the socialist left, having already endorsed the principle of equal pay for equal work, rhetorically the Great Depression did not cause either the Socialist or Communist parties to change course. Notably, in 1936 Léon Blum took the symbolic step of appointing Suzanne Lacore, Irène Joliot-Curie, and Cécile Brunschvicg as deputy ministers. Critics, however, attacked this as tokenism.[62] Blum strengthened this impression with his flippant remark in 1937 that he had realized sexual equality with Lacore, Joliot-Curie, and Brunschvicg's appointments. The fact that Joliot-Curie, the deputy minister for scientific research and a Nobel prize winner, resigned in August 1936 after less than three months on the job because she had not been given anything to do and had never been assigned an office also seems suggestive.[63] Beyond Blum's grand gesture, moreover, the Popular Front did not do much for women workers. As Frader and Linda Clark emphasize, respectively, women did not reap the benefits of the Matignon Accords, and the Popular Front did not open the upper echelons of the civil service to female employees: the glass ceiling remained firmly in place.[64]

Clearly, left- and right-wing conceptions of gender were central to the obstacles women continued to face in the workplace. The privileging of the breadwinner ideal despite the fact that men's wages were generally insufficient to support families put women between a rock and a hard place, the parties and leagues' theoretical commitment to equal pay for equal work notwithstanding. Gender also combined with racialism across the political spectrum in discussions of another topic that could both benefit and harm women workers: the perceived need to "protect" them from the harmful effects of labor.

"Protective legislation" of this kind flourished and multiplied in the late nineteenth and early twentieth centuries. It could take two forms. The first involved restrictions on women's work. A law of 1874, for example, prevented girls younger than twenty-one from working at night or from working underground at any time in mines, pits, and quarries; 1892 legislation extended the restriction from night work to all women and limited their working day to eleven hours; and the introduction of the eight-hour workday for all workers in 1919 also prohibited women from engaging in various types of work. The second form of protective legislation centered on the provision of maternity benefits and services in the workplace designed to support motherhood, such as crèches, daycares, or designated spaces for breastfeeding. Thus, a 1909 law guaranteed women would not lose their job following maternity leave and a 1913 bill specified women could take up to four weeks of unpaid maternity leave prior to their due dates and had to take four unpaid weeks off after giving birth. In all cases, race and gender were central to these efforts. Seeing women primarily as mothers, reformers worried that laboring too hard enervated them and, when pregnant, their fetuses; plus legislators feared that women after giving birth had neither the time nor the strength to care for their infants properly. These issues, most concluded, contributed to France's high rate of infant mortality and therefore depopulation, and, for those with a racialist bent, its racial degeneration as well.[65]

This logic, with differing emphases depending on the commentator and her or his political convictions, continued in the interwar period. Communists, for example, consistently urged more "protection" for expectant mothers in the workplace and assailed the capitalist system for failing to safeguard working mothers. Berthe Fouchère writing under her pseudonym Irma Taury put it thus: "It is ['the capitalist regime'] that keeps pregnant women at the factory when complete rest is what is needed for both her and her unborn child."[66] This Communist critique of capitalism was coupled with concrete proposals: the Communist Party "demand[ed] the protection of maternity by obliging employers to create breastfeeding rooms and crèches, in requiring the state to pay four months maternity benefits at full salary, two months before and two months after births, to working women."[67] These grievances and demands remained largely unchanged in the 1930s and were, for example, outlined again by Josette Billoux in 1933.[68]

The Socialists, however, followed a slightly different trajectory from their Communist counterparts. They remained largely silent on the issue of "protective" measures in the 1920s while occasionally commenting approvingly on the existing legislation.[69] By the 1930s, however, the Socialists began to draw followers' attention more consistently to the need for greater protection of women and maternity in the workplace. Louise Saumoneau, for example, proposed, as per the party's platform, that women be given six weeks off prior to and eight weeks off after giving birth. She stipulated that those women should be "financially supported" without saying that they should continue to receive their full wage, as the Communists urged, and without indicating whether employers or the state should be responsible for the payment of such support.[70] Writing in the same space as Saumoneau in *Le Populaire,* the "Women's Tribune," Cypriane Fel repeated the call for "The Defense of Women," and linked three problems that she saw as intertwined: the ravages of capitalism that made it necessary for women to work to survive, the inadequate protection of pregnant women and mothers in the workplace, and the pervasion of "scourges" like alcoholism, slums, and tuberculosis.[71] Gender thus informed Fel's thinking in that she viewed the situation through a lens colored by the assumption that ideally women would not have to work. A eugenicist mentality—that she shared with Saumoneau—was likewise apparent and helped drive her desire to protect women in the workplace.

The Radicals and right-wing parties focused less on the need for "protective legislation" than the socialist left. That said, such commentary as did appear was similar in important respects. Addressing supporters in 1934, for example, Radical leader Édouard Daladier placed "the protection of women and children" alongside improving "hygiene" as among his key goals.[72] That same year a senator in Belgium brought forward a bill proposing to ban mothers from working altogether. This prompted *Le Petit Démocrate* to opine that the best means of protecting mothers and children was to give the former the means to stay out of the labor market through family allowances—this would make coercive measures unnecessary.[73] Fascist Paul Marion, meanwhile, listed the protection of women in the workplace as a crucial aim of the Parti populaire français and connected this explicitly to women's status as "progenitors of the race."[74] In short, while devoid of critiques of capitalism, commentary on the center, right, and far right, like that offered on the left, was shaped by both gender and conceptions of race.

What effect did this discussion of protective legislation have on working women? It may have motivated some employers to offer better maternity benefits and services for mothers voluntarily. It certainly reinforced the perception of feminine difference and weakness, casting employers, politicians, and the government as the protectors of women in a paternalist fashion. The discussion also provides a glimpse at how the equation of motherhood and women was a double-edged sword for women workers. On the one hand, motherhood could be marshaled to improve conditions for women in sometimes significant ways; on the other, if nearly everyone adhered to the breadwinner ideal and saw women's work as undesirable and a temporary necessity or nuisance that impeded women's true "natural" function of motherhood then that doubtless hindered claims to other advances such as equal pay for equal work. Herein the historian catches a glimpse, in other words, of the logic that made the parties and leagues' commitments to equal pay and other measures almost purely rhetorical.

In sum, at the level of parties' policies there was slow and limited progress on issues related to women's work. Across the political spectrum there was a grudging realization that women in the workplace appeared to be there to stay, at least for the time being. Thus, while all parties and leagues adhered to the breadwinner ideal they also, with the exceptions of the Croix de feu and Radical Party, came by the mid-1930s to embrace the principle of equal pay for equal work, and many pundits showed at least a modicum of sensitivity to the challenges faced by women in the workforce. On the ground, however, this shifting attitude on the part of France's politicos made little impact: real change would have to wait until the post–World War II years.

THE SEX TRADE

If most of interwar France's politicians and commentators came, by the 1930s, to accept the idea of women working they were nearly united throughout the interwar years in their condemnation of prostitution. Sympathy for this particular group of "public women" existed but even sympathizers viewed sex trade workers as passive victims in need of protection rather than as agents with a measure of control over their own lives. In this case, as in the case of women working generally, conceptions of both gender and race shaped opinions across the spectrum.

In France, the state had long chosen to regulate rather than prohibit prostitution. In metropolitan France prostitution was not legalized but in practice from 1802 to 1946 sex trade workers and brothels were allowed to operate as long as they registered with police and women submitted to inspections for venereal diseases.[75] In the colonies the government not only regulated brothels but ran them for French military officers and officials as well as for indigenous soldiers. Most famously, the French administration in Morocco built and maintained "Bousbir" in Casablanca in the 1920s, a self-contained complex complete with shops, a café, and a cinema, where two hundred government-paid sex trade workers served soldiers and colonial administrators.[76] This system of government brothels was introduced to France itself during World War I, at least partly to direct the sexual energies of colonial soldiers toward sex trade workers and away from "good" French women.[77]

Socialists and Communists reveled in attacking the government for its complicity in prostitution. Bigot, for example, ridiculed the *président du conseil* Georges Clemenceau by satirizing his nickname, "Father Victory," dubbing him instead the "Father of Prostitution." She also played on popular fears of contagion, notably by asking how many fathers had returned to their homes "diseased" thanks to the services offered in state brothels, and she called this phenomenon "another jewel on the crown of Victory."[78] Less wittily in a long and racist rant Socialist feminist Louise Bodin vented her anger at the military for providing white prostitutes for the colonial troops stationed in Europe. For this "horrible crime against white women and civilization," she blamed "Sacré-Cœur [Marshal Ferdinand] Foch."[79] Bodin and others' racialist fears of colonial troops evoked the paranoia around "white slavery" that raged in the late nineteenth and early twentieth centuries.[80] At *L'Ère nouvelle* Radical Fanny Clar likewise fretted, albeit minus Bodin's racism, about human traffickers enticing or coercing young French girls into Argentine brothels.[81]

In the 1920s, as with the campaign for equal pay Socialists and especially Communists assured their readers that the blight of prostitution would be eliminated by the socialist revolution. As Communist Noëlie Drous assured her readers, the "causes" of prostitution "will disappear with the bourgeois regime."[82] Accordingly, many looked to the Soviet Union as a harbinger of things to come. Jean Longuet proclaimed that despite reactionaries' depictions of the U.S.S.R. as a "Bolshevik hell" there were "NO MORE PROSTITUTES!" in Petrograd thanks to the Bolsheviks' suppression of the "hideous" institution of prostitution, and Katia Palianoff declared that following the October Revolution women "abandoned" the sex trade in droves.[83] By the 1930s, commentators realized that despite such declarations the sex trade persisted in the Soviet Union. In 1932 Communist Jeanne Dupont nonetheless assured her readers that prostitution had been a much graver problem in tsarist Russia than it was in the Soviet Union: thanks to programs during the Russian Civil War reeducating sex trade workers in concentration camps most had seen the error of their ways.[84] As another *L'Ouvrière* contributor explained, prostitution had been eliminated after the Revolution but had reappeared thanks to the difficult economic conditions created in the Soviet Union by the capitalist world's isolation of the country.[85] In 1935, long-time *Le Populaire* contributor Dr. Emmeline Weill-Raynal had a slightly different explanation for the persistence of the world's oldest profession in the U.S.S.R.: "the depraved and the perverse . . . prefer to earn their living by selling their bodies and are nearly impossible to re-educate."[86]

Whatever the situation may have been in the putative workers' paradise, Communists and Socialists remained convinced that the suppression of the sex trade in France should be the goal. Socialist Elisabeth Renaud summarized Socialists and Communists' logic on the subject of regulating the sex trade succinctly: "The regulation of prostitution is a betrayal of public health, it is an outrage to morality, it is a violation of women's liberty."[87] Opposition to regulating the sex trade was widely shared. In the 1930s the "Temporary Union for the Suppression of the Regulation of Prostitution and Trafficking in Women" brought many notables from across the political spectrum together in common cause. Its officers and committee of honor included prominent feminists Ghénia Avril de Sainte Croix, Marcelle Legrand-Falco, Elisabeth Fonsèque, and Maria Vérone, as well as the Archbishop of Paris Cardinal Jean Verdier, the well-known and respected Catholic politician and commentator Dr. Marc Sangnier, Fédération républicaine leader Louis Marin, Démocrate populaire professor Paul Gemaehling of the University of Strasbourg, Radical senators Louis Martin and Justin Godart, and Socialist Party members Victor Basch and Marius Moutet.[88]

What motivated these diverse individuals was likely not identical, however. In 1925, the Seventeenth Annual Federal Festival of Gymnastics was held in Strasbourg, for which sixteen thousand boys and young men descended on the city, where they were quartered at the university. Paul Gemaehling's wife, Margueritte, unhappily reported the events that followed for readers of *Le Petit Démocrate*. Unfortunately, "not 200 metres from the University, and even closer to some schools," the city's red light district could be found. Predictably, some of the boys did find it throughout the weekend—a veritable "rush" of them in fact. Indeed, despite the "courageous" efforts of their chaperones to "save at least the youngest of these children," from temptation, many escaped their elders' watchful eyes and "experienced the most shameful initiations of the type that corrupt either the soul or the body, or both simultaneously, for a lifetime." Gemaehling called for women, as "mothers, educators, and guardians of the nation's morality," to protect "the future of the race" by campaigning for the criminalization of the sex trade and the end of the state regulation of brothels.[89] She did not, it seems, poll either the boys or the sex trade workers for their opinions on the matter.

As Gemaehling's disquiet suggests, the key motivation for the right in calling for the suppression of the sex trade was to protect "the race" and to raise the birthrate. Exactly how suppressing the trade would help France produce more babies was not explicitly outlined, but presumably pundits believed men would have reproductive sex with their "legitimate" partners more frequently if denied access to sex trade workers, and certainly they hoped that criminalization would decrease the spread of syphilis and other venereal diseases, which most thought inhibited healthy reproduction. That the demographic and health of the race was foremost in most right-wing commentators' minds was clear from the fact that exhortations to suppress the sex trade also called for the repression of pornography, contraceptive literature, and abortion.[90] The connection between the fight to raise the birthrate and the suppression of the sex trade was clear in the Fédération républicaine's 1934 program, which placed its call for the elimination of "prostitution" among its demands for other measures designed to fight depopulation.[91]

The supporters of regulating the sex trade mostly kept their opinions to themselves, no doubt recognizing that voicing them too loudly might cost them or their party votes. But they must have represented a majority in the Chamber of Deputies because there was no change to France's regulation of the sex trade in the interwar years despite an attempt by the minister of health (and eugenicist), Henri Sellier, to abolish the practice in 1936. Nor did Vichy offer the system's critics any satisfaction: not only did Marshal Pétain's government not crack down on the sex trade, but it legalized brothels much to the disgust of Paul Gemaehling among others.[92] When proponents of regulation did defend the practice their argument usually hinged on two themes. First, they normally admitted that the sex trade was a regrettable institution but took the pragmatic position that the only thing worse than regulation would be criminalization, as it would drive the sex trade underground, thereby placing both sex workers and their customers at risk. Second, they argued that the imperative should be to reduce the spread of venereal diseases and that, though the sex trade was deplorable it was better to reduce the harm it caused than to ignore it.[93]

The discussion of the sex trade, in short, while being similarly shaped by conceptions of race and gender as discussions of women working generally, had a particularly unreal quality. Few and far between were accounts exploring the lived conditions of sex workers,[94] and reports or essays giving voice to women in the sex trade themselves were nonexistent. All presumed to speak for the subjects; all assumed women sex trade workers' passivity (with the exception of Weill-Raynal, who allowed that some were depraved and perverse); and none considered them as workers per se. Sex workers, like working women generally then, were perceived to be women forced into public space and in their case a degrading profession against their will. In the ideal society they would not exist and all women would be safely within the protective embrace of the home.

MISOGYNY AND ANTIFEMINISM

There is a considerable literature suggesting that the growing presence of women in public space as workers, sex workers, and political activists triggered a misogynist backlash—in a process of gender boundary marking—meant to force women to retreat to domestic space. Judith Walkowitz's brilliant *City of Dreadful Delight*, for example, discusses how newspapers and social commentators cast the "Jack the Ripper" narrative as a warning to women, particularly working-class shopgirls, about the dangers of venturing figuratively into male-dominated public space and literally across the class boundaries of London's neighborhoods.[95] In post–World War I France, meanwhile, Roberts's celebrated work suggests that French men returned from the war embittered by their experiences and eager for the solace of *le foyer* only to find that their newly emancipated mothers, wives, girlfriends, and sisters had cut their hair and taken men's jobs. As Roberts and others maintain, this masculine resentment led to a predominantly right-wing antifeminist campaign to return women to their homes, particularly around the politics of pronatalism: this trend found its most vehement expression among the fascists, such as Antoine Rédier and the Légion of the 1920s.[96]

There was, beyond a doubt, an "antifeminist" reaction on the far right (and on the right generally), which did look for women to return to their supposedly traditional roles. Certainly, if one restricts one's research to fascist intellectuals, individuals such as the Parti populaire français's (until 1938) Pierre Drieu La Rochelle provide ample fodder for the contention that fascism was in some respects a misogynist reaction. Drieu's signature novel, for example, *Gilles,* features a seemingly endless parade of sexual liaisons for the title character, who is given to utterances like, "This woman was foul . . . she thought of nothing but eating and drinking."[97] Louis-Ferdinand Céline's work likewise evinces a marked misogyny,[98] and while Robert Brasillach's fiction certainly does not contain the sort of vicious language typical of Drieu, his female characters generally lack depth, and since it is the men and not the women in his novels who seem erotically charged, some, including Jean-Paul Sartre, have insinuated that Brasillach was a homosexual.[99]

Beyond the intellectuals, however, while there is little doubt that the Croix de feu and Parti populaire français demonstrated a form of hypermasculinity, there is scant evidence that misogyny was any more present in either organization than in the more moderate parties on the center-right or left. In all of the right-wing parties isolated incidents of misogyny can be found, but the general impression is one of veneration for women, particularly for women as mothers. True, commentators in both the Croix de feu and Parti populaire français believed that a woman's place was in the home, but this was not at all different from the other political formations. Colonel de La Rocque and his followers, or Doriot and his, felt that in an ideal society women would keep the home; it does not necessarily follow that they hated women.

When antifeminism reared its head in the right-wing parties and press, it was usually overtly political and directed against left-wing figures and feminists. The Alliance démocratique's Jean Crussot, for instance, wrote a facetious piece addressed to "Madame N. . ., Feminist." In this, he expressed surprise at her attractiveness and pointedly patronized her by insisting on using the traditional terms Madame and Mademoiselle.[100] Crussot thereby belittled the feminist project and insinuated that feminists were typically ugly and masculine.

At *La Nation,* meanwhile, Jean Le Mee's tirades against left-wing teachers had a notably antifeminist tone. His rants against the "Feminist Groups for Secular Education" were especially vicious and carried on from at least 1927 to 1932. His outrage toward these women touched on a variety of themes, including their campaigns for sexual education, their propagation of revolution in the classroom, and their refusal to promote nationalism. An article on November 1,1930, was typical, where Le Mee commented on the group's national congress in Marseille: "A teacher from the Indre, comrade Pierrette Rouquet, gave a statement in favor of 'free motherhood' and apologized for teenaged-mothers." Le Mee found this legitimization of impropriety appalling and called for Rouquet to be fired as unfit to teach.[101]

L'Émancipation nationale did feature pieces that could be read as misogynist invective. These, like those above, were political in nature. The most compelling example was Yves Sicard's article "*Milicienne!* . . . The Unbelievable Adventure of a Depraved Young Girl Who Gave the Coup de Grâce to the Victims of the Reds." This fantastical account discussed the case of "Mademoiselle Christiane X," whom Sicard described as a "superb monster" and "young harpy." X was a dedicated young Communist who trained to kill on the streets of Paris and admitted to Sicard that she had participated in the murder of two old women before setting off to Spain, where she had been part of a crack execution squad. While Sicard expressed horror at this story and did so by contrasting X's feminine appearance with her horrendous pursuits, his real revulsion was saved for the Communist Party for creating this "excellent specimen of what communism can do with a young French girl."[102] In sum, this was a parable meant to caution *pères de famille* to protect their daughters from Communist influence as much as a misogynist rant.

Certainly, it is true that fascists tended to blame women for France's declining birthrate. Again, however, so too did others. Maurice Rondet-Saint of the *Alliance démocratique* typified this phenomenon. While purporting to denounce the loose morality and hedonism of all young people as at fault for depopulation, he conjured images of young women almost exclusively. Thus he attacked the modern cinema, "where topless women have become as indispensable as the projectionist" and lamented the state of France's beaches, where "young girls walk around with the minimum of clothing showing the maximum of skin whether it is beautiful or not, white or red, or smooth or hairy."[103] The shameless modern woman thus became a cipher for the decadence Rondet-Saint saw as leading France astray. This was part and parcel of the broad rejection of the *femme moderne,* or *garçonne,* whom the right reviled for violating gender roles and destabilizing the traditional family.[104]

Present and at times prominent though antifeminism and misogyny were on the right, it was equally visible on the left. The Radical Party has long been recognized as a haven for misogynists of the worst kind, including the infamous Senator Raymond Duplantier, who, invoking Madeleine Pelletier's desire to destigmatize prostitution, opposed women's suffrage because, among other reasons, he worried that on election day men would go to their favorite brothels only to find them closed so their "inhabitants" could exercise their suffrage. This remark was notably greeted with "smiles and exclamations," by Duplantier's fellow senators. When Louis Martin (also a Radical) interjected that most women in prostitution had been coerced in some fashion, Duplantier disagreed, saying that prostitutes entered the profession willingly, often due to their being too lazy to do legitimate work. He then proclaimed, again to smiles: "These ladies want to be deputies? Well, let them remain . . . what they are!"[105]

Duplantier's was a celebrated case, but as vile as his rhetoric was, it was not beyond the bounds of acceptable leftist discourse, as witnessed by the chuckles he received in the Senate. Charles Régismanset, a frequent contributor to *L'Ère nouvelle,* was similarly misogynistic. Régismanset most often printed columns meant to be humorous, called, "Contradictions," which featured a list of supposed incongruities and jokes. Witness this sample of Régismanset's prose: "When a woman is raped or assaulted by a satyr, society always screams for justice, but the victim rarely does. Was it not Catherine of Russia who said, knowledgably, that a woman is never raped the entire time?"[106] "Feminism—and I mean by that a certain hateful and discontented cannibalism—has no other excuse than the ugliness and disgrace of a great many of its female adepts";[107] "Certain women for whom indifference equals kindness don't give themselves, they let themselves be taken";[108] "Your daughter is mute and you're complaining?"[109] These deeply misogynist observations appeared on the first page of one of the center-left's most influential tribunes. So too did the Carlo Rim cartoon (fig. 5.1) that appeared in the November 24, 1929, edition of *L'Ère nouvelle.* This was meant to denigrate

Louis Marin and the Fédération républicaine for the continuing squabbles of their parliamentary group, known as the Union républicaine et démocrate.[110] However, it also revealed both Rim and the editors' comfort with depicting a naked woman being filleted by the butcher, Marin, on the front page of the newspaper (oddly, this woman appears to have been both Marianne and the embodiment of the Union, an especially convoluted piece of imagery). The pornographic nature of this image was doubly shocking as *L'Ère nouvelle* rarely printed any cartoons. Perhaps it should not have been. The paper's editor at the time of Rim's cartoon was noted Radical Georges Ponsot, who had earlier written an article pining for the days when men could murder their unfaithful wives without threat of punishment. This article was a particularly deranged example of the postwar wave of misogyny that Roberts documents, as Ponsot ranted semicoherently against women "chasing males from their positions" in a postwar social order turned upside down.[111]

Fig. 5.1. *L'Ère Nouvelle,* November 24, 1929, 1.

Fig. 5.2. *Le Populaire,* July 17, 1932, 1.

Nor was antifeminism the exclusive domain of the Radicals. A particular tendency among both Socialists and Communists was to portray women as the embodiment of bourgeois decadence. Figure 5.2 appeared in *Le Populaire;* it contrasted the working-class women on the left who were willing to mend their hats so they would serve for another season (embodying the proper feminine spirit of self-sacrifice) with the bourgeois woman on the right, adorned in a fur and ordering "a little hat in the depression style, madame, with orchid leaves and crow feathers." This woman's decadence symbolized the injustice behind the Great Depression to Socialist readers.

This image at least provided a counterexample of suitable femininity—other instances were less equivocal. One of Socialist Charles Vérècque's poems, for example, contained the following stanza, decrying the injustice of workers' exploitation:

> You must enrich your boss,
> Who, long ago, became a baron,
> He must have jewels for his wife

Who does not hide her emotion,
I will use rags, I will.
That she would hold disgusting![112]

The poem is addressed to a male worker ("mon homme"), and his sufferings are contrasted with the extravagance of the boss's wife who "must have jewels." It is her unseemly greed that causes his misery.

Communist Marie Roncière likewise employed this device of the decadent *bourgeoise*. She scornfully and sarcastically outlined middle-class women's activities, explaining that they had no time to be mothers as well:

> The bourgeois woman is very busy, if we are to believe Marcel Prévost, overcome even by her social responsibilities: visits/dinners, theater, directing the household, watching over numerous servants, balancing a budget that is rarely in accord with the lifestyle she wants to lead, frequently trying out complicated make-up and washing regimens, very long spa treatments: baths, massages, manicures, pedicures, hair-stylings, etc. . . . And she must also keep up a fastidious correspondence, read society journals, fashionable books, and be up to date on all the gossip, and all the past, present or . . . future scandals!
>
> Poor woman! With such a *burden* can she really also think of motherhood?[113]

In short, antifeminism and misogyny were not unique to the right. While the foci of male discontent could sometimes be different—extravagant bourgeois women for Socialists and Communists, selfish and sterile modern women for the right, for example—there was also considerable overlap as Ponsot and others' complaints about women working demonstrate. Certainly, this widespread antifeminism and sometimes outright misogyny must have discouraged many women from entering male domains: women knew that if they dared to demand the franchise, for example, they would be called "whores" or worse by those like Duplantier. The largely male sentinels at the gates to public space were vigorous in their defense of male privilege.

WOMEN IN POLITICS

What is quite amazing given the often hostile climate to women in public was that despite Duplantier and others' efforts to silence and intimidate women, they forced their way into France's political parties and leagues in unprecedented numbers in the interwar years. Women made vital contributions to France's political formations out of all proportion to their numbers: in every case, prominent women took leadership positions and helped shape militants' opinions on the pages of the parties and leagues' newspapers and propaganda.

As Kevin Passmore and Caroline Campbell illustrate, the Croix de feu was the first French political party to have a significant female membership with over a hundred thousand women adherents. Further, these women undertook the social outreach programs that, especially post-1936, the Parti social français leadership saw as key to its success.[114] These included the activities of the Joan of Arc Medico-Social Association, staffed by women, which provided home visits, held clinics, ran a pharmacy, and maintained the Allées rest home.[115] In addition, there was also a simple "social services" division (divided later into the Civil Action Group and the Social Action Group), which acted as a kind of private welfare office and seems also to have been a feminine domain. Its agents evaluated the worthiness of "clients," allotted funds to them based on those evaluations, and monitored their subsequent progress.[116] There was also, of course, the Feminine Section of the party, which maintained its own apparatus and, most interestingly, ran the Croix de feu's youth camps and activities, reflecting the fact that looking after children was considered a woman's job.[117] This vast empire of feminine activity was, moreover, supervised by Antoinette de Préval, a trusted lieutenant of Colonel de La Rocque, and Campbell has recently argued that de Préval enjoyed considerable freedom of action within her domain.[118] In short, there were many different roles within the movement that women could and did fill. Granted, these were limited within the confines of so-called properly feminine pursuits, representing an extension of the role of mother to the public sphere, but that does not negate the fact that thousands of women in the Croix de feu became politically involved and had their own role in a political endeavor validated.

The same, to a much lesser degree, can be said of the Parti populaire français. It too had a feminine section, although much less successful.[119] Further, the section also seems to have run its youth organization and summer camps.[120] Beyond that, however, little is known, and it must be said that the party's feminine section was much less visible in its publications than its Croix de feu counterpart.

While women in the Croix de feu, in particular, entered politics in robust numbers, the novelty of this was not absolute. The other parties, including those on the center-right, also witnessed women found their own groups, newspapers, and activities—the real innovation of the Croix de feu lay in the scope of its women's organizations, which was indeed unique.

On the right, the Parti démocrate populaire, in particular, anticipated the Croix de feu. This may have been due to the party's social Catholicism, which the Croix de feu shared to a considerable degree. As early as the party's founding year, for example, in 1925, *Le Petit Démocrate* reported on meetings of the Social and Civic Action Group of Marseille, which appears to have been constituted by women.[121] Indeed, as Jean-Claude Delbreil points out, Marseille was Chapuis's hometown, and so from the outset she was the outstanding personality in the party's feminine section and in its mobilization of women.[122] In late 1925, with Chapuis the key figure, the feminine section, calling itself "The Civil and Social Feminine Union" (UFCS), held its inaugural congress in Paris just before Christmas. Interestingly, the UFCS, in spite of Chapuis's suffragism, avoided declaring itself in favor of women's suffrage, and instead proclaimed that it saw one of its tasks as to prepare women for the vote.[123] It also came out in support of the maintenance of mothers in the home and of the breadwinner wage; the title of the article covering this congress was "For the restoration of *le foyer*": clearly, this was not a radical feminist organization. Still, on the right, the Parti démocrate populaire seems to have been the first mainstream party to mobilize women and the significance of this innovation should not be underestimated. As Delbreil comments, the UFCS remained a fairly docile organization until 1935, when Christiane d'Hellencourt assumed the presidency and it was renamed "The National Feminine Federation."[124] Thereafter, instead of simply meeting periodically in its local sections to discuss suffrage and social issues, the federation took a more active role in agitating for women's suffrage, and in fundraising and other activities for the party.[125] This change, in fact, was reflected on the "Our *Foyer*" page of *Le Petit Démocrate,* which in early 1936 shifted its tone considerably from covering safely "feminine" topics such as housekeeping and cooking to more political ones such as the need to reform France's civil code to emancipate women fully. Even so, while the UFCS and its successor displayed considerable vitality, and markedly more than the other republican right parties' organizations, given the limited success of the party generally, a couple of thousand women (if that many) were likely all the Parti démocrate populaire ever managed to rally to its banner.

In addition to its own organization, the Parti démocrate populaire also maintained close ties to the National Union for Women's Vote (UNVF), a conservative feminist organization with, like the party, a strongly Catholic character.[126] The party newspaper consistently advertised UNVF activities, and writers and leaders expressed approval for the group's agenda.[127] The conservative feminism espoused by the UNVF, in fact, fit perfectly with the Parti démocrate populaire's own women in its traditional view of the family but nonetheless provided forceful (within the confines of bourgeois respectability) advocacy for women's rights.[128]

Indeed, the UNVF is a good indicator of the homogeneity of the republican right in terms both of the depth of its commitment to feminism and its feminine ideal. Edmée de la Rochefoucauld, for instance, who succeeded Madame Le Vert Chotard as president of the group in 1930, wrote Pierre-Étienne Flandin in 1933 congratulating him for his election as president of the Alliance démocratique in glowing terms and thanking him for his mandating that women could join the party as full-fledged members. Flandin responded by suggesting the two sit down to discuss collaboration between the new party and UNVF, indicating both the Alliance's comfort level with the UNVF's outlook and the UNVF's closeness not just to the Parti démocrate populaire but the Alliance démocratique as well.[129] Thereafter, the Alliance démocratique, like the Parti démocrate populaire, gave the UNVF good press.[130] The Fédération républicaine, meanwhile, likewise commented favorably on the UNVF's activities:[131] this was hardly surprising given that Blanche Lescouvé, the most prominent woman in the party, was a former lieutenant of Le Vert Chotard's.[132]

Just as the Alliance démocratique and Fédération républicaine shared in the Parti démocrate populaire's support for the UNVF, so too did they follow its lead in organizing women. The Alliance seems to have been the most lackadaisical of the three republican right parties in its approach to women. This was so despite the touted feminism of Flandin and the prominence of the formidable Yvonne Foinant, who, in addition to running her own company, was also president of the Ardennes section of the French Union for Women's Suffrage,[133] a more centrist organization than the UNVF. In 1935, the League for the Civil and Civic Emancipation of the French Woman" was born, the de facto feminine section of the party. Unsurprisingly, Foinant was elected president, while her collaborator, Ginette Petit, became the secretary-general; equally expectedly, this group evinced exactly the same conservative feminist ethos found in the UFCS and UNVF, expressing support for suffrage but emphasizing more strongly the need for women to return to the home.[134] Notably, despite the fact that the league was fairly active,[135] it was ignored more often than not in the party press; only when Foinant forced feminist issues onto the agenda, as she did at the 1937 party congress, did *L'Alliance démocratique* take notice.[136] Tellingly, despite promising in 1935 to carry a women's page,[137] the paper never did so with any regularity. Perhaps this apathy explains the occasionally frustrated tone of Foinant's correspondence to Flandin,[138] and Donald Wileman's lack of comment on women within the party.[139] In truth, the Alliance's women's organization was probably quite small—one might speculate a few hundred members—given the elitist tone and focus of its efforts. Still, the Alliance démocratique did have a women's organization that provided an outlet for female activism, even if whether or not feminine efforts were valued by the party's male leaders remained at best an open question.

Like the Alliance démocratique, the Fédération républicaine only belatedly formed a feminine section in 1935. However, this group did have its own paper, *Le Devoir des femmes,* and by 1936 it also boasted sections in sixty-five departments.[140] Its founding manifesto called for women's suffrage but typically devoted more print to calling for measures to defend the traditional family.[141] The party did call on members of the feminine section to volunteer for Fédération candidates' campaigns,[142] but otherwise, what activities party women engaged in remain unclear. Lacking the mass organization of the Croix de feu and espousing a traditionalist view of women's roles that did not normally lend itself to female political involvement, the Fédération républicaine's local women's sections probably did little more than meet semiregularly to discuss women's issues, whether political or domestic. That this was at best modestly successful is clear in that *Le Devoir des femmes* had only 1,625 subscribers in 1936,[143] reducing the paper's editors to pleading with male party members, in *La Nation,* to buy their wives subscriptions.[144] It seems likely, therefore, that the Fédération's feminine section never enjoyed more than, at most, a couple of thousand members.

So, while it is true that the Croix de feu (and to a lesser extent, the Parti populaire français) broke new ground in its mobilization of women—by using them as social workers and medical caregivers and by organizing them at a young age—the republican right, especially the Parti démocrate populaire, set the stage for this development with its own organizations. Further, the caregiving motherly ideal embodied in the Croix de feu and Parti populaire français's women's roles, was entirely consistent with the feminine ideal on the republican right. It is unlikely that anyone in the Alliance démocratique, Parti démocrate populaire, or Fédération républicaine would have been taken aback by fascist women's activities. That said, the extent of women's involvement in the Croix de feu, in particular, was novel and should be recognized as such. It was also specifically fascist in that it was part and parcel of the movement's budding totalitarianism—it was a crucial component of the effort to construct a counter-society. As Daniella Sarnoff remarks, this placed fascist women at "the center of [French] fascism."[145]

As on the right, all the left-wing parties sought, at one time or another, to mobilize women under their banners. Organizations for women existed on the left earlier than on the right. These organizations engaged in activities sometimes quite similar to their right-wing counterparts. Equally, although the parties met with limited success in mobilizing women, through their activism leftist women were at the center of their parties' lives and agendas.

In the department of the Seine at least, the Communists seem to have had a feminine section from their earliest days. The section apparently met to discuss their agenda for the Communist Party's 1921 national congress that year in Marseille.[146] One suspects they were disappointed at the results of that congress: in four days worth of covering it, the only mention *L'Humanité* made of any women or women's issues was to report that Lucie Colliard had expressed her regret that more women had not participated.[147] This dearth of success was typical of the Communists' experiences in recruiting women. *L'Ouvrière,* for example, founded in 1922 with high expectations about its potential to recruit women to the party,[148] was perpetually in financial trouble and closed down in 1927 owing to insufficient funds.[149] That this was as much to do with a failure to build circulation as with a lack of enthusiasm from the Politburo is clear: in 1923 the paper claimed a readership of only 2,500.[150] The newspaper reappeared in May 1930,[151] but continued to be greeted by unresponsiveness both from potential readers and from the party's leadership. At the end of 1935,[152] after 135 issues of the post-1930 edition, the Politburo decided to shut *L'Ouvrière* down permanently. The dismissive attitude with which they did so was captured by their suggestion that readers' needs could be more than adequately met through subscribing to the Communist International's women's journal.[153] This decision must have been all the more galling to Communist women as it came in the midst of the party's great expansion during the Popular Front;[154] funds, for once, should have been available.

Failure, in fact, characterized the Communist Party's advances to women for a long time. In 1922, the feminine secretariat admitted its inability to draw women into the party, an inability it attributed to women's frustratingly apolitical attitudes.[155] Nonetheless, the party's women persisted and the feminine section continued to report regularly at party congresses and, just as regularly, lamented its insignificant membership and slow recruitment.[156]

The tone changed somewhat with the advent of the Popular Front. In 1936, Daniel Renoult boasted at a public meeting of Communist women that the party was attracting scores of French women to its ranks.[157] Moreover, that same year, the party founded the Jeunes filles de France to much fanfare.[158] As seen in chapter 2, Danielle Casanova became the secretary-general of this group, and it began to hold annual congresses in 1937. That the Jeunes filles de France confined itself to roles strikingly similar to those of right-wing women was clear. For example, during the Spanish Civil War the group was very active fundraising to mail condensed milk to Spain for starving republican babies.[159] This is not to deny that this was a worthy humanitarian endeavor, but it is nonetheless notable that Communist women took charge of this problem while Communist men were encouraged to enlist in the international brigades. This was so, moreover, despite the fact that Spanish women did fight in the Civil War.[160] This was also a provocative mirror reflection of the later Croix de feu, Parti populaire français, Fédération républicaine, and Parti démocrate populaire women's campaigns to send care packages to France's men at the front during World War II,[161] suggesting the proximity of even the Communists' feminine ideal with that on the right, including the fascist right. The partial exception of the post-1936 years aside, there is little evidence to contradict Reynolds's assertion that the Communist Party remained overwhelmingly male, even in its ascendancy.[162] Laird Boswell estimates that women made up 1.1 percent of party members in the Corrèze.[163]

The Socialist Party was not much more successful in its efforts. As early as 1918, Annette Charreau was stressing the urgency of the need for the then-unified party to recruit women given the fact (so she thought) that women's suffrage would soon be realized. She, like many after her, stressed that the best way to go about this was for Socialist men to convince their wives and girlfriends to join.[164] Charreau also wrote an admiring column about the British Labour Party's successful enrollment of women, and she detailed how it attached feminine sections to each and every party section.[165] Her implication was clear: the Socialists should follow the Labour Party's lead.

In 1919, as part of its outreach to women, the party celebrated "Women's Day" with a conference in Paris where notables like Marcel Cachin, Suzanne Girault, Albert Thomas, and Alice Jouenne addressed the crowd; Cachin's theme, suitably, was how the advancement of capitalism had led to an ever greater subjugation of women.[166]

There was indication of dissatisfaction among Socialist women, however, about the party's failure to respond to Charreau's call more enthusiastically. Bigot, for example, complained bitterly about the decision not to send any representatives to a 1919 meeting of international socialist women in Southampton, England, and felt it reflected the wider Socialist antipathy toward women's activism.[167] Likewise, Charreau regretted the attitudes of some of her male comrades in opposition to Louise Saumoneau and two other women's candidacies for a position on the National Council because in their minds, "the task was beyond the strength of a woman."[168]

By 1922 the Group of Socialist Women had been founded, with Saumoneau presiding.[169] And, of course, the group had Saumoneau's journal, the monthly *La Femme Socialiste,* at its disposal.[170] The Group of Socialist Women was very much the descendant of the Feminist and Socialist Group, founded in 1899 by Saumoneau and Elisabeth Renaud, and followed their strict privileging of their socialism over their feminism accordingly.[171] The logic was indistinguishable from that in the Communist Party: the socialist revolution would break women's chains; therefore, all efforts should be directed toward furthering that rather than improving the status of women within the capitalist Third Republic. Later neo-Socialist and fascist Marcel Déat explained the logic succinctly, saying the party "does not need to devote itself to a specifically feminist propaganda, as its doctrine is broadly human."[172] Still, Saumoneau was not shy about the need for a separate women's organization within the party. As she explained, while in theory the "doors" to the party sections were "open to women," in practice, thanks to the hostility and ignorance of local male party officials and activists, women found those doors impassable. Feminine sections, Saumoneau hoped, would help foster a more inclusive attitude.[173] That this was less than a raging success was more than evidenced by the following facts: the Women's Group did not hold a national congress until 1930, eight years after its founding,[174] at the 1931 party congress in Bordeaux, Saumoneau still felt compelled to justify the need for a women's organization,[175] and the Group's secretary-general, Suzanne Buisson, eclipsing Saumoneau as the party's dominant female personality by the early 1930s, annually chided the party's men for their failure to support efforts to lure women.[176] No doubt, this unspectacular record was also due, at least in part, to the group's own insistence that only women who were already party members be admitted, a policy at odds with the stated goal of attracting women to socialism through the group's activities.[177] It is somewhat sad to see Buisson boasting in 1933, eleven years after the Group of Socialist Women's inauguration, of there being thirteen federations across the country, including one in the Somme with forty-five members. Moreover, according to Buisson's own figures, this paltry total represented a dramatic increase over the previous year's, a fact that highlighted the group's long-term underachievement more than its relative short-term success.[178]

As for the Communist Party, the Popular Front years saw a mild surge in Socialist activity as the party tried harder to draw women to its cause. For example, the National Council of Socialist Women, the repackaged Group of Socialist Women, launched a new journal in 1936, *La tribune des femmes Socialistes,* as its official monthly, possibly due to Saumoneau's (and therefore *La Femme Socialiste*'s) increasing isolation within the party.[179] More spectacular still was Blum's appointment of Brunschvicg, Lacore, and Joliot-Curie as deputy ministers.[180] But despite these efforts, in 1937 Buisson was still complaining of women's lack of representation and general invisibility within the party. The evidence, then, as with the Communist Party, confirms Reynolds's assertion that the Socialist Party too was largely unable to attract female members.[181]

The Radicals, predictably, were no better. As Serge Berstein adroitly points out, until 1924–25, it is fair to say that the Radical Party had not given so much as a thought to admitting women members. It was the party's 1924 Congress that passed then Secretary-General Félix Bouffandeau's resolution to permit women's entry by a thin majority. Thereafter, the party did come to boast some impressive female talents such as Suzanne Schreiber (who became a vice-president of the party's executive committee in 1926), Brunschvicg, Marcelle Kraemer-Bach, and Éliane Brault, but on the whole its record was unimpressive. The percentage of women on the executive committee from 1922 to 1938 provides an accurate synopsis of the place of women in the party: in that time there were 6,984 delegates to the committee, including exactly fifty-three women, or 0.75 percent of the total.[182] Moreover, the party put forth zero effort to mobilize women. It had a "National Mixed Committee," founded in 1925, where Brault emerged as the dominant female personality by the early 1930s. However, the committee's activities were confined to Paris, and it was not a mass organization, performing only mildly politicized charitable work. It also reflected the two themes of Radicals' organization of women: it replicated the party's middle-class base and hence remained inaccessible to the broader public; and it included men who held all the key positions within the institution.[183] That men dominated this organization despite the abundance of female talent available within the party is doubly revealing of the Radicals' deep ambivalence about mobilizing women. By 1938 there was a women's organization called The Radical-Socialist Women, with Kraemer-Bach as its president, but this group's activities remain obscure and one can only presume its success was limited.[184]

All the parties then, tried to mobilize women, albeit halfheartedly in some cases. While the record of the parties in recruiting women in large numbers was pretty spotty, with really only the Croix de feu enjoying sustained success, it is nevertheless true that women played important roles in all the parties and leagues.

One of the most striking things to any present-day reader of the interwar political press is the prominence of women contributors, both eminent and obscure. Every party and league featured a roster of women reporters and analysts who debated and thereby helped shape the parties' understanding and policies on the issues of the day. Alongside contributions from well-known feminists, leaders, or journalists like Antoinette de Préval, Dora Sabiani, Madame Le Vert Chotard, Edmée de la Rochefoucauld, Blanche Lescouvé, Ginette Petit, Christiane d'Hellencourt, Germaine Chapuis, Yvonne Foinant, Cécile Brunschvicg, Éliane Brault, Marcelle Kraemer-Bach, Suzanne Buisson, Elisabeth Renaud, Louise Saumoneau, Lydia Lainé, Séverine, Louise Bodin, Berthe Fouchère, Marthe Bigot, and Danielle Casanova appeared the voices of literally hundreds of women—lesser lights in the parties and leagues who made vital contributions to their organizations and to the political life of the country. Dozens of them are featured throughout this manuscript. Some like Emmeline Weill-Raynal, Jenny Héricourt, or Madeleine Pelletier were doctors who sought to lend their expertise to issues of public interest; others like *Le Petit Démocrate*'s Annie or *L'Ère nouvelle*'s Fanny Clar addressed themselves largely to their women readers' concerns; others like Germaine Peyroles at *Le Petit Démocrate* or the Communist Party's Marie Bréant weighed in on the political issues of the day; and still others appear fleetingly, reporting on obscure items or analyzing particular problems before disappearing again from the printed record. While these women were as diverse as the political organizations to which they belonged, and in fact, many offered opinions that were largely indistinct from those of their male counterparts, there is simply no doubt that Sîan Reynolds is correct to assert women's profound involvement in interwar politics despite their not exercising the suffrage or appearing in large numbers among most of the parties and leagues' membership rolls.[185] These women deserve to be rescued from the "enormous condescension of posterity";[186] in the words of little-known Socialist Marthe Louis-Lévy they "raise[d] their voice" to "say their piece" and shaped their lives and society accordingly.[187]

CONCLUSION

Women in public space and roles generated a great deal of discussion in interwar France. The political parties, for their part, included their share of antifeminists and misogynists who actively sought to prevent women from intruding into perceived male preserves. The Pierre Drieu La Rochelles and Raymond Duplantiers were at the extreme edge of a considerable group of political men who were at best deeply ambivalent about the emergence of the *femme moderne* and used misogynist invective to try to exclude women from work, politics, and the public sphere.

Despite that, thanks to pressure from below from outstanding figures like Louise Saumoneau, Marcelle Kraemer-Bach, and Antoinette de Préval as well as from hundreds of less-well-known women in their ranks, there was progress for women among the interwar parties and leagues. On the issue of women working, for example, despite the onset of the Great Depression, which created considerable popular hostility to women working, there was a clear change over time toward acceptance of not just the presence of women in the workforce but also the principle of equal pay for equal work. Admittedly, the goal for conservatives and socialists alike remained a society where exigent circumstances did not force women to work—the assumption that women did not choose to work freely was nearly universal. Progress, moreover, was halting and limited by the bipartisan adherence to the breadwinner ideal as well as the perception of women as passive; prostitution, for instance, was envisioned as representing a failure of state paternalism with sex trade workers themselves cast as silent and inactive victims; yet, the evolution in the parties and leagues' attitudes was buttressed by the growing inclusion of women, most spectacularly in the Croix de feu. Tens of thousands of women joined France's political parties and leagues in the interwar years, giving weight to women's claims for full inclusion in the body politic in the process: the evolution of the accepted wisdom on women's work shows the impact the entry of women in such large numbers had on political discourse.

6

"VERITABLE PRISONERS OF THEIR SEX"

GENDER AND RACE IN THE DEBATES OVER WOMEN'S SUFFRAGE

As with the issues of birth control, family allocations, and abortion, widespread concerns regarding gender and race informed the discussion of women's suffrage and the family vote in interwar France. Women, of course, did not gain the vote in France until April 21, 1944, when it was decreed by the provisional government headed by Charles de Gaulle from Algiers.[1] The failure of women to win the vote in the interwar period, or, more accurately, of French politicians to concede it to them, has sparked widespread deliberation among historians. Explanations of this apparent anomaly have run the gamut from examinations of the flawed equality of difference ideology predominant in French feminism of the era,[2] to studies of the indifference or outright hostility of French politicians of various stripes to women's emancipation,[3] to analyses of the masculinism inherent in French republicanism.[4]

This chapter falls largely within the latter two traditions. While interwar relational feminists' arguments were no doubt problematic, as Joan Scott suggests, because of their biological essentialism, it would be ahistorical to expect them to have embraced the iconoclastic Madeleine Pelletier's call for absolute and ungendered equality.[5] It is unfair to castigate feminists such as Radical Cécile Brunschvicg or Socialist-sympathizing Maria Vérone for possessing the mentality of their time, however accurate it might be to point out that their brand of feminism was theoretically problematic. Moreover, "relational feminists"[6] who built their case for women's rights on essentializing conceptions of women as biologically different but equal dominated across the western world, and yet women in other national contexts received the right to vote;[7] hence, the cause of France's delinquency must have been something other than the relational feminism—and corresponding gender conservatism—of French feminists.

Instead, one must look to politics to explain the lateness of women's political emancipation in France. France's politicians, from right to left, failed

French women. Historians have studied the failings of the Socialist Party in this regard,[8] as well as the Communist Party's ultimate shortcomings,[9] and most observers emphasize the obstreperous and dishonorable role of the Radicals, particularly in the Senate,[10] but no one has yet conducted an in-depth organization-by-organization analysis of the arguments for and against women's suffrage.

Such a survey proves revealing. All parties and leagues examined, with the notable exceptions of the Radicals and the Parti populaire français, officially endorsed women's suffrage at some point in the interwar period, yet all parties, without exception, did very little to promote its enactment.[11] So the question is: why was there this dichotomy? Why did French politicians, so often eager to portray themselves as the champions of women's rights, in fact do next to nothing to further the suffragist cause and, in many cases, obstruct that cause whenever possible?

The reasons varied. For one, Scott and Judith Stone seem right to suggest that French republicanism, with its emphasis on the free-thinking male individual as the body politic's key constituent, found it exceedingly difficult to deal with the feminist challenge.[12] This led to the pervasion of a particularly masculine conception of citizenship. In addition, this republican masculinity entailed not just rights but duties: duties that it was believed only men could perform. The French Revolution, after all, brought not only Liberty and Equality, but also Fraternity, which implies brotherly solidarity and the privileging of duties over rights.[13] Herein lay the seeds of the masculine variety of self-abnegation so central to French conceptions of republican citizenship. Women were simply not believed capable of assuming a complete individuality and thus of becoming responsibly masculine citizens. They were, in fact, constrained by their bodies, "veritable prisoners of their sex," as the novelist and performer Sidonie-Gabrielle Colette allegedly put it.[14] This uncertainty about women's suitability for the rigors of republican politics, or, as frequently, certainty about their unsuitability, led to an endless series of suggestions that women needed a period of apprenticeship during which they would be educated in order that they should exercise their suffrage appropriately. Obstructions of this nature were found intermittently across the political spectrum, but most frequently in those parties most closely associated with republicanism, including the Fédération républicaine, the Parti démocrate populaire, the Alliance démocratique, the Radical Party, and, especially by the late 1930s, the Socialist Party.

The notion that, as Fédération républicaine Senator Alexandre Lefas put it, "Duties come before rights"[15] handicapped the feminist agenda. If women wanted to become full citizens, they had to behave as did, at least in theory, male republicans, sacrificing their interests for the Republic. Far too often, women found that this meant shelving their feminist objectives, and especially their demands for the franchise, so that their parties could pursue other supposedly more pressing matters.

Gender played another, even more obvious role. As seen in preceding chapters, all parties and leagues, by the 1930s, agreed that women's proper place was in the home. Women's primary social function, it was believed, was bearing and raising children and caring for their husbands' and families' needs. This was part of the all-pervasive breadwinner ideal, wherein the masculine complement to this traditional femininity was a man who went forth into the workforce to earn his family's keep. With such a conception of gender and family relations, it was thoroughly consistent that French politicians would also believe that the breadwinner should exercise the vote on behalf of his charges, including his wife. It was better a good French woman remain unpolluted by the rough waters of politics: it was her man's responsibility to act for and thus shield her from this heavy burden. A desire to maintain this patriarchal structure in politics underlay both the otherwise curious lack of enthusiasm for women's suffrage among those like Léon Blum and, more clearly, the violent misogyny of people such as Radical senator Raymond Duplantier.

Most obviously, this breadwinner discourse was evident in the campaign for the family vote, which, although it was most prominent on the right, also gained supporters on the left. The family vote was also an issue deeply infused with the anxieties about racial and national regeneration discussed above. In giving the breadwinner more power, it was thought, men would be encouraged to have more children. But race also permeated discussions of women's suffrage more generally: as men worried that politically emancipated women might not make the best of wives, so too they fretted that women's suffrage would drive the final nail into the French race's proverbial coffin. Women who voted, many French politicians felt, would have fewer babies and thus bring disaster.

More crassly political considerations also played their part. Most famously, members of the Radical Party, and, it should be said, the Socialist Party, believed that women would be more likely to vote for the right due to their greater religiosity compared to men. The Church, it was claimed, would use its influence over infantile women voters to fill the Chamber of Deputies and the Senate with antirepublican men of the right and thereby destroy the Republic. This argument seems so patently fraudulent that one cannot help but question its sincerity. Yet, it was omnipresent, which suggests that, even if for many commentators the specter of a royalist or fascist takeover proved a convenient pretext to deny women the vote, most genuinely perceived in women's suffrage a shift to the right and a concomitant decline in their party's electoral fortunes. Since the Radicals, and to some degree the Socialists, saw themselves as the only true republicans, this led to quixotic and alarmist claims that in the name of republican defense one must oppose women's suffrage.[16] Of course, the authors of the declarations of fidelity to the cause of women's political emancipation found on the right were probably similarly convinced of women's conservatism. This may have colored their thinking as well.

It is also important to note that the proponents of women's suffrage were no more emancipated from gender and race than their opposites. If women's suffrage would be, in the minds of many, a good thing, for example, it was because it would allow French women to be better mothers and thereby improve racial hygiene; or it would permit the extension of feminine maternity to the public realm, where it was assumed that women's influence would have a salubrious effect on a host of social problems, especially "social scourges."[17] In other words, race and gender determined and framed the interwar debates on women's and familial suffrage no matter the discussant's perspective.

Finally, as on other issues, the preponderance of women's voices in the debate over women's suffrage is noteworthy. In all, there are thirty-nine different women or groups of women cited in this chapter, and there are many more whose voices were recorded as part of the research. It is thus certainly the case that women engaged in this debate disproportionately in their respective parties and leagues. What they said varied widely. Some raised distinct voices, pushed for women's suffrage, and urged their organizations to be proactive in its pursuit; some used their position as women to oppose women's suffrage; and some joined the discussion but offered commentary that differed little from their male counterparts. Regardless of what they said, however, women shaped the debate over women's suffrage in diverse ways and demonstrated their agency in so doing.

THE CASE FOR WOMEN'S SUFFRAGE

As mentioned above, all the parties, with the exception of the Radicals and the Parti populaire français, endorsed women's suffrage. Jules Guesde's Workers' Party, the forerunner to the Socialist Party, first included women's suffrage as part of its program in 1879,[18] and as early as the 1910–14 period, eighty-five of 103 Socialist deputies consistently supported the suffragists' cause.[19] The Communists could claim a share of this heritage and offered their support for the enfranchisement of women from the Communist Party's inception in late 1920.[20] The Radicals, while they never adopted women's suffrage as part of their platform, could boast several of its most prominent proponents among their ranks, including Cécile Brunschvicg, the head of the French Union for Women's Suffrage, and Senator Louis Martin. The Alliance démocratique included strong language in its founding manifesto in support of women voting and could point to the fact that its leader, Pierre-Étienne Flandin, had reported favorably in 1919 for the Chamber of Deputies' commission on universal suffrage on women receiving the municipal vote (Flandin claimed that he had recommended a gradual emancipation of women in order to get the bill past the Senate).[21] The Parti démocrate populaire was less forceful, but equally unequivocal at its founding congress.[22] Fédération républicaine chief Louis Marin had perhaps the most solid pro-suffrage credentials of any of the party leaders, having been a champion of the cause since the 1910s.[23] Moreover, the Fédération contained other key figures calling for the enfranchisement of French women, and it included an appeal for women's suffrage in its official program from 1928 onward.[24] The fascist groups were less enamored of the notion of women casting ballots, due, undoubtedly, to their rigidifying gender politics and their general distaste for democracy. The Croix de feu supported women voting in municipal elections as a precursor to their complete emancipation, but only if this measure was accompanied by the family vote.[25] The movement for the most part, however, simply ignored the issue; debates of it were largely absent from *Le Flambeau*'s pages.[26] The Parti populaire français, meanwhile, did not include women's suffrage among its initial aims,[27] and it also largely disregarded the issue, declaring itself neither for nor against it. The attitude of the party, however, might have been best encapsulated by Yves Dautun's idealized interviewee, Claudine, who labeled suffragists "ridiculous" and "odious."[28] Despite this lack of enthusiasm on the extreme right, however, what is remarkable, considering the failure to legislate the measure, is the widespread and bipartisan support that women's suffrage apparently enjoyed. Correspondingly, there was no shortage of arguments in favor of it.

Despite the justifiably jaundiced view adopted by most historians of the left's handling of the suffrage issue, at times leftists, particularly Communists and Socialists, did make forceful cases in favor of women's enfranchisement. It was, after all, Socialist Alexandre Bracke who brought forward the bill, adopted by the Chamber of Deputies in 1919, rejecting Flandin's measure to give women the municipal vote and granting them instead full and equal political status. By any measure, Bracke's speech in support of his motion was impassioned and reasoned, if somewhat brief,[29] and the Socialist deputies voted for his successful motion.[30] This first attempt at enfranchising women in the interwar period, however, was crushed by the Senate's refusal in 1922, by 156 votes to 131, to even consider it (though the senators did, in fact, discuss the issue at length before reaching this decision).[31] Sadly, this was the closest that the Third Republic ever came to achieving truly universal adult suffrage.

Bracke's enthusiasm was not entirely disinterested. As he himself had said a couple of months earlier, given that the parties of the extremes were the most enthusiastic about and adept at organizing women, it was natural for the Socialists (this was prior to the split at Tours) to expect female voters to support them at the expense of the centrist Radicals. The lesson for the Socialist Party, Bracke said, was to be energetic in both the recruitment of women and the pursuit of their suffrage.[32]

This argument of Bracke's typified one strand among women's suffrage's supporters: many believed on both the left and the right that women would vote disproportionately for their party and championed the measure accordingly. This was, of course, self-interested and in total contradiction to the widespread espousal of selflessness and bipartisanship, but then, it was no doubt felt best not to be too rigid in the interpretation and application of this ethos. Socialist Annette Charreau, for instance, pointedly outlined the favorable results of the British Labour Party's efforts at organizing women.[33] Ferdinand Buisson, in fact, offered a variation on this theme in 1910 when he filed his 275-page report to the Chamber recommending the deputies pass a bill on women's suffrage. Buisson sought to reassure those fearful of the Catholic menace by cataloging at length the number of prominent women since 1789 who had worked in the service of the Republic.[34] In other words,

Buisson suggested, women made good republicans and could be trusted with the vote. As Socialist Rachel Lempereur declared, "Women will vote, and they will vote Socialist."[35]

The right, with more realistic hopes than the left of gaining at the ballot box from women's involvement, was understandably circumspect: one searches in vain for an explicit statement that a right-wing party backed women's suffrage because it sought a boost to its electoral fortunes. No one wanted to give fodder to those opposed to women's suffrage because of the supposed counter-revolutionary threat. What one does find, in contrast, are a plethora of assurances that women's enfranchisement would herald the realization of cherished right-wing goals. As Germaine Chapuis of the Parti démocrate populaire put it, for instance, women's suffrage would prove a happy development for "the destiny of the family."[36] Marcel Petitjean of the Fédération républicaine, in fact, highlighted the frustration of the party's agenda as one of the primary reasons to extend the suffrage to women, implying, thereby, that, were women allowed to vote, this agenda would be enacted.[37] Blanche Lescouvé assured her Fédération républicaine readership that as voters, women would "exercise the happiest influence on the life of our country. [We will] defend [our] familial, social, and national ideal."[38] Likewise, a Croix de feu propagandist mentioned a desire to combat the Communist threat as his primary motivation for joining the Parti social français and then called for the enactment of women's suffrage, the family vote, and the obligatory vote as though he thought these measures would stem the red tide.[39] Yvonne Foinant of the Alliance démocratique, meanwhile, suggested in 1936 that the Popular Front was alienating French mothers with its inflationary policies and declared this all the more reason why women should be given the vote: in order that they be able to help remove the Blum government from office.[40] André Tardieu, thoroughly antidemocratic by the late 1930s, also felt that women would further the right's agenda. As he stipulated, "If [the two houses of parliament] wanted a truly loyal regime, they would enact, in addition to proportional representation: 1) women's vote 2) the family vote of the father for his children 3) the obligatory vote."[41] Nor was Tardieu the only figure of questionable republican sympathies to hint at women's right-wing proclivities. Ramon Fernandez of the Parti populaire français informed his readers that French women were flocking to the party in droves, a fact he felt boded well for the party in the event of their enfranchisement.[42] Perhaps Fédération républicaine deputy L. Camuzet came closest to an avowal of the self-interest of the right with regard to women's suffrage when he wrote that "women are generally attached to order, to respect for the family and property, and to the national spirit."[43] In short, it is not too cynical to claim that while democratic and egalitarian principles influenced many right-wing commentators' thinking, a measure of partisan self-interest also had an impact.

The argument that an idealist would hope to find, that women should be given the vote because it was just, long overdue, and in keeping with republican traditions, appeared on both the left and the right. Buisson, to his credit, made these points in his 1910 treatise,[44] and other leftists followed his lead thereafter. It must be said, however, that these principled arguments came more consistently from leftist women than men. Marthe Bigot, for instance, declared in 1919 that it was the Socialist Party's "duty" to affirm once and for all its unequivocal support for women's enfranchisement as a question of justice.[45] Using similar language in 1925, Socialist Jeanne Mureine argued that women's suffrage was a matter of "justice" and chided France's politicians for producing a seemingly never-ending stream of spurious objections to it.[46] Echoing Mureine, Fanny Clar likewise declared herself tired of French men's "pretexts" for allowing the "injustice" of women's disenfranchisement to continue.[47] Some men also emphasized these themes. For instance, Radical senator Louis Martin, the most consistent champion of women's suffrage in the upper chamber until his defeat in 1935, constantly emphasized that principle, conscience, and fairness demanded the extension of the franchise.[48] Similarly, Louis Andrieux, the Radical and *doyen d'âge* in 1924 in the Chamber of Deputies, said that he refused to allow the need for a bill for women's suffrage, a "law of justice," to go unremembered,[49] and Flandin, as if not to let the right be outdone, declared moving toward a truly universal suffrage an "oeuvre of justice" in 1918.[50] In other words, some suitably principled language was uttered regarding women's emancipation, and there were some who defined the issue as a question of individual rights.

Over time, as, to the surprise of most observers, women's suffrage remained a promise unfulfilled, a series of more detailed and revealing arguments developed in favor of women's suffrage. These were more visibly gendered than those discussed above. For example, commentators of all political persuasions proclaimed that, as women now worked outside the home in sizable numbers, they ought to be allowed to have a say in the direction of the country. That this line of reasoning both mistakenly assumed that women's participation in the workforce was a new phenomenon engendered by the war—when, in fact, France had long led the industrialized world in rates of female gainful employment[51]—and implied that women who remained in the home, those oft-celebrated paragons of femininity, were somehow less deserving of the vote than their working counterparts does not seem to have occurred to most commentators.[52] Germaine Chapuis of the Parti démocrate populaire, for instance, listed women's increasing participation in the workforce among her reasons to enact women's suffrage.[53] Likewise, Fédération républicaine observer Jean Corbière explained that as, out of necessity, women were undertaking paid labor they "had professional interests to defend" and thus required the franchise.[54] In the Alliance démocratique Yvonne Foinant gave her 1934 report on the status of women's work and noted the absurdity of the fact that 37 percent of French women worked outside the home and yet were denied a political voice.[55] It is possible that the appearance of this argument on the right reflected the class biases of the right-wing parties. As Linda Clark makes clear, for example, professional women made significant inroads into previously male preserves in the interwar period;[56] perhaps such women evoked more sympathy from the right than working-class women toiling in factories who had been more typical pre–World War I.

While the left was absent the class bias found on the right, the logic that women worked and therefore should be able to vote was similarly prevalent. Socialist Cypriane Fel, for example, decried the inability of working women to defend their interests via the ballot box and stated that the development of the modern capitalist economy necessitated their inclusion in the body politic.[57] Even Communists repeated this problematic trope. "Angelica" of *L'Ouvrière* railed that it was particularly unjust that women be denied the vote given there were, she claimed, 3,500,000 women now in the workforce who earned wages and paid taxes,[58] and Marcel Cachin finished a detailed analysis of women in the workforce by concluding that, as they now worked in significant numbers, they needed the franchise.[59] One cannot but question the force of this particular argument—that women needed to vote because they worked—given that, as seen in previous chapters, commentators of diverse politics held, especially by the mid-1930s, that women's proper place was in the home as auxiliaries to their men. If only women who worked truly needed the vote, and if the predominant desire of French politicians was to eliminate the need for women's employment, then one must assume that, if French politicians felt they could be successful in returning France to that imagined time when hardworking male breadwinners supported their families unaided by their wives, they must have thought the need for women's suffrage was not altogether pressing. At the very least, commentators like Cachin seem to have thought women's voting an evil born of necessity and not principle. Furthermore, this particular argument for women's suffrage reveals the degree to which conceptions of citizenship commingled with the breadwinner ideal and therefore masculinity. It was apparently in becoming more like breadwinners, in assuming the masculine role of wage earning, that women took the first step toward citizenship.

Breadwinning was one of the duties of the French citizen. Another duty was serving one's country in wartime, and this provided the grounds for an additional argument in favor of women's enfranchisement: that French women had done their duty to the nation during World War I and thus deserved the vote. Jules Siegfried made this case most forcefully in 1919. Siegfried, the husband of feminist Julie Siegfried and the father of famed political geographer André Siegfried, was a republican conservative and member of the Alliance républicaine et démocratique, who had proven his fealty to the Republic by his defense of Dreyfus. An octogenarian by the end of the war, Siegfried was the interwar Chamber of Deputies' first doyen d'âge. He used the occasion of his speech to the Chamber to make the case for women's suffrage:

> France showed what she is capable of during the war; our men, on the front, by their qualities of intelligence, sacrifice, and energy, have won the world's admiration; our women too, in their way, were on the front, in giving without faltering what they cherished most to the fatherland.
>
> Everywhere they replaced men who had left for the war and showed by their endurance and other faculties aroused by tragic circumstances that the hour has sounded to integrate them, in a definitive fashion, in public life by placing the ballot in their hands.[60]

In other words, women had lived up to that third component of the republican triad: fraternity. They had done their duty to France and thus proven worthy of citizenship.

Once again, this logic was one found across the political spectrum. Siegfried, a man of the center-right, may have set the tune, but conservatives joined with leftists in singing along. Radical senator Fernand Merlin, for example, evoked women's contribution to the war effort in rebutting fellow Radical Alexandre Bérard's condemnation of women's suffrage in 1922.[61] Ultraconservative Marie Maugeret, meanwhile, also highlighted women's war service as a reason for their inclusion in politics and, remarking on the bipartisan nature of her argument, added that "even" the Socialists agreed with her on this point.[62] Indeed they did. Pierre Picard, for example, attacked a proposition to give only war widows the vote on the grounds that all women had done their duty during the war and thus all merited the suffrage.[63] The Communists, understandably, given their vehement denunciations of the war effort in the 1920s, did not use this line of reasoning, but they did offer a variation of it. Marguerite Faussecave, for example, in a typical Communist piece celebrating the emancipation of women in the Soviet Union, carefully pointed out that women had been on the frontlines during the October Revolution and thus were justly rewarded by Lenin following its success.[64] This story line was in fact repeated most years around the anniversary of the Bolsheviks' seizure of power.[65] In the Communist lexicon, in other words, the Revolution displaced the war in the narrative of women's deliverance, but it was still in assuming manly responsibilities that women proved their merit and thus established that they warranted full political inclusion.

Another argument that proponents of women's suffrage advanced along bipartisan lines was an answer to one of the principal objections to their enfranchisement. Opponents often claimed that women were unprepared for the vote and that they would not, therefore, cast their ballots responsibly. To answer this infantilizing and patronizing charge, sponsors of the measure countered that, in fact, women were well prepared for the vote and, if anything, more likely than men to be sensible in its exercise. Again, this was a gendered discourse. Behaving responsibly was required of breadwinners, who had to remember that they acted not just for themselves but for the collective good of their families and society. This was a masculine "duty," much like serving in wartime, that accompanied the rights granted to French citizens during the French Revolution. Thus, women had to be shown to be suitably responsible before they could be trusted with the vote. Catholic feminist Adrienne Cambry pursued this line in her "Letter to an Elector" in 1925, as she pointed out that it was incongruous that republican men claimed women lacked the needed gravitas to acquire citizenship yet, at the same time, lauded their wives for their ability to organize and manage the home.[66] Similarly, Alliance démocratique sympathizer and the president of the Feminine Union of Liberal and Commercial Career Women, Marcelle Genetelli, insisted that if women could run businesses competently surely they could be trusted at the polls.[67] This was, in fact, a running theme in the *Alliance,* once again reflecting the middle- and upper-class clientele of the party, as Yvonne Foinant, a businesswoman herself, consistently drew attention to women's commercial successes and outlined the implication that women were clearly ready to conduct themselves maturely in politics. In fact, in a 1934 piece, she urged businesswomen to vote in the Commerce Tribunal elections of that year as was their right, telling them, "Women, do your duty as electors."[68]

This sort of logic was not as foreign to left-wing circles as one might imagine. While Radicals, Communists, and Socialists did not, certainly, hold aloft businesswomen in the manner of the *Alliance démocratique,* they did try to play up, when in favor of women's suffrage, women's preparedness for the vote. Radical Éliane Brault offered a sterling example of this tendency in 1932 when she pointed out that suffragists' adult comportment in the gallery during the Senate debates on women's suffrage that year showed their readiness for the vote: "Conscious of the grave hours that the country is enduring, the listeners have shown through their calm and their irreproachable conduct that they share the government's preoccupations. Even though their feminine sensibility was put to a tough test, they did not permit themselves any demonstration."[69] In other words, Brault suggested, women had learned their lesson and would not be repeating the apparently shameful outburst of 1922 when, following the refusal to consider Bracke's bill in the upper house, several suffragists caused a commotion in the gallery resulting in one protester's expulsion,[70] or the 1928 demonstration outside the Luxembourg Palace when Maria Vérone and others were arrested for disturbing public order.[71] Women had grown up and could now enjoy the benefits of adulthood. The Socialist Party too adopted this masculinist discourse of republican "duties" and "responsibilities," and so its pro-suffrage adherents sought to prove women capable in both respects. Marthe Louis-Lévy, for instance, proclaimed, "It is urgent to give our campaigns [for women's suffrage] the sense of their responsibility. This is the only way to prepare our numerous militants, conscious of their duties."[72] A Communist piece in *L'Ouvrière* actually went so far as to suggest that only women who worked, and who had accordingly demonstrated the required sense of responsibility, should be granted the vote. The author was explicit in stating this absurd notion's purpose: to keep bourgeois women, not likely to be Communist supporters, disenfranchised.[73]

Another counter to the argument that women were inherently irresponsible —that they were essentially the "weaker sex"—was to concentrate on other categories of presumed incompetents. Surely, for example, women were no less capable of voting than alcoholics? And yet these exercised the rights of citizenship while women did not. Radical Léon Accambray, for instance, opposed Henri Roulleaux-Dugage's proposal in 1923 to append a proposal for the family vote onto the bill for women's suffrage in municipal elections on the grounds that "fathers of families can be alcoholics"; therefore, he felt it would be counterproductive to jeopardize perfectly healthy women's chances of winning the vote by simultaneously proposing that these degenerate men cast multiple ballots.[74] Likewise, Socialist Louise Brunet, in reporting on a feminist meeting in Paris's nineteenth arrondissement, recorded that "everyone was agreed that France, the home of civilization, cannot permit any longer that the alcoholic and half-crazy votes weigh in the national balance for or against peace, while the opinions of educated and intelligent women, of all the mothers of French families, are rejected concerning the essential questions that touch on the vitality and the greatness of the country."[75] *La Nation* ran a piece claiming to understand women's frustration at having to endure the "inarticulate cries" of some male electors: "You . . . are indignant, at once at the weakness of the tranquil mass of men and at the bestiality that reveals itself, so promptly and odiously, in the souls of poor men made tipsy by alcohol or hatred." How absurd that such men should vote while women could not, implied the author.[76] It was, however, perhaps André Gide who provided the most poignant rebuttal to those who posited women's biologically defined incapability: "The less intelligent a man is, the stupider women seem to him."[77]

Somewhat less provocatively, backers of women's suffrage frequently sought to demonstrate that women had voted elsewhere without negative effect. This tradition, in fact, had its genesis in Buisson's seminal 1910 report, where he devoted no fewer than 113 pages to the evolution of women's rights and political emancipation in countries as diverse as Bulgaria and Canada in an attempt to shame French politicians at the realization that France, the proud guarantor of European republicanism, was lagging behind in the fight to liberate women.[78] Given that Buisson's report was never discussed in the Chamber and that women's suffrage did not get its hearing until 1919, one must assume that a sense of shame was not especially widespread among French deputies. Still, others perpetuated his tactic. Marguerite de Witt-Schlumberger, for instance, the president of the French Union for Women's Suffrage, pursued this line in a 1919 epistle, as did Cécile Brunschvicg, who lamented that "it is humiliating to think that French women—daughters of the country of the Revolution and the Declaration of the Rights of Man—in the year 1919 of our grace are still reduced to asking for 'the rights of woman.'"[79] Similarly, Louis Martin, in his prolonged 1922 plea for women's suffrage, claimed that France's international reputation was suffering due to the senators' reluctance and the nation's resultant tardiness to render French women as full citizens,[80] and Radical feminist Germaine Malaterre-Sellier lamented that France stood far behind India and even Fascist Italy in its enfranchisement of women.[81] The Communist Party, of course, prior to the Popular Front reveled in France's delinquency. Ultra-leftist Suzanne Girault, for example, who had been for all intents and purposes the party's second-in-command from 1923 to 1925,[82] exulted that "in most of the countries of Europe, the bourgeoisie has conceded this terrain. In France, the question is still unresolved. Our country of so-called democracy finds itself neck and neck with the most backward countries in this domain as in so many others."[83] But this was a peculiarly Communist tendency; much more common were articles of the type run by *Le Populaire* in 1923 that disparaged France's record next to Germany's regarding women's suffrage, intending, like Buisson, to inspire French men to embrace the reform.[84] The choice of Germany as a comparator was not accidental. Not only did the Weimar constitution grant women the suffrage on an equal basis to men, but the notion that Germany, the country of Prussian militarism and authoritarianism, was more advanced democratically than republican France was well-designed to offend most French men's sensibilities.

Apostles of women's suffrage also used more positive but obviously gendered claims to make their case. One such was a consistent assertion that endowing women with the vote would further the cause of peace. This was consonant with the image of women-as-mothers who inclined naturally to pacifism. Being mothers, it was assumed, French women would naturally pursue peace to save their sons from being slaughtered in a rerun of 1914–18. Thus, their inclusion in the body politic could literally be the difference between life and death for hundreds of thousands of French men. Radical Party feminist Yvonne Netter, for example, rejoiced in the high rate among female students of participation in the pacifist movement and claimed that it was to serve the nation by battling for peace and disarmament that these young women wanted the vote.[85] The Group of Socialist Women, meanwhile, assigned new secretary Suzanne Buisson to organize a propaganda campaign to push for peace and the suffrage in 1930, as though the two were somehow linked.[86] Parti démocrate populaire secretary Jean Raymond-Laurent likewise insisted that "the day after a war that left so many French homes in grief" was the perfect moment to embrace women's suffrage and thereby avoid a recurrence of armed conflict.[87] The Catholic politician sounded remarkably similar to an author at *L'Humanité* who informed women that "they would have to unite with their companions . . . against the murderous [French] wars of Syria and Morocco . . . [and] for the conquest of women's political rights."[88] Even the Parti populaire français, which never endorsed women's suffrage, used the same line of reasoning to explain its women's political involvement: they joined the party in order to help Jacques Doriot preserve European peace.[89]

Equally consistent with the hegemonic conception of femininity shared, in the mid-1930s, by all political factions, was the line of reasoning that women should be enfranchised because, once empowered with the vote, they could more ably combat "social scourges." Thus, suffrage was seen as the means through which women could best exert their specifically feminine and maternal influence for the betterment of the nation and race. This was consistent with relational feminism, which sought to lay claim to rights for women based on their biological difference, especially on women's maternity and unique motherly qualities.[90] Veteran Fédération républicaine president Auguste Isaac's defense of women's suffrage and the family vote in the Chamber of Deputies in 1923 epitomized this tendency: "The right to suffrage that has been given to them in other countries has provided women the means to obtain very useful reforms in the domains of hygiene and morality. It has permitted them to struggle effectively against certain scourges, certain abuses, to bring an end, notably, to the intolerable situation of women who are victims of their alcoholic husbands."[91] Thus, women's suffrage would benefit the French race and society, and not women alone. It was, therefore, worthy of enactment. In this logic, Isaac echoed Louis Martin, who a year and a half earlier had staked women's claim to the vote on the grounds that armed with it, they could help eradicate "tuberculosis, alcoholism, syphilis, prostitution, [and] the infections of slums."[92] Indeed, women's suffrage was seen as a panacea by its proponents. Voting women were conjectured as purifying angels who would descend from the heavens and cleanse France of its ills. In 1919 French Socialist women, for example, making their case for an "International Charter of Women," akin to the Charter of Work, stated the following: "Creators, educators, protectors of the race; enemies by nature of violence; . . . women will know how to struggle against social ills: pauperism, debauchery, prostitution, syphilis, tuberculosis, war."[93] This racialist concern and conviction that women were the guarantors of racial hygiene was equally apparent in Siegfried's famous address that same year. Stating that women could help their men in facing up to the many duties confronting them in the postwar era, Siegfried pronounced, "Among these duties the struggle against alcoholism, this internal enemy that we must vanquish at all costs, stands in the first rank, because it means discord in the home, the compromising of the race, this beautiful French race that we must revivify and multiply in the physical as in the intellectual and moral orders."[94] As Germaine Chapuis asked, if women were given the vote, would they not "change plenty of things? In doing so, would they not serve with the same blow the family and the entire race?"[95]

THE CASE AGAINST WOMEN'S SUFFRAGE

While the case for women's suffrage was evidently racialized and gender-specific, the case against it was no different. That said, far and away the most frequent objection to women's voting, and one that was specific to the left, was more purely political in nature. Republicans, and especially members of the Radical Party, feared that as women attended church more faithfully than men, the Catholic Church would be able to use its influence on women voters to elect antirepublicans to the Chamber of Deputies and so initiate the downfall of the Republic. This argument was prominent in the Senate's three discussions of and refusals to consider bills for women's suffrage in 1922, 1929, and 1932, and it could plausibly be fingered as the primary reason for the Senate's obstructionism. Radical senator Alexandre Bérard, for instance, an ardent opponent of women's suffrage and the reporter for the commission on universal suffrage in 1922, outlined his many reservations and placed the specter of the Catholic Church acting through ill-prepared women at the forefront.[96] Senator François Labrousse, who, like Bérard, evinced a marked misogyny, echoed this concern.[97] In 1932, Louis Tissier again conjured up the Catholic menace,[98] as did René Héry, the reporter on this occasion,[99] and Armand Calmel.[100]

But it was not only Radical senators who made this argument. Indeed, the Ligue des droits de l'homme, dominated by Radicals in the 1920s but increasingly by Socialists in the 1930s, offered only token gestures in support of women's suffrage. That the league's thinking was tempered by fears of the Catholic menace was evident, as in 1935 when Suzanne Collette and Odette René-Bloch, the only two women on the league's forty-eight-member central committee, wondered why so little had been done of late for women's suffrage and were treated to angry and patronizing discourses on how the league had always been women's greatest champions and how the moment was inopportune to enfranchise women.[101] In other words, the men of the central committee, erstwhile champions of human rights, wanted to deny women the vote because they were afraid of whom they would vote for. This should not have taken Collette or René-Bloch by surprise. In 1929 Victor Basch, the league's president after 1926 and a prominent member of the Socialist Party, wrote a column for *La Volonté* ostensibly in favor of women's political emancipation. Toward the end of the article, however, readers found him identifying the influence of Catholicism on French women and their expected right-wing leanings as voters, as the primary reason behind women's failure to gain the vote:

> There is the crux of the problem. One must admit that it is not easy to dismiss.
>
> I am one of those, it is well known, who are passionately attached to the primacy of secular power over spiritual power and who are profoundly convinced that secular schools, the only schools of tolerance, are the foundation upon which all democratic republics rest. And I am also one of those who believe that it is possible that the granting of suffrage to women will lead to right-wing majorities whose first move, in effect, will be to destroy the secular education system.[102]

Basch then proceeded to explain that this was why he supported only a gradual process of incorporating women into the body politic, a position adopted by the league in 1924. Not only was this in contradiction with the league's universalist principles, but the 1924 resolution was actually a retreat from positions adopted in the prewar period.[103] Given this fact, it was more than a little disingenuous of league secretary Henri Guernut to call on the Senate to be "wise" in 1932 and give women the municipal vote. Particularly nervy was that Guernut presented this as a compromise between principled proponents of women's suffrage like himself and those afraid of the chimera of a Catholic resurgence through women's ballots.[104]

Indeed, leftist women allowed at times that there was some force to this concern. J. Christin, for instance, the woman principal of the École Xavier-Jouvin in Grenoble, while arguing vehemently for the vote, confessed that the Catholic menace was a legitimate worry although she did blame republican men for this because they did not send their daughters to secular schools.[105] According to *La Lumière* in 1935, in fact, republican feminists recognized the danger to the Republic and accordingly agreed with their male leaders that the postponement of their goals was for the best.[106] Socialist Berthe Fouchère followed leader Léon Blum,[107] when she admitted that women's Catholicism was a problem and agitated for more political education for women prior to their being given the suffrage.[108] In fact, the Socialist Party's record as a whole on women's suffrage was barely more respectable than the Radicals'. In 1932, only five of nine Socialist senators voted in favor of women voting despite the party's official position.[109] As a retired civil servant wrote to Flandin in 1917, women's suffrage would "lead surely *to the death of the Republic*":[110] this thinking no doubt influenced leftist women as it did men, if somewhat less consistently. Gabrielle Esther Moyse, then the president of the Group of Radical-Socialist Women, wrote Flandin in 1917: "It would be *criminal* to talk about the feminine vote before the end of the war."[111] Best to postpone the discussion for another, undetermined time.

So the Socialists and the Radicals had, on the whole, undistinguished records regarding women's suffrage. What about the Communists? Were they also afraid of the Catholic menace? Their record, in fact, mirrored the familiar interwar Communist evolution. While as early as 1924, there were signs that the Communists were not entirely pleased at the prospect of women voting due to their perceived reactionary tendencies,[112] from 1921 to roughly 1934, the Communists were generally uncompromising in their support for women's suffrage, with the important caveat that women would not truly be emancipated until the coming Communist revolution. However, with the adoption of the Popular Front strategy and the ensuing embrace of republicanism, the Communists, both because of their wish not to agitate the Radicals and because they adopted wholeheartedly the traditional gender politics that had long been present in the party, abandoned the suffragists.[113] Accordingly, the Popular Front program made no mention of women's suffrage.[114] Léon Blum ignored the issue in his first speech as premier in the Chamber, which was all the more noteworthy as he was quite detailed and explicit regarding other planned reforms,[115] and Blum, with Communist support, tried to buy the feminists' acquiescence by his appointment of three women as deputy ministers. Moreover, when the final Third Republican bill for women's suffrage passed in the Chamber by a vote of 409 to 0, Blum's entire cabinet was to be found among the ninety-four deputies who abstained.[116]

Of course, the threat of Catholic reaction was not women's suffrage's opponents' only complaint. Like their opposites who claimed that women were sufficiently mature to exercise the vote responsibly, women's suffrage's detractors subscribed to a masculinist vision of citizenship, except that they believed that women could not live up to their ideal, that they were, in fact, inherently irrational, irresponsible, and immature. This represented an infantilization of women that cast them as childlike and incapable of fully formed individuality. Pierre-Étienne Flandin in fact, that self-advertised champion of women's suffrage, revealed his own suspicions regarding women's suitability and preparedness in 1919 in the Chamber, when, in response to Louis Andrieux, who had debunked the notion that women should begin with the municipal vote by stating that there were plenty of men who were not necessarily ideal voters either, he exclaimed, "Mr. Andrieux has denounced male voters as too frequently ignorant. But is this a reason to aggravate the harm and to double it with ignorant female voters?"[117] Conservative Edmond Lefebvre du Prey,[118] who later also opposed women's suffrage as a senator,[119] was even more unequivocal in his opposition. First, he outlined that there were jobs, such as nursing, which called for feminine qualities like nurturing and care giving and masculine equivalents that required mental or physical rigor. Then he reminded his listeners that while women had assumed male work during the war, that had been an unnatural state of affairs necessitated by circumstances; and did they not, he queried, remember how tired French women had seemed as a result? Finally, he concluded this portion of his address by stating that "from the physical point of view, a woman's inferiority is incontestable. Her nature does not permit her to undertake the exercise of functions destined to last too long. Her intelligence, however lively it might be, is not oriented in the same fashion as a man's."[120] In short, women were by nature unable to be full citizens.

This argument, moreover, reappeared in various forms throughout the interwar period. It was, it should be noted, the domain of open opponents to the reform and therefore did not find its way into the Socialist or Communist presses, which is not to say that Socialist or Communist foes of the measure did not subscribe to this line of thinking. Radicals, on the other hand, could give free reign to their prejudices. Georges Ponsot, for example, the influential editorialist at *L'Ère nouvelle,* wrote a few columns in the early 1920s in support of women's suffrage,[121] but by 1925 he was emerging as a determined adversary of the measure. In March 1925, a Ponsot article appeared that worried about the Catholic menace, "We must, claim the feminists, liberate her [woman] from the hands of her husband. Evidently, in order to put her in the hands of the priest."[122] This signaled a sea change not only in Ponsot's outlook but also in *L'Ère nouvelle*'s more generally. Ponsot's analysis, such as it was, of the reactionary Paul von Hindenburg's election as president of the Weimar Republic amounted to a denunciation of the childish women voters whom he labeled responsible for the field marshal's success. Ponsot believed that women were totally incapable of rational action and that, essentially, they had been wowed by Hindenburg's military uniform:

> Women have shown, one more time, that they are deprived of all political sense and that they make determinations in their political activities according to the lightness of their spirit.
>
> Women like war and warriors, panache, whistling fifes, beating tambourines, military stripes, old military stripes like those of the marshal, decorations, parades of goose-stepping soldiers, revenge, eternal revenge (until all countries are vanquished, including the victors who are ruined); women love a military man, the general in a cavalry uniform on a black horse.[123]

It seems that Ponsot did not subscribe to the dominant perception of women as naturally pacifist. On the contrary, he viewed them as starry-eyed and vacuous beings, easily led down the proverbial garden path. Male voters would have been more discerning, apparently, even though millions of men had voted for Hindenburg as well.

Jean Ernest-Charles, another Radical who wrote for *L'Ère nouvelle,* agreed unreservedly with Ponsot. He felt that feminists did not deserve the vote as they seemed too obsessed with their own desires and not the good of the Republic. Only when they evinced the citizenly virtue of self-abnegation in the service of Marianne would their claims to the vote merit attention.[124] In the 1930s, "Norpois," who wrote for the "Our Echoes" section, which resembled the *faits divers* of other publications, took up this mantle at *L'Ère nouvelle.* Over the years, Norpois asserted variously that irresponsible women voters had brought Hitler to power,[125] that women did not elect each other as their representatives in countries where they exercised the franchise and therefore, clearly, they recognized their own unsuitability for public office,[126] that women should realize that if they got the vote they would have to accept being eligible for capital punishment like other citizens (he made this point twice),[127] that suffragists had shown themselves ill-equipped for the vote through their irresponsible demonstrations in and around the Senate,[128] that women were too impressionable and would vote for the Communists,[129] and that none other than Queen Victoria of England had opposed feminism as dangerous for democracy.[130] The "new era" at *L'Ère nouvelle* was apparently not going to include female electors. Put together, this hodgepodge of objections amounted to a coherent critique of women as unable to meet the standards of French citizenship. Women were simply too frail, too impressionable, and too inept to vote. Herein lay the trap, or paradox as Scott would define it, of relational feminism. By admitting that women were different, relational feminists opened the door to claims of women's inherent inferiority or unsuitability for the franchise.[131]

It was in answer to such concerns that the various proposals for a gradual emancipation of women appeared. It was thought that this would ease men's anxieties about the potential toppling of the Republic through female ballots. Only after women had shown themselves trustworthy at the municipal level for an indeterminate amount of time would they then be allowed to vote in national elections. This, for example, was Flandin's logic in 1919,[132] Victor Basch's in 1929,[133] and while it was not explicitly Louis Marin's rationale as he proposed women be given the municipal vote in 1924 for the 1925 elections, many who rallied to his cause did point out the advantages to this gradual approach.[134] The municipal vote would, it was hoped, provide unskilled women voters with a necessary apprenticeship. In one Radical deputy's words, "Frenchwomen must prepare themselves progressively in the exercise of political rights."[135]

Put otherwise, women had to prove themselves capable of the citizen's duties before receiving "his" rights. They had to demonstrate, in particular, sufficient selflessness in order to merit the vote. This allowed French politicians to label feminists, in particular, as unfit for citizenship if they pressed their "selfish" agenda too hard. In turn, male leaders urged their parties' women to subordinate and postpone their ambitions in the name and tradition of republican defense. During the height of the Popular Front interlude, for example, *L'Alliance démocratique* published a call for women to join the party; however, about midway through, readers found the following passage: "But the *Alliance* could never forget that you mean to place *the general interest of France* ahead of your own properly feminine aspirations."[136] The message was that women should, in order to prove themselves worthy of their male forebears such as the defenders of Captain Dreyfus, for the time being set aside their own desires for the greater good.[137]

One noteworthy Radical Party variation on the appraisal of women as unsuitable voters was that they could not perform the duties of citizenship: namely, women could not serve in the military, which was compulsory for all men. It was this claim that women's suffrage's proponents tried to counter, as shown above, by pointing to women's wartime service. Ponsot raised this objection several times. He was particularly fond of mocking the suffragists for not demanding this "duty" as they demanded their political "rights."[138] Senator Hugues Le Roux likewise listed this among his objections in 1922.[139] Jean Corbière of the Fédération républicaine, in fact, named Radicals Charles Régismanset, whose misogyny was explored in chapter 5, Alexandre Bérard, François Labrousse, René Héry, and Louis Tissier as all forwarding this "stupid argument."[140] Stupid it may have been given that the exclusion of women from military service rested upon the same gendered prejudices as those that kept them from voting, but it was nonetheless consistent with the French tradition whereby the rights of citizenship were conditional upon attendant duties.

Another popular adaptation of this line of reasoning that women were not suited for the franchise was to claim that the majority of women did not actually want to vote. Once again, this tactic had a long pedigree: Lefebvre du Prey dwelled on it at some length in 1919, for instance, insisting that were a referendum held inquiring after French women's attitudes it would show them largely hostile to their own enfranchisement.[141] Alexandre Bérard parroted this view in 1922, stating simply, "The immense majority of Frenchwomen themselves would return the present that some want to give them. The women of France do not want the ballot."[142] *L'Ère nouvelle* contributor Charles-Henry repeated this mantra in 1925,[143] as did Tissier in the Senate in 1932.[144] Feminists and their supporters, in fact, expended considerable effort to rebut this allegation, thereby demonstrating its pervasiveness and power, writing articles repudiating it;[145] they organized opinion polls to demonstrate both that the population at large supported women's suffrage and that women specifically did.[146] The most succinct and elegant response was, however, provided by Socialist deputy (and eugenicist) Armand Charpentier, who actually affirmed that women were largely uninterested in their own emancipation, but queried, "Slaves, beaten down by their enslavement, did not demand their liberty. Was this justification to continue their enslavement?"[147]

Charpentier's language approached Marxist rhetoric about the enslavement of the working class. In fact, there was one particularly Marxist line on women's suffrage, which, if not exactly in opposition to the measure, posited its worthlessness and, therefore, no doubt drained away much-needed support and energy from suffragists' cause. Essentially, Communists until the mid-1930s offered support for women's suffrage but continually asserted its uselessness: true emancipation would come only with the Communist utopia. Charles Rappoport, for instance, offered such reasoning to the readers of *L'Ouvrière.*[148] Indeed *L'Ouvrière,* perhaps seeking to shore up its Communist credentials and guard itself from being labeled a haven for bourgeois feminists,[149] carried such analyses frequently. As Marguerite Michard lectured feminists disillusioned with the two-facedness of French parliamentarians who promised reform and never delivered, "We suggest [a solution] to them that we know is infallible: THE DICTATORSHIP OF THE PROLETARIAT."[150] The Communist Party required its members to follow Louise Bodin's simple dictum: "Feminism? No. Communism? Yes."[151] This subjugation of the feminist agenda within Communist rhetoric contributed to the marginalization of women generally in the party and prepared the ground for the transition to familialism in the 1930s. It does not negate, on the one hand, the fact that the Communists performed some noteworthy services for the suffragist cause, such as putting forward three bills for women's suffrage, in 1924, 1927, and 1928,[152] and fielding women candidates in assorted elections;[153] on the other hand, it does help explicate the limitations of Communist commitment to winning women the vote and the silence of the Popular Front on the issue.

Concern for the future of the race underlay much of the protest against women's political emancipation. In particular, deputies, senators, and others alleged that, were women given the vote, this would force them outside the home and thereby discourage them from having babies. Presumably, although the argument was never well-articulated, these naysayers meant that giving women the franchise would encourage their integration into the public sphere, a process they deemed detrimental to their maternal instincts. The alternative, that they thought French women's leaving their homes for a few hours to vote would cause them to have fewer babies, is ridiculous but nonetheless possible. Whatever the precise logic, these commentators revealed their equation of women with mothers, an equation they shared with relational feminists and most supporters of women's suffrage. A woman's "maternal duty" or "familial duty"[154] was, after all, both a "social duty"[155] and an "imperious" one.[156] To neglect it for the sake of casting a vote would have been the height of selfishness and therefore anathema to the discourse of republican citizenship. In the 1919 discussion in the Chamber, in fact, several of women's suffrage's proponents, including Flandin, Siegfried, and Fernand Merlin, anticipated this line of attack and so sought to preempt it by arguing that voting would, on the contrary, encourage women to procreate as they would feel more secure in the belief that their children would be raised in a just society free from the plague of war (because, of course, women as mothers inclined to pacifism).[157] Nor did these gentlemen's adversaries disappoint. In 1922, Senator François Labrousse complained bitterly of the negative impact of the "blonde revolution" initiated by feminism, stating that it had made maternity a "disagreeable accessory" in women's eyes, that in Sweden where women voted the number of celibate women had caused a "social wound," and that in Oregon the previous year, where women had been voting in state elections since 1913, there had been 980 marriages and 720 divorces. In short, Labrousse concluded, "Women's suffrage would be, in my view, gravely imprudent."[158] Senator Joseph Massabuau agreed with Labrousse and exclaimed, "Women who want the vote know how to do everything except have children!"[159] In 1925, Radical deputy Roger Lafagette expressed the pronatalist anxiety concisely, drawing out the argument a bit further than most of his colleagues. He perceived women's suffrage as one more step toward women's general emancipation, which would lead to them pursuing careers and achieving equality in the workplace instead of focusing on childbearing and rearing: "She [a generic woman] will bring to her new preoccupations that passionate ardor that our cradles are currently lacking. As a bureaucrat, she will legitimately dream of a promotion that a pregnancy could compromise; as a propagandist, she will find the outlet for the capacity for devotion and sacrifice that lies within her."[160] In other words, women's suffrage could only mean the further deterioration of France's feeble birthrate, imperiling the French nation and race.

Concern for racial and national regeneration led to another campaign that could be seen as either an impediment or complement to the cause of women's suffrage: the quest for the family vote. The family vote was a right-wing domain: none of the parties of the left adopted it as a plank in their platforms, and bills proposing it were consistently generated on the right. The left rejected the family vote for somewhat cynical reasons. Fathers of large families tended to be rural and Catholic; therefore, commentators remarked, giving them supplemental ballots might not be such a good idea.[161] The left's suspicions, no doubt, were heightened by the royalist *Action française*'s endorsement of the family vote,[162] and the Croix de feu and Parti populaire français's following suit in the 1930s.[163] The fascistic Jeunesses patriotes and Solidarité française likewise embraced the measure.[164] The first serious proposition for the family vote in the interwar years came from Fédération républicaine deputy Henri Roulleaux-Dugage in 1919. Roulleaux-Dugage's proposal was typical in its gendered assumptions and aims: fathers would get an extra vote for each member of their families. Mothers would vote only in the event of fathers' deaths.[165] This formula was, additionally, replicated later that year by Senator Philippe de Las Cases, who went on to be a stalwart of the Parti démocrate populaire.[166] The Alliance démocratique was noticeably less active than the Fédération républicaine or Parti démocrate populaire in the campaign for the family vote, but the party nonetheless consistently listed its enactment as a priority.[167] This may have been due, at least in part, to Paul Reynaud, as he seems to have worked to ensure that the issue remained on the Alliance's agenda.[168] But the Fédération républicaine and the Parti démocrate populaire were undoubtedly the family vote's most adamant proponents. That a desire to revivify the race was Roulleaux-Dugage and others' primary motivation was obvious and usually explicit. *L'Action française* paraphrased Roulleaux-Dugage's rationale for the family vote in 1922 thusly: "France is depopulating; we have to remedy this at any cost. In 1870 there were 3.33 births per union, in 1913 the number fell to 2.48, and in 1920 to 1.34."[169] Roulleaux-Dugage and other key backers of the family vote like Georges Pernot believed that giving fathers extra votes would both motivate them to have children and, more broadly, render French politics more communitarian and less individualistic. The Fédération's Pernot crusaded, for example, for a complete overhaul of French society on familial lines. A disciple of the conservative social theorist Frédéric Le Play's, he believed that France had lost its way in 1789 when it placed the emphasis on the rights of the individual;[170] instead, he suggested, the family's rights should come foremost in policy decisions. The figure of the *père de famille,* he maintained, would be essential to this transformation. In 1939, as the last of many proposals to implement the family vote arose, Henri Roulleaux-Dugage's brother Georges, who had assumed his seat in the Chamber upon his sibling's death in 1932, summed up the logic succinctly:

> Nothing stable can be maintained in the state so long as we have not recognized and given to the family, on the electoral field, its legitimate place in the economic and social life of the country.
>
> The declining birthrate is the great drama of our modern France, the most dangerous menace that threatens our future.[171]

Whether or not the family vote detracted from the suffragists' cause is an open question. Some feminists certainly thought so. *L'Ouvrière,* for example, opined that propositions for fathers to wield multiple votes were wrongheaded and distracted observers from the real injustice of women's political degradation.[172] More interestingly still, women members of the Parti démocrate populaire showed considerable discontent in the 1930s with various conservative propositions for the family vote. Germaine Chapuis, for instance, complained that while the family vote was all well and good, it should not obscure the need to enfranchise women first and foremost.[173] Regarding a 1936 proposal, Germaine Peyroles likewise, while insisting that she did not think Louis Duval-Arnould, who had put it forward, had meant it to torpedo the momentum for women's suffrage then building, argued that it had done just that and pointed out that many committed opponents of women voting mysteriously rallied to Duval-Arnould's banner. In her words, "Linking the question of women's suffrage to that of familial suffrage seems inopportune and maladroit to us."[174] Chapuis and Peyroles were largely ignored. Even in their own party opinion makers continued not only to propose the two in tandem but also to suggest that the family vote was in fact a necessary corollary to women's suffrage. This was so, the argument went, because the family vote would offset the individualism spread through the extension of ballot box to French women with the increased influence of fathers of families, who would inject French political life with the necessary familial serum.[175] That conservatives, to whom the image of the mother in the home was sacrosanct, would evince more enthusiasm for the family vote than women's suffrage was congruent with their worldview. That it was these people, whose commitment to women's emancipation was often, apparently, skin-deep, who were suffragists' most consistent defenders speaks volumes about the frailty of women's suffrage's political support and offers a partial explanation for the failure of the Third Republic to incorporate women into the body politic. For the sponsors of family suffrage, their conceptions of gender and race trumped their commitment, such as it was, to women's enfranchisement.

Misogyny naturally also played a role in the opposition to women's suffrage. To what degree this was true is difficult to discern, of course, given that many misogynists no doubt successfully disguised their prejudices and seemingly opposed women's emancipation on other grounds. Still, particularly with the discussion detailed above regarding the natural unsuitability of women for the vote, a belief in women's inherent inferiority was distinctly apparent and that conviction sometimes betrayed a deeper contempt for women. Several senators, for example, slipped rather easily between supposedly principled objections to women's suffrage and blatantly misogynist rants. François Labrousse, for instance, made several controversial statements in his 1922 speech against women's suffrage in the Senate. He invoked the Adam and Eve legend to prove that women could not be trusted; he reminded listeners of the "tough frankness of Proudhon," the nineteenth-century socialist and infamous antifeminist whose legacy was key, according to Anne-Marie Sohn, to the rude welcome given to women workers by the French trade union movement;[176] he derided women's accomplishments abroad, claiming that where women had been given the vote they had achieved nothing; he described women's suffrage as a step "on the slow march to sterility"; he inveighed against women's emotionality; he warned of a return to a primitive matriarchy; and he concluded his soliloquy with the following words: "As a man, I refuse to gamble the race; as a citizen, I refuse to gamble the family; as a republican, I do not want to gamble the philosophy, the spirit, nor the very form of the Republic."[177] During the next round of that same discussion, Alexandre Bérard made a derogatory reference to the feminists and suffragists who had addressed the Chamber of Deputies, and exclaimed, "I declare to you, sirs, and many of you will be with me, that for the future of the French race, for the greatness of our fatherland, we are more inclined to side with the woman who has breastfed thirteen children than with those who insulted her from the height of the tribune in the Chamber." One version of femininity was worthy, in other words, and did not assert itself in the public sphere; another, offered by upstart feminists, was contemptible and to concede its proponents the vote would embolden its champions. That this was a popular notion in the Senate was signaled by the apparently warm applause Bérard received upon making this statement. Moreover, the senator countered the argument that women had earned the vote by their wartime sacrifices, and he continued, "In the United States, women's suffrage was judged at the moment when the American republic came to our side in the war in defense of justice and liberty. On that day, in the Washington congress, while the question was being discussed, there sat just one woman; she did not want to take a side either for or against the war; she contented herself with weeping, establishing thus that her feminine nerves alone determined her will."[178] Women, in Bérard's mind, were inescapably feminine and therefore weak-willed and inapt for citizenship. Had women been in charge, he implied, the United States would have left France to its fate in 1917.

As vicious as these statements were, they paled in comparison to those that followed in 1932. Perhaps the most infamous misogynist in interwar France, barring possibly Pierre Drieu La Rochelle, made his reputation in the Senate's debates on women's suffrage that year. Again, as in 1922, the culprit was a Radical: Senator Raymond Duplantier. Duplantier's speech outlining his stance against women's enfranchisement was magnificent in its violence. He scorned feminists as representing only a vocal minority of French women and noted that their discourse had "an aggressive and violent allure," implying thereby their lack of femininity. He then proceeded to outline his own masculinist conception of citizenship, perfectly in tune with that discussed at length above, wherein the vote was "a function, a charge, and a public commission" and not a "right." Women were incapable, he asserted, of assuming this heavy "responsibility." Duplantier went on thereafter, apparently to smiles among his colleagues, to attack the notion that women would profitably combat alcoholism once armed with the vote by saying that there were far more alcoholic women than men; he added that in the United States, the rate of prostitution went up dramatically after women gained the vote. He continued to link women's voting to prostitution, and suffragists to prostitutes by extension, by attacking Madeleine Pelletier for wanting to deregulate the sex trade and asking rhetorically whether French parliamentarians really wanted to hand the ballot "to all the women who give themselves to prostitution."He also asserted that in Paris "a very great number of women live from prostitution" due to their "laziness" and linked these estimated fifteen thousand to eighteen thousand sex workers to the "amazons" of the commune.[179] Aside from an occasional interjection from Louis Martin, Duplantier provoked no rebuke from his colleagues. In fact, he drew smiles.

In the end Duplantier paid for his invective. In 1935, Louise Weiss and her fledgling organization "New Woman" ensured his defeat in the partial renewal of the Senate that year by giving his more intemperate remarks as wide a circulation as possible.[180] But Duplantier was not the only senator to distinguish himself by his misogyny in the 1932 debates. In fact, in the tradition of his predecessor Alexandre Bérard, the reporter for the commission on universal suffrage Radical René Héry also exposed his misogynist tendencies. Héry claimed that all women lacked "genius" and proceeded to use the example of Marie-Antoinette to demonstrate women's incapacity for the vote and, most tellingly, the irreconcilability of the feminine with citizenship:

> She committed, in her political activity, specifically feminine mistakes. And we are talking here about a superior woman. When faced with the most tragic difficulties, she did not know how to use the exceptional assistance available to the royal cause. A man of genius like Mirabeau horrified her; La Fayette, a man of prominence and a force to be reckoned with, seemed ridiculous to her; and then there was the unhappy Barnave to whom she would not even deign to lower her eyes; such were the men whom Marie-Antoinette, woman politician and sovereign who wanted to seize the reins of the state and to save the imperiled monarchy, pushed aside due to feminine caprice, feminine frivolity, feminine custom.[181]

Historians generally believe that Louis XVI committed a few errors in judgment as well, but Héry did not offer his mistakes as proof of men's unsuitability for citizenship. Rather, much as had revolutionary propagandists in the 1780s and 1790s,[182] he singled out Marie-Antoinette, "a superior woman['s]" blunders, to show that all women were innately limited by their femininity and therefore could not be trusted with the vote.

Women too were occasionally co-opted by such antifeminism. Communist Francine Duclos, for instance, concentrating on the reviled bourgeois woman-as-decadent trope, wondered whether the Communist Party had sufficiently considered the ramifications of such "objects of luxury" voting: "One cannot talk to her about her rights or her duties. She does not know them, she is born for 'pleasure,' for the life of adventure that intoxicates her and she aspires to nothing more."[183] This, in all likelihood, betrayed more Duclos's class hatred than misogyny, but it does show a degree of internalization, on her part, of the notion that at least some women represented weakness and were therefore unlikely to use their "rights" responsibly or fulfill their "duties" competently. Germaine Sillon, another Communist writer, also exposed a belief that women were childlike and therefore not ready for the vote. In writing about the consequence of women's voting on their mentality, she offered the hope that: "We would grow up, in a way, and we would certainly gain a little of that virility in our ideas that is currently missing."[184] These were hardly the grounds on which to convince uncertain Communist men of women's equality. A piece in *L'Ère nouvelle* by Janine Louis-Merlet displayed an analogous lack of confidence in women's abilities. As the author frankly admitted, "I estimate that woman is not made physiologically to lead a life equal to that of man."[185]

The most unhinged example of misogyny vis-à-vis women's suffrage came courtesy of Georges Ponsot and the famed novelist and performer Colette. In an attack on the idea of women's voting, suffragists, feminism, and women in general, Ponsot let the words of Colette explain that women were not fully human:

> During a minimum period of three days, which returns at regular intervals twelve times per year, a woman is no longer a woman. She is a savage beast. She is a periodic slave. She is an unbalanced, exasperated being. She no longer has control of herself. She is incapable of all serious work. She is, as Marguerite Moreno so justly says of my poor and charming Annie de Pêne,[186] 'indulgent towards blackguards, severe towards honest men' . . . I see, sir, around me, the most composed, the most virile women lose, during the time that you know of, all good sense and conduct themselves like veritable prisoners of their sex.
>
> *I tremble,* you see, *I tremble* at the idea that, in a parliamentary commission or in a jury, an important decision with ramifications for the state or a man's head could depend on a woman tortured by the physiological demon. It is impossible that women could take charge usefully of the affairs of the country when they have their . . . possessions.[187]

Whether or not Ponsot recorded Colette's words faithfully is unknown, but it is true that she was not a suffragist.[188] Either way, Ponsot seconded Colette and told his reader, "*I tremble,* I too, *I tremble.*" While Ponsot and apparently

Colette's anxieties seem absurd and were certainly more explicit than other opponents' of women's suffrage, they were nonetheless widely shared, in a milder form, by many French politicians. Women were, indeed, "prisoners of their sex": in the minds of the arbiters of their fate, women's biologically determined femininity rendered them inferior and unable to perform the duties of a French citizen. It placed citizenship beyond their limited reach.

THE ACHIEVEMENT OF SUFFRAGE IN 1944

At first glance, the achievement of women's suffrage in 1944 seems remarkable. As of 1939 there was no reason for optimism that the enactment of women's suffrage was imminent. This begs the question: why, if the enfranchisement of women seemed a nearly impossible dream in 1939, was it achieved just five years later?

Historians' conclusions on this question are interesting. Notably, they emphasize that in the period leading up to and during the Liberation men, including male politicians and commentators in the press, continued to have the same reservations about women's suffrage as previously. In fact, as Joan Tumblety demonstrates, the discussion of the pros and cons of women's suffrage in the Liberation era rehearsed the arguments of the interwar period.[189] Despite this, the provisional government of Charles de Gaulle took the momentous step of enfranchising adult women nonetheless. Ironically given the role that his party colleagues in the upper chamber had played in obstructing women's emancipation, the commission that recommended the measure was headed by a Radical senator, Paul Giacobbi.[190] The commission decided to recommend giving the ballot to women for, apparently, three reasons—a rationale that was shared by de Gaulle when he signed women's suffrage into law on April 21, 1944. First, just like those in the interwar period who argued that women's service during World War I showed that they could perform citizenly duties responsibly and so deserved the vote, many felt that women's activity in the Resistance, where they fought alongside men as equals showed that French women were ready to cast ballots. Second, while women guilty of "horizontal collaboration" with Germans had their heads shorn and found themselves convicted of "national degradation" and therefore stripped of their political rights, "good" French women who had been sexually and symbolically faithful, embodied by those widowed by the war, deserved to be rewarded with the franchise. Third, many in the provisional government as well as the commentariat saw giving women the suffrage as a way of distinguishing democratic Liberation France from the autocratic Vichy regime and as necessary to bringing France in line with its western allies, particularly Britain and the United States, where women had exercised the vote for well over twenty years. As Kelly Ricciardi Colvin astutely notes, absent from this reasoning was the idea that women's suffrage was a right; rather, women got the vote because they "deserved" it. Moreover, opinion had not really changed in France or among the country's political leaders: it was international circumstances that necessitated the enactment of women's suffrage.[191] The implication seems inescapable, therefore, that in a different international context—and certainly absent the events of World War II—French women would likely not have achieved the vote even in 1944 for the same array of reasons as during the interwar years.

CONCLUSION

Despite that somewhat depressing conclusion, however, the achievement of women's suffrage in 1944 should be seen as just that: an achievement, attained through the long years of struggle by male and female suffragists, but particularly by the many women who, through their activity in suffragist organizations as well as the political parties and leagues, kept women's suffrage firmly on the agenda. Without the constant pressure from below that these women of diverse political persuasions applied in the interwar years and before, it is a near certainty that women's suffrage would not have come to pass in 1944.

The delay in French women's attainment of the vote, on the other hand, was the fault of intransigent or indifferent male politicians. No French government ever made women's suffrage a question of confidence, and no French politician, save perhaps Louis Martin, proved willing to jeopardize his career for the suffragists' cause. Furthermore, a group of senators, primarily composed of Radicals but also including Socialists and some conservatives, successfully blocked women's access to the city. That a cohort of old men in an indirectly elected chamber of parliament were able to exercise such undue influence regarding what should have been seen as a question of justice underscores the thinness of the support among France's political elite for women's enfranchisement. In fact, it is difficult to gauge the sincerity of even those deputies who voted for women's suffrage. Republican-Socialist Victor Augagneur, for example, who sounded an awful lot like an opponent of women's suffrage in 1919, suddenly seemed a good deal keener when informed by Alexandre Varenne that the Senate's own commission of universal suffrage had just rejected a similar proposal from Martin.[192] He subsequently voted in favor of Alexandre Bracke's motion to enfranchise women.[193] Can he and those like him really be counted among women's suffrage's supporters? It seems more likely that he cast his vote secure in the knowledge that the passage of women's suffrage in the Chamber of Deputies was an illusory victory, destined to be thwarted by the Senate. Likewise, on the right, men like Henri Roulleaux-Dugage, Louis Duval-Arnould, François de La Rocque, and Georges Pernot demonstrated their clear preference for the family vote, a measure much more consistent with the primacy of fathers of families as posited in their glorification of male breadwinners. These men were able to bleed support from women's cause at crucial moments, playing as they did to widely shared prejudices.

Given the importance of high politics to suffragists' temporary defeat, it is of paramount importance to understand properly the debate about women's suffrage in political circles. To do so, a gender analysis is required. In examining both the cases for and against enfranchising French women, it becomes apparent that, despite their divergent perspectives on women's voting, the two sides shared many values and mentalities. Both, for example, argued on racialist lines. Proponents felt women's suffrage would be beneficial to racial hygiene; opponents believed, on the contrary, that it would be detrimental. Regardless, the two camps were united in their pursuit of racial regeneration. Both also shared a very traditional conception of femininity. Opponents thought women inherently weak and held that their femininity precluded their political emancipation. Those in favor of giving the vote to women, however, held that the extension of their uniquely feminine influence to the public arena would prove uplifting: women would, in this view, apply their maternal instincts to the welfare of the nation. Neither side, it should be noted, believed that women were absolutely equal to men; even suffragists (with rare exceptions) thought them to be different but equal, bringing weaknesses and strengths to the political table unique to their sex. They adopted, in effect, the relational feminist line.

This was, as Joan Scott might put it, a paradox on offer. Given the conflation of masculinity with citizenship, the significance attached to the performance of manly duties in the spirit of fraternity in the republican creed, the deep-seated belief that women's primary social function was motherhood, and the resultant view that mothers needed to return to the home to have more babies for the good of the French race and nation, suffrage's backers proved powerless to overcome the obstacles placed in their path in the interwar years. When feminists attempted to do so, they were susceptible to accusations of selfishness, which implied, by extension, their unworthiness as citizens. While blame for the delay in passing women's suffrage in France should be placed where it belongs—with the male politicians—it is nonetheless true that in adopting the "different but equal" line, as was inevitable given the context of the period, women's suffrage's advocates had conceded critical ground to the case against them: they had accepted the hegemonic racialist and gendered framework of interwar French politics. This framework was not friendly to women's voting.

Thus, cry as Louis Marin might in 1925 that "the ballot is given to human beings in the city as an inherent right,"[194] French republicanism was so innately masculinist that it could not incorporate women without the profound change in circumstances that World War II engendered. In the republic of men, women were literally prisoners of their sex, bound and chained by the imagined limitations of their femininity.

Conclusion

Politicians' conceptions of gender and race had a profound impact in interwar France. As this study of the Communist Party, the Socialist Party, the Radical and Radical-Socialist Party, the Alliance démocratique, the Fédération républicaine, the Parti démocrate populaire, the Croix de feu/Parti social français, and the Parti populaire français makes clear, gender and race informed the parties' mobilizations of men and women, their politics, their policies, and their political identities.

In the interwar Republic, political actors of all stripes had a near-obsession with virtue. These virtues defined citizenship and were usually sex-specific. Selflessness, in particular, was the most eminent of the citizenly virtues. French men of both the left and the right aspired to self-abnegation in the performance of their fatherly, brotherly, and citizenly duties. On the right, this meant that men looked after their families without thinking of their own needs, while also disinterestedly following the lead of their political, social, and economic betters. On the left, French men showed their selflessness in politics somewhat differently. Thus, the Radical Party urged its men to selflessness in defense of the Republic and republican institutions like the secular education system, while the Socialist and Communist parties in the 1920s exalted men who showed self-abnegation in pursuit of socialist revolution, at least until the Popular Front when they too came to embrace the Republic. Regardless of where they stood on the political spectrum, meanwhile, all the parties and leagues embraced the breadwinner ideal; this was especially pronounced in the 1930s following the onset of the Great Depression.

For women across the political spectrum, meanwhile, selflessness meant something else altogether. Selfless women, rather than taking decisions for the welfare of their families and society, showed their self-abnegation by having and raising their children and being dutiful wives. For the republican parties, this amounted to embracing republican motherhood. Not surprisingly, given the nearly universal purchase of the view of women as defined by motherhood, virtues understood to be specifically feminine were likewise associated with maternity. Accordingly, commentators believed that the ideal woman was pure, chaste outside of marriage, inherently nurturing, and pacifistic.

If commentators thought women to be pacifists by nature, the same was not true of the fascist and Communist new men. The fascist new man, promoted by both the Croix de feu and the Parti populaire français, was a virile, physical, anti-intellectual, and potentially violent individual who knew his place in the social hierarchy and followed his political chiefs to whatever end—presumably in counter-revolutionary struggle and the establishment of an authoritarian state. The Communist new man was both similar and different. He too embodied a youthful, virile masculinity, but rather than respecting hierarchy and social order, Communists envisioned him as a shock troop of socialist revolution. Yet, despite this glaring difference from the fascist new man the Communist one too required a militaristic discipline. These new radical militarized masculinities were no doubt in part the product of the Great War, which traumatized French society and brutalized many young men who came of age, politically, in the interwar years. Both the Communist and fascist variations on the new man, moreover, proved highly influential, inspiring imitators even within the republican mainstream. Thus, while the breadwinner ideal remained hegemonic, even within the Communist and fascist parties and leagues, interwar France nevertheless witnessed a creeping totalitarianization of political gender identities that reflected the increasing attempt to monopolize and politicize party members' leisure time seemingly from the cradle to the grave.

This new man also represented the fusion of the two seemingly contradictory gender traditions of the French right and left: conservatives' paternalism and leftists' fraternalism. In the Alliance démocratique, the Parti démocrate populaire, and the Fédération républicaine a hierarchical ethos predominated, modeled on the traditional family wherein social betters and party leaders reigned supreme over their charges, who followed their fathers' lead, safe in the knowledge that "father knows best." On the left meanwhile, at least in theory, a discourse of fraternity preponderated. French men were invited to participate in the parties' political projects as equal but manly partners, united by their shared enterprise and, in the Socialist and Communist parties, by class identity. The fascists wedded these gendered appeals, maintaining the familial and essentially authoritarian model of the right while using the language, symbolism, and rituals of fraternity to gather recruits and motivate adherents.

Alongside the rise of fascism and the new man came the ascendance of racialism. In keeping with Francine Muël-Dreyfus's finding that asserting gender hierarchy legitimates and invigorates other forms of domination,[1] the emerging consensus concerning women's place in the home and men's status as breadwinner accompanied a bipartisan adherence, by the era of the Popular Front, to the goal of raising the birthrate and ensuring the future of the French race. These twin ambitions—keeping women at home to raise children and boosting France's fertility were, moreover, seen as complementary. By the mid-1930s, they provoked elements within all the parties to advocate a range of policies including family allocations, the breadwinner wage, the suppression of birth control and its literature, the suppression of the sex trade, the construction of hygienic public housing, the criminalization of abortion, the extension of maternity leave and benefits, the promotion of physical education, the restriction of nonwhite immigration, and the family vote. The politics of gender and race intersected, dominated a wide spectrum of Third Republican debate, and paved the way for the racist and exclusionary dominion of Vichy France.

This intersection of gender and race had especially profound implications for French women. The convergence, most pronounced in the 1930s with the onset of the Great Depression and the rise of the Popular Front, upon a startlingly traditional model of femininity in particular, a convergence motivated in part by concern for the race, had profound repercussions. These included a push for women's retreat from the public world of work and the suppression of conflicting versions of femininity and womanhood, most notably in the Communist Party. The meeting of conservative gender and racial agendas, furthermore, generated considerable hostility to women in public space—whether that meant hostility toward women working, voting, or engaging in political activism. The misogyny of Raymond Duplantier and others was but the most obvious sign of this antifeminist and racially motivated backlash.

Despite this fact, there is something heroic about the story of women and politics in interwar France. French women, facing considerable hostility from many corners, continued to work for pay in large numbers, including during the Depression. Women activists, moreover, pushed their way definitively into France's political parties and leagues during this period. All of the seventeen newspapers sampled for this study, most of which were directly affiliated with the parties and leagues, featured women contributors prominently, and the 1930s, in particular, witnessed a remarkable influx of women into politics as members of parties and leagues. The Croix de feu was the most notable organization in this respect, but other groups witnessed similar if less pronounced phenomena. In addition, while it is true that some of the time women's voices were indistinct from men's, there were important counterexamples. The women in French politics, ranging from those who held leadership positions in their respective parties and leagues to lesser known newspaper contributors and party members, successfully pressured their organizations to adopt positions seemingly at odds with the breadwinner ideology, such as endorsing the principle of equal pay for equal work. They were pioneers and laid the groundwork for the further gains French women made in the post–World War II era, May 1968, and beyond.

On the issue of women's suffrage too, women played a critical role. The case against women's suffrage was, like the adoption of pronatalism and the diverse policies examined herein, largely a product of the convergence of gender and racial discourses mentioned above. France's male politicians believed fervently in the biological difference of the sexes and the need for more French babies, and for many this implied the unfitness of women for the rigors of the franchise. Women were supposedly virtuous, motherly, emotional rather than intellectual, and politically naïve; it was thought best that they not vote. Without the pressure from below provided by the constant stream of suffragist articles and letters penned principally by women, it seems very likely that women's suffrage would simply have slipped off the political agenda in interwar France. That in the face of a political, social, and cultural context that was increasingly hostile to women's suffrage, particularly after the onset of the Great Depression and during the crisis years of the mid- to late 1930s, women's suffrage remained one of the burning questions of the age is a testament to the strength of these women. In that light, while it is true that the Third Republic self-destructed having never enfranchised the more than 50 percent of the population who were female, the enfranchisement of women on April 21, 1944, should be interpreted as a victory won by women suffragists and their male collaborators.

Hence, analyzing the gender and racial discourses of interwar France's political parties and leagues changes the historiographical picture of the period. The Popular Front, often portrayed as a period of profound political cleavage between the left and right, appears also to have witnessed the Communists, Socialists, and Radicals unite with conservatives in pursuit of a deeply problematic agenda of racial hygiene and gender orthodoxy. Understanding gender and race properly, moreover, facilitates historians' comprehension of the mentalities of French politicians, political party members, and voters, and, despite the prevailing masculinism of the parties, renders perceptible the contributions of women to French political life. It, in short, helps historians to understand important issues of the era better, including the denial of women's suffrage, as well as what transpired after July 10, 1940.

★ ★ ★

Logic would seem to dictate that the interwar period came to a close on September 1, 1939, with the German invasion of Poland or perhaps two days later when the French came to Poland's aid and declared war on Nazi Germany. However, July 10, 1940, when the National Assembly—still populated exclusively by men—abrogated the Third Republic's constitution and voted full powers to Marshal Philippe Pétain, is when the interwar Republic ended definitively. In the context of defeat many of the themes evident on November 11, 1918, reappeared, if in a distorted form. Indeed, the Alliance démocratique's Paul Reynaud, the *president du conseil* as of March 1940, heralded the emergence of a more authoritarian and intolerant France at the precise moment when the military catastrophe of the German breakthrough started to become clear. On May 16, the very day that the Allies ordered a general retreat from Belgium, Erwin Rommel began his thrust to the west to try to encircle British and French forces, and the new British prime minister, Winston Churchill, arrived in Paris for a summit with Reynaud,[2] the *president du conseil* addressed the Senate. He hinted darkly that the defense of the fatherland was not going well and then suggested that desperate times called for desperate measures:

> We must not be satisfied with vague hopes or words. Our soldiers are fighting. French blood is being spilled. The period we are about to live through may be totally unlike that which has come before it. We will be called to take measures that would have seemed revolutionary yesterday.
>
> We might have to change everything, our methods, our men. (Lively applause.)
>
> For failure, the punishment will be swift: death. (New applause.)[3]

As the hopelessness of the situation became obvious Reynaud returned to the Senate five days later. In an attempt to rally the senators' morale, he referenced the facts that Pétain had joined the government as the deputy *président du conseil* and General Maxime Weygand had replaced Maurice Gamelin as the commander of France's armed forces.[4] These measures had long been called for by the right, who worshiped Pétain, in particular as the savior of France in World War I. While it would be going too far to say that contemporaries saw the ascent of Pétain and Weygand to power as spelling the doom of the Republic, Pétain's views on the need for greater "authority" in government were widely known. Combine this with Reynaud's ruminations about the need for "revolutionary measures" and change was certainly in the air. Both Pétain and Weygand, of course, went on to play central roles in Vichy. Moreover, in his address to the Senate Reynaud returned to his call for severe punishment for those who had betrayed or failed the nation and connected their punishment to France's survival:

> Failure will not be tolerated.
>
> Death is an inadequate punishment for all crimes committed against the vital interests of the country.
>
> Therefore, while our soldiers are dying there will be no dilatory procedures for traitors, saboteurs, or cowards.[5]

As he was willing to throw due process out the window as "dilatory," it was clear that Reynaud envisioned harsh measures for enemies of the nation. Little did he know he would soon be victimized by similar suggestions that he had somehow failed in his citizenly responsibilities.

On July 10, before the constitutional law effectively dissolving the Republic was even deposited for discussion, Pierre Laval, executed after the Liberation for his crimes of collaboration, established the tenor of the day.[6] Édouard Herriot and Jules Jeanneney, the Radical speakers of the Chamber of Deputies and Senate, respectively, raised a protest against the looming deliberation transpiring in the absence of those such as Reynaud, conservative Georges Mandel, the Fédération républicaine's Joseph Denais, Radical Yvon Delbos, and Socialist Jammy Schmidt. These men, in good conscience and on the orders of the government of the day, had boarded the *Massilia,* a ship bound for Algiers, in order to carry on the war effort from the colonies. Laval responded to Herriot and Jeanneney's entreaty thusly:

> I was not a member of the government at the moment when these events transpired and when this departure took place; but I do remember precisely that, if I am correct, the members of the government had considered the transfer of the seat of government from Bordeaux to Perpignan, a noble and wise idea —and this will not surprise you—suggested by Marshal Pétain, who said: "No matter what happens, me, I will stay amidst my fellow citizens." (*Applause.*)
>
> I myself had occasion to say that it was not in fleeing France that one helps her.[7]

Laval's words, like Reynaud's before them, were an inversion of Georges Clemenceau's and Paul Deschanel's on November 11, 1918. Where Clemenceau and Deschanel had applauded the "superhuman courage" of French soldiers in performing their citizenly duty to defend the fatherland, Laval attacked the masculinity and patriotic bona fides of those who had failed France and had fled her shores in a supposedly cowardly fashion. In a prelude to the politics of exclusion that soon dominated in Vichy France, he implied that Reynaud, who had in fact led France against Germany with considerable aplomb,[8] and his compatriots were unworthy citizens: they had abandoned France in her hour of need, unlike Marshal Pétain who had remained "with his fellow citizens." The National Assembly, in other words, did not need to concern itself with their absence as they had betrayed the nation. Laval thereby used the discourse of manly citizenship against his enemies to devastating effect. Nor was he the only one to do so. Prior to the historic vote of full powers to Pétain, Radical Fernand Bouisson, a former speaker of the Chamber of Deputies and briefly a *president du conseil,* insisted angrily that all those who abstained from voting should have their names published (presumably so that their cowardice and abdication of citizenly duty would be public knowledge). His motion passed. Reynaud's assertion on May 16 that "we will overcome this peril united" thus proved mistaken.[9] And so, by a vote of 569 to 80, the Republic fell on its proverbial sword. The final exchange of the debate captured the isolation of the opposition as well as the discursive displacement of the Republic by the nation:

> Mr. Pierre Laval, deputy-*président du conseil.* Sirs, in the name of Marshal Pétain, I thank you for France! (*Lively applause.*)
>
> Mr. Marcel Astier. Long live the Republic just the same!
>
> *Numerous voices.* Long live France![10]

The French Republic had come full circle from Clemenceau and Deschanel's triumphalism. Yet, in 1940 as in 1918, although in the crucible of defeat rather than victory, conceptions of gender and race once again framed the French political leadership's understanding, interpretation, and handling of the crisis. Sadly, by August 1940 racists such as the Parti populaire français's Maurice Sicard were calling for Jewish citizens to be punished collectively for having caused the defeat, and by 1942 the deportation of French Jews to Auschwitz had begun. Not coincidentally, in that same year Vichy made performing abortions a capital crime, confirming once again the intimate connections between race, gender, and nation in the minds of France's political leaders and illustrating the devastating effects these connections could produce for minorities and French women.[11]

NOTES

ACRONYMS

AD—Alliance démocratique
AF—Action française
ARD—Alliance républicaine démocratique
CdF—Croix de feu
CGT—Confédération générale du travail (public sector union)
CGTU—Confédération générale du travail unitaire (Communist offshoot of the CGT)
FR—Fédération républicaine
FST— Fédération sportive du travail (Communist sporting organization)
JFdF—Jeunes filles de France (Communist girls' organization)
JFF—Jeunes filles françaises (PPF girls' organization)
JGS—Jeunes gardes Socialistes
LRN—Ligue républicaine nationale (Alexandre Millerand's league)
PCF—Section française de l'internationale communiste (French Communist Party)
PDP—Parti démocrate populaire
PPF—Parti populaire français
PSF—Parti social français
SFIO—Section française de l'internationale ouvrière (French Socialist Party)
UFCS—Union féminine civique et sociale (PDP women's organization)
UNVF—Union nationale pour le vote des femmes
UPJF—Union populaire de la jeunesse française (PPF youth group)

INTRODUCTION

1. *Président du conseil* refers to the first minister of the government.

2. Benjamin F. Martin, *France and the Après-Guerre, 1918–1924: Illusions and Disillusionment* (Baton Rouge: Louisiana State University Press, 1999), 16–17.

3. For an examination of the Republic's attempt to reintegrate Alsace post-1918, particularly Alsatian women, see Elizabeth Vlossak, *Marianne or Germania? Nationalizing Women in Alsace, 1870–1946* (Oxford: Oxford University Press, 2010), 168–252.

4. *Président de la chambre* means speaker of the house, in this case, the speaker of the Chamber of Deputies.

5. "Communication du gouvernement," *Journal officiel de la République française. Débats parlementaires. Chambre des députés* [hereafter *Journal officiel, Chambre*], November 11, 1918, 2298–3000. For the similar discussion in the Senate, see "Allocutions de M. le président du sénat et de M. le président du conseil. Ministre de la guerre," *Journal officiel de la République française. Débats parlementaires. Sénat* [hereafter *Journal officiel, Sénat*], November 11, 1918, 741. Italics in original.

6. Avner Ben-Amos demonstrates in his study of French state funerals that "great men" displaced monarchs as the symbols of the nation under the Republic. These men, because they had theoretically attained their status through merit, held out the promise to other male citizens that they too could achieve greatness and thus immortality, thereby building republican consensus and national cohesion: Avner Ben-Amos, *Funerals, Politics, and Memory in Modern France, 1789–1996* (Oxford: Oxford University Press, 2000), 22–23.

7. Deschanel and Clemenceau had in fact dueled in the 1890s, when Clemenceau, the superior swordsman, roundly defeated his opponent but satisfied himself with a nick above Deschanel's eye: Martin, *France and the Après-Guerre*, 14.

8. This phrase is actually borrowed from Linda Kerber, *Women of the Republic: Intellect and Ideology in Revolutionary America* (Chapel Hill: University of North Carolina Press, 1980).

9. Joan B. Landes, *Women and the Public Sphere in the Age of the French Revolution* (Ithaca, NY: Cornell University Press, 1988), and *Visualizing the Nation: Gender, Representation, and Revolution in Eighteenth-Century France* (Ithaca, NY: Cornell University Press, 2001), 135–68.

10. Judith Surkis, *Sexing the Citizen: Morality and Masculinity in France, 1870–1920* (Ithaca, NY: Cornell University Press, 2006); Patricia A. Tilburg, *Colette's Republic: Work, Gender, and Popular Culture in France, 1870–1914* (New York: Berghahn, 2010), 23–74. See also Judith Stone, "Republican Ideology, Gender, and Class: France, 1860s–1914," in *Gender and Class in Modern Europe*, ed. Laura L. Frader and Sonya O. Rose (Ithaca, NY: Cornell University Press, 1996), 238–59.

11. For relational feminism, see Karen Offen, "Defining Feminism: A Comparative Historical Approach," *Journal of Women in Culture and Society* 14, no. 1 (Autumn 1988): 135. For a sample of Offen's work on relational feminists, see Karen Offen, "Ernest Legouvé and the Doctrine of 'Equality in Difference' for Women: A Case Study of Male Feminism in Nineteenth-Century French Thought," *Journal of Modern History* 58, no. 2 (June 1986): 452–84, "Depopulation, Nationalism, and Feminism in Fin-de-Siecle France," *American Historical Review* 89, no. 3 (June 1984): 648–76, and "Body Politics: Women, Work and the Politics of Motherhood in France, 1920–1950," in *Maternity and Gender Policies: Women and the Rise of the European Welfare States, 1880s–1950s*, ed. Gisela Bock and Pat Thane (New York: Routledge, 1991), 138–59.

12. Joan Wallach Scott, *Only Paradoxes to Offer: French Feminists and the Rights of Man* (Cambridge: Harvard University Press, 1996), *passim.*

13. Francine Muël-Dreyfus, *Vichy and the Eternal Feminine: A Contribution to a Sociology of Gender* (Durham, NC: Duke University Press, 2001), *passim.*

14. Laura Levine Frader, *Breadwinners and Citizens: Gender in the Making of the French Social Model* (Durham, NC: Duke University Press, 2008); Kristen Stromberg Childers, *Fathers, Families, and the State in France, 1914–1945* (Ithaca, NY: Cornell University Press, 2003), 12–81.

15. Rachel G. Fuchs, *Contested Paternity: Constructing Families in Modern France* (Baltimore: Johns Hopkins University Press, 2008), 59–239.

16. Elisa Camiscioli, *Reproducing the French Race: Immigration, Intimacy, and Embodiment in the Early Twentieth Century* (Durham, NC: Duke University Press, 2009).

17. Frader, *Breadwinners and Citizens*, 31–34, 42–45.

18. Vicki Caron, *Uneasy Asylum: France and the Jewish Refugee Crisis, 1933–1942* (Stanford, CA: Stanford University Press, 1999), 75–80.

19. Ibid, 81–86.

20. "Radical" refers here to Sarraut's being a member of the Radical and Radical-Socialist Party.

21.Clifford Rosenberg, "Albert Sarraut and Republican Racial Thought," in *Race in France: Interdisciplinary Perspectives on the Politics of Difference,* ed. Herrick Chapman and Laura L. Frader (New York: Berghahn, 2004), 36–53.

22. Mary Dewhurst Lewis, "The Strangeness of Foreigners: Policing Migration and Nation in Interwar Marseille," in *Race in France: Interdisciplinary Perspectives on the Politics of Difference,* ed. Herrick Chapman and Laura L. Frader (New York: Berghahn, 2004), 77–107.

23. Anne Carol, *L'Histoire de l'eugénisme en France: Les médecins et la procréation, XIXe–XXe siècle* (Paris: Éditions du Seuil, 1995), 80; Rachel G. Fuchs, "France in a Comparative Perspective," in *Gender and the Politics of Social Reform in France, 1870–1914,* ed. Elinor Accampo, Rachel G. Fuchs, and Mary Lynn Stewart (Baltimore: Johns Hopkins University Press, 1995), 176–77; William H. Schneider, *Quality and Quantity: The Quest for Biological Regeneration in Twentieth-Century France* (Cambridge: Cambridge University Press, 1990), 89–90.

24. See, for example, Roger-Henri Guerrand and Christine Moissinac, *Henri Sellier: Urbaniste et réformateur social* (Paris: Éditions la découverte, 2005).

25. Andrès Horacio Reggiani, *God's Eugenicist: Alexis Carrel and the Sociobiology of Decline* (New York: Berghahn, 2007), 59–84.

26. See also Geoff Read, "'Citizens Useful to Their Country and to Humanity': The Convergence of Eugenics and Pro-Natalism in Interwar French Politics, 1918–1940," *Canadian Bulletin of Medical History* 29, no. 2 (Fall 2012): 171–95.

27. Carole Reynaud Paligot, *La République raciale: Paradigme racial et idéologie républicaine (1860–1930)* (Paris: Presses universitaires de France, 2006). See also Claude Blanckaert, "Of Monstrous Métis? Hybridity, Fear of Miscegenation, and Patriotism from Buffon to Paul Broca," in *The Color of Liberty: Histories of Race in France,* ed. Sue Peabody and Tyler Stovall (Durham, NC: Duke University Press, 2003), 42–70.

28. Carole Reynaud Paligot, *Races, racisme et antiracisme dans les années 1930* (Paris: Presses universitaires de France, 2007).

29. Camiscioli, *Reproducing the French Race,* 21–49; Cheryl Ann Koos, "Engendering Reaction: The Politics of Pro-natalism and Family in France, 1919–1944" (PhD diss.: History Department, University of Southern California, 1997), 11–12; Miranda Pollard, *Reign of Virtue: Mobilizing Gender in Vichy France* (Chicago: University of Chicago Press, 1998), 9–41.

30. Cheryl Koos, "'On les aura!' The Gendered Politics of Abortion and the Alliance nationale contre la dépopulation, 1938–1944," *Modern and Contemporary France* 7, no. 1 (1999): 21–33.

31. Elinor Accampo, *Blessed Motherhood, Bitter Fruit: Nelly Roussel and the Politics of Female Pain in Third Republic France* (Baltimore: Johns Hopkins University Press, 2006), 42, 215. See also Roger-Henri Guerrand and Francis Ronsin, *Le Sexe apprivoisé: Jeanne Humbert et la lutte pour le contrôle des naissances* (Paris: Éditions la découverte, 1990); Angus McLaren, *Sexuality and Social Order: The Debate over the Fertility of Women and Workers in France, 1770–1920* (New York: Holmes & Meier, 1983), 93–121.

32. See, for example, Kevin Passmore, "Boy Scouting for Grown-ups? Paramilitarism in the Croix de Feu and the Parti Social Français," *French Historical Studies* 19, no. 2 (Autumn 1995), 527–57.

33. Perhaps the most influential scholar regarding the "fascist new man" has been George L. Mosse. See George L. Mosse, *Masses and Man: Nationalist and Fascist Perceptions of Reality* (New York: Howard Fertig, 1980), 87, 165–67, and *The Image of Man: The Creation of Modern Masculinity* (Oxford: Oxford University Press, 1996), 155–80.

34. Klaus Theweleit, *Male Fantasies, Volume 1: Women, Floods, Bodies, History* (Minneapolis: University of Minnesota Press, 1987), and *Volume 2, Male Bodies: Psychoanalyzing the White Terror* (Minneapolis: University of Minnesota Press, 1989).

35. Julie V. Gottlieb, *Feminine Fascism: Women in Britain's Fascist Movement* (London: I. B. Tauris, 2000).

36. Caroline Jane Campbell, "Women and Men in French Authoritarianism: Gender in the Croix de Feu and Parti Social Français, 1927–1945" (PhD diss.: Iowa City, History Dept., University of Iowa, 2009), 1–39. See also Caroline Campbell, "Women and Gender in the Croix de Feu and the Parti Social Français: Creating a Nationalist Youth Culture, 1927–1939," *Proceedings of the Western Society for French History* 36 (2008): 249–64.

37. The one fascistic organization which did have an inarguably mass base, with nearly 1 million members in 1938, was the Croix de feu, which morphed into the Parti social français (PSF) in 1936. See Sean Kennedy, *Reconciling France against Democracy: The Croix de Feu and the Parti Social Français, 1927–1945* (Montreal: McGill-Queen's University Press, 2007), 4.

38. Robert A. Nye, *Masculinity and Male Codes of Honor in Modern France* (New York: Oxford University Press, 1993).

39. The four most notable exceptions are Childers, *Fathers, Families, and the State*, 42–81; Frader, *Breadwinners and Citizens;* Mary Louise Roberts, *Civilization without Sexes: Reconstructing Gender in Postwar France, 1917–1927* (Chicago: University of Chicago Press, 1994); Joan Tumblety, *Remaking the Male Body: Masculinity and the Uses of Physical Culture in Interwar and Vichy France* (Oxford: Oxford University Press, 2012).

40. Christopher E. Forth, *The Dreyfus Affair and the Crisis of French Manhood* (Baltimore: John Hopkins University Press, 2004).

41. Joan Wallach Scott, *Gender and the Politics of History*, revised ed. (New York: Columbia University Press, 1999), 28–50.

42. Regarding more traditional histories, see, for example, Serge Berstein, *Histoire du Parti radical: La recherche de l'âge d'or* (Paris: Presses de la Fondation nationale des sciences politiques, 1980); Jean-Paul Brunet, *Jacques Doriot: Du communisme au fascisme* (Paris: Balland, 1986); Jean-Claude Delbreil, *Centrisme et démocratie-chrétienne en France: Le Parti démocrate populaire des origines au M.R.P.* (Paris: Publications de la Sorbonne, 1990); Alan Douglas, *From Fascism to Libertarian Communism: Georges Valois against the Third Republic* (Berkeley: University of California Press, 1992); William D. Irvine, *French Conservatism in Crisis: The Republican Federation of France in the 1930s* (Baton Rouge: Louisiana State University Press, 1979); Paul Jankowski, *Communism and Collaboration: Simon Sabiani and Politics in Marseille, 1919–1944* (New Haven. CT: Yale University Press, 1989); Kennedy, *Reconciling France against Democracy;* Laurent Kestel, *La conversion politique: Doriot, le PPF et la question du fascisme français* (Paris: Éditions raisons d'agir, 2012); Jean Lacouture, *Léon Blum* (New York: Holmes & Meier, 1982); Peter J. Larmour, *The French Radical Party of the 1930s* (Stanford, CA: Stanford University Press, 1964); Edward Mortimer, *The Rise of the French Communist Party, 1920–1947* (London: Faber & Faber, 1984); Jacques Nobécourt, *Le Colonel de La Rocque, 1885–1946, ou les pièges du nationalisme chrétien* (Paris: Libraire Fayard, 1996); Robert Soucy, *French Fascism: The Second Wave, 1933–1939* (New

Haven, CT: Yale University Press, 1995); Donald G. Wileman, "L'Alliance républicaine démocratique: The Dead Centre of French Politics, 1901–1947" (PhD diss., York University, Toronto, 1988).

43. Encouragingly, Samuel Kalman's book on the far right includes an excellent chapter on gender: Samuel Kalman, *The Extreme Right in Interwar France* (London: Ashgate, 2008), 111–44.

44. Lucia Re, "Fascist Theories of 'Woman' and the Construction of Gender," in *Mothers of Invention: Women, Italian Fascism, and Culture,* ed. Robin Pickering-Iazzi (Minneapolis: University of Minnesota Press, 1995), 76–99; David Carroll, *French Literary Fascism: Nationalism, Anti-Semitism, and the Ideology of Culture* (Princeton. NJ: Princeton University Press, 1995), 147–70.

45. See, for example, Mary Jean Green, "Gender, Fascism, and the Croix de Feu: The Women's Pages of *Le Flambeau,*" *French Cultural Studies* 8, no. 2 (1997): 229–39; Daniella Sarnoff, "In the Cervix of the Nation: Women in French Fascism, 1919–1939" (PhD diss., Boston College, 2001).

46. Obituaries, in fact, proved an especially fruitful source, particularly for the exploration of masculinity. In Janice Hume's words, "An obituary distills the essence of a citizen's life, and because it is a commemoration as well as a life chronicle, it reflects what society values and wants to remember about that person's history." Obituaries thus make superb sources for gender historians. Janice Hume, *Obituaries in American Culture* (Jackson: University Press of Mississippi, 2000), 12. See also: Mushira Eid, *The World of Obituaries: Gender across Cultures and over Time* (Detroit: Wayne State University Press, 2002).

47. Paul Jankowski, *Stavisky: A Confidence Man in the Republic of Virtue* (Ithaca, NY: Cornell University Press, 2002).

48. The Popular Front was a coalition of the Radical-Socialist, Socialist, and Communist parties formed to combat fascism in 1935; a Popular Front government featuring Radicals and Socialists in power with the support of the Communists took power in the spring of 1936: Julian Jackson, *The Popular Front in France: Defending Democracy, 1934–1938* (Cambridge: Cambridge University Press, 1990).

49. This difference, as Miranda Pollard discusses, helped to mark the break between the Third Republic and the Vichy regime, as Philippe Pétain positioned himself as the father of the nation: Miranda Pollard, "In the Name of the Father: Male Masculinities in Vichy France," in *French Masculinities: History, Culture, and Politics,* ed. Christopher E. Forth and Bertrand Taithe (New York: Palgrave Macmillan, 2007), 141–56.

50. Mosse, *Masses and Man,* 87, 165–167, and *The Image of Man,* 155–80.

51. Mosse, *The Image of Man,* 107–32.

52. Mona L. Siegel, *The Moral Disarmament of France: Education, Pacifism, and Patriotism, 1914–1940* (Cambridge: Cambridge University Press, 2004), 19–220. "Integral" pacifists were those who wished to avoid war at all costs.

53. See, for example, Charles Rearick, *The French in Love and War: Popular Culture in the Era of the World Wars* (New Haven, CT: Yale University Press, 1997), 205–41; Mortimer, *The Rise of the French Communist Party,* 226–67.

54. Marie-Monique Huss, "Pronatalism in the Interwar Period in France," *Journal of Contemporary History* 25 (1990): 42.

55. Sîan Reynolds, *France between the Wars: Gender and Politics* (London: Routledge, 1996), 156–82.

56. Mary Lynn Stewart's work, for example, provides an interesting glimpse of how France's politicians tried, mostly unsuccessfully, to reconcile their traditionalist visions of femininity with the need for women to work and the desire to protect their children (and so safeguard the race): Mary Lynn Stewart, *Women, Work, and the French State: Labour Protection and Social Patriarchy, 1879–1914* (Montreal: McGill-Queen's University Press, 1989).

57. Christine Bard and Jean-Louis Robert, "The French Communist Party and Women, 1920–1939: From Feminism to 'Familialism,'" in *Women and Socialism/Socialism and Women*, ed. Helmut Gruber and Pamela Graves (Providence: Berghahn, 1998), 321–47; Campbell, "Women and Men in French Authoritarianism"; Helmut Gruber, "French Women in the Crossfire of Class, Sex, Maternity and Citizenship," in *Women and Socialism/Socialism and Women*, ed.Helmut Gruber and Pamela Graves (Providence, RI: Berghahn, 1998), 279–320; Sarnoff, "In the Cervix of the Nation."

58. See, for example, Wileman, "L'Alliance républicaine démocratique"; Larmour, *The French Radical Party.*

59. Delbreil, *Centrisme et démocratie-chrétienne en France;* Berstein, *Histoire du Parti radical;* Irvine, *French Conservatism in Crisis;* Mortimer, *The Rise of the French Communist Party.*

60. Daniella Sarnoff, "Interwar Fascism and the Franchise: Women's Suffrage and the *Ligues,*" *Historical Reflections/Réflexions historiques* 34, no. 2 (Summer 2008): 112–33. See also Christine Bard, *Les filles de Marianne: Histoire des féminismes, 1914–1940* (Paris: Libraire Arthème Fayard, 1995); Steven C. Hause with Anne R. Kenney, *Women's Suffrage and Social Politics in the French Third Republic* (Princeton, NJ: Princeton University Press, 1984); Sîan Reynolds, "Marianne's Citizens? Women, the Republic, and Universal Suffrage in France," in *Women, State and Revolution: Essays on Power and Gender in Europe Since 1789*, ed. Sîan Reynolds (Brighton: Wheatsheaf, 1986), 101–22; Paul Smith, *Feminism and the Third Republic: Women's Political and Civil Rights in France, 1918–1945* (Oxford: Clarendon Press, 1999); Charles Sowerwine, *Les femmes et le socialisme: Un siècle d'histoire* (Paris: Presses de la Fondation nationale des sciences-politiques, 1978).

61. Joan Scott, "Gender: A Useful Category of Historical Analysis," *American Historical Review* 91, no. 5 (December 1986): 1067.

62. R. W. Connell, *Masculinities* (Berkeley: University of California Press, 1995), 71.

63. Scott, *Gender and the Politics of History,* 28–50.

64. See, for example, Kathleen Canning, *Languages of Labour and Gender: Female Factory Work in Germany, 1850–1914* (Ithaca, NY: Cornell University Press, 1996).

65. See, for example, Michele Haapamaki, "Writers in Arms and the Just War: The Spanish Civil War, Literary Activism, and Leftist Masculinity," *Left History* 10, no. 2 (2005): 33–52; or the essays in Stefan Dudink, Karen Hagemann, and John Tosh, eds., *Masculinities in Politics and War: Gendering Modern History* (Manchester: Manchester University Press, 2004).

66. Lisa Cody, "This Sex Which Seems to Have Won: The Emergence of Masculinity as a Category of Historical Analysis," *Radical History Review* 61 (1995): 166–74.

67. Connell, *Masculinities,* 35–37; Judith Butler, *Gender Trouble: Feminism and the Subversion of Identity,* revised edition (New York: Routledge, 1999), vii–xxvi.

68. Scott, "Gender: A Useful Category," 1074.

69. Paligot, *La république raciale,* 9–31, 151–220.

70. Paligot, *Races, racisme, et anti-racisme,* 5–59.

71. Pierre-André Taguieff, *La Force du préjugé: Essai sur le racisme et ses doubles* (Paris: Éditions la découverte, 1987), 31. Translated by Geoff Read.

72. Ibid, 314. Translated by Geoff Read.

73. See Roger Griffin, *The Nature of Fascism* (New York: St. Martin's Press, 1991); Stanley G. Payne, *Fascism: Comparison, and Definition* (Madison: University of Wisconsin Press, 1980).

74. Robert O. Paxton, *The Anatomy of Fascism* (New York: Vintage, 2004), 218.

75. See William D. Irvine, "Fascism in France and the Strange Case of the Croix de Feu," *Journal of Modern History* 63, no. 2 (June 1991): 271–95; Kalman, *The Extreme Right in Interwar France,* 13–60; Albert Kéchichian, *Les Croix de feu à l'âge des fascismes* (Paris: Champ Vallon, 2006); Kennedy, *Reconciling France against Democracy,* 6–7; Nobécourt, *Le Colonel de La Rocque;* Passmore, "Boy Scouting for Grown-Ups?" 527–57; Geoff Read, "'He Is Depending on You': Militarism, Martyrdom and the Appeal to Manliness in the Case of France's 'Croix de Feu,' 1931–1940," *Journal of the Canadian Historical Association* 19 (2005): 261–92; René Rémond, *Les Droites en France* (Paris: Aubier, 1982); Michel Winock, *Nationalisme, Antisémitisme et Fascisme en France* (Paris: Éditions du Seuil, 1990); Soucy, *French Fascism,* 104–203; Zeev Sternhell, *Neither Right nor Left: Fascist Ideology in France* (Los Angeles: University of California Press, 1986).

76. Paxton, *Anatomy of Fascism,* 69–71.

77. Ibid., 14–23.

78. Byron Criddle, "Electoral Systems in France," *Parliamentary Affairs* 45, no. 1 (1992): 109.

79. Mortimer, *The Rise of the French Communist Party,* 19, 45.

80. Comintern refers to the Communist International, by which the Bolsheviks sought to discipline and control communist parties worldwide.

81. Mortimer, *The Rise of the French Communist Party,* 68.

82. Ibid., 113.

83. Ibid., 248–51.

84. Bard and Robert, "The French Communist Party and Women," 328. The journal itself claimed 2,500 subscribers in 1923: "Ce que les femmes doivent faire pour que leur journal vive et se développe," *L'Ouvrière: Organe des travailleuses manuelles et intellectuelles* [hereafter *L'Ouvrière*], April 14, 1923, 1.

85. Mortimer, *The Rise of the French Communist Party,* 68.

86. Lacouture, *Léon Blum,* 196.

87. Ibid., 243.

88. Ibid., 151.

89. Compère-Morel, "40,000 abonnés!" *Le Populaire: Quotidien du Parti socialiste (S.F.I.O.)* [hereafter *Le Populaire*], January 31, 1932, 1. The total number of papers sold including subscriptions was near eighty thousand per issue in 1932. See a chart featured in *Le Populaire* of August 24, 1932, 1.

90. Larmour, *The French Radical Party,* 22.

91. Ibid., 202.

92. Lacouture, *Léon Blum,* 244.

93. Larmour, *The French Radical Party,* 55–56.

94. Wileman, "L'Alliance républicaine démocratique."

95. Ibid., 131–34.

96. Ibid., 212–16.

97. Irvine, *French Conservatism in Crisis,* 27–31.

98. "Bloc national" refers to a coalition of right-wing parties, groups, and individuals that took power in the 1919 elections.

99. The PDP elected twenty-three deputies in both the 1932 and 1936 elections: "Résultats officiels des élections communiqués par le ministère de l'Intérieur," *Le Populaire,* May 5. 1936, 1.

100. Delbreil, *Centrisme et démocratie-chrétienne en France,* 11–13.

101. The "Cartel des gauches" refers to the left-wing coalition that took power in the 1924 elections. The Socialists supported the cartel but did not participate in government while the Communists, in keeping with their intransigence in the 1920s, did not support it. This meant that the Radicals dominated the Cartel des gauches government.

102. Delbreil, *Centrisme et démocratie-chrétienne en France,* 11–17.

103. Kennedy, *Reconciling France against Democracy,* 4.

104. Soucy, *French Fascism,* 36, 108.

105. Robert Soucy and W. D. Irvine are foremost among the former group. See: Soucy, *French Fascism,* 104–203; Irvine, "Fascism in France and the Strange Case of the Croix de Feu." The latter group includes Kéchichian, *Les Croix de feu à l'âge des fascismes;* Nobécourt, *Le Colonel de La Rocque;* Rémond, *Les Droites en France;* Sternhell, *Neither Right nor Left.* Kevin Passmore holds the middle ground, arguing that the Croix de feu was fascist, but that the Parti social français was not: Passmore, "Boy Scouting for Grown-Ups?" 527–57. Sean Kennedy meanwhile, insists on the antidemocratic and authoritarian nature of the movement, but argues it was not exactly fascist: Kennedy, *Reconciling France against Democracy.* Kalman joins Kennedy in suggesting the debate over the movement's fascism has run its course: Kalman, *The Extreme Right in Interwar France,* 39–57.

106. Brunet, *Jacques Doriot,* 228–29.

CHAPTER ONE

1. Karen Offen, message posted to H-France under subject heading "Masculinity and Dreyfus Affair," August 23, 2004, https://lists.uakron.edu/sympa/arc/h-france/2004-08/msg00074.html (accessed September 1, 2009).

2. Jankowski, *Stavisky.*

3. Albert Lebrun, "Le voyage de M. Albert Lebrun à Montélimar: Inaugurant le monument élevé à la mémoire d'Émile Loubet, le président de la République déclare que le devoir, aujourd'hui, est de subordonner les intérêts particuliers à la notion du salut public," *L'Ère nouvelle: Organe de l'entente des gauches* [hereafter *L'Ère nouvelle*], April 3, 1939, 1, 3.

4. Paris, Institut des Sciences-Politiques, letter dated October 13, 1936, from François de La Rocque to Raymond Guenard, in carton 24 of the François de La Rocque papers [hereafter ISP LR/carton number].

5. "Communication du gouvernement," *Journal officiel, Chambre,* January 22, 1920, 15–16.

6. Louis Marin, "Adieu à Charles de Lasteyrie," *La Nation: Organe de la Fédération républicaine de France* [hereafter *La Nation*], July 11,1936, 533.

7. Paris, Archives nationales de France, letter dated April 21, 1936, from Henri Bergson to André Tardieu, in carton 119 of the André Tardieu papers [hereafter ANF AP 324/carton number]. Bergson was a philosopher who emphasized the irrational as a motive force, and George Mosse, for one, sees him as an important intellectual progenitor of the emotive appeals of fascism: Mosse, *Masses and Man,* 199. Indeed, Andrès Reggiani emphasizes the proximity of Alexis Carrel's views to Bergson's. Bergson praised Carrel's book, *L'homme, cet inconnu,* which

included passages favoring "negative" eugenic measures as well as a dictatorship of technocratic elites: Reggiani, *God's Eugenicist*, 76.

8. Judith F. Stone, "The Republican Brotherhood: Gender and Ideology," in *Gender and the Politics of Social Reform in France, 1870–1914*, ed. Elinor A. Accampo, Rachel G. Fuchs, and Mary Lynn Stewart (Baltimore: Johns Hopkins University Press, 1996), 48–49.

9. Mortimer, *The Rise of the French Communist Party*, 123.

10. Boris Souvarine, "Illitch, cher Illitch," *L'Humanité: Organe central du Parti communiste (S.F.I.C.)* [hereafter *L'Humanité*], January 27, 1924, 1.

11. See, for example: Paris, Archives nationales de France, letter dated February 14, 1934, from Marcel Sauqé to Édouard Daladier, in carton 4 of the Edouard Daladier papers [hereafter ANF AP 496/carton number].

12. Paris, Archives nationales de France, text of a speech delivered at the "Soirée solennelle de la Mutualité," on October 13, 1938, Marcel Cachin, "Paul Vaillant-Couturier: Homme de la paix," in carton 9 of the Marcel Cachin Papers [hereafter referred to as ANF AP 447/carton number].

13. See, for example, the following text of either a speech or an editorial about an upcoming congress of the Confédération générale du travail ouvrière: "Le prochain congrès des syndicats révolutionnaires français," September 1927, in ANF AP 447/14.

14. Paris, Archives nationales de France, a red poster titled "Remerciements," dated 1932 in carton 11 of the Vincent Auriol Papers [hereafter referred to as ANF AP 552/carton number].

15. "Nécrologie: Madame Paul Duguet," *Le Petit Démocrate: Journal démocrate populaire* [hereafter *Le Petit Démocrate*], September 29, 1929, 5.

16. See, for example, "Nécrologie : Mort de Mme P. Sauvage," *L'Alliance démocratique*, March 20, 1936, 1; or the following photo of a female member of the Executive Committee: "Mme Perreau-Chandet," *L'Alliance démocratique*, December 11, 1936, 1.

17. Fernande Hartmann, "La famille et l'éducation des femmes," *Le Devoir des femmes: Revue mensuelle de la section féminine de la Fédération républicaine de France* [hereafter *Le Devoir des femmes*], July–August 1937, 12–13.

18. Marie Maugeret, "Questions féminines et questions féministes: Notre programme," *Questions féminines et questions féministes*, December 15, 1924, 1.

19. Smith, *Feminism and the Third Republic*, 34–36. The title *Le Droit des femmes* can actually be traced all the way back to the second Empire, as it was the name chosen by early feminists Léon Richer and Maria Desraismes for their journal: Sowerine, *Les femmes et le socialisme*, 10. Vérone argued for women's full civic equality within marriage on the basis that women were refusing to wed so as not to give up their rights: Andrea Mansker, *Sex, Honor, and Citizenship in Early Third Republic France* (New York: Palgrave MacMillan, 2011), 163–92.

20. A. Lefas, "Le devoir prime le droit: Devoir d'abord!" *Le Devoir des femmes*, May 20, 1935, 1.

21. "Section féminine," *Le Flambeau: Organe du mouvement Croix de feu* [hereafter *Le Flambeau*], July 1, 1934, 3.

22. "Paula Wallisch," *La Femme Socialiste: Organe d'éducation de propagande et d'action Socialiste* [hereafter *La Femme Socialiste*], May 15, 1934, 2–3.

23. Georges Boris, "Thérèse Blum," *La Lumière: Le grand hebdomadaire des gauches* [hereafter *La Lumière*], January 28, 1938, 1.

24. René Remond with Aline Coutrot, *Les Catholiques, le communisme et les crises, 1929–1939* (Paris: Armand Colin, 1960), 21–39.

25. "Exemples de leçons de vertu de mes parents ou de mes maîtres (pensées de l'empereur Marc-Aurèle)," *Le Devoir des femmes,* January 15, 1936, 5.

26. Letter dated September 20. 1931, from Paul Doumer to André Tardieu, ANF AP 324/118.

27. Transcript of the "Réunion du comité exécutif du 8 Octobre 1936," in ISP LR/15. Capitalization in original.

28. Jacques Doriot, "Les 11, 12 et 13 mars, notre parti tient à Paris ses assises nationales populaires françaises," *L'Émancipation nationale: Hebdomadaire du Parti populaire français* [hereafter *L'Émancipation nationale*], March 4, 1938, 1.

29. Alfred Bayet, "Emile Glay: Un grand ouvrier de l'idée laïque," *La Lumière,* February 29, 1936, 1–2.

30. "Nécrologie," *La Femme Socialiste,* December 1933, 6–8.

31. "Sa mère : Une visite chez la mère de notre camarade Staline," *L'Ouvrière,* November 30, 1935, 2.

32. Letter dated October 28, 1934, from A. Bernard to Édouard Daladier, ANF AP 496/6.

33. Undated note from Marcel Cachin to "Zizi," ANF AP 447/10.

34. Paul Faure, "La mort de l'apôtre," *Le Populaire,* July 29, 1922, 2.

35. Marcel Cachin, "Sangfroid," *L'Humanité,* March 16, 1920, 1, May 10, 1920, 1, *and* September 30, 1920, 1. Cachin was at this time still a member of the SFIO as the schism between the SFIO adherents to the Second International and the PCF supporters of the Third did not take place until December 1920.

36. André Février, "Sang-froid et courage!" *Le Populaire,* March 20, 1937, 1.

37. "Discussion, après demande de discussion immédiate, d'un projet de loi monétaire, modifié par le Sénat," *Journal officiel, Chambre,* September 30, 1936, 2860.

38. EN, "Courage et sang-froid," *L'Ère nouvelle,* May 14, 1940, 1.

39. A. Champetier de Ribes, "1936," *Le Petit Démocrate,* 5 January 1936, 1.

40. François de La Rocque, "Sang-froid," *Le Flambeau,* July 1, 1934, 1.

41. Maurice Lebrun, "Les gardes mobiles se constituent une armée d'élite mais ce sont aussi des hommes," *L'Émancipation nationale,* May 2, 1937, 4.

42. Landes, *Women and the Public Sphere.*

43. Frader, *Breadwinners and Citizens,* 51–102.

44. Childers, *Fathers, Families, and the State,* 4.

45. "Paternité," *Le Petit Démocrate,* February 3, 1929, 4.

46. Paris, Archives nationales de France, letter dated December 20, 1920, from Louis Marin to 'Mon Colonel,' in carton 228 of the Louis Marin papers [hereafter ANF AP 317/carton number].

47. Paris, Archives nationales de France, letter dated 1924 from le Comte de Montenon to Alexandre Millerand, in carton 109 of the Alexandre Millerand Papers [hereafter ANF AP 470/carton number].

48. Alexandre Bérard, "Communication relative au décès de M. Desgranges, Sénateur de Saône-et-Loire," *Journal officiel, Sénat,* March 15, 1921, 238.

49. Fernand Bouisson, "Décès d'un Député," *Journal officiel, Chambre,* April 18, 1930, 1981.

50. See, for example, the text of a speech he gave to the workers at Peugeot: P.G., "Quand Jacques Doriot parle de la famille," *L'Émancipation nationale,* April 10, 1937, 8.

51. François de La Rocque, "A ceux d'après-guerre: Aux F.F.C.F.," *Le Flambeau,* November 1, 1932, 8. Emphasis in original.

52. See, for example, a series of reports to La Rocque such as one marked: "Cas D . . ." which summarized the personal circumstances of given members and their families and the actions taken by the party's organs on their behalf in carton 87/88 in the François de La Rocque Papers, Archives nationales de France [hereafter ANF AP 451/carton number].

53. Letter dated October 6, 1937, from A. de Préval to Miss de Gimard, ANF AP 451/163.

54. I. Montaudoin, "Le foyer des moins de treize ans," *Le Flambeau*, January 1, 1935, 4. Victoria de Grazia has identified this usurpation of the father's role by the party or state as a key feature of Italian fascism. See Victoria de Grazia, *How Fascism Ruled Women: Italy, 1922–1945* (Berkeley: University of California Press, 1991), 77–115.

55. Text of speech, Édouard Daladier, "Allocution radiodiffusée de M. Édouard Daladier, Président du conseil," ANF AP 496/16.

56. Letter dated October 30, 1939, from Vincent Auriol to Monsieur le Ministre de la guerre et de la défense nationale, ANF AP 552/27.

57. Paul Vaillant-Couturier, "Ce qu'ils n'ont pas vu à Moscou: Les enfants et les parents," *L'Humanité*, January 7, 1933, 1–2.

58. See, for example, Antoine Valbert, "La dépopulation française," *L'Humanité*, January 6, 1924, 4.

59. Manuscript, Louis Marin, "Sainte Margueritte, vierge et martyre," ANF AP 317/250.

60. Annie, "Petite causerie: Fiançailles," *Le Petit Démocrate*, March 31, 1929, 4.

61. This appeared in two publications: François de La Rocque, "À mes filles étudiantes," *L'Étudiant social: Organe de la réconciliation française chez les étudiants*, February 1939, 1, ISP LR/15; François de La Rocque, "À mes filles étudiantes," *Pourquoi s'en faire T.V.B.: Organe de la réconciliation française chez les étudiantes*, April 1938, ANF AP 451/114.

62. Fanny Clar, "La femme et la vie: De quelques préjugés dangereux," *L'Ère nouvelle*, August 7, 1931, 1–2. Clar recognized and argued that this supposed celebration of women served only to subjugate passive women to active men.

63. Alice Jouenne, "Tribune féministe: La journée des femmes," *Le Populaire*, March 9, 1919, 2.

64. Marcel Cachin, "Lénine, Karl Liebknecht et Rosa Luxembourg toujours vivants en nos cœurs," *L'Humanité*, January 21, 1939, 2.

65. Paul Guitard, "Josephine Baker, fille sauvage," *L'Humanité*, June 10, 1926, 4. Guitard would later move into the camp of the fascist Parti populaire français.

66. Rearick, *The French in Love and War*, 81–82.

67. Louise Saumoneau, "Confiance," *La Femme Socialiste*, August 1931, 1.

68. Léon Blum, *Du mariage* (Paris: Imprimerie de St. Denis, 1937), 5–12.

69. Louise Bodin, "Adam et Eve," *Le Populaire*, October 26, 1919, 1. Berthe Fouchère, under the pseudonym Irma Taury, also argued for young girls to receive sexual education: Irma Taury, "L'éducation sociale de la jeune fille," *L'Ouvrière*, July 7, 1923, 1. Communists, especially in the early 1920s, proved the most nonconformist in their thinking. See "La vie familiale: Le lit," *L'Ouvrière*, May 15, 1924, 2.

70. See, for example, Sowerine, *Les femmes et le socialisme*, Bard, *Les filles de Marianne*, 367, 394–95; Scott, *Only Paradoxes to Offer*, 125–60.

71. Doctoresse Pelletier, "De la prostitution," *L'Ouvrière*, March 8, 1924, 3.

72. McLaren, *Sexuality and Social Order*, 180–81.

73. Ibid., 77–88.

74. Dr. J. Héricourt, "L'éducation sexuelle de la jeunesse: Il faut prendre garde à ses conséquences morales et physiologiques," *La Lumière,* October 22, 1927, 11.

75. Danièle Vindor, "Pour nos filles," *Le Populaire,* October 14, 1922, 4.

76. See Richard D. Sonn, *Sex, Violence, and the Avant-Garde: Anarchism in Interwar France* (University Park: Pennsylvania State University Press, 2010), 99–116.

77. Alice Jouenne, "La femme et l'école," *Le Populaire,* July 5, 1934, 4.

78. "Nécrologie," *Le Petit Démocrate,* March 11, 1928, 5.

79. Yves Dautun, "France, qu'as-tu fait de ta jeunesse? (suite)" *L'Émancipation nationale,* April 14, 1939, 7–8.

80. J.L., "Inquiétude de la jeune fille française devant l'avenir," *L'Alliance démocratique,* January 24, 1936, 3.

81. Sarnoff, "In the Cervix of the Nation."

82. P., "Nécrologie: Madame Paul Duguet," *Le Petit Démocrate,* September 29, 1929, 5.

83. Henri Schulz, "Conseils à une mère Socialiste—I," *Le Populaire,* July 27, 1919, 3.

84. The women's page was founded in 1922 : L'administration, "Une bonne surprise," *Le Populaire,* October 13, 1922, 1.

85. See, for example, Docteur Weill-Raynal, "N'envoyez point prématurément les nouveau-nés en nourrice," *Le Populaire,* October 7, 1928, 4. The Weill-Raynal clan appears to have been well-represented in the SFIO. The Weill-Raynals included Étienne, Emmeline, who served on the National Committee of Socialist Women, and Sara.

86. Maupassant was a celebrated nineteenth-century French short story writer. It is possible that this was actually authored by someone else who was just using his name. For a biography of Maupassant, see Bernard Valette, *Guy de Maupassant: Une vie* (Paris: Études littéraires, 1993).

87. Guy de Maupassant, "Un parricide," *L'Ouvrière,* September 10, 1925, 2–3.

88. Letter dated 1927 from Marcel Cachin to Lilite Cachin, ANF AP 447/10.

89. Maurice Thorez, *Fils du peuple* (Paris: Editions Sociales, 1970), 16–17.

90. "Discussion de propositions de loi relatives à l'élection et à l'éligibilité des femmes," *Journal officiel, Sénat,* November 7, 1922, 1298–1299.

91. Janine Louis-Merlet, "Le vote des femmes," *L'Ère nouvelle,* March 31, 1928, 1.

92. Letter dated February 9, 1934, from Sibille Brésart to Édouard Daladier, ANF AP 496/4.

93. S.G.Mgr. Julien, "La mission familiale de la femme: L'éducation de la femme d'aujourd'hui," *Le Petit Démocrate,* August 14, 1927, 4.

94. Princesse de Robech, "Le rôle des femmes dans le miracle canadien," *Le Devoir des femmes,* June 20, 1935, 5–6.

95. Marie Rabaté, "Les boy-scouts: Organisation pré-fasciste de la jeunesse," *L'Humanité,* June 4, 1933, 4.

96. Gabrielle Bouet- - - [three letters illegible], "L'éducation des jeunesses," *L'Humanité,* August 20, 1922, 4.

97. Berthe Fouchère, "Tribune des femmes Socialistes: Adelheid Popp est morte," *Le Populaire,* April 9, 1939, 8.

98. Maud-Puy, "Les femmes Radicales: Notre appel aux républicains n'est pas resté sans écho," *L'Ère nouvelle,* January 16,1933, 3. Historians have remarked upon this role of mothers as evangelists for the secular faith: Surkis, *Sexing the Citizen,* 21–42; Tilburg, *Colette's Republic,* 24.

99. Dr. Paul Boyer, "Pour les autres," *Le Réveil,* May 26, 1918, 1, in ANF/470, AP/102.

100. "Suite de la discussion de la proposition de loi tendant à accorder aux femmes le droit de vote dans certaines élections," *Journal officiel, Chambre,* May 12, 1919, 2300. For Du Prey's membership in the Alliance, see a party report: Paris, Bibliothèque nationale de France, "Alliance démocratique (Parti des républicains de gauche et des républicains radicaux)," undated, in carton 1 of the Alliance démocratique et républicain papers [hereafter BNF/37620/carton number].

101. Gabriel Péri, "Mamans de France! Les mamans d'Espagne vous demandent du lait pour leurs petits: Dimanche prochain, faites votre devoir comme les combattants de la liberté font le leur," *L'Humanité,* October 18, 1938, 1, 3.

102. For the Croix de feu see a report by R. Fallay, "Rapport sur la fédération de la Somme," March 4, 1940, ANF AP 451/29; for the Parti démocrate populaire, see S.L., "Pour nos mobilisés: Le comité du 'colis Palatine'—son but, son organisation, ses intentions," *Le Petit Démocrate,* April 1, 1940, 3; for the Fédération républicaine, see "La page du soldat 'sans famille,'" *Le Devoir des femmes,* January–February 1940, 5–6; for the Parti populaire français, see "Colis de Noël pour nos soldats," *L'Émancipation nationale,* November 24, 1939, 6.

103. Maurice Vincent, "1870–1914–1939," *Bulletin trihebdomadaire de la presse démocratique française,* September 14, 1939, 2, BNF/37260/2.

104. "A une mère française," *La Nation,* September 28, 1929, 912.

105. Marie-Thérèse Archambault, "Pour la paix: Devant le malaise actuel," *Le Petit Démocrate,* March 8, 1931, 4.

106. Pamphlet dated 1934, "Gala tricolore," ANF AP 451/87/88.

107. Fly sheet, "Femmes Françaises," ANF AP 451/ 82/83.

108. Paul Schue, "The Prodigal Sons of Communism: Parti Populaire Français Narratives of Communist Recruitment for the Spanish Civil War and the Everyday Functioning of Party Ideology," *French Historical Studies* 24, no. 1 (Winter 2001): 87–111.

109. J.R., "'Thorez, rendez-moi mon enfant!' Dit une mère d'un gars de 18 ans, parti pour l'Espagne," *L'Émancipation nationale,* December 12, 1936, 5.

110. Chamine, "Les évadés de l'enfer espagnol: Cinq jeunes ouvriers français enrôlés dans les milices internationales dénoncent la barbarie soviétique et la lâcheté des gouvernementaux," *L'Émancipation nationale,* January 16, 1937, 5.

111. Pierre Drieu La Rochelle, "Réponse à une femme," *L'Émancipation nationale,* December 5, 1936, 8.

112. See, for example, Pierre Drieu La Rochelle, *L'Homme à cheval,* 3rd ed. (Paris: Gallimard, 1943).

113. L.-A. Gremilly, "Les droits de la femme: Une grande manifestation—les résultats du congrès de Genève," *L'Ère nouvelle,* June 21, 1920, 1–2.

114. Noel, "Les femmes et la paix," *L'Ère nouvelle,* December 13, 1931, 2. Malaterre-Sellier was a vice-president of the Union française pour le suffrage des femmes: Smith, *Feminism and the Third Republic,* 25.

CHAPTER TWO

1. A third group, headed by Karl Marx's grandson Jean Longuet and Paul Faure, wished initially to join the Third International with some conditions but reconsidered after an uncompromising and bellicose address by Comintern secretary Grigory Zinoviev. Longuet, Faure, and

their followers thus also remained in the Socialist Party and became the de facto leaders of the party's left wing: Joel Colton, *Léon Blum: Humanist in Politics*, 2nd ed. (Durham, NC: Duke University Press, 1987), 48–54.

2. See, for example, Mosse, *The Image of Man*, 13–14.

3. Mary Louise Roberts, *Disruptive Acts: The New Woman in Fin-de-Siècle France* (Chicago: University of Chicago Press, 2002), 19–47.

4. For Nelly Roussel, see Accampo, *Blessed Motherhood, Bitter Fruit*, esp. 35–69.

5. Katia Palianoff, "Les ouvrières de la Russie des Soviets," *L'Ouvrière*, March 18, 1922, 2–3.

6. Katia Palianoff, "Les ouvrières de la Russie des Soviets," *L'Ouvrière*, March 25, 1922, 2–3.

7. Katia Palianoff, "Les ouvrières de la Russie des Soviets," *L'Ouvrière*, April 8, 1922, 3.

8. Germaine Sillon, "La femme et le communisme," *L'Ouvrière*, November 2, 1923, 1–2.

9. Germaine Sillon, "La jeune fille accomplie," *L'Ouvrière*, September 22, 1923, 2.

10. "L'héroïque dévouement d'une ouvrière," *L'Ouvrière*, November 6, 1924, 3.

11. "Pour sauver son mari, une jeune ouvrière donne huit fois son sang," *L'Ouvrière*, December 23, 1926, 4.

12. Jeanne Vendras, "Le devoir de la femme," *L'Ouvrière*, January 13, 1927, 2.

13. C.F. de la R.P., "Soutenons dans la lutte, notre camarade Suzanne Girault," *L'Ouvrière*, July 31, 1930, 1.

14. "Le bonheur des femmes," *L'Ouvrière*, August 25, 1923, 2.

15. Agnes, "Aux mères abandonnées," *L'Ouvrière*, July 16, 1925, 1.

16. Germaine V. . . , "Mauvaise mère," *L'Ouvrière*, June 18, 1925, 1.

17. Les Jeunesses Communistes, "Appel aux jeunes ouvrières," *L'Humanité*, February 28, 1926, 4.

18. Marcel Cachin, "Aux journés d'amitié des 16, 17, et 18 avril les Jeunes filles de France vont formuler leurs espoirs et chanter le printemps," *L'Humanité*, April 16, 1938, 1–2. Cachin incorrectly dated the founding of the JFF as 1928.

19. See, for example, the following untitled photographs: *L'Ouvrière*, November 30, 1930, 4, and September 15, 1935, 4.

20. Susan B. Whitney, "Embracing the Status Quo: French Communists, Young Women and the Popular Front," *Journal of Social History* 30, no. 1 (Autumn 1996): 29–53.

21. "Journée internationale des femmes," *L'Ouvrière*, March 11, 1922, 4.

22. "Une municipalité Communiste: St. Ouen," *L'Ouvrière*, October 7, 1922, 2.

23. Clamamus, "La protection de la mère et de l'enfant," *L'Ouvrière*, August 15, 1933, 1–2.

24. The first issue featuring this section appeared on May 31, 1934.

25. See A. Gilles, "Terme! Taudis! Habitations à bon marché: L'angoissante question du terme!" *L'Ouvrière*, January 31, 1933, 1.

26. Marguerite Michard, "La duperie fasciste sur le retour de la femme au foyer," *L'Ouvrière*, January 31, 1935, 1.

27. Marcel Martinet, "Séverine," *L'Humanité*, July 17, 1921, 4.

28. *L'Humanité*, November 21, 1935, 4.

29. See, for example, Frader, *Breadwinners and Citizens*, 193–227.

30. See, for example, L.-A. Pagès, "Pour lutter contre le chômage—le retour de la mère au foyer: Une très opportune enquête de l'Union féminine civique et sociale," *Le Petit Démocrate*, November 1, 1931, 2.

31. In typical fashion, this was signaled by a wave of purges and counterpurges within the party's leadership: Mortimer, *The Rise of the French Communist Party*, 98–130.

32. See also Bard and Robert, "The French Communist Party and Women," 339–341. François Delpla has similarly concluded that at about 1935 the Communists' discussions of female sexuality became much more conventional: François Delpla with Jean-Gabriel Foucaud, "Les communistes français et la sexualité (1932–1938)," *Le Mouvement social* 91 (April–June 1975): 133–42.

33. Nenassou, "Ce qu'une femme doit savoir," *Le Flambeau,* July 1, 1934, 6.

34. Mary Jean Green, "The Bouboule Novels: Constructing a French Fascist Woman," in *Gender and Fascism in Modern France,* ed. Melanie Hawthorne and Richard Golsan (Hanover: University Press of New England, 1997), 49–68.

35. For a discussion of Dora's father's career, see Jankowski, *Communism and Collaboration.* For the text of a report Dora made to the party youth congress, see Dora Sabiani, "Jeunes filles françaises," *L'Émancipation nationale,* April 21, 1939, 7.

36. Jacqueline Girard, "Jeunes filles françaises," *L'Émancipation nationale,* April 28, 1939, 8.

37. Jacques Cartonnet, "L'Union sportive des jeunesses françaises doit être le refuge de tous les jeunes," *L'Émancipation nationale,* March 4, 1938, 2; Jacqueline Girard, "Jeunes filles françaises," *L'Émancipation nationale,* May 5, 1939, 8.

38. Ph. L. de Villeneuve Breix, "Les fils de Croix de feu," *Le Flambeau,* July 1930, 4.

39. François de La Rocque, "À ceux d'après-guerre: Aux F.F.C.F.," *Le Flambeau,* November 1932, 8. See also the group's regulations dated 1935, "Règlement général de l'association 'Les fils et filles de Croix de feu,'" ISP LR/6/54.

40. See memo dated October 1935, "Création des groupes C et des foyers des jeunes filles (Jeunes filles de 14 à 25 ans)," ANF AP 451/93.

41. See memo dated 1937, "Colonies de vacances," ANF AP 451/133.

42. "Pourquoi ce bulletin?" *Organe de la réconciliation française chez les étudiantes,* April 1937, 1–2, ANF AP 451/114.

43. Sarnoff, "In the Cervix of the Nation," 44–46.

44. See S.M., "Jeunes filles de France," *L'Émancipation nationale,* July 16, 1938, 2.

45. See a photograph with that caption: *L'Émancipation nationale,* June 12, 1937, 8.

46. Surkis, *Sexing the Citizen;* Stone, "Republican Ideology, Gender and Class." See also Tilburg, *Colette's Republic,* 46–74. Andrea Mansker illustrates how feminists challenged the male code of honor and citizenship in the early Third Republic: Mansker, *Sex, Honor, and Citizenship,* 5–22, 193–233.

47. The memorials to these two men in their respective legislative chambers were interesting for how their eulogizers tactfully overlooked their problematic histories to include them in the discursive pantheon of servants to the Republic and/or France: M. Jenouvrier, "Communication relative au décès de M. Dominique Delahaye, Sénateur de Maine-et-Loire," *Journal officiel, Sénat,* January 12, 1932, 4–5; Fernand Bouisson, "Décès d'un député," *Journal officiel, Chambre,* June 23, 1933, 3053–3054. In a sign of his authoritarianism, the *Croix de feu* also mourned Ferrette's passing on the pages of *Le Flambeau:* "Les grands morts du mois," *Le Flambeau,* July 1933, 8.

48. Albert Treint, "Les jeunes sont l'avenir du communisme," *L'Humanité,* August 5, 1923, 1. Treint helped to purge Trotskyists like Boris Souvarine from the party in the mid-1920s, which did not save him from being so purged shortly afterward: Mortimer, The Rise of *the French Communist Party,* 139.

49. "Les deux congrès," *L'Humanité,* January 20, 1925, 1.

50. Susan B. Whitney, *Mobilizing Youth: Communists and Catholics in Interwar France* (Durham, NC: Duke University Press, 2009), 51–79.

51. Amedée Dunois, "Contre nos jeunes," *L'Humanité,* May 22, 1921, 1.

52. Uncharacteristically, the party expressed regret at her departure. See Louise Bodin, "Lettre ouverte à Séverine," *L'Humanité,* February 10, 1923, 1.

53. Séverine, "Allez-vous les laisser mourir?" *L'Humanité,* May 27, 1921, 1.

54. Maurice Lebrun, "Au secours d'un courageux militant! Lucien Carré fait route vers le bagne de Mécharia," *L'Humanité,* November 19, 1931, 1.

55. See, for example, "Arrestation de Gabriel Péri," *L'Humanité,* March 22, 1923, 1.

56. Newspaper clipping, Gabriel Péri, "Morts pour la France: Lettres des condamnés à mort," ANF AP 447/10.

57. Brunet, *Jacques Doriot,* 488–89.

58. Jacques Doriot, "Soutenez les Jeunesses Communistes," *L'Humanité,* September 4, 1924, 1.

59. Mortimer, *The Rise of the French Communist Party,* 254.

60. Fernand Desprès, "La colonie de vacances de Bobigny: Les enfants s'installent," *L'Humanité,* August 13, 1923, 2.

61. "En vacances: Le retour des enfants de l'Île de Ré," *L'Humanité,* September 21, 1925, 2.

62. Jacques Doriot, "La semaine internationale de la jeunesse," *L'Humanité,* August 26, 1924, 1.

63. Jacques Doriot, "Voltaire Radi," *L'Humanité,* December 1, 1925, 1.

64. Marie Rabaté, "Les Boy Scouts: Organisation pré-fasciste de la jeunesse," *L'Humanité,* June 4, 1933, 4.

65. "Pourquoi nous fondons *La Lumière,*" *La Lumière,* May 14, 1927, 3.

66. "Communication du gouvernement," *Journal officiel, Chambre,* April 12, 1938, 1148.

67. "Communication du gouvernement," *Journal officiel, Chambre,* September 2, 1939, 1950–52.

68. Text of speech, Édouard Daladier, "Allocution radiodiffusée de M. Édouard Daladier, Président du conseil," ANF AP 496/16.

69. Suzanne Lacore, "La guerre: Action féminine," *Le Populaire,* September 4, 1929, 1–2.

70. Suzanne Renaud, "Tribune des femmes Socialistes: Pour une éducation fraternelle," *Le Populaire,* May 20, 1934, 4.

71. " Les tâches du militant," *Le Populaire,* February 11, 1934, 1.

72. La fédération des Jeunesses Communistes, "Fédération nationale des jeunesses Communistes: Manifeste aux conscrits—Jeune ouvrier! Jeune paysan!" *L'Humanité,* March 11, 1923, 5.

73. See "Jacques Doriot condamné à 4 mois de prison," *L'Humanité.* December 22, 1923, 1; Albert Treint, "Jacques Doriot condamné, notre propagande continue," *L'Humanité,* December 28, 1923, 1.

74. "Les valets de répression se sont surpassés: 4 ans de prison à André Marty," *L'Humanité,* December 15, 928, 1.

75. Forth, *The Dreyfus Affair and the Crisis of French Manhood,* 203–34.

76. Tumblety, *Remaking the Male Body,* 133–204.

77. Paul Vaillant-Couturier, "Le sport et la révolution," *L'Humanité,* July 8, 1923, 1.

78. L. Robert, "'Le muscle' ou comment la bourgeoisie se sert du sport pour sa propagande," *L'Humanité,* January 13, 1927, 4.

79. Jacques Doriot, "La semaine internationale des jeunes," *L'Humanité,* August 26, 1924, 1.

80. This was an omission that cost the German Social Democratic Party dearly as the Communists and Nazis turned many workers away from Weimar democracy through their takeover of popular sporting events. Such was the case, for example, with the Nazification of the Eilen-

riede motorcycle races: Adelheid von Saldern, "Cultural Conflicts, Popular Mass Culture, and the Question of Nazi Success: The Eilenriede Motorcycle Races, 1924–1939," *German Studies Review* 15, no. 2 (May 1992): 317–38. For a discussion of, among other things, the politicization of popular sport in the 1930s in France, see Joan Tumblety, "The Soccer World Cup of 1938: Politics, Spectacles, and 'la Culture Physique' in Interwar France," *French Historical Studies* 31, no. 1 (Winter 2008): 77–116.

81. Un correspondant de Fontenay-Sous-Bois, "Naissance de la F.S.T.," *L'Humanité,* December 26, 1928, 4.

82. See, for example, Marcel Cachin, "Aujourd'hui: Le sport ouvrier," *L'Humanité,* August 14, 1926, 1.

83. See, for example, "Colmar en fête accueille 5.000 gymnastes travaillistes," *L'Humanité,* August 15, 1938, 6.

84. "Nécrologie: Funérailles civiles de notre petit camarade Lucien Thorez," *L'Humanité,* April 21, 1938, 2.

85. *L'Humanité,* May 1, 1934, 6.

86. Manuscript, Marcel Cachin, "L'Impérialisme français contre l'U.R.S.S.," ANF AP 447/11.

87. Undated letter from Madame Cachin to unknown, ANF AP 447/11.

88. M. Magnien, "Vive l'armée rouge, rempart de la liberté et de la paix: L'URSS veut la paix mais écrasera ceux qui voudront l'attaquer," *L'Humanité,* February 21, 1939, 8.

89. This is a term used by labor historians and others to refer to those (male) workers who, thanks to the successes of unionism, enjoyed breadwinner status. See, for example, Thomas Dunk, "Remaking the Working Class: Experience, Class Consciousness, and the Industrial Adjustment Process," *American Ethnologist* 29, no. 4 (2002): 880.

90. Henri Barbé, "La cinquième congrès de la jeunesse Communiste s'ouvre aujourd'hui," *L'Humanité,* August 15, 1926, 1.

91. See Paul Guitard, "Hier, cloture . . . Le Tour de France est mort. À bas le Tour de France!" *L'Humanité,* July 18, 1927, 4, and "Plus de mille délégués de l'U.P.J.F assisteront au congrès de Marseille: Le chef sera présent aux trois journées," *L'Émancipation nationale,* April 7, 1939, 1.

92. See Maurice Lebrun, "Le même jour à la même heure," *L'Émancipation nationale,* October 17, 1936, 6.

93. Laurent Kestel makes this point: Kestel, *La conversion politique.*

94. Paul Guitard, "Le style, c'est l'homme," *L'Émancipation nationale,* April 22, 1938, 8.

95. Mosse, *Masses and Man,* 185.

96. "Action, éducation, distraction, tel est le programme de l'Union populaire de la jeunesse française," *L'Émancipation nationale,* October 10, 1936, 6.

97. J.-M. Aimot, "Constituons partout des sections de pionniers de Jacques Doriot," *L'Émancipation nationale,* December 5, 1936, 2.

98. Henri Barbé, "Le journal des jeunes: Vive *Jeunesse de France*!" *L'Émancipation nationale,* April 17, 1937, 6.

99. Jacques Cartonnet, "L'Union sportive des jeunesses françaises doit être le refuge de tous les jeunes," *L'Émancipation nationale,* March 4, 1938, 2.

100. Henri Lebre, "Au camp de vacances de la Ferté-Milon: Doriot chez les enfants," *L'Émancipation nationale,* August 27, 1937, 8.

101. Ivan Sicard et al., "Les jeunes du l'U.P.J.F. mourront, s'il le faut, pour la France," *L'Émancipation nationale,* September 1, 1939, 15.

102. Passmore, "Boy Scouting for Grown-Ups?" 544–46.

103. See, for example, Demos., "Les grandes manoeuvres de la guerre civile," *L'Ère nouvelle,* September 30, 1935, 3.

104. See Serge Berstein, *Le 6 février* (Paris: Editions Gallimard, 1975). For an excellent history of the Stavisky scandal, see Jankowski, *Stavisky.*

105. Passmore, "Boy Scouting for Grown-Ups?" 533. Chris Millington finds that the ostensibly apolitical veterans' group the Union nationale des combattants was also deeply implicated in the riot: Chris Millington, *From Victory to Vichy: Veterans in Inter-War France* (Manchester: Manchester University Press, 2012), 52–82.

106. Circular dated April 25, 1933, François de La Rocque, "Instruction urgente au sujet de l'activité générale de l'association," ANF AP 451/81. The "first time" presumably was during World War I.

107. Forth, *The Dreyfus Affair and the Crisis of French Manhood,* 203–34.

108. See contents of ANF AP 451/114/133.

109. Document dated 1935, "Groupe A (mixte) (moins de 13 ans)," ANF AP 451/93.

110. See, for example, Carroll, *French Literary Fascism,* 147–170; Tumblety, *Remaking the Male Body,* 179–200.

111. Jean-Paul Sartre, "Qu'est-ce qu'un collaborateur?" in Jean-Paul Sartre, *Situations, III* (Paris: Gallimard, 1949), 43–61; Theodor Adorno, *Minima Moralia: Reflections from Damaged Life* (Surrey: Gresham Press, 1974), 45–46.

112. See Andrew Hewitt, *Political Inversions: Homosexuality, Fascism, and the Modernist Imaginary* (Stanford, CA: Stanford University Press, 1996); Alice Kaplan, *The Collaborator: The Trial and Execution of Robert Brasillach* (Chicago: University of Chicago Press, 2000), 7–9.

113. Ph. L. de Villeneuve Breix, "Les fils de 'Croix de feu,'" *Le Flambeau,* July 1930, 4.

114. See, for example, "Programme de février des F.F.C.F.B.," *Le Flambeau,* February 1. 1933, 8.

115. Text of a speech dated May 16, 1939, G. A. Maire, "Discours," ANF AP 451/155. Jacques Nobécourt emphasizes that this organization's purpose was to mobilize and organize children, and to give them, in Maire's words, "the taste for physical education linked to moral values." Nobécourt, *Le Colonel de La Rocque,* 658.

116. Jean Bernard, "11 November 1938," *L'Étudiant social,* November 1938, 2, ANF AP 451/105. Drieu La Rochelle contrasted the vigorous PPF with the indolent, feminine bourgeois men of the Republic, in Pierre Drieu La Rochelle, "Nous et la bourgeoisie," *L'Émancipation nationale,* April 3, 1937, 2.

117. Report dated March 4, 1940, R. Fallay, "Rapport sur la fédération de la Somme," ISP LR/29. Armand Lanoux of the PPF likewise extolled the virtues of toy soldiers as they instilled in children a thirst for action and adventure: Armand Lanoux, "Monde des jouets reflet le monde des hommes," *L'Émancipation nationale,* December 30, 1938, 8.

118. Cheryl Koos, "The (Anti) Republican Right and the Gendered Politics of the Family: The Case of Louis Duval-Arnould and Georges Pernot" (paper presented at the annual meeting of the Society for French Historical Studies, June 2004, in Paris, France).

119. "Nos militants," *Le Petit Démocrate,* October 30, 1927, 5.

120. This could lead to odd circumstances, such as in 1936 when the "*Doyen d'âge,*" Maurice Le Corbeiller, had to explain awkwardly that the four Deputies older than he had either recently passed on or fallen gravely ill, and thus he had been rushed into service and his speech was ill-prepared: "Allocution de M. le président," *Journal officiel, Chambre,* January 14, 1936, 1–2.

121. "Trêve du peuple," *Le Flambeau,* March 14, 1936, 1.

122. The trifecta "Libery, Equality, Fraternity," is found on the face of many public buildings in France.

123. François de La Rocque, "Esprit Croix de feu," *Le Flambeau,* July 4, 1936, 1.

124. Millington, *From Victory to Vichy,* 2–3.

125. J.-M. Aimot, "Le camping au P.P.F.: Le peuple doyen de l'Europe retrouvera sa jeunesse sous la tente," *L'Émancipation nationale,* April 3, 1937, 7.

126. See, for example, François de La Rocque, "Note aux présidents," November 13, 1933, AN 451AP/81; Letter from Deléglise to François de La Rocque, July 1932, AN 451 AP/91.

127. "Albert Roux, mort pour la France," *L'Émancipation nationale,* November 3, 1939, 1.

128. This odd title would seem to be a reference to the fact that the original Croix de feu members—all veterans—had to have been recipients of a medal or other distinction for their service in World War I in order to gain admission to the organization. It also borrowed from the subtitle of the Legion of Honor. See an undated list of the movement's statutes, "Mouvement social français des Croix de feu," ISP LR/6.

129. All Croix de feu members wore an insignia, as opposed to a full-blown uniform. See undated list of statutes: "Les Croix de feu et briscards: Statuts," ISP LR/6.

130. See a lyric sheet by Marcel Dambrine, "Les Croix de feu: Chanson marche officielle de l'association des décorés au péril de leur vie" (Toulouse: Editions de "L'Oie du Capitole"), ANF AP 451/82/83.

131. Paris, Archives nationales de France, letter dated July 25, 1932, from François de La Rocque to Édouard Daladier, ANF AP 496/1. .

132. Bertrand de Jouvenel, "En revenant de Teruel," *L'Émancipation nationale,* January 7, 1938, 8. Bertrand's father had been married to Gabrielle-Sidonie Colette from 1912 to 1925: Tilburg, *Colette's Republic,* 125–27.

133. Pierre Drieu La Rochelle, *Gilles* (Paris: Editions Gallimard, 1939).

134. "Un nouveau martyr," *Le Flambeau,* August 22, 1936, 1. Samuel Houston Goodfellow briefly comments on this incident in the context of Alsatian fascism (Muntz was active on the Alsatian far right): Samuel Houston Goodfellow, *Between the Swastika and the Cross of Lorraine: Fascisms in Interwar Alsace* (Dekalb: Northern Illinois University Press, 1999), 138.

135. "Les émouvantes obsèques de Victor Muntz," *Le Flambeau,* September 5, 1936, 2.

136. "Une tête, des muscles: Conduisant les militants du P.P.F., notre chef Jacques Doriot repousse à coups de poing les communistes, armés de poignards et de matraques," *L'Émancipation nationale,* September 5, 1936, 1–2.

137. Sean Kennedy, "The Croix de Feu, the Parti Social Français, and the Politics of Aviation, 1931–1939," *French Historical Studies* 23, no. 2 (Spring 2000), 373–99. For the links between aviation and fascism more broadly, see Colin Cook, "The Myth of the Aviator and the Flight to Fascism," *History Today* 53, no. 12 (December 2003): 36–42.

138. Kennedy, *Reconciling France against Democracy,* 111–12.

139. Minutes dated July 10, 1936, "Réunion constitutive du Parti social français," ISP LR/15.

140. Sîan Reynolds makes an interesting observation about Mermoz's death: that, while when he died he was proclaimed as a masculine hero, when female pilots similarly perished in pursuit of glory they were criticized for orphaning their children and abandoning their homes: Reynolds, *France between the Wars,* 79.

141. François de La Rocque, "Un Chef: Mermoz," *Le Flambeau,* December 19, 1936, 1.

142. "Les Aero-Clubs Jean Mermoz," *Le Flambeau,* February 13, 1937, 5.

143. "Jeunes hommes de France: Écoutez . . . Mermoz, votre guide," *Le Flambeau,* May 1, 1937, 5.

144. Sean Kennedy in conversation with the author, June 2004.

145. Bernard Boringe, "'Mes Vols,' par Mermoz," *Le Petit Journal,* July 14, 1937, 5. This piece was actually a sort of preview of and promotion for a book of Mermoz's accounts of his adventures.

146. Jean Bernard, "Son exemple," *L'Étudiant social,* December 1938, 1; François de La Rocque, *Au service de l'avenir: Réflexions en montagne* (Paris: Société d'Edition et d'Abonnement, 1946), iii.

147. Claude Popelin and Jacques Doriot, "Mermoz: Héros français du vingtième siècle," *L'Émancipation nationale,* December 12, 1936, 8; Jean Lafarge, "Mermoz," *L'Émancipation nationale,* July 21, 1939, 6.

148. Jacques Cartonnet, "L'Union sportive des jeunesses françaises doit être le refuge de tous les jeunes," *L'Émancipation nationale,* March 4, 1938, 2; Henri Lebre, "Au camp des vacances de Ferté-Milon: Doriot chez les enfants," *L'Émancipation nationale,* August 27, 1937, 8.

149. Passmore discusses this: Passmore, "Boy Scouting for Grown-Ups?" 535–36.

150. Text of speech, François de La Rocque, "Discours du Colonel, Bordeaux, 5 Aout 1937," ISP LR/20.

151. See, for example, Pierre Drieu La Rochelle, *Doriot ou la vie d'un ouvrier français* (Paris: Les Éditions populaires françaises, 1936).

152. See, for example, "Jacques Doriot donne à tous l'exemple de l'activité," *L'Émancipation nationale,* December 24, 1937, 6.

153. See, for example, "Règlement général de l'association 'Les fils et filles de Croix de feu,'" February 17, 1935, ANF AP 451/6.

154. Kennedy, *Reconciling France against Democracy,* 267–68.

155. "Parti populaire français: Instructions provisoires pour la constitution des sections locales et des fédérations départementales du parti," *L'Émancipation nationale,* July 4, 1936, 2.

156. There is scant evidence of the mobilization of women by the PPF, as seen in chap. 5.

157. "Le conseil national du parti," *L'Émancipation nationale,* March 19, 1938, 12.

158. Philippe Burrin, *La dérive fasciste: Doriot, Déat, Bergery, 1933–1945* (Paris: Éditions du Seuil, 1986).

159. "Décès d'un député," *Journal officiel, Chambre,* April 11, 1940, 667–68.

160. Text of a speech, Édouard Daladier, "Discours de Vichy," ANF AP 496/2.

161. Berstein, *Histoire du Parti radical,* 238–39.

162. See, for example, Justin Godart, "Scoutisme," *L'Ère nouvelle,* September 11, 1921, 1.

163. Bergery was also a former Socialist, having stood for the SFIO in the 1919 general election: "Pour les élections de demain: Les candidats Socialistes pour les secteurs de la Seine," *L'Humanité,* November, 11–15, 1919, 1.

164. Larmour, *The French Radical Party,* 39–40. It should be noted that, especially with regard to the Radical Party, "youth" was a relative term. It usually denoted an ill-defined age group ranging from older teenagers right up to men in their early thirties.

165. Ibid., 221–32.

166. Ibid., 231.

167. Roland Manescau, "Ce que pensent nos militants: Les ennemis de la nation et de la

République," *L'Ère nouvelle,* January 21, 1935, 3. It is unclear whether Manescau was referring to fascists or Communists: likely, he meant both.

168. Roland Manescau, "Ce que pensent nos militants: Au seuil de la victoire," *L'Ère nouvelle,* November 3, 1936, 3.

169. Soucy, *French Fascism,* 29.

170. "A travers les départements: Jeune homme, réfléchis!" *L'Ère nouvelle,* November 15, 1937, 3.

171. "Ce que pensent nos militants: L'hommage des jeunes à Louis Besse," *L'Ère nouvelle,* January 18, 1937, 3.

172. Kevin Passmore, *From Liberalism to Fascism: The Right in a French Province, 1928–1939* (Cambridge: Cambridge University Press, 1997), 274.

173. "La conférence nationale des Jeunesses Socialistes de France: La question de l'adhésion à l'internationale communiste," *L'Humanité,* November 1, 1920, 1–2.

174. See, for example, Emile Bardiès, "La semaine d'études des Jeunesses Socialistes: La première journée," *Le Populaire,* August 6, 1930, 6.

175. R. Dumon, "La voix des jeunes: Le 10e congrès national des Jeunesses Socialistes," *Le Populaire,* January 7, 1931, 6.

176. Ibid.

177. Letter dated November 4, 1927, from Suzanne Caille to Léon Blum, ANF AP 570/7.

178. Louis Levy, "Nos jeunesses," *Le Populaire,* February 2, 1930, 1–2.

179. See, for example, R. Dumontier, "Le problème de la jeunesse: Les jeunes et la crise," *Le Populaire,* July 19, 1933, 6.

180. Eugène Aubey, "Jeunesses Socialistes," *Le Populaire,* February 20, 1940, 4.

181. Bernard Chochoy, "Tribune du Parti: Nos Jeunesses Socialistes devant les problèmes de la discipline et de l'unité," *Le Populaire,* February 17, 1938, 4.

182. Paul Faure, "Le foyer des jeunes," *Le Populaire,* December 7, 1931, 1; Paul Faure, "Le foyer des jeunes," *La Femme Socialiste,* February–March 1932, 6.

183. André Botta, "Au camp de Draveil," *Le Populaire,* August 14, 1932, 6.

184. Chagneau, "Chronique estudiantine: La culture des masses," *Le Populaire,* July 26, 1936, 4.

185. Pierre Hanon, "Le congrès de la Fédération nationale des étudiants Socialistes," *Le Populaire,* February 20, 1939, 4.

186. F.L., "Aidez les Jeunesses Socialistes," *Le Populaire,* July 22, 1937, 4.

187. Le secrétariat régional des J.G.S., "J.G.S.! Aux jeunes pour la défense du prolétariat," *Le Populaire,* January 16, 1934, 6.

188. Paul Faure, "La politique Socialiste: Jeunes gardes," *Le Populaire,* January 29, 1934, 1.

189. "Dimanche prochain à Creil: Grand rassemblement national des Jeunes gardes Socialistes," *Le Populaire,* March 25, 1937, 1.

190. "Pour l'Espagne républicaine: Tous les groupes de Faucons rouges participeront demain à la journée nationale de solidarité," *Le Populaire,* December 25, 1937, 1.

191. "Les Faucons rouges sont rentrés," *Le Populaire,* August 27, 1938, 8.

192. Pierre Marie, "Avant le congrès de l'U.S.S.G.T.," *Le Populaire,* November 6, 1933, 4.

193. R. L.-M., "Une réalisation Socialiste: La garderie d'enfants de Monceau-les-Mines," *Le Populaire,* June 17, 1934, 5.

194. "Le manifeste constitutif de la Jeunesse républicaine française," *L'Alliance démocratique,* March 7, 1934, 2.

195. Louis Bour, "Appel aux jeunes: Il nous faut un journal," *Le Petit Démocrate,* January 27, 1935, 3.

196. Delbreil, *Centrisme et démocratie-chrétienne en France,* 59.

197. Ibid., 317–62.

198. Irvine, *French Conservatism in Crisis,* 32–33.

199. Ibid., 98–126.

200. Ibid, 105–8; Kennedy, *Reconciling France,* 33–34; see the LRN's founding manifesto entitled "Manifeste de la Ligue républicaine nationale. Texte définitif," in ANF/AP470/87; Wileman, "L'Alliance républicaine démocratique," 226–27.

201. Goodfellow, *Between the Swastika;* Passmore, *From Liberalism to Fascism.*

202. Carmen Callil, *Bad Faith: A Forgotten History of Family, Fatherland, and Vichy France* (New York: Knopf, 2006), 103.

203. A. Cavaille-Coll, "Les combattants et le devoir présent," *La Nation,* April 24, 1926, 355.

204. Louis Marin to Louis Adt, February 9, 1935, ANF AP 317/215.

205. "Extraits du programme de politique intérieur," ANF AP 317/265.

206. "Annexe au procès verbal," *Journal officiel, Chambre,* July 10, 1940, 826–27. One should be careful not to overstate the importance of this vote's utility in uncovering politicians' or parties' democratic sensibilities. Many seem to have voted as they did believing that Pétain would negotiate an armistice with the Germans and then reestablish at least a semblance of democracy. Also, while Marin abstained, most other Fédération parliamentarians did not, including Georges Roulleaux-Dugage. For a discussion of the varied rationales behind supporting Pétain in June 1940, see William D. Irvine, "Domestic Politics and the Fall of France in 1940," *Historical Reflections/Réflexions Historiques* 22, no. 1 (1996): 77–90.

207. See, for example, Paxton, *The Anatomy of Fascism,* 5, 27.

208. Herbert Luethy, *France against Herself* (New York: Meridians, 1955), 77.

CHAPTER THREE

1. Callil, *Bad Faith;* Kaplan, *The Collaborator.*

2. For a recent and excellent synopsis of the worst of the Nazis' racially motivated crimes, see Richard J. Evans, *The Third Reich at War* (New York: Penguin, 2008), 3–105, 217–432, 541–646. Michael Marrus and Robert O. Paxton, *Vichy France and the Jews* (Stanford, CA: Stanford University Press, 1995), remains the best work on Vichy's collaboration with the Holocaust and the Nazis' other racially motivated crimes.

3. On Céline, Drieu La Rochelle, and Maurras see Carroll, *French Literary Fascism,* 71–96, 125–221; Sandrine Sanos, *The Aesthetics of Hate: Far-Right Intellectuals, Anti-Semitism and Gender in 1930s France* (Stanford, CA: Stanford University Press, 2012), 158–93. On Daudet, see Alister Kershaw, *An Introduction to Léon Daudet, with Selections from His Memoirs* (Francestown, NH: Typographeum, 1988).

4. Catherine Collomp, "Regard sur les politiques de l'immigration: Le Marché du travail en France et aux Etats-Unis, 1880–1930," *Annales, Histoire, Sciences Sociales* 51 (September–October 1996): 1107–1135; Gérard Noiriel, *Les origines républicaines de Vichy* (Paris: Éditions Hachette, 1999); Rosenberg, "Albert Sarraut," 36–53.

5. Pierre Lainé, "L'invasion de la Géorgie racontée par un témoin: Les représentants diplomatiques français ont été au-dessous de leur tâche," *Le Populaire,* March 25, 1921, 1.

6. Drieu La Rochelle, *Doriot ou la vie d'un ouvrier français,* 22; Robert Cornilleau, "Le maître de la terre," *Le Petit Démocrate,* August 8, 1920, 1.

7. Three million immigrants, or 7 percent of the population, entered the country from the end of World War I to 1931 alone: Rosenberg, "Albert Sarraut," 36.

8. Christopher E. Forth, "*La Civilisation* and Its Discontents: Modernity, Manhood, and the Body in the Early Third Republic," in *French Masculinities: History, Culture, and Politics,* ed. Christopher E. Forth and Bertrand Taithe (New York: Palgrave Macmillan, 2007), 84–102.

9. R. Le Bon, "Pour l'avenir de la race: L'industrie moderne doit favoriser les sports," *L'Ère nouvelle,* September 3, 1929, 1–2.

10. Édouard Herriot, *Pourquoi je suis radical-socialiste* (Paris: Éditions de France, 1928), 168–69, 180.

11. Georges Faugère, "La culture physique et le sport," *L'Ère nouvelle,* April 22, 1927, 1–2.

12. J. Ernest-Charles, "Éducation physique," *L'Ère nouvelle,* March 6, 1937, 1.

13. André Glarner, "Il faut que le front populaire mette les sports à la portée de tous: Un programme grandiose pour l'éducation physique de la jeunesse," *La Lumière,* May 23, 1936, 4.

14. Danièle Vindor, "Contre la mollesse," *Le Populaire,* March 24, 1923, 5.

15. Marie inaugurated the sports section with this column: Pierre Marie, "Notre point de vue: Les Socialistes et le sport," *Le Populaire,* January 24, 1927, 4.

16. Pierre Marie, "La culture physique au secours de la santé," *Le Populaire,* March 14, 1932, 4.

17. Pierre Marie, "Toujours l'alcoolisme," *Le Populaire,* July 4, 1938, 6.

18. Paul Vaillant-Couturier, "Le sport et la révolution," *L'Humanité,* July 8, 1923, 1.

19. Branger, "La mortalité infantile," *Le Populaire,* April 14, 1923, 3. As Rachel Fuchs notes, the Socialists' complaint about women working right up until giving birth had nineteenth-century origins among reformers and populationists such as Paul Strauss: Rachel G. Fuchs, "The Right to Life: Paul Strauss and the Politics of Motherhood," in *Gender and the Politics of Social Reform in France, 1870–1914,* ed. Elinor A. Accampo, Rachel G. Fuchs, and Mary Lynn Stewart (Baltimore: Johns Hopkins University Press, 1995), 95.

20. Jean Alessandri, "Un important problème social: La protection de l'enfance commence dès la maternité," *Le Populaire,* December 29, 1937, 8.

21. Bertine, "Maternité," *L'Ère nouvelle,* January 20, 1930, 2.

22. Nanterre, France. Letter dated February 15, 1936, from Joseph Garat to M. le Juge, Bibliothèque de documentation internationale et contemporain, Ligue des droits de l'homme papers, carton 5 (hereafter BDIC FdeltaRes798/carton number).

23. Marcel Cachin, "Ce que le communisme fera pour la femme," *L'Humanité,* February 28, 1926, 4.

24. "Chez tous les peuples, c'est dans la famille que se sont acquises et cultivées les aptitudes et les vertus de la race," *Le Devoir des femmes,* April 1937, 7–8.

25. Raoul de Warren, "Pour la protection de l'enfance," *La Nation,* February 8, 1930, 133–34.

26. Frader, *Breadwinners and Citizens,* 11–12, 15, 87–92.

27. Ibid., 208–9.

28. Caron, *Uneasy Asylum,* 210.

29. "Le péril jaune à Limehouse," *Le Populaire,* October 7, 1920, 2. See also "Le péril jaune," *Le Populaire,* December 19, 1920, 2.

30. See pamphlet "Le programme Socialiste," 1924, in ANF AP/552/5.

31. See Frader, *Breadwinners and Citizens,* 159.

32. Pierre Mille, "Colonisation étrangère en France," *L'Ère nouvelle,* April 29, 1937, 1; Norpois, "Le chômage et les étrangers," *L'Ère nouvelle,* July 20, 1937, 2.

33. "Suite de la discussion d'une proposition de loi relative au suffrage des femmes," *Journal officiel, Chambre,* December 11, 1923, 4017.

34. "Kabyles" refers to the Kabyle or Berber people of Algeria.

35. Camiscioli, *Reproducing the French Race,* 21–49.

36. Étienne-Martin Saint-Léon, "D'abord vivre . . . puisque la France se dépeuple faut-il faire appel à l'immigration étrangère?" *Le Petit Démocrate,* October 26, 1924, 1–2; Jean Bourdon, "Soyons clairvoyants dans notre hospitalité: L'immigration étrangère—peut-elle reconstituer la population française?" *La Nation,* June 26, 1926, 555–56.

37. "Invasion étrangère," *Le Flambeau,* December 1, 1933, 3.

38. E. Anxionnat, "Xénophobes?" *Le Flambeau,* November 1, 1932, 1.

39. Pierre Drieu La Rochelle, "L'atroce réalité," *L'Émancipation nationale,* August 6, 1937, 4.

40. "Folle ivresse," *La Nation,* April 3, 1926, 290.

41. Jacques Doriot, "Le P.P.F. s'est battu pour la paix, pour l'honneur: Le message du chef du parti," *L'Émancipation nationale,* October 7, 1938, 6. Capitalization in original.

42. "Impôt du sang" was a common expression for the blood sacrifice required to defend the nation in war.

43. Jacques St.-Germain, "Il faut régler le grave problème des commerçants étrangers," *L'Émancipation nationale,* January 26, 1940, 5. While less extreme, an unsettlingly similar logic was put forward by the Alliance démocratique's Pierre Auscher: "Les étrangers contre les commerçants français," *Bulletin trihebdomadaire de la presse démocratique française,* March 1, 1939, 6, in BNF/37260/5.

44. St.-Germain referenced the fact that while the French branch of the Rothschild family was ensconced in Paris the family as a whole made a lot of money financing the British war machine during the Napoleonic era. In general, the prominence of the Rothschilds in international finance made them a favorite target of the anti-Semitic right, beginning at least in the 1880s and 1890s; the Radicals were also known to target the Rothschilds as one of the hated "200 families" who supposedly dominated France: Michel Winock, "Joan of Arc," in *Realms of Memory: The Construction of the French Past, vol. 3: Symbols,* ed. Pierre Nora (New York: Columbia University Press, 1992), 463; Rearick, *The French in Love and War,* 189.

45. Bertrand Taithe, *The Killer Trail: A Colonial Scandal in the Heart of Africa* (Oxford: Oxford University Press, 2009), 42–67.

46. Camiscioli, *Reproducing the French Race,* 99–128; Paligot, *Races, racisme et anti-racisme,* 89–146. Robert Aldrich argues further that in the colonialist imagination of Hubert Lyautey and others, the colonies acted as a proving ground for a rebirth of French masculinity: Robert Aldrich, "Colonial Man," in *French Masculinities: History, Culture, and Politics,* ed. Christopher E. Forth and Bertrand Taithe (New York: Palgrave Macmillan, 2007), 123–40.

47. Alice L. Conklin, Sarah Fishman, and Robert Zaretsky, *France and Its Empire since 1870* (Oxford: Oxford University Press, 2011), 170–72.

48. "Allocutions de M. le président et de M. le président du conseil," *Journal officiel, Chambre,* December 11, 1918, 3309.

49. Herman Lebovics, *Imperialism and the Corruption of Democracies* (Durham, NC: Duke University Press, 2006), 60–86.

50. Taithe, *The Killer Trail,* 74–75.

51. "La France et les faibles," *L'Ère nouvelle,* January 7, 1920, 1.

52. "Suite de la discussion d'une interpellation," *Journal officiel, Chambre,* March 20, 1922, 928.

53. "Allocution de M. le Président," *Journal officiel, Chambre,* January 10, 1939, 3. Needless to say, France had not always or even usually treated the empire's "exotic peoples" with "kindness and respect."

54. Louis Marin, twelve-page manuscript titled "Discours à l'inhumation des cendres du Maréchal Lyautey," October 30, 1935, pp. 5, 8–9: ANF AP 317/220.

55. Edward Berenson, *Heroes of Empire: Five Charismatic Men and the Conquest of Africa* (Berkeley: University of California Press, 2010), 228–62.

56. Cécile de Corlieu, "Aux états-généraux du féminisme: Quelques impressions," *Le Petit Démocrate,* June 21, 1931, 4.

57. Pauline Le Cormier, "Au continent noir," *Le Petit Démocrate,* July 1, 1934, 3. Party notable Paul Archambault touched on similar themes: Paul Archambault, "Les problèmes de l'empire française: L'Afrique noire et la famille chrétienne," *Le Petit Démocrate,* August 28, 1938, 2.

58. The Republican Socialists were a loosely affiliated group of deputies who occupied the margins between the right wing of the Socialist Party and the left wing of the Radical Party. They were usually exiles or dissidents from one or the other organization: Berstein, *Histoire du Parti radical,* 118.

59. Victor Augagneur, "La question des métis," *L'Ère nouvelle,* June 28, 1926, 1, and July 5, 1926, 1.

60. Pierre Mille, "Les métis," *L'Ère nouvelle,* April 15, 1937, 1.

61. Ch. Chenet, "Le rôle de la femme française aux colonies: Protection des enfants métis abandonnés," *Le Devoir des femmes,* February 15, 1936, 8.

62. Carol, *L'Histoire de l'eugénisme en France,* 106.

63. Yvonne-Edmond Foinant, "Discours de Madame Edmond Foinant, Presidente de la 'Femme française,' au Congrès de Bourg-en-Bresse le dimanche 8 novembre 1936," *L'Alliance démocratique,* November 20, 1936, 6.

64. Pierre Mille, "Variétés: Les femmes musulmanes . . . aux deux bouts de notre Afrique du nord," *L'Ère nouvelle,* May 26, 1939, 1–2.

65. "Communication relative au décès de M. Auber, sénateur de La Réunion," *Journal officiel, Chambre,* June 7, 1928, 963–64. Doumer was referring specifically to La Réunion.

66. See, for example, Taithe, *The Killer Trail,* 136–67.

67. See, for example, Bertram Wyatt-Brown, *Honor and Violence in the Old South* (New York: Oxford University Press, 1986), 191–92; Christopher Hibbert, *The Great Mutiny: India, 1857* (London: Penguin, 1978), 37–39; Sara Carter, *Capturing Women: The Manipulation of Cultural Imagery in Canada's Prairie West* (Montreal: McGill-Queen's University Press, 1997), 48–86.

68. See Richard S. Fogarty, *Race and War in France: Colonial Subjects in the French Army, 1914–1918* (Baltimore: Johns Hopkins University Press, 2008), 202–29.

69. Conklin, Fishman, and Zaretsky, *France and Its Empire,* 169.

70. In fact, the French army did organize brothels staffed by European women for colonial troops in Europe both during World War I and after, which caused a great deal of public outrage: Camiscioli, *Reproducing the French Race,* 117.

71. This referred to the "Hamitic" hypothesis, developed by John Hanning Speke in the 1860s. Speke argued that a Caucasoid people originating in Ethiopia had brought civilization

to central Africa and that these people were the progeny of Ham, cursed by Noah for Ham's having publicly disgraced himself. See Philip Gourevitch, *We Wish to Inform You that Tomorrow We Will Be Killed with Our Families: Stories from Rwanda* (New York: Farrar, Strauss & Giroux, 1998), 50–53.

72. Louise Bodin, "Infâmes, infâmies!" *Le Populaire,* April 21, 1920, 1. Italics in original.

73. Lacouture, *Léon Blum,* 24–25.

74. As quoted in Ernest R. May, *Strange Victory: Hitler's Conquest of France* (New York: Hill & Wang, 2000), 323.

75. As quoted in Kalman, *The Extreme Right in Interwar France,* 205.

76. Charles Régismanset, "Contradictions," *L'Ère nouvelle,* April 24, 1931, 1, and "Contradictions," *L'Ère nouvelle,* May 27, 1932, 1.

77. Léo-Abel Gaboriaud, "Propos d'un incroyant: Enterrons l'anticléricalisme," *L'Ère nouvelle,* May 25, 1937, 1.

78. Léo-Abel Gaboriaud, "Le socialisme devant la réligion et les femmes," *L'Ère nouvelle,* April 15, 1940, 1. See also "Propos d'un incroyant: Mort de Cardinal Verdier," *L'Ère nouvelle,* April 12, 1940, 1.

79. Pierre Mille, "Les juifs et la colonisation: Tout le monde est d'accord que la France qui a déjà reçu trois millions d'étrangers 'a fait son plein,'" *L'Ère nouvelle,* December 23, 1938, 1. See also Pierre Mille, "Les juifs et Madagascar," *L'Ère nouvelle,* February 7, 1937, 1–2, and "Émigration juive," *L'Ère nouvelle,* February 8, 1939, 1.

80. Joan Tumblety, "Revenge of the Fascist Knights: Masculine Identities in *Je suis partout,* 1940–1944," *Modern and Contemporary France* 7, no. 1 (1999): 11–20. See also Sanos, *The Aesthetics of Hate,* 194–244.

81. See Laurent Kestel, "The Emergence of Anti-Semitism in the Parti Populaire Français: Party Intellectuals, Peripheral Figures, and National Leaders," *French History* 19, no. 3 (September 2005): 364–84.

82. See, for example, Carroll, *French Literary Fascism,* 147–70.

83. Pierre Drieu La Rochelle, "A propos du racisme," *L'Émancipation nationale,* July 29, 1938, 2.

84. Abremski was certainly an interesting aberration. He was memorialized in the same hypermasculine and hyperpatriotic terms as other *Parti populaire français* militants: Jacques Doriot, "Abremski disparaît . . . ," *L'Émancipation nationale,* February 11, 1938, 1, 8.

85. Kestel, "The Emergence of Anti-Semitism," 375.

86. See, for example, Maurice Ivan Sicard, "Lettre à M. le procureur de la République pour retrouver le juif Weisskopf," *L'Émancipation nationale,* August 5, 1940, 1.

87. For the intersection of anti-Semitism and masculinity in the case of the Dreyfus Affair, see: Forth, *The Dreyfus Affair and the Crisis of French Manhood,* 21–59.

88. Pamphlet titled "Buts généraux de Croix de feu," ANF AP 451/81.

89. Letter dated October 25, 1935, from le Chef de la Propagande to "Cher Camarade,"ISP LR/10.

90. Text, François de La Rocque, "Extraits du discours prononcé par le Colonel de la Rocque au Congrès départemental du Rhône du 14 Février 1937," ISP LR/20.

91. Kalman, *The Extreme Right in Interwar France,* 223.

92. Ibid., 216.

93. Ibid., 207–17; Kestel, "The Emergence of Anti-Semitism."

94. Paul Archambault, "Le monde juif et son destin," *Le Petit Démocrate,* June 12, 1938, 1.

95. See an internal LRN report dated January 5, 1926: Emmanuel Brousse, "Rapport de fin d'année," ANF AP 470/87.

96. Irvine, *French Conservatism in Crisis,* 14–16.

97. Ibid., 114.

98. See, for example, "Provocation à l'assassinat!" *L'Alliance démocratique,* March 1, 1935, 1. For an occasion when Flandin defended himself, by proxy, from charges of anti-Semitism, see Emmanuel Berl, "M. P.-E. Flandin et l'antisémitisme," *L'Alliance démocratique,* September 30–October 14, 1938, 5.

99. Soucy, *French Fascism,* 152–58.

100. Victor Basch, "Pour la liberté individuelle dans nos colonies," *La Volonté,* August 4, 1930, in BDIC/FdeltaRES 798/9.

101. Yvon Delbos, "Les massacres juifs," *L'Ère nouvelle,* February 15, 1920, 1.

102. "Doriot c'est La Rocque, La Rocque c'est Doriot: Ils provoquent au pogrome en Afrique du nord," *La Lumière,* December 5, 1936, 1,3; L.P., "Les Croix de feu antisémites: L'intervention du Colonel de La Rocque dans les élections algériennes," *La Lumière,* May 2, 1936, 3.

103. Léo-Ab Gaboriaud, "Propos d'un incroyant: Sur la mort du Cardinal Verdier," *L'Ère nouvelle,* April 12, 1940, 1.

104. J.-B. Séverac, "La politique Socialiste: Racisme, antisémitisme et socialisme," *Le Populaire,* June 20, 1939, 1.

105. K. K., "États-Unis: La malheureuse situation de la femme nègre," *L'Ouvrière,* September 9, 1926, 4.

106. Maurice Thorez, *Fils du peuple,* 169.

107. "L'Alliance et les élections au bureau de la chambre des députés: Mm. Louis Rollin et Gratien Candace sont élus vice-présidents, M. Raymon Lachal est élu secretaire," *L'Alliance démocratique,* January 14, 1938, 1.

108. Antoinette de Préval to Madame Perrineau, March 26, 1937, ANF AP/451/62.

109. Le Docteur Djilali Bentami, "Justice aux musulmans," *L'Émancipation nationale,* December 2, 1938, 2. This inclusive attitude, admittedly, was more than offset by an accompanying spike in the party's anti-Semitism, which Kestel suggests party leaders saw as a recruiting tool in the North African colony: Kestel, "The Emergence of Anti-Semitism," 378–82.

110. France Duspay, "C'est la guerre: Auprès de ma blonde," *L'Émancipation nationale,* March 1, 1940, 7.

111. See, for example, Barbara A. Yates, "White Views of Black Minds: Schooling in King Leopold's Congo," *History of Education Quarterly* 20, no. 1 (Spring 1980): 27–50.

CHAPTER FOUR

1. "Berceaux vides," *L'Émancipation nationale,* August 29, 1936, 6. See also "Berceaux vides," *L'Émancipation nationale,* September 5, 1936, 6.

2. For example, see Anne Cova, "French Feminism and Maternity: Theories and Policies, 1890–1918," in *Maternity and Gender Policies: Women and the Rise of the European Welfare States, 1880s–1950s,* ed. Gisela Bock and Pat Thane (New York: Routledge, 1991), 119–37; Cheryl Koos, "Gender, Anti-Individualism, and Nationalism: The Alliance Nationale and the Pronatalist Backlash against the *Femme moderne,* 1933–1940," *French Historical Studies* 19, no. 3 (Spring

1996): 699–723; Eric Jennings, "Discours corporatiste, propagande nataliste, et contrôle social sous Vichy," *Revue d'histoire moderne et contemporaine* 49, no. 4 (2002): 101–31; Richard Tomlinson, "The 'Disappearance' of France: French Politics and the Birth Rate," *Historical Journal* 28, no. 2 (1985) 405–15; Huss, "Pronatalism in the Interwar Period in France," 35–68.

3. There has been some commentary on this. See Guerrand and Ronsin, *Le sexe apprivoisé*, 118–19; Offen, "Body Politics," 148–49; Bard and Robert, "The French Communist Party and Women," 321–47.

4. Camiscioli, *Reproducing the French Race.*

5. Koos, "Gender, Anti-individualism, and Nationalism," 711.

6. Susan Pedersen, *Family, Dependence, and the Origins of the Welfare State: Britain and France, 1914–1945* (Cambridge: Cambridge University Press, 1993), 60.

7. Clive Ponting, *A Green History of the World: The Environment and the Collapse of Great Civilizations* (London: Penguin, 1991), 148–49.

8. Robert Talmy, *Histoire du mouvement familial en France (1896–1939)* (Aubenas: Union nationale des associations familiales, 1962), 66–69.

9. Koos, "Engendering Reaction," 35.

10. This organization was founded in 1880 as a socialist women's organization by Léonie Rouzade: Sowerwine, *Les femmes et le socialisme,* 20. Given its preoccupation with pronatalism and the fact that it invited Fédération républicaine leader Louis Marin to sit at the table of honor alongside Albert Lebrun, the president of the Republic, at its fiftieth anniversary dinner in 1931, the Union seems to have drifted significantly to the right. See letter dated July 11, 1931 from Madame Delsart to Louis Marin, ANF AP 317/228.

11. Un Mutualiste, "Mutualité maternelle," *Le Petit Démocrate,* January 4, 1920, 1.

12. "Des chiffres éloquents: Ce que la guerre a coûté," *L'Ère nouvelle,* February 27, 1921, 1.

13. Millardet, "L'exposition de la dépopulation: Pour la famille—pour l'enfance," *L'Ère nouvelle,* June 16, 1921, 2.

14. "La population de l'Allemagne en 1924, a augmenté de 500.000 Habitants," *Le Petit Démocrate,* July 26, 1925, 3.

15. "Allocution de M. le doyen d'âge," *Journal officiel, Chambre,* January 8, 1924, 1–2.

16. "Blue horizon" referred to the high number of military men wearing blue uniforms sitting in the Chamber. These men were nearly entirely of the right. See Martin, *France and the Après-Guerre,* 50.

17. Koos, "The (Anti)Republican Right and the Gendered Politics of the Family."

18. Irène, "Chronique de la mode: Le mariage, fiançailles, usages, préparatifs," *La Nation,* March 6, 1926, 216.

19. As quoted in Marie Maugeret, "Regards sur le passé," *Questions féminines et questions féministes,* May 15, 1928, 137.

20. Report, Le Lieutenant Colonel Blaison, *Rapport sur les prix de vertu* (Paris, Nancy, and Strasbourg : Imprimerie Berger-Levrault, 1928), 19–23, ANF AP 317/22.

21. Offen, "Body Politics," 138.

22. Chiara Saraceno, "Redefining Maternity and Paternity: Gender, Pro-natalism and Social Policies in Fascist Italy," in *Maternity and Gender Policies: Women and the Rise of the European Welfare States, 1880s–1950s,* ed. Gisela Bock and Pat Thane (New York: 1991), 196–212; Ute Frevert, *Women in German History: From Bourgeois Emancipation to Sexual Liberation* (Oxford: Berg, 1990), 232–33. For an interview that provides an interesting glimpse of the impact of such

awards, see Alison Owings, *Frauen: German Women Recall the Third Reich* (New Brunswick, NJ: Rutgers University Press, 1995), 17–31.

23. Marthe Bigot, "Encore la répopulation," *Le Populaire*, September 28, 1919, 2.

24. "Hypocrisie bourgeoise," *L'Humanité*, March 17, 1925, 5.

25. Sixte-Quenin, "Noël! Noël! Pour les familles nombreuses," *L'Humanité*, December 25, 1919, 1.

26. Sixte-Quenin, "Impudence et imprudence," *L'Humanité*, June 30, 1920, 1.

27. "Luttons pour la protection de la maternité! Que fait la loi française pour l'ouvrière mère," *L'Ouvrière*, March 26, 1925, 4.

28. "La philanthropie intéressée," *L'Humanité*, January 2, 1932, 1.

29. Jean Longuet, "Pour sauver l'enfance ouvrière," *Le Populaire*, January 17, 1919, 1.

30. François de La Rocque, "La défense nationale: Est-elle assurée?" *Le Flambeau*, November 1, 1929, 3.

31. Sixte-Quenin, "Tribune du parti: Contre les familles nombreuses," *Le Populaire*, October 5, 1934, 6.

32. Dr. Weill-Raynal, "Propos du Docteur: Fécondité!" *Le Populaire*, August 2, 1936, 5. George Alter outlines the three main theories of fertility decline, all of which maintain that parents make a rational choice based on a cost-benefit analysis of the economic advantages and disadvantages of childbearing: George Alter, "Theories of Fertility Decline: A Nonspecialist's Guide to the Current Debate," in *The European Experience of Declining Fertility, 1850–1970: The Quiet Revolution*, ed. John R. Gillis, Louise A. Tilly, and David Levine (Cambridge: Blackwell, 1992), 13–30.

33. "Rien ne brisera le front populaire: Rapport de Maurice Thorez, Secrétaire Général du parti Communiste français, à la conférence nationale de Montreuil, le 22 Janvier 1937," *L'Humanité*, January 24, 1937, 7.

34. "Maurice Thorez, parrain du 15e enfant d'une famille Ardennaise," *L'Humanité*, July 1, 1939, 2.

35. For a detailed analysis of the Communist Party's transition to a "national party," see Mortimer, *The Rise of the French Communist Party*, 195–395.

36. Bard and Robert, "The French Communist Party and Women," 339–41. Eric Weitz argues that this change in outlook was also part of a strategy to attract more popular support: Eric D. Weitz, "The Heroic Man and the Ever-Changing Woman: Gender and Politics in European Communism, 1917–1950," in *Gender and Class in Modern Europe*, ed. Laura L. Frader and Sonya O. Rose (Ithaca, NY: Cornell University Press, 1996), 340–44.

37. In the context of 1939, this led Faure to advocate surrendering to Germany rather than resisting the Nazi invasion. For an explanation of the term, see: Norman Ingram, "'Nous allons vers les monastères': French Pacifism and the Crisis of the Second World War," in *Crisis and Renewal in France, 1918–1962*, ed. Kenneth Mouré and Martin S. Alexander (New York: Berghahn, 2002), 133.

38. Paul Faure, "La politique Socialiste: Les problèmes de la démographie," *Le Populaire*, July 12, 1939, 1.

39. Carol, *L'Histoire de l'eugénisme en France*, 9.

40. Ibid., 17–65; Camiscioli, *Reproducing the French Race*, 75–80; Paligot, *La République raciale*, 9–88; Schneider, *Quality and Quantity*, 55–83. Puericulture was a term coined by Parisian physician Alfred Caron in 1858 and championed by obstetrician Adolphe Pinard in the late nine-

teenth century. It referred to a scientific approach to pre- and postnatal care: see Schneider, *Quality and Quantity,* 63–65.

41. Francis Galton, "Eugenics: Its Definition, Scope, and Aims," *American Journal of Sociology* 10, no. 1 (July 1904): 1.

42. As quoted in Carol, *L'Histoire de l'eugénisme en France,* 137.

43. Ibid, 247–48.

44. Paligot, *Races, racisme et antiracisme,* 47–48.

45. Reggiani, *God's Eugenicist,* 127–57. See also Read, "'Citizens Useful to Their Country and to Humanity.'"

46. Henry Spont, "Pour l'avenir de la race," *L'Ère nouvelle,* November 10, 1922, 1.

47. Fuchs, "The Right to Life," 82–105.

48. See "L'allaitement maternel diminue la mortalité infantile: Comment il faut l'encourager," *Le Petit Démocrate,* January 13, 1924, 2; Fuchs, "France in a Comparative Perspective," 173–75.

49. Louis Duval-Arnould, "Agriculture et natalité," *La Nation,* November 27, 1926, 1095–1096.

50. Camiscioli, *Reproducing the French Race,* 21–49.

51. Maurice Rondet-Saint, "Natalité," *L'Alliance démocratique,* February 5–12, 1937, 2.

52. Gustave Gautherot, "Rapport sur la politique sociale," *Congrès national 1938 de la Fédération républicaine de France* (Paris: February 1939), 70.

53. Jacques Doriot, "Nous voulons refaire la France," *L'Émancipation nationale,* March 19, 1938, 7.

54. Amélie Vincent, "Tribune des femmes Socialistes: Défendons le foyer," *Le Populaire,* October 23, 1938, 8.

55. Henri Sellier, "Ce que le code de la famille a malheureusement négligé," *La Lumière,* February 23, 1940, 3.

56. As quoted in Guerrand and Moissinac, *Henri Sellier,* 158.

57. Ibid., 91–190.

58. Reggiani, *God's Eugenicist,* 145–46.

59. Carol, *L'Histoire de l'eugénisme en France,* 309.

60. Louise Saumoneau, "Nous ne voulons plus voir," *La Femme Socialiste,* May 1929, 1.

61. Armand Charpentier, "La guerre et la natalité," *Le Populaire,* March 3, 1920, 1.

62. Alice Jouenne, "Avant la géhenne," *La Femme Socialiste,* December 1934, 1.

63. McLaren, *Sexuality and Social Order,* 99–100; Accampo, *Blessed Motherhood, Bitter Fruit,* 42–43; Christiane Demeulenaere-Douyere, *Paul Robin, 1837–1912: Un militant de la liberté et du bonheur (La France au fil des siècles)* (Paris: Publisud, 1994).

64. Dr. Toulouse, "Comment repeupler?" *L'Ère nouvelle,* February 7, 1920, 1. For Toulouse's relationship with Sellier, see Guerrand and Moissinac, *Henri Sellier,* 157.

65. Denise Moran, "Un péril qui va grandissant: Le nombre des enfants anormaux a doublé depuis 1914—ces enfants, si on ne les soigne pas, constituent une charge pour la société et un danger public," *La Lumière,* July 30, 1927, 10.

66. Schneider, *Quantity and Quality,* 11–12.

67. Henri Michel, "Hygiène et natalité," *L'Ère nouvelle,* April 17, 1929, 1.

68. Daniel Pick, *Faces of Degeneration: A European Disorder, 1848–1918* (Cambridge: Cambridge University Press, 1989), 43, 98.

69. Judith Surkis, "Enemies Within: Venereal Disease and the Defense of French Masculinity between the Wars." In *French Masculinities: History, Culture, and Politics,* ed. Christopher E. Forth and Bertrand Taithe (New York: Palgrave Macmillan, 2007), 103–23.

70. Doctoresse Nadia, "Quelques réflexions sur la syphilis," *L'Ouvrière,* December 4, 1924, 2.

71. Georges Levy, "Budget et syphilis," *L'Humanité,* January 7, 1922, 1.

72. Iwan Bloch, *The Sexual Life of Our Time: In Its Relations to Modern Civilization,* trans. M. Eden Paul M. D. (London: Rebman, 1937), 373–74. Fournier advocated the sterilization of syphilitics: Carol, *L'Histoire de l'eugénisme en France,* 56.

73. Roberts, *Civilization without Sexes,* 197, 320.

74. See the U.S. National Institute of Allergies and Infectious Diseases' Web site: http://www.niaid.nih.gov/topics/syphilis/understanding/Pages/transmission.aspx (accessed June 11, 2012); and the U.S. National Library of Medicine's Medline Plus Web page: http://www.nlm.nih.gov/medlineplus/ency/article/001344.htm (accessed June 11, 2012).

75. "Séance de l'après-midi: Le programme du parti," *Le Petit Démocrate,* November 23, 1924, 2–3.

76. L. Camuzet, "Pas de démocratie sans pitié pour les malheureux: Protégeons les familles françaises," *La Nation,* October 22, 1927, 1027–1028.

77. "Pour une politique française," *Le Flambeau,* November 14, 1936, 3.

78. Text dated May 16, 1939, G. A. Maire, "Discours," ANF AP 451/155. Capitalization in original.

79. Koos, "Engendering Reaction," 193–221.

80. Guerrand and Moissinac, *Henri Sellier,* 151–53. The authors speculate that it might have been his friendship with Strölin that saved Sellier from being sent to a concentration camp during the Nazi occupation.

81. Ibid., 158. On Carrel see Reggiani, *God's Eugenicist;* Andrés Horacio Reggiani, "Alexis Carrel, the Unknown: Eugenics and Population Research under Vichy," *French Historical Studies* 25, no. 2 (Spring 2002): 331–56.

82. See Edwin Black, *War against the Weak: Eugenics and America's Campaign to Create a Master Race* (New York: Four Walls Eight Windows, 2003); Phillip R. Reilly, *The Surgical Solution: A History of Involuntary Sterilization in the United States* (Baltimore: Johns Hopkins University Press, 1991); Stefan Kuhl, *The Nazi Connection: Eugenics, American Racism, and German National Socialism* (New York: Oxford University Press, 1994); Robert Jay Lifton, *The Nazi Doctors: Medical Killing and the Psychology of Genocide* (New York: Basic Books, 1986).

83. Paxton and Marrus, *Vichy France and the Jews.*

84. Childers, *Fathers, Families, and the State,* 125; Muël-Dreyfus, *Vichy and the Eternal Feminine,* 255–310.

85. Paligot, *Races, racisme et antiracisme,* 49–58.

86. "Discussion de propositions de loi relatives aux familles nombreuses," *Journal officiel, Chambre,* March 10, 1921, 1192.

87. Ibid., 1186, 1190.

88. "Suite de la discussion de plusieurs propositions de loi concernant l'assistance aux familles nombreuses," *Journal officiel, Chambre,* March 23, 1921, 1366, and March 24, 1921, 1410.

89. See the minutes of the "Commission féministe: Séance du 17 janvier 1928,"BDIC FdeltaRes798/9. This commission attracted some impressive talent including Cécile Brunschvicg and Marcelle Kraemer-Bach, who were present at the meeting, and Germaine Malaterre-Sellier, Suzanne Schreiber, and Jane Misme, who were absent.

90. They did meet roughly a month later when they resolved to send the French banks a reminder that women were not legally obligated to get their husbands' permission to open bank accounts: minutes, "Commission féministe: Séance du 24 février 1928," BDIC FdeltaRes798/9. For an outline of the general lack of enthusiasm in the League for women's suffrage, see William D. Irvine, "Women's Right and the Rights of Man," in *Crisis and Renewal in France, 1918–1962*, ed. Kenneth Mouré and Martin S. Alexander (New York: Berghahn, 2002), 46–65.

91. Letter dated February 8, 1928, from Victor Basch to M. le Ministre de Finances, BDIC FdeltaRes798/98.

92. Georges Pernot, "Pour la répopulation de la France: Les allocations aux familles nombreuses," *La Nation*, November 10, 1925, 180.

93. According to Laura Frader, mothers and fathers were eligible for these "*sursalaires familiales*": Laura L. Frader, "Engendering Work and Wages: The French Labor Movement and the Family Wage," in *Gender and Class in Modern Europe*, ed. Laura L. Frader and Sonya O. Rose (Ithaca, NY: Cornell University Press, 1996), 158.

94. Louis Siefridt, "Les allocations familiales doivent devenir obligatoires," *Le Petit Démocrate*, June 14, 1925, 3; "Les allocations familiales sont en progression constante et rapide," *Le Petit Démocrate*, July 4, 1926, 3.

95. See Alexandre Duval, "Labourage et pâturage . . . les allocations familiales en agriculture," *La Nation*, July 17, 1926, 637–38; Jean Lerolle, "La politique sociale," *Le Petit Démocrate*, November 25, 1928, 5.

96. "Un important progrès dans la législation sociale—la chambre a voté les allocations familiales obligatoires: la première initiative en revient à Jean Lerolle et au groupe des députés démocrates populaires," *Le Petit Démocrate*, May 17, 1931, 3. In truth, there were so many exceptions to these "obligatory" allocations that their utility was bound to be limited.

97. Raoul de Warren, "Vote de la loi sur les allocations familiales," *La Nation*, February 27, 1932, 203–4.

98. "Les allocations familiales," *L'Ère nouvelle*, October 27, 1920, 4; Henri Michel, "Pour relever la natalité française. Les allocations familiales: Les résultats obtenus.—l'avenir," *L'Ère nouvelle*, April 29, 1930, 1–2.

99. Louise Bodin, "Le million de la répopulation," *Le Populaire*, September 6, 1920, 1.

100. Marthe Bigot, "Charges familiales," *L'Ouvrière*, August 5, 1922, 1.

101. Eugène-Georges, " L'Évolution économique et la vie ouvrière: Les allocations familiales," *Le Populaire*, April 6, 1930, 5.

102. Fernand Fontenoy, "La bataille des 'textiles' du Nord: Des 'allocations familiales' à la 'prime de fidélité . . .' ou les véritables buts de la 'philanthropie patronale,'" *L'Humanité*, September 8, 1930, 1.

103. B. Cattaneo, "Les allocations familiales," *L'Humanité*, March 19, 1933, 5.

104. Sixte-Quenin, "Tribune du Parti," *Le Populaire*, October 5, 1934, 6.

105. J. Ernest-Charles, "Allocations familiales," *L'Ère nouvelle*, April 12, 1935, 1.

106. Frader, "Engendering Work and Wages," 161.

107. Paul Vaillant-Couturier, "Au secours de la famille: Réponse à M. Boverat, nataliste," *L'Humanité*, December 22, 1935, 2.

108. Jacques Duclos, "Pour faire payer les riches, réforme fiscale: Le système fiscal et la défense de la famille," *L'Humanité*, December 28, 1936, 1–2.

109. "La mise en vigueur des allocations familiales en agriculture: Par décret, les taux ont été fixés sur les mêmes bases que pour l'industrie et le commerce," *Le Populaire,* November 21, 1936, 4.

110. Jean Lagarigue, "Une mesure juste: Les allocations familiales," *L'Émancipation nationale,* January 16, 1937, 6.

111. See Renaud Jean, "Les allocations familiales et l'agriculture," *L'Humanité,* April 4. 1938, 7; S. Blanchet, "Les allocations familiales en agriculture: Mêmes allocations pour toutes les familles nombreuses, à quelque profession et même à quelque situation sociale qu'elles appartiennent," *Le Populaire,* December 12, 1937, 5; A., " Que fait-on pour protéger les familles nombreuses? Les paysans sont sacrifiés," *L'Ère nouvelle,* February 11, 1938, 1; Pierre Trémintin, "Le drame de la terre et les allocations familiales," *Le Petit Démocrate,* May 8, 1938, 1; "Les allocations familiales en agriculture," *L'Alliance démocratique,*September 2–9, 1938, 274–75; Alexandre Duval, "La famille et le budget," *La Nation,* December 17, 1938, 812; J. Chamdes, "Il faut soutenir et sauver la famille: Sans enfants, la nation est en péril mortel—ayons une politique du foyer," *Le Flambeau,* April 17, 1937, 4; Jacques Doriot, "Nous voulons refaire la France," *L'Émancipation nationale,* March 19, 1938, 7.

112. Michel Rius, "Les ouvriers agricoles veulent des allocations familiales," *L'Humanité,* April 20, 1936, 5.

113. "Discussion, après demande de discussion immédiate, d'une proposition de loi tendant à étendre aux métayers le bénéfice des allocations familiales," *Journal officiel, Chambre,* March 19, 1937, 1119–1124. Monnet was in fact driving the car from which Léon Blum was pried and subsequently beaten by an angry right-wing mob including many Camelots du Roy of the Action Française on February 13, 1936: Lacouture, *Léon Blum,* 225–26.

114. Offen, "Body Politics," 150.

115. Gaston Doumergue, "Emploi des femmes en couches," *La Femme Socialiste,* June 1928, 2.

116. Paul Faure, "Le massacre des gosses," *La Femme Socialiste,* October 1929, 1; "La mère et l'enfant en U.R.S.S.," *L'Humanité,* March 10, 1931, 4.

117. Rachel G. Fuchs, *Poor and Pregnant in Paris: Strategies for Survival in the Nineteenth Century* (New Brunswick, NJ: Rutgers University Press, 1992), 142–44.

118. "Il faut des crèches et des garderies pour les jeunes enfants," *L'Ouvrière,* September 1, 1923, 2.

119. Charles Huzo, "Ce que la ville de Paris a réalisé pour les familles nombreuses," *L'Ère nouvelle,* December 9, 1927, 2.

120. Pacaud, "Les crèches et les garderies dans les hôpitaux," *L'Ouvrière,* January 15, 1931, 3.

121. J.B., "Dans l'assistance publique: Comment on encourage les familles nombreuses," *Le Populaire,* March 7, 1931, 6.

122. Pierre Semard, "L'aide à la famille, la défense de la femme et de l'enfant: Ce que le groupe Communiste propose," *L'Humanité,* April 27, 1938, 7.

123. *Parti démocrate populaire: Déclaration et documents* (Paris: Éditions du Parti démocrate populaire, 1930), 18.

124. "Manifeste féminin," *Le Petit Démocrate,* December 10, 1933, 3.

125. La Fédération républicaine de France, *Extraits du programme de politique sociale* (Paris, 1935), 3–4, ANF AP 317/265.

126. Letter dated November 21, 1935, from François de La Rocque to M. le Préfet de Police, ANF AP 451/ 87/88.

127. Letter dated November 21, 1935, from François de La Rocque to M. le Préfet de Police, ANF AP 451/ 87/88. This was a separate letter, or at least a separate draft of a letter, from the previous reference.

128. Letter dated April 25, 1938, from M. Danner to Antoinette de Préval, ANF AP 451/133.

129. Jeanne Vaillant, "Femme 1936: Pour les enfants de St. Denis," *L'Émancipation nationale,* August 1, 1936, 6.

130. Maurice Guérin, "Une large brèche est ouverte dans le système individualiste libéral par le code de la famille. Il ne reste plus qu'à l'agrandir pour y faire passer tout l'ordre personnaliste communautaire," *Le Petit Démocrate,* August 13, 1939, 2.

131. Offen, "Body Politics," 150.

132. Andrès Horacio Reggiani, "Birthing the French Welfare State: Political Crises, Population and Public Health, 1914–1960» (PhD diss.: History Department, State University of New York at Stony Brook, 1998), 147.

133. Childers, *Fathers, Families, and the State,* 40. An Alliance démocratique press report contradicts Childers, stating that Reynaud opposed the code: Marcel Ventenat, "Une oeuvre de justice sociale," *Bulletin trihebdomadaire de la presse démocratique française,* August 7, 1939, 3, BNF 37260/5. A PPF report prior to the code's issue likewise maintained that Daladier and Reynaud were quarreling over the birth premiums with Daladier in favor and Reynaud opposed: J.-M. Aimot, "M. Léon Blum rêve d'agitation tandis que M. Paul Reynaud sabote le code de la famille et que M. Daladier décide de ne rien décider, sinon la prorogation . . .," *L'Émancipation nationale,* July 14, 1939, 2. A quarrel seems likely, given the intense enmity between Daladier and Reynaud that Ernest May documents: May, *Strange Victory,* 184, 325–36.

134. Guérin, "Une large brèche." As with the 1932 Family Allowance Act the Parti démocrate populaire and the Fédération républicaine both claimed that the ideas behind the code were originally theirs: Marcel Petitjean, "Le code de la famille et la Fédération," *La Nation,* August 12, 1939, 501–502; Pierre Le Morin, "Les démocrates populaires ont pris une part importante à la réparation du Code de la Famille," *Le Petit Démocrate,* August 27, 1939, 1.

135. Jean Garchery, "Lancune dans le 'Code de la Famille,'" *Le Populaire,* August 2, 1939, 4.

136. Édouard Storace, "Code de la Famille: Allocations familiales," *L'Humanité,* August 1, 1939, 1–2.

137. For Italy, see De Grazia, *How Fascism Ruled Women,* 41–115; Saraceno, "Redefining Maternity and Paternity."

138. "Scrutin (N. 166)," *Journal officiel, Chambre,* July 23, 1920, 3096–3097. Strangely, André Tardieu and Raoul Péret joined Paul-Boncour in abstaining.

139. "Reprise de la discussion de la proposition de loi tendant à la répression des avortements criminels," *Journal officiel, Chambre,* July 23, 1920, 3074–3075.

140. Dr. Georges Thibout, "Ce que le parlement a fait pour la famille," *Le Petit Démocrate,* March 30, 1924, 1.

141. Georges Pernot, "Pour l'assainissement . . . moral: La lutte contre les publications obscènes," *La Nation,* January 23, 1926, 3.

142. Pick, *Faces of Degeneration,* 176–93; William Greenslade, *Degeneration, Culture, and the Novel, 1880–1940* (Cambridge: Cambridge University Press, 1994), 211–33. For a history of cultural understandings of masturbation, largely in the western world, see Thomas W. Laqueur, *Solitary Sex: A Cultural History of Masturbation* (New York: Zone Books, 2003).

143. Louise Bodin, "De la limitation des enfants," *Le Populaire*, January 31, 1920, 1.

144. Armand Charpentier, "Vie chère et famille nombreuse," *Le Populaire*, September 19, 1920, 1.

145. Sixte-Quenin, for example, mocked the Action française's Léon Daudet's pronatalism and moralizing: Sixte-Quenin, "Ce pornographe est surpopulateur," *Le Populaire*, June 12, 1922, 1.

146. Blum, *Du mariage*, 324.

147. "Avortements," *Le Populaire*, April 7, 1922, 2. See also "Un scandale en banlieue: Avortement et chantage," *Le Populaire*, November 1, 1922, 1.

148. "Suite de la discussion du projet du loi modifiant les dispositions de l'article 317 du code pénal sur l'avortement," *Journal officiel, Chambre*, January 12, 1923, 53–60.

149. Reynolds, *France between the Wars*, 18.

150. "Les femmes devant la justice," *L'Ouvrière*, July 8, 1922, 1.

151. Marthe Arendsee, "Une intéressante campagne des femmes communistes," *L'Ouvrière*, March 18, 1922, 4. See also Suzanne Girault, "L'avortement: Deux politiques," *L'Ouvrière*, July 1, 1922, 1.

152. Victor Méric, "Criminels," *L'Humanité*, January 10, 1922, 1.

153. "L'avortement et la loi d'amnistie," *L'Ouvrière*, August 14, 1924, 1–2.

154. "La politique féminine du ministère Herriot," *L'Ouvrière*, June 26, 1924, 1.

155. "Un médecin parisien condamné comme avorteur," *L'Humanité*, May 19, 1926, 3.

156. "Plutôt l'avortement!" *L'Ouvrière*, October 20, 1923, 2.

157. "Pour les filles-mères," *La Femme Socialiste*, January 1927, 2.

158. Marguerite Michard, "Le capitalisme assassine en série," *L'Ouvrière*, May 1931, 2.

159. "Arrachons l'avortement légal," *L'Ouvrière*, November 15, 1932, 1.

160. Clamamus, "La protection de la mère et de l'enfant," *L'Ouvrière*, August 15, 1933, 1–2.

161. "Renée Bourdon, la jeune femme trouvée morte sur un trottoir Parisien a succombé à des manoeuvres abortives," *L'Humanité*, May 6, 1939, 2.

162. Denise Moran, "Faut-il légaliser l'avortement? Dans les pays où l'avortement est puni, les naissances diminuent; en Russie, où il est actuellement réglementé, elles augmentent," *La Lumière*, July 22, 1933, 10, and "Faut-il autoriser l'avortement? En Russie, où il est autorisé sous le contrôle de l'état, il ne comporte presque plus de risques et il est en décroissance," *La Lumière*, July 29, 1933, 10. These articles argued for the legalization of abortion on pronatalist grounds. Moran held that the criminalization of abortion actually lowered the birthrate because of the number of women who died or became sterile due to illegal procedures.

163. "La sage-femme menait grande vie . . . elle avait installé à Paris deux officines d'avortements: ELLE EST EN PRISON,," *Le Populaire*, November 8, 1932, 1–2.

164. See pamphlet, "Programme de l'Alliance démocratique, parti républicain démocratique et social," BNF 37260/1.

165. Custos, "Le bien-être matériel est une condition de l'ordre social: La protection de la famille," *La Nation*, January 28, 1928, 92.

166. "Une brochure d'actualité: Vers plus de justice sociale . . . Mais par quelle route?"*Le Petit Démocrate*, March 15, 1925, 1–2.

167. Dr. Gaston Guigon, "La croisade des berceaux II," *L'Émancipation nationale*, August 4, 1939, 14.

168. S.M., "Jeunes filles de France," *L'Émancipation nationale*, July 16, 1938, 2.

169. Kalman, *The Extreme Right in Interwar France*, 147.

170. Cova, "French Feminism and Maternity," 128–29.

171. Pollard, *Reign of Virtue,* 174–94.

172. "Vive le 'Parti populaire français,'" *L'Émancipation nationale,* 4 July 1936, 1, 7.

173. See Philippe Burrin, *France under the Germans: Collaboration and Compromise* (New York: New Press, 1995), 156–59, 171.

174. See, for example, Rearick, *The French in Love and War,* 205–41; Jackson, *The Politics of Depression in France,* 113–33.

CHAPTER FIVE

1. Frader, *Breadwinners and Citizens,* 47; see also Linda L. Clark, *The Rise of Professional Women in France: Gender and Public Administration since 1830* (Cambridge: Cambridge University Press, 2000), 171–206.

2. Roger Biles, *A New Deal for the American People* (Dekalb: Northern Illinois University Press, 1991), 202–3.

3. Jean-Louis Robert, "Women and Work in France during the First World War," in *The Upheaval of War: Family, Work, and Welfare in Europe,* ed. Richard Wall and Jay Winter (Cambridge: Cambridge University Press, 1988), 253.

4. Ibid, 262–63.

5. Ibid.

6. Roger Besnard, "Pour les femmes fonctionnaires," *L'Ère nouvelle,* February 13, 1927, 2.

7. Manuscript, Louis Marin, "Le retour de la femme au foyer," ANF AP 317/250. This essay can be dated from the 1920s as it is covered in editorial notes from Georges Ducrocq, who died in 1927.

8. Louis Blain, "Comment le problème des salaires se pose dans la famille ouvrière," *Le Petit Démocrate,* June 6, 1926, 3.

9. Elinor Accampo, *Industrialization, Family Life, and Class Relations: Saint Chamond, 1815–1914* (Berkeley: University of California Press, 1989), 111–37.

10. Joseph Danel, "La femme et la profession: Quelles professions ouvrir aux femmes? Comment les y orienter?" *Le Petit Démocrate,* August 14, 1927, 4.

11. Annie, "Petite causerie: Le choix d'une situation," *Le Petit Démocrate,* November 10, 1929, 4.

12. E.B., "La femme, essentiellement épouse et mère, doit pouvoir rester au foyer familial: Pour la suppression du travail salarié de la femme, véritable plaie de l'économie moderne," *Le Petit Démocrate,* October 19, 1930, 4.

13. L.-A. Pagès, "Pour lutter contre le chômage—le retour de la mère au foyer: Une très opportune enquête de l'Union féminine civique et sociale," *Le Petit Démocrate,* November 1, 1931, 2.

14. Raoul de Warren, "Le salaire des femmes travaillant à domicile," *La Nation,* March 22, 1930, 279.

15. Raoul de Warren, "Comment organiser le travail de la femme," *La Nation,* March 28, 1931, 306.

16. Gustave Rouanet, "À la chambre: Pour que les mobilisés retrouvent leurs emplois," *L'Humanité,* November 14, 1918, 2.

17. Roberts, *Civilization without Sexes.*

18. Louise Saumoneau, "Organisation syndicale des ouvrières," *La Femme Socialiste,* March 1919, 1–2.

19. Marthe Bigot, "Pour les élections: Le droit des femmes," *L'Humanité,* October 18, 1919, 2.

20. Pierre Semard, "La femme et le parti Communiste," *L'Humanité,* November 8, 1924, 1.

21. See, for example, "La femme policier," *Le Populaire,* October 21, 1922, 4.

22. Suzanne Buisson, "Le travail féminin et la crise," *Le Populaire,* September 1, 1935, 4.

23. "Pour la défense des chômeuses," *L'Humanité,* June 19, 1934, 5.

24. Le comité directeur, "Pour la journée internationale des femmes: Lettre ouverte au parti Socialiste (S.F.I.O.), à la C.G.T. et à la C.G.T.U.," *L'Humanité,* February 26, 1924, 1–2.

25. "A travail égal, salaire égal," *La Femme Socialiste,* September 1929, 4.

26. "L'exploitation du travail féminin: À travail égal, salaire égal. Le travail des femmes peut valoir celui des hommes," *Le Populaire,* February 19, 1929, 5.

27. See, for example, Besnard, "Pour les femmes fonctionnaires."

28. Herriot, *Pourquoi je suis Radical-socialiste,* 59.

29. Monette Thomas, "Les femmes et les huit heures," *Le Populaire,* May 1, 1919, 2.

30. William D. Irvine, *Between Justice and Politics: The Ligue des Droits de l'Homme, 1898–1945* (Stanford, CA: Stanford University Press, 2007), 9.

31. Émile Kahn, "Ouvrières à domicile," *Le Populaire,* August 13, 1929, 2.

32. Germaine Fauchère, "La femme au labeur: L'infirmière," *Le Populaire,* December 5, 1931, 1–2.

33. "La femme au travail," *La Femme Socialiste*, June 1933, 5.

34. In fact, as Ruth Schwartz Cohen has demonstrated in the American context, such developments often only burdened women further: Ruth Schwartz Cohen, *More Work for Mother: The Ironies of Household Technology from the Open Hearth to the Microwave* (New York: Basic Books, 1983).

35. Anita Coder, "L'éducation Communiste des femmes: Pourquoi? Par quels moyens?" *L'Ouvrière,* October 21, 1922, 1.

36. Marthe Bigot, "Pour l'organisation rationnelle du travail: Forces gaspillées," *L'Ouvrière,* September 2, 1922, 1.

37. Marcelle Le Guen, "Il faut alléger la tâche de la femme au foyer," *L'Ouvrière,* November 27, 1924, 2.

38. A.T., "Pire que sous Poincaré," *L'Humanité,* April 19, 1925, 1. While women could not vote, the Communist Party exploited the fact that they were not explicitly forbidden from standing for public office. This loophole was later closed.

39. Charlotte Davy, "Femme, n'accepte plus un salaire d'appoint," *L'Ouvrière,* February 17, 1927, 1.

40. Alexandra Kollontaï, "La femme et la révolution russe," *L'Ouvrière,* November 6, 1924, 1.

41. Kollontaï was, in fact, the only member of the 1917 central committee, besides Stalin himself, to survive the 1930s. See Beryl Williams, "Kollontai and After: Women in the Russian Revolution," in *Women, State and Revolution: Essays on Power and Gender in Europe since 1789,* ed. Sîan Reynolds (Brighton: Wheatsheaf Books, 1986), 60–80.

42. Manuscript, Marcel Cachin, "La situation de la femme en travail," ANF AP 447/11.

43. Marcel Bidoux, "Le fait social: Le foyer perdu," *Le Populaire,* September 9, 1932, 6.

44. Suzanne Buisson, "Tribune des femmes Socialistes: La question des salaires féminins au comité des travailleuses," *Le Populaire,* August 8, 1937, 5.

45. Frader, *Breadwinners and Citizens,* 15–18.

46. Henriette Langlade, "La femme moderne: Une militante," *Le Populaire,* April 4, 1931, 1–2.

47. Adrienne Montegudet, "Les problèmes du congrès de Saint-Étienne: Une commission syndicale féminine est-elle bien utile?" *L'Humanité,* June 15, 1922, 4.

48. Fanny Clar, "La femme et la vie," *L'Ère nouvelle,* March 29, 1927, 2.

49. Fanny Clar, "La femme et la vie," *L'Ère nouvelle,* January 10, 1928, 2.

50. See, for example, Germaine Chapuis, "La Femme dans la vie civique: Pourquoi nous sommes partisans du suffrage féminin," *Le Petit Démocrate,* April 12, 1931, 3. Chapuis was also an ardent champion of women's suffrage, as discussed in chapter 6.

51. Hause with Kenney, *Women's Suffrage and Social Politics,* 251.

52. "Manifeste féminin," *Le Petit Démocrate,* December 10, 1933, 3.

53. *L'Alliance démocratique : Ce qu'elle est, ce qu'elle veut* (Paris: Imprimerie Spéciale de L'Alliance démocratique, 1933), 11.

54. "La C.G.P.F. avec nous," *L'Alliance démocratique,* December 9–16, 1938, 3.

55. La Fédération républicaine de France, *Extraits du programme de politique sociale,* 5.

56. See Frevert, *Women in German History,* 217–39; De Grazia, *How Fascism Ruled Women,* 166–200.

57. "Pour une politique française," *Le Flambeau,* November 14, 1936, 3.

58. Paul Marion, "Les principes du programme," *L'Émancipation nationale,* March 26, 1938, 4–6.

59. Jeanne Vaillant, "Femme 1936 : Les assistantes sociales," *L'Émancipation nationale,* July 11, 1936, 6, and "Femme 1936: L'assistante sociale," *L'Émancipation nationale,* July 18, 1936, 6; Jean Clairy, "Sa femme et sa dactylo," *L'Émancipation nationale,* August 1, 1936, 6; D., "Le travail des femmes," *L'Émancipation nationale,* January 26, 1940, 4.

60. Chamine, "Femme 1936: Le coeur à l'ouvrage," *L'Émancipation nationale,* December 5, 1936, 2. Two PDP authors did likewise: Pauline Le Cormier, "Le congrès de la mère au foyer ou la justice en marche," *Le Petit Démocrate,* July 2, 1933, 3; Christiane d'Hellencourt, "La femme et le travail," *Le Petit Démocrate,* February 9, 1936, 3.

61. Paxton, *The Anatomy of Fascism,* 114–47.

62. See, for example, letter dated March 19, 1938, from Yvonne Foinant to Pierre-Étienne Flandin, BNF 37260/7; Mme André Parmentier, "Rapport sur l'activité de la section féminine de la Fédération républicaine de France," *La Nation,* February 28, 1939, 112. The congress that this report was from took place in late 1938.

63. Gruber, "French Women in the Crossfire," 287, 292–93.

64. Frader, *Breadwinners and Citizens,* 224; Clark, *The Rise of Professional Women in France,* 171–206.

65. Elinor A. Accampo, "Gender, Social Policy, and the Formation of the Third Republic: An Introduction," in *Gender and the Politics of Social Reform in France, 1870–1914,* ed. Elinor A. Accampo, Rachel G. Fuchs, and Mary Lynn Stewart (Baltimore: Johns Hopkins University Press, 1995), 8–10.

66. Irma Taury, "Les causes de la mortalité infantile," *L'Ouvrière,* April 7, 1923, 1.

67. "Comment les nationalistes envisagent la protection de la maternité," *L'Humanité,* April 26, 1925, 5.

68. Josette Billoux, "Les femmes travailleuses dans la bataille," *L'Humanité,* March 12, 1933, 4.

69. "Droit ouvrier: La protection de la maternité à l'usine," *Le Populaire,* October 10, 1928, 5.

70. Louise Saumoneau, "Tribune des femmes Socialistes: Protection de la maternité," *Le Populaire,* August 27, 1933, 4.

71. Cypriane Fel, "Tribune des femmes Socialistes: La défense de la femme," *Le Populaire,* May 29, 1938, 8.

72. Édouard Daladier, "Discours," dated 1934, ANF 496AP/2.

73. M. G., "Faut-il interdire le travail de la mère hors du foyer?" *Le Petit Démocrate,* September 23, 1934, 3.

74. Paul Marion, "Les principes du programme," *L'Émancipation nationale,* March 26, 1938, 5.

75. Camiscioli, *Reproducing the French Race,* 102.

76. Ibid., 123.

77. Ibid., 117–26.

78. Marthe Bigot, "Le père le Victoire: Père de la prostitution," *Le Populaire,* May 29, 1919, 2.

79. Louise Bodin, "Infâmes, infamies," *Le Populaire,* April 21, 1920, 1.

80. Camiscioli, *Reproducing the French Race,* 99–128.

81. Fanny Clar, "La Femme et la vie," *L'Ère nouvelle,* August 23, 1927, 1–2.

82. Noëlie Drous, "De la prostitution," *L'Ouvrière,* April 8, 1922, 1.

83. Jean Longuet, "Dans 'l'enfer Bolchevik': Ce qu'a vu un visiteur récent—ni voleurs, ni prostituées—l'ordre et la tranquilité," *Le Populaire,* May 21, 1919, 1, capitalization in original; Katia Palianoff, "Les ouvrières et de la Russie des Soviets," *L'Ouvrière,* April 8, 1922, 3.

84. Jeanne Dupont, "La prostitution en U.R.S.S.," *L'Ouvrière,* August 31, 1932, 2.

85. B.K., "La femme en Russie Soviétique," *L'Ouvrière,* November 12, 1925, 4.

86. Dr. Weill-Raynal, "Le prophylactorium féminin de Moscou," *Le Populaire,* November 3, 1935, 6.

87. Elisabeth Renaud, "La réglementation de la prostitution," *La Femme Socialiste,* November 1919, 1–2.

88. Letter from Madame Legrand-Falco to Victor Basch, December 31. 1934, BDIC FdeltaRES 798/71

89. Margueritte Gemaehling, "À propos des incidents de Strasbourg—Pour nos enfants et pour l'avenir de la race : La suppression d'un régime immoral," *Le Petit Démocrate,* July 12, 1925, 1–2.

90. See, for example, Custos, "Le bien-être matériel est une condition de l'ordre social," 92.

91. "Extraits du programme de politique sociale," *La Nation,* February 17, 1934, 136.

92. Pollard, *Reign of Virtue,* 67–68.

93. See, for example, "Glanes . . . La justice et les réalistes," *Le Petit Démocrate,* September 17, 1933, 3.

94. Elisabeth Renaud's multipart exploration of the regulation of prostitution was a partial exception. For part III, see E. Renaud, "La réglementation de la prostitution, III," *La Femme Socialiste,* 5 May 1920, 1–2.

95. Judith R. Walkowitz, *City of Dreadful Delight: Narratives of Sexual Danger in Late-Victorian London* (Chicago: University of Chicago Press, 1992), 191–228.

96. Roberts, *Civilization without Sexes,* 120–47; Cheryl Koos, "Fascism, Fatherhood, and the Family in Interwar France: The Case of Antoine Rédier and the Légion," *Journal of Family History* 24, no. 3 (1999): 317–29.

97. Drieu La Rochelle, *Gilles,* 19.

98. Green, "The Bouboule Novels," 49; Sanos, *The Aesthetics of Hate,* 162–63.

99. Sartre, "Qu'est-ce qu'un collaborateur?" 43–61.

100. Jean Crussot, "Propos d'un provincial: Lettre à madame N. . . , féministe," *L'Alliance démocratique*, October 11, 1935, 1.

101. Jean Le Mee, "Contre la famille et contre la patrie," *La Nation*, November 1, 1930, 1045. The Feminist Groups for Secular Education peaked in 1927 with 1,074 members in 42 sections across France: Siegel, *The Moral Disarmament of France*, 112.

102. Yves Sicard, "Milicienne! . . . L'invraisemblable aventure d'une jeune dépravée qui donnait le coup de grâce aux victimes des 'rouges,'" *L'Émancipation nationale*, April 3, 1937, 8.

103. Maurice Rondet-Saint, "Un angoissant problème: La dénatalité vue sous son vrai jour," *L'Alliance démocratique*, June 12, 1936, 3.

104. Roberts deals with this at length: Roberts, *Civilization without Sexes*, 17–87.

105. "Suite de la première délibération sur le droit de vote et d'éligibilité des femmes," *Journal officiel, Sénat*, June 28, 1932, 961–969.

106. Charles Régismanset, "Contradictions," *L'Ère nouvelle*, September 9, 1930, 1.

107. Charles Régismanset, "Contradictions," *L'Ère nouvelle*, March 13, 1931, 1.

108. Charles Régismanset, "Contradictions," *L'Ère nouvelle*, August 15–16,1932, 1.

109. Charles Régismanset, "Contradictions," *L'Ère nouvelle*, May 12, 1933, 1.

110. For a thorough discussion of the infighting in the Union républicaine et démocrate, see Irvine, *French Conservatism in Crisis*, 51–60.

111. Georges Ponsot, "Tue-le!" *L'Ère nouvelle*, August 25, 1920, 1.

112. Charles Vérècque, "Le coin des poètes," *La Femme Socialiste*, July 1934, 6.

113. Marie Roncière, "La maternité dans la bourgeoisie et dans la classe ouvrière," *L'Ouvrière*, January 7, 1926, 1–2. Italics in original.

114. Kevin Passmore, "'Planting the Tricolor in the Citadels of Communism': Women's Social Action in the Croix de feu and Parti social français," *Journal of Modern History* 71, no. 4 (1999): 814–51. See page 817 for membership figures; Campbell, "Women and Gender in the Croix de Feu."

115. For the minutes from the group's constitutive meeting, see minutes dated December 23, 1936, "Réunion constitutive de l'Association médico-sociale 'Jeanne d'Arc,'" ANF AP 451/163.

116. For a series of reports to the "Service social" in 1936, see ANF AP 451/87/88.

117. "Section féminine," *Le Flambeau*, October 5, 1935, 2.

118. Campbell, "Women and Gender in the Croix de Feu," 249–64.

119. "Sections féminines," *L'Émancipation nationale*, July 24, 1937, 6.

120. "Au camp de vacances de la Ferté-Milon: Doriot chez les enfants," *L'Émancipation nationale*, August 27, 1937, 8.

121. "Bouches-du-Rhône: Au groupement d'action civique et sociale de Marseille," *Le Petit Démocrate*, August 23, 1925, 4.

122. Delbreil, *Centrisme et démocratie-chrétienne en France*, 57.

123. E.-A Baudouin, "Pour la restauraton du foyer: Les travaux du premier congrès de l'Union féminine civique et sociale," *Le Petit Démocrate*, January 24, 1926, 6.

124. Delbreil, *Centrisme et démocratie chrétienne en France*, 58. See also J.T., "Votre fédération: Au comité directeur féminin du Parti démocrate populaire," *Le Petit Démocrate*, August 4, 1935, 3. D'Hellencourt resigned in 1937.

125. See, for example, "Vers plus de justice électorale—un grand meeting pour le vote des femmes, réunissant tous les partis politiques, s'est tenu à Paris," *Le Petit Démocrate*, June 7,

1936; “La Fédération féminine du P.D.P. Organise . . . la Vente-Kermesse,” *Le Petit Démocrate*, December 11, 1938, 3.

126. Party secretary-general Jean Raymond-Laurent discussed, briefly, the party’s ties to the UNVF: Raymond-Laurent, “L’activité du Parti,” *Le Petit Démocrate*, November 21, 1926, 1–4.

127. See, for example, “L’Union nationale pour le vote des femmes,” *Le Petit Démocrate*, June 7, 1925, 2; “Les congrès féminins: À l’Union nationale pour le vote des femmes,” *Le Petit Démocrate*, March 3, 1935, 3.

128. See, for example, the text of a speech given by Madame Le Vert Chotard, the UNVF’s president until 1930, at the 1928 “Joan of Arc Conference,” a reunion bringing right-wing feminists together: Madame Le Vert Chotard, “Le féminisme,” *Questions féminines et questions féministes*, September–October 1928, 238–41. The choice of Joan of Arc as a unifying symbol signified the conservative political orientation of the conference.

129. Letter dated March 31, 1933, from Edmée de La Rochefoucauld to Pierre-Étienne Flandin, March 31, 1933, and letter dated April 11, 1933, from Pierre-Étienne Flandin to Edmée de La Rochefoucauld, BNF 37260/1. Further suggesting the interconnectedness of the right, Marie-Thérèse Moreau was a member of the UNVF in the 1920s and also the head of the feminine section of the fascistic Jeunesses patriotes (JP). Similarly, Hélène Fortoul variously belonged to the JP, the UNVF, and the Fédération républicaine: Sarnoff, “Interwar Fascism and the Franchise,” 114; Hélène Fortoul, untitled tribute to Blanche Lescouvé, *Le Devoir des femmes*, July–August 1937, 1–2.

130. See, for example, “Union nationale pour le vote des femmes: Congrès d’études des problèmes nationaux,” *L’Alliance démocratique*, January 24, 1934, 2; “Union nationale pour le vote des femmes,” *L’Alliance démocratique*, February 21, 1934, 2.

131. “Le suffrage féminin et l’actualité,” *La Nation*, July 8, 1933, 422.

132. Smith, *Feminism and the Third Republic*, 93. Lescouvé died in 1937.

133. “Congrès national de l’Alliance démocratique à Arras, les 2, 3 et 4 Novembre Prochain: La main-d’oeuvre féminine (rapporteur: mme Ed. Foinant),” *L’Alliance démocratique*, October 31, 1934, 2; “Et si les femmes votent: Les partis de gauche ont le devoir de les préparer à ce rôle,” *La Lumière*, July 7, 1934, 6.

134. Ginette Petit, “Les buts de la <Ligue de la femme française>: Rapport présenté par madame PETIT, secrétaire de la <Femme française>,” *L’Alliance démocratique*, November 22, 1935, 5.

135. Smith, *Feminism and the Third Republic*, 88–89.

136. “Motion concernant les droits civils de la femme: Congrès de Bourg 1936 de l’Alliance démocratique,” *L’Alliance démocratique*, May 21, 1937, 3.

137. Yvonne Foinant, “Tribune de la femme: Un appel,” *L’Alliance démocratique*, October 4, 1935, 3.

138. Letter dated December 1938 from Yvonne Foinant to Pierre-Étienne Flandin, BNF 37260/7.

139. Wileman, “L’Alliance républicaine démocratique.”

140. Irvine, *French Conservatism in Crisis*, 31.

141. “Section féminine de la Fédération républicaine de France, parti républicain national,” *Le Devoir des femmes*, February 16, 1935, 15–16.

142. Le Bureau de la S.F., “Femmes de France,” *Le Devoir des femmes*, March 15, 1936, 1–2.

143. Irvine, *French Conservatism in Crisis*, 31.

144. "Appel de notre section féminine," *La Nation,* November 13, 1936, 1856.

145. Sarnoff, "In the Cervix of the Nation," 1–2.

146. "Fédération de la Seine (S.F.I.C.): Femmes Communistes," *L'Humanité,* December 19, 1921, 1.

147. "Le congrès de Marseille a pris fin," *L'Humanité,* December 31, 1921, 1–2.

148. See Louise Bodin's enthusiastic and hopeful call for its founding: Louise Bodin, "Un journal Communiste pour les femmes," *L'Humanité,* October 17, 1921, 1.

149. "A toutes nos camarades, à nos lectrices, aux 'amies de l'Ouvrière,'" *L'Ouvrière,* March 31, 1927, 1.

150. "Ce que les femmes doivent faire pour que leur journal vive et se développe," *L'Ouvrière,* April 14, 1923, 1.

151. "L'Ouvrière réparait," *L'Ouvrière,* May 1, 1930, 1.

152. For specialists who notice the discrepancy: Sîan Reynolds mistakenly gives the year of the paper's closing as 1934: Reynolds, *France between the Wars,* 172.

153. "'L'Ouvrière' sera suspendue à partir du 1er Janvier, 1936," *L'Ouvrière,* December 31, 1935, 1.

154. By September 1936, the party claimed 536,000 members: "536.000," *L'Humanité,* September 6, 1936, 1.

155. "Rapport du secrétariat féminin," *L'Ouvrière,* September 23, 1922, 2.

156. See, for example, "La résolution féminine," *L'Humanité,* January 12, 1924, 4.

157. "Une belle assemblée des femmes Communistes de l'est parisien," *L'Humanité,* September 3, 1936, 4.

158. "Les jeunes filles de France vont tenir leur premier congrès," *L'Humanité,* December 17, 1936, 4.

159. Gabriel Péri, "Mamans de France! Les mamans d'Espagne vous demandent du lait pour leurs petits: Dimanche prochain, faites votre devoir comme les combattants de la liberté font le leur," *L'Humanité,* October 18, 1938, 1, 3.

160. See, for example, Robert W. Kern, "Anarchist Principles and Spanish Reality: Emma Goldman as a Participant in the Civil War, 1936–1939," *Journal of Contemporary History* 11 (1976): 237–59.

161. For the Croix de feu, see a report by R. Fallay, "Rapport sur la fédération de la Somme," March 4, 1940, ANF AP 451/29; for the Parti démocrate populaire, see S. L., "Pour nos mobilisés: Le comité du 'colis Palatine'—son but, son organisation, ses intentions," *Le Petit Démocrate,* April 1, 1940, 3; for the Fédération républicaine, see "La page du soldat 'sans famille,'" *Le Devoir des femmes,* January–February 1940, 5–6; for the Parti populaire français, see : "Colis de Noël pour nos soldats," *L'Émancipation nationale,* November 24, 1939, 6.

162. Reynolds, *France between the Wars,* 173–74.

163. Laird Boswell, *Rural Communism in France, 1920–1939* (Ithaca, NY: Cornell University Press, 1998), 178–79.

164. Annette Charreau, "Tribune féministe: Le recrutement féminin," *L'Humanité,* December 8, 1918, 2.

165. Annette Charreau, "Tribune féministe: Les femmes dans le 'Labour Party,'" *L'Humanité,* December 29, 1918, 2.

166. "La journée des femmes," *L'Humanité,* April 29, 1919, 2.

167. Marthe Bigot, "Le mouvement Socialiste féministe," *Le Populaire,* July 20, 1919, 2.

168. Annette Charreau, "Tribune féministe: Déléguées femmes et femmes de délégués," *L'Humanité,* July 27, 1919, 2.

169. "Statuts des femmes Socialistes," *La Femme Socialiste,* November 1922, 3–4.

170. Saumoneau took over the editorship in 1923: Sowerine, *Les femmes et le socialisme,* 218.

171. Hause with Kenney, *Women's Suffrage and Social Politics,* 68–70.

172. "Mouvement féminin ouvrier et Socialiste," *La Femme Socialiste,* January 1931, 1–2. For a thorough discussion of Déat's inglorious career, see Burrin, *La dérive fasciste.*

173. Louise Saumoneau, "Pourquoi une organisation de femmes Socialistes?" *La Femme Socialiste,* August 15, 1922, 3.

174. This conference was amicable but revealed a split within the group, between those favouring women's emancipation and equality, behind the secretary-general Buisson, and those who saw themselves as agitating for the maintenance of the mother in the home and the breadwinner wage, behind Lydia Lainé: "La propagande féminine: La première assemblée générale du groupe des femmes," *Le Populaire,* December 17, 1930, 6.

175. Louise Saumoneau, "Études et documents: De l'organisation des femmes Socialistes," *La Femme Socialiste,* March 1931, 2–4.

176. See, for example, "Troisième journée du 29e journée du congrès national du parti Socialiste," *Le Populaire,* June 1, 1932, 1–2. This complaint also appeared in "Woman and the Home": M. Ballot, "Tribune des femmes Socialistes: Recrutement féminin," *Le Populaire,* July 31, 1932, 4.

177. "Études et documents: De l'organisation des femmes Socialistes," *La Femme Socialiste,* February 1931, 3–4.

178. Suzanne Buisson, "Tribune des femmes Socialistes: Premier bilan, Les femmes viennent au parti Socialiste," *Le Populaire,* April 16, 1933, 4.

179. Suzanne Buisson, "Notre journal est paru," *Le Populaire,* January 19, 1936, 5.

180. Reynolds, *France between the Wars,* 150.

181. Ibid., 171.

182. Berstein, *Histoire du Parti radical,* 235–39.

183. Maud-Puy, "Les femmes Radicales: Notre appel aux républicains n'est pas resté sans écho," *L'Ère nouvelle,* January 16, 1933, 3.

184. "Les femmes Radicales," *L'Ère nouvelle,* November 7, 1938, 3.

185. Reynolds, *France between the Wars,* 156–57.

186. E. P. Thompson, *The Making of the English Working Class* (London: Penguin, 1991), 12.

187. Marthe Louis-Lévy, "Tribune des femmes Socialistes: Et le vote des femmes?" *Le Populaire,* January 29, 1939, 8.

CHAPTER SIX

1. Reynolds, *France between the Wars,* 215.
2. See, for example, Scott, *Only Paradoxes to Offer,* 125–60.
3. See, for example, Smith, *Feminism and the Third Republic.*
4. See, for example, Surkis, *Sexing the Citizen.*
5. Scott, *Only Paradoxes to Offer,* 125–60.
6. Offen, "Defining Feminism," 135–50.
7. See, for example, Ida Blom, "Voluntary Motherhood 1900–1930: Theories and Politics of

a Norwegian Feminist in an International Perspective," in *Maternity and Gender Policies: Women and the Rise of the European Welfare States, 1880s–1950s*, ed. Gisela Bock and Pat Thane (New York: Routledge, 1991), 21–39.

8. Gruber, "French Women in the Crossfire," 279–320; Sowerwine, *Les femmes et le socialisme.*

9. Bard and Robert, "The French Communist Party and Women," 321–47.

10. See, for example, Smith, *Feminism and the Third Republic*, 151–56.

11. In Daniella Sarnoff's examination of the far right, which includes some formations not examined herein, she finds that the Solidarité française, the Jeunesses patriotes, and the Croix de feu supported women's suffrage while the Faisceau was opposed and the Francistes took no explicit position on the question: Sarnoff, "Interwar Fascism and the Franchise."

12. Scott, *Only Paradoxes to Offer;* Stone, "Republican Ideology, Gender, and Class," 238–59.

13. Ozouf, "Liberty, Equality, Fraternity," 86–89.

14. As quoted in, Georges Ponsot, "Êtes-vous féministe?" *L'Ère nouvelle*, April 15, 1927, 1.

15. A. Lefas, "Le devoir prime le droit: Devoir d'abord!" *Le Devoir des femmes*, May 20, 1935, 1.

16. In the first election (1946) in which Frenchwomen voted, the right did, in fact, do slightly better with women voters than men. The disparity disappeared thereafter. Jane Jenson, "The Liberation and New Rights for French Women," in *Behind the Lines: Gender and the Two World Wars*, ed. Margaret Randolph Higonnet et al. (New Haven, CT: Yale University Press, 1987), 279.

17. See, for example, "Manifeste féminin," *Le Petit Démocrate*, December 10, 1933, 3.

18. Sowerwine, *Les femmes et le socialisme*, 16.

19. Hause with Kenney, *Women's Suffrage and Social Politics*, 157.

20. Louise Bodin, "Un journal Communiste pour les femmes," *L'Humanité*, October 17, 1921, 1.

21. See the following pamphlet: "L'Alliance démocratique: Ce qu'elle est, ce qu'elle veut" (Paris : Imprimerie spéciale de l'Alliance démocratique, 1933), 11.

22. "Séance de l'après-midi : Le programme du parti," *Le Petit Démocrate*, November 23, 1924, 2–3.

23. Smith, *Feminism and the Third Republic*, 90.

24. "Déclaration sur la politique générale du parti," *La Nation*, December 22, 1928, 1202.

25. See the following fourteen-page brochure dated 1935: "Programmes?" ANF AP 451/82/83. Also Sarnoff, "Interwar Fascism and the Franchise," 127–29.

26. La Rocque claimed in 1944 that he had always supported women's suffrage, but the evidence does not support this assertion: La Rocque, *Au service de l'avenir*, 94.

27. "Vive le 'Parti populaire français,'" *L'Émancipation nationale*, July 4, 1936, 1.

28. Yves Dautun, "France, qu'as-tu fait de ta jeunesse? (suite)" *L'Émancipation nationale*, April 21, 1939, 2.

29. "Discussion de la proposition de loi tendant à accorder aux femmes le droit de vote dans certaines élections," *Journal officiel, Chambre*, May 8, 1919, 2231–2233.

30. "Scrutin (N.904)," *Journal officiel, Chambre*, May 15, 1919, 2365–2366.

31. "Discussion relative à l'électorat et à l'éligibilité des femmes," *Journal officiel, Sénat*, November 22, 1922, 1379.

32. Alexandre Bracke, "Les femmes au parlement," *L'Humanité*, February 23, 1919, 1.

33. Annette Charreau, "Tribune féministe: Les femmes dans le 'Labour Party,'" *L'Humanité*, December 29, 1918, 2.

34. Ferdinand Buisson, "Rapport fait au nom de la commission du suffrage universel chargée d'examiner la proposition de loi tendant à accorder le droit de vote aux femmes, dans les

élections aux conseils municipaux, aux conseils d'arrondissement et aux conseils généraux," June 10, 1910, 8–27, Paris, Bibliothèque nationale de France, carton 86 of the Pierre-Étienne Flandin Papers[hereafter referred to as BNF 31357/carton number].

35. Rachel Lempereur, "Les femmes voteront, et voteront socialiste," *Le Populaire,* June 30, 1935, 4.

36. "Au cercles d'études politiques et sociales de Marseille: Le vote des femmes," *Le Petit Démocrate,* February 13, 1927, 4.

37. Marcel Petitjean, "Pour le suffrage universel intégral," *La Nation,* April 18, 1931, 369–70.

38. Blanche Lescouvé, "Aux femmes françaises," *Le Devoir des femmes,* February 16, 1935, 4.

39. Pamphlet: "Pourquoi j'ai adhéré au Parti social français" (Paris: Siège social, 1936), 12, ISP LR/28.

40. Yvonne-Edmond Foinant, "Discours de Madame Édmond Foinant, Presidente de la 'Femme française,' au congrès de Bourg-en-Bresse le dimanche 8 Novembre 1936," *Alliance démocratique,* November 20, 1936, 6.

41. André Tardieu, "La farce de la réforme éléctorale," *Nord-est: Reims,* July 2, 1939, page unknown, ANF AP 324/136. Some, like Tardieu, believed that all citizens should be forced to vote.

42. Fernandez did not endorse women's suffrage in this piece. Ramon Fernandez, "Rayonnement du P.P.F.: Lorsqu'il s'agit de la vie de notre grand parti, les femmes ne marchandent jamais leur dévouement, et leur peine," *L'Émancipation nationale,* November 12, 1937, 2.

43. L. Camuzet, "Pas de démocratie sans participation des femmes: Suffrages nécessaires," *La Nation,* March 12, 1927, 250.

44. Ferdinand Buisson, "Rapport fait au nom du commission de la suffrage universel," 153.

45. Marthe Bigot, "Pour les élections: Les droits des femmes," *L'Humanité,* October 18, 1919, 2.

46. Marie-Jeanne Mureine, "Pour le vote des femmes," *L'Ère nouvelle,* May 7, 1925, 4.

47. Fanny Clar, "La femme et la vie: Voulez-vous . . .," *L'Ère nouvelle,* April 17, 1936, 3.

48. "Discussion de propositions de loi relatives à l'élection et à l'éligibilité des femmes," *Journal officiel, Sénat,* November 7, 1922, 1298.

49. "Allocution de M. le doyen d'age," *Journal officiel, Chambre,* January 8, 1924, 1–2.

50. This is from Flandin's report from the commission on universal suffrage: "Rapport fait au nom de la commission du suffrage universel et ayant pour objet de compléter le rapport de la précédente législature, repris le 16 Juin 1914, sur la proposition de loi de M. Dussaussoy tendant à accorder aux femmes le droit de vote dans les élections aux conseils municipaux aux conseils d'arrondissement et aux conseils généraux," *Journal officiel, Chambre,* October 18, 1918, 2, BNF 31357/86.

51. Frader, "Engendering Work and Wages," 148.

52. Flandin actually raised and deconstructed the 'red herring' that women in the home did not have interests to defend via the vote: Flandin, "Rapport fait au nom de la commission du suffrage universel," 4–5.

53. Germaine Chapuis, "La femme dans la vie civique: Pourquoi nous sommes partisans du suffrage féminin," *Le Petit Démocrate,* April 12, 1931, 3.

54. Jean Corbière, "Les françaises doivent voter," *La Nation,* February 9, 1935, 87.

55. "Congrès national de l'Alliance démocratique à Arras, les 2, 3 et 4 novembre prochain: La main-d'oeuvre feminine (rapporteur: mme Ed. Foinant)," *L'Alliance démocratique,* October 31, 1934, 2.

56. Clark, *The Rise of Professional Women in France,* 141–70.

57. Cypriane Fel, "Tribune des femmes socialistes: La défense de la femme," *Le Populaire,* May 29, 1938, 8.

58. Angelica, "Le parti communiste et le droit de vote," *L'Ouvrière,* March 15, 1932, 1–2.

59. See manuscript: Marcel Cachin, "La situation de la femme en travail," ANF AP 447/11.

60. "Allocution de M. le Président d'âge," *Journal officiel, Chambre,* January 14, 1919, 10.

61. "Suite de la discussion relative à l'électorat et à l'éligibilité des femmes," *Journal officiel, Sénat,* November 16, 1922, 1356.

62. Marie Maugeret, "À batons rompus," *Questions féminines et questions féministes,* March 15, 1928, 71.

63. Pierre Picard, "Pour sauver le bloc national, faire voter des femmes: Seulement celles que l'on suppose sous la domination des curés," *Le Populaire,* April 4, 1923, 1.

64. Marguerite Faussecave, "Les femmes et la révolution d'octobre," *L'Humanité,* November 7, 1925, 6.

65. See, for example, the 1926 equivalent to Faussecave's 1925 missive: "Novembre 1917–novembre 1926: Le pouvoir des soviets a tout fait pour que la femme soit l'égale de l'homme," *L'Humanité,* November 11, 1926, 4.

66. Adrienne Cambry, "Lettre à un électeur," *Questions féminines et questions féministes,* October 15, 1925, 2.

67. Marcelle Genetelli, "Femmes de commerçants, femmes commerçantes," *L'Alliance démocratique,* April 29, 1938, 1.

68. Un appel aux femmes commerçantes," *L'Alliance démocratique,* August 29, 1934, 2.

69. Éliane Brault, "La femme devant le sénat: Militants, aidez-nous!" *L'Ère nouvelle,* July 11, 1932, 3.

70. "Discussion relative à l'électorat et l'éligibilité des femmes," *Journal officiel, Sénat,* November 22, 1922, 1379.

71. "Suffragists: Mme Maria Vérone arrêtée arbitrairement porte plainte contre un commissaire de police," *Le Populaire,* November 10, 1928, 3.

72. Marthe Louis-Lévy, "Tribune des femmes socialistes: Et le vote des femmes?" *Le Populaire,* January 29, 1939, 8.

73. L.-C. Calas, "Notre pointe de vue sur le droit de vote," *L'Ouvrière,* July 15, 1930, 1–2.

74. "Suite de la discussion d'une proposition relative au suffrage des femmes," *Journal officiel, Chambre,* December 13, 1923, 4087.

75. Louise Brunet, "Pour le suffrage des femmes," *Le Populaire,* November 21, 1921, 2.

76. "À une future éléctrice," *La Nation,* May 14, 1932, 480.

77. As quoted in Denise Moran, "En déniant aux femmes l'aptitude au vote le sénat a pris une position indéfendable: Mais si à l'heure actuelle les femmes votaient, la réaction ne triompherait-elle pas?" *La Lumière,* July 16, 1932, 14.

78. Ferdinand Buisson, "Rapport fait au nom de la commission de suffrage universel," 28–141.

79. These were among a series of excerpts authored by French feminists in the following article: "Les femmes et le droit de vote," *L'Humanité,* May 19, 1919, 2.

80. "Discussion de propositions de loi," 1304.

81. Germaine Malaterre-Sellier, "C'est aux républicains et non aux réactionnaires qu'il appartient de donner le droit de vote aux femmes," *La Lumière,* January 7, 1928, 12.

82. Bard and Robert, "The French Communist Party and Women," 324. Along with then party secretary Albert Treint, Girault oversaw the Bolshevization of the party.

83. Suzanne Girault, "Pour le prolétariat, le droit de vote des femmes est une revendication de classe," *L'Ouvrière,* February 24, 1927, 1.

84. "Les droits politiques des femmes allemandes," *Le Populaire,* September 12, 1923, 4.

85. Yvonne Netter, "Les étudiantes et la paix," *L'Ère nouvelle,* December 12, 1925, 1–2.

86. Louise Saumoneau, "Au travail," *La Femme Socialiste,* November 1930, 1.

87. "Vers plus de justice électorale—pour le suffrage féminin: Le Conseil général de la Seine vote à l'unanimité un voeu déposé par Raymond-Laurent," *Le Petit Démocrate,* July 30, 1933, 2, 5.

88. B.P., "Le fascisme libérateur," *L'Humanité,* February 14, 1926, 4.

89. Chamine, "Pourquois je suis venue à Doriot," *L'Émancipation nationale,* 10 July 1937, 5. Notably, preserving European peace in the party's vision later entailed joining the Nazi invasion of the Soviet Union as part of the Anti-Bolshevik Legion: Robert O. Paxton, *Vichy France: Old Guard and New Order, 1940–1944,* new ed. (New York: Columbia University Press, 2001), 254.

90. Offen, "Defining Feminism," 135–50.

91. "Suite de la discussion d'une proposition de loi relative au suffrage des femmes," *Journal officiel, Chambre,* December 11, 1923, 4025.

92. "Discussion de propositions de loi," 1299.

93. "Tribune féministe: Une charte internationale de la femme," *L'Humanité,* April 17, 1919, 2.

94. "Allocution de M. le président d'age," 10.

95. Germaine Chapuis, "La femme dans la vie civique: Pourquoi nous sommes partisanes du suffrage féminin," *Le Petit Démocrate,* September 20, 1931, 3.

96. "Suite de la discussion relative à l'électorat et l'éligibilité des femmes," *Journal officiel, Sénat,* November 16, 1922, 1354–1355.

97. "Suite de la discussion relative à l'élection et à l'éligibilité des femmes," *Journal officiel, Sénat,* November 14, 1922, 1347.

98. "Discussion d'une proposition de loi sur le vote des femmes," *Journal officiel, Sénat,* June 23. 1932, 945.

99. "Suite de la discussion d'une proposition de loi sur le vote des femmes," *Journal officiel, Sénat,* July 7. 1932, 1035.

100. "Suite de la discussion d'une proposition de loi sur le vote des femmes," *Journal officiel, Sénat,* July 3, 1932, 1017–1018.

101. Irvine, "Women's Right and the 'Rights of Man,'" 55.

102. Victor Basch, "Le droit des femmes au suffrage," *La Volonté,* June 2, 1929, 1–2, BDIC FdeltaRes798/3.

103. Irvine, "Women's Right and the 'Rights of Man,'" 52.

104. Henri Guernut, "Le vote des femmes: Par où commencer?" *L'Ère nouvelle,* June 26, 1932, 1.

105. "Réponses à des amis," *L'Ère nouvelle,* March 24, 1925, 2.

106. La Lumière, "Aux républicains! Les féministes de gauche ne voudront pas servir les desseins du cléricalisme et du fascisme," *La Lumière,* March 9, 1935, 1–2.

107. Léon Blum, "Notre programme: Le suffrage des femmes," *Le Populaire,* December 24, 1927, 1. Blum supported women's suffrage. However, he also confessed that women's suffrage had been bad for the Belgian Socialists and the British Labour Party and said the SFIO must work harder to indoctrinate women before they got the vote.

108. Berthe Fouchère, "La femme et la laïcité," *Le Populaire,* May 14, 1936, 4.

109. Gruber, "French Women in the Crossfire," 293.

110. Letter dated March 8, 1917, from L. Thibaud to Pierre-Étienne Flandin, BNF 31357/86. Emphasis in original.

111. Letter dated August 7, 1917, from Gabrielle-Esther Moyse to Pierre-Étienne Flandin, BNF 31357/86. Emphasis in original.

112. "La femme comme électrice," *L'Ouvrière,* May 8, 1924, 4; "La femme peut devenir un élément contre-révolutionnaire dangéreux," *L'Ouvrière,* March 8, 1924, 1.

113. For a brief discussion of this, see Bard and Robert, "The French Communist Party and Women," 335–36.

114. Gruber, "French Women in the Crossfire," 285.

115. "Communication du gouvernement," *Journal officiel, Chambre,* June 6, 1936, 1315–1316.

116. Ibid., 293.

117. "Suite de la discussion de la proposition de loi tendant à accorder aux femmes le droit de vote dans certaines élections," *Journal officiel, Chambre,* May 12, 1919, 2354.

118. Lefebvre du Prey sat in the Chamber with the deputies of the Groupe de L'entente républicaine démocratique, most of whom were members of the Fédération républicaine. It is likely that he was also a member of the FR: "Listes électorales des membres des groupes, remises au Président de la chambre, le 20 mars 1919, en exécution de l'article 12 du règlement," *Journal officiel, Chambre,* March 20, 1919, 1354–1355.

119. "Suite de la discussion d'une proposition de loi," 1042–1044.

120. "Suite de la discussion de la proposition de loi tendant à accorder aux femmes le droit de vote dans certaines élections," *Journal officiel, Chambre,* May 15, 1919, 2301.

121. See Georges Ponsot, "Le vote des femmes," *L'Ère nouvelle,* November 4, 1920, 1; Georges Ponsot, "La fronde," *L'Ère nouvelle,* November 29, 1920, 1, and"Notes," *L'Ère nouvelle,* November 18, 1922, 1.

122. Georges Ponsot, "Le féminisme intégral," *L'Ère nouvelle,* March 18, 1925, 1.

123. Georges Ponsot, "Les femmes ont élu Hindenburg," *L'Ère nouvelle,* April 29, 1925, 1.

124. J. Ernest-Charles, "La république des femmes,"*L'Ère nouvelle,* November 18, 1928, 2.

125. Norpois, "Les femmes qui votent," *L'Ère nouvelle,* September 1, 1934, 2.

126. Norpois, "Les femmes n'ont pas confiance en elles-mêmes," *L'Ère nouvelle,* November 25, 1934, 2.

127. Norpois, "La peine de mort," *L'Ère nouvelle,* December 20, 1934, 2, and "Les femmes et l'égalité," *L'Ère nouvelle,* June 17, 1936, 2.

128. Norpois, "L'électorat municipal," *L'Ère nouvelle,* December 26, 1934, 2.

129. Norpois, "Le vote des femmes," *L'Ère nouvelle,* February 20, 1935, 2.

130. Norpois, "Les femmes et les élections," *L'Ère nouvelle,* October 17, 1937, 2.

131. Scott, *Only Paradoxes to Offer.*

132. "Suite de la discussion de la proposition de loi," 2354.

133. Basch, "Le droit des femmes au suffrage," 1.

134. Pierre Trémintin, "Aurons-nous le vote municipal des femmes en 1925?" *Le Petit Démocrate,* December 28, 1924, 1. As Trémintin remarked, Ferdinand Buisson also made this argument in the Chamber.

135. "Discussion de plusieurs propositions de loi tendant à donner aux femmes l'électorat et l'éligibilité," *Journal officiel, Chambre,* March 31, 1925, 1951. The speaker was M. Vermare.

136. "Message aux femmes de France," *L'Alliance démocratique,* June 5, 1936, 3. Italics in original.

137. Steven Hause remarks on this leftist duplicity in an earlier context: Hause with Kenney, *Women's Suffrage and Social Politics,* 8.

138. See, for example, Georges Ponsot, "L'égalité des sexes," *L'Ère nouvelle,* May 31, 1926, 1, and "La femme et l'armée," *L'Ère nouvelle,* June 2, 1926, 1.

139. "Suite de la discussion relative à l'élection et l'éligibilité des femmes," *Journal officiel, Sénat,* November 10, 1922, 1349.

140. Jean Corbière, "Les Françaises doivent voter," *La Nation,* February 9, 1935, 87.

141. "Suite de la discussion de la proposition de loi," 2299.

142. H.V., "Les femmes doivent-elles voter? M. Alexandre Bérard nous dit pourquoi il s'opposera, avec la majorité du sénat, à une réforme 'inopportune,'" *L'Ère nouvelle,* November 5, 1922, 1.

143. Charles-Henry, "Le vote des femmes est un piège à républicains," *L'Ère nouvelle,* March 17, 1925, 2.

144. "Discussion d'une proposition de loi," 944–45.

145. Martha Desrumeaux, "Les femmes veulent le droit de vote," *L'Ouvrière,* April 15, 1935, 1, 3; Roseline, "Et le vote des femmes? Interrogées, les femmes qui travaillent au village, à l'usine, au bureau, sont favorables au droit de suffrage," *Le Populaire,* December 30, 1927, 2.

146. Hause with Kenney, *Women's Suffrage and Social Politics,* 232–33.

147. Armand Charpentier, "Le vote des femmes," *L'Ère nouvelle,* December 15, 1922, 1.

148. Charles Rappoport, "La société capitaliste et le problème de la femme," *L'Ouvrière,* March 11, 1922, 1.

149. This strategy was unsuccessful. The newspaper was so labeled during the Bolshevization of the party and shut down in 1926 (temporarily as it turned out): Bard and Robert, "The French Communist Party and Women," 323.

150. Marguerite Michard, "Mesdames les féministes se réveillent . . . ," *L'Ouvrière,* May 7. 1925, 2. Capitalization in original.

151. Louise Bodin, "Féminisme? Non. Communisme? Oui," *L'Humanité,* June 4, 1926, 1.

152. Bard and Robert, "The French Communist Party and Women," 338.

153. Marthe Bigot, for example, stood for election as a municipal councillor in 1922: "Aux Enfants-Rouges Marthe Bigot conserve toutes ses voix: Une défaite du bloc," *L'Humanité,* April 3, 1922, 1; Lucie Colliard, "À propos du candidature," *L'Ouvrière,* March 25, 1922, 1.

154. Flandin used both these terms in his 1918 report to describe motherhood: "Rapport fait au nom de la commission du suffrage universel," 5, 10.

155. This is how motherhood was referred to in a Parti social français monthly bulletin for its social services. See bulletin dated May 1938, "Service social,"ANF AP 451/133. This phrase was also used in "Honorons la famille française," *La Nation,* September 21, 1929, 906; Pauline Blanc, "A propos de l'interview du professeur Pinard: La législation soviétique a fait de la femme l'égale de l'homme," *L'Humanité,* January 5, 1928, 4.

156. "Tribune féministe: Une charte internationale de la femme," *L'Humanité,* April 17, 1919, 2.

157. "Discussion de la proposition de loi," 2228–2242.

158. "Suite de la discussion relative à l'élection et à l'éligibilité des femmes," *Journal Officiel, Sénat,* November 14, 1922, 1344–1347.

159. "Discussion relative à l'électorat et l'éligibilité des femmes," 1375.

160. "Suite de la discussion de plusieurs propositions de loi tendant à donner aux femmes l'électorat et l'éligibilité," *Journal officiel, Chambre,* April 2, 1925, 2061.

161. See, for example, J. Lebas, "Le suffrage familial," *Le Populaire*, January 31, 1922, 1; Germaine Sillon, "Sur le vote familial," *L'Ouvrière*, August 4, 1923, 1. The left also liked to point out that many of these fathers were unworthy of special consideration, being drunkards, laggards, and bad fathers. See, for example, Jarjaille, "Pour le vote familial," *Le Populaire*, August 29, 1934, 2.

162. Charles Maurras, "La politique," *L'Action française*, December 10, 1920, 1.

163. For the Croix de feu, see a brochure dated 1935: "Programmes?" 9, ANF AP 451/82/83; or the Parti social français's sixty-four-page program *Le Parti social français: Une mystique, un programme* (Paris: 1936), 34–35, in ISP LR/28. For the Parti populaire français, see "Leur code de la famille . . . et le nôtre," *L'Émancipation nationale*, August 11, 1939, 6–7.

164. Sarnoff, "Interwar Fascism and the Franchise," 115, 118.

165. "Suite de la discussion de la proposition de loi de M. Charles Benoist et plusieurs de ses collègues portant modification aux lois organiques sur l'élection des députés et tendant à établir le scrutin de liste avec représentation proportionelle," *Journal officiel, Chambre*, April 4, 1919, 1705–1707.

166. "Dépôt d'un projet de loi," *Journal officiel, Sénat*, July 11, 1919, 1119.

167. "Manifeste de l'Alliance démocratique," *L'Alliance démocratique*, May 9, 1934, 1.

168. "Au comité directeur," *L'Alliance démocratique*, May 9, 1934, 2. Reynaud headed a more conservative, nationalistic wing of the party than that which favored the centrist Pierre-Étienne Flandin. See Wileman, "L'Alliance républicaine démocratique," 172.

169. "Le vote familial: Une conférence de M. Roulleaux-Dugage," *L'Action française*, February 1, 1922, 2.

170. This was typical of the pronatalist movement. See Koos, "Gender, Anti-Individualism, and Nationalism," 699–723.

171. Georges Roulleaux-Dugage, "La réforme électorale et le vote familial," *Le Devoir des femmes*, March 3, 1939, 1.

172. "Le suffrage des femmes," *L'Ouvrière*, December 15, 1923, 1.

173. Germaine Chapuis, "Tribune libre: À propos du suffrage familial. Il doit s'intégrer dans une réforme générale de nos institutions et trouver place dans la représentation des forces collectives de la nation," *Le Petit Démocrate*, August 6, 1933, 1–2.

174. Germaine Peyroles, "Pour le vote féminin: Vote féminin, vote familial," *Le Petit Démocrate*, November 15, 1936, 3.

175. André Toulemon, "Le suffrage universel et la famille," *Le Petit Démocrate*, July 4, 1937, 3.

176. Anne-Marie Sohn, "Exemplarité et limites de la participation féminine à la vie syndicale: Les institutrices de la C.G.T.U.," *Revue d`histoire moderne et contemporaine* 24 (1977): 391. Pierre-Joseph Proudhon called women's emancipation a "pornocracy," opposed women's suffrage, labeled abortion "murder," attacked birth control as detracting from the spirit of sacrifice needed for the socialist revolution, and named women a "separate species" that men would do well to steer clear of. See McLaren, *Sexuality and Social Order*, 79–86.

177. "Suite de la discussion relative à l'élection et à l'éligibilité des femmes," *Journal Officiel, Sénat*, November 14, 1922, 1344–1347.

178. "Suite de la discussion relative à l'élection et à l'éligibilité des femmes," *Journal Officiel, Sénat*, November 16, 1922, 1354–1355.

179. "Suite de la première déliberation," 963–69.

180. Smith, *Feminism and the Third Republic*, 34; Gruber, "French Women in the Crossfire," 295.

181. "Suite de la discussion d'une proposition de loi sur le vote des femmes," *Journal officiel, Sénat,* July 7, 1932, 1031.

182. See Elizabeth Colwill, "Just another *Citoyenne?* Marie-Antoinette on Trial, 1790–1793," *History Workshop Journal* 28 (Autumn 1989): 63–87.

183. Francine Duclos, "Le vote et la femme," *L'Ouvrière,* September 2, 1922, 3.

184. Germaine Sillon, "Sur le vote des femmes," *L'Ouvrière,* May 15, 1924, 1.

185. Janine Louis-Merlet, "Le vote des femmes," *L'Ère nouvelle,* March 31, 1928, 1.

186. A good friend of Colette's. See Colette, *Lettres à Annie de Pêne et Germaine Beaumont* (Paris: Flammarion, 1995).

187. Ponsot, "Êtes-vous féministe?" 1. Italics and second ellipsis in original.

188. Tilburg, *Colette's Republic,* 12–13.

189. Joan Tumblety, "Responses to Women's Enfranchisement in France, 1944–1945," *Women's Studies International Forum* 26, no. 5 (2003): 483–90.

190. Ibid, 484.

191. Kelly Ricciardi Colvin, "Solidarity or Suspicion: Gender, Enfranchisement, and Popular Culture in Liberation France," *Journal of Women's History* 24, no. 2 (Summer 2012): 94–97.

192. "Suite de la discussion de la proposition de loi tendant à accorder aux femmes le droit de vote dans certaines élections," *Journal Officiel, Chambre,* May 12, 1919, 2303–2306.

193. "Scrutin (N.904)," *Journal officiel, Chambre,* May 15, 1919, 2365–2366.

194. "Discussion de plusieurs propositions de loi," 1958.

CONCLUSION

1. Muël-Dreyfus, *Vichy and the Eternal Feminine.*

2. Julian Jackson, *The Fall of France: The Nazi Invasion of 1940* (Oxford: Oxford University Press, 2003), 54–56, 86.

3. "Communication du gouvernement," *Journal officiel, Sénat,* May 16, 1940, 765–66.

4. Jackson, *The Fall of France,* 129.

5. "Communication du gouvernement," *Journal officiel, Sénat,* May 21, 1940, 335–37.

6. Burrin, *France under the Germans,* 455.

7. "Incident," *Journal officiel de la République française, Débats parlementaires, Assemblée nationale,* July 10, 1940, 821–22.

8. May, *Strange Victory,* 324–41.

9. "Communication du gouvernement," *Journal officiel, Chambre,* May 16, 1940, 765–66.

10. "Dépôt du project de loi constitutionelle," *Journal officiel, Assemblée nationale,* July 10, 1940, 823–25. Astier was a Radical senator and voted against granting Pétain full powers. See "Annexe au procès-verbal," *Journal officiel, Assemblée nationale,* July 10, 1940, 826–27, 285.

11. Sicard, "Lettre à M. le procureur de la République"; Peter Longerich, *Holocaust: The Nazi Persecution and Murder of the Jews* (Oxford: Oxford University Press, 2010), 392; Pollard, *Reign of Virtue,* 174.

INDEX

Note: Page numbers in *italics* refer to illustrations; those followed by "n" indicate endnotes.